OTHER OWNERSHIP RIGHTS

WATER RIGHTS

1. Riparian Doctrine: Water belongs to the owners of land bordering the watercourse.
   a. Natural Flow: Riparian owner is entitled to water without diminution in its quantity.
   b. Reasonable Use: Riparian owner must share with other riparian owners and is entitled only to reasonable use.
2. Prior Appropriation Doctrine: An individual may divert and use water whether or not she borders the watercourse; individual rights are established by actual use.

▼

RIGHT TO LATERAL AND SUBJACENT SUPPORT

Strict liability for owner of land whose excavations cause a neighboring parcel to subside, or which damage buildings on adjacent land.

GIFTS

IN GENERAL

1. *Definition:* A gratuitous voluntary lifetime transfer of property from a donor to donee.
2. Requirements:
   a. Present intent to make a gift;
   b. Delivery by donor; and
   c. Acceptance by donee
3. Classification:
   a. *inter vivos:* Made during donor's lifetime; irrevocable unless donor retains right to revoke.
   b. *gifts causa mortis:* Lifetime gift by donor in contemplation of impending death.
      i. Contemplation of impending death;
      ii. Automatic revocation if donor survives peril;
      iii. Ambiguity of donor's intent; and
      iv. Death from different peril.

INTEREST IN LAND: EST

TYPE	
PRESENT POSSESSORY ESTATES –	
FEE SIMPLE ABSOLUTE:	
FEE SIMPLE DETERMINABLE:	Right given by a grantor
FEE SIMPLE ON CONDITION SUBSEQUENT:	Right given by a grantor
FEE TAIL (FEE SIMPLE CONDITIONAL):	Right given by a grantor
LIFE ESTATE:	Right given by a grantor
CONCURRENT ESTATES – *Property interest in land currently possessed by several individuals at the same time,*	
TENANCY IN COMMON:	Deed, will, or law of intestate succession
JOINT TENANCY:	Deed and will, but not by intestate succession; requires the following Four Unities: **1.** Time: Co-tenants acquire at same time **2.** Title: Interests acquired under same instrument **3.** Interest: Co-tenants have exactly same interest **4.** Possession: Co-tenants each have possession of entire estate
TENANCY BY ENTIRETY:	Deed, will, or law of intestate succession
LEASEHOLDS (LANDLORD AND TENANT) – *Interest in land according to the terms of a lease agreement, in t*	
PERIODIC TENANCY:	Created by lease; contractual agreement
TENANCY FOR YEARS:	Created by lease; contractual agreement
TENANCY AT WILL:	Created by lease; contractual agreement
TENANCY AT SUFFERANCE:	Created by operation of law when tenant wrongfully remains in possession after end of lawful lease term
FUTURE INTERESTS – *An interest in property that is not presently possessory, but will come into possession s*	
REVERSION (IN GRANTOR):	Automatically at end of transferred estate or by express reservation by grantor after transferring title
POSSIBILITY OF REVERTER (IN GRANTOR):	Occurrence of event terminating a fee simple determinable
RIGHT OF ENTRY (IN GRANTOR):	Occurrence of condition terminating a fee simple on condition subsequent
EXECUTORY INTEREST (IN GRANTEE):	Occurrence of condition as specified by grantor
REMAINDERS (IN GRANTEE):	Occurrence of limitation (not a condition) terminating a prior possessory estate simultaneously created

b. Interest in Property: A BFP has superior rights to others claiming an interest in the same property, including the actual owner, where the BFP takes possession in good faith and pays value.

2. Adverse Possessor (AP):
   a. *Definition*: One who takes possession contrary to the possessory rights of another. Requires that possession by the AP throughout the entire statutory period required be:
      i. Actual; open and notorious; exclusive; continuous; and hostile under Claim of Right.
   b. Interest in Property: Adverse possessor acquires superior title good against all the world.

LANDLORD AND TENANT

THE LEASE

The interest in property between a landlord and tenant is controlled by the lease.

1. For a proper lease:
   a. Formal lease requirements:
      i. Identification of landlord and tenant;
      ii. Adequate description of the premises;
      iii. Amount of rent/dates to pay rent (if no rent amount, reasonable value); and
      iv. Duration of lease.
   b. Statute of Frauds (if lease > 1 year):
      i. Must be in writing; and
      ii. Signed by the party to be charged.
2. The lease terms create the type of estate ("leasehold").
   a. Periodic Tenancy: Right to occupy tenancy for fixed period (year, month, week, or day).
   b. Tenancy for Years: Right to occupy tenancy beginning on a fixed date and ending on a fixed date.
   c. Tenancy at Will: Right to occupy tenancy "at will" as long as both landlord and tenant so desire.
   d. Tenancy at Sufferance: Holdover tenant is treated as trespasser and evicted, or new periodic tenancy is imposed.
3. The lease defines rights and duties between Landlord and Tenant.
   a. *Example*: All L's duties are done in exchange for T's payment of rent, if landlord breaches duties, tenant can withhold rent, if T breaches duties (e.g., fails to pay rent), L can evict.
   b. Lease terms/duties are independent:
      i. Failure to perform by one party does not excuse other party from performing.
      ii. Exception: if warranty of habitability is breached.
4. Other legal considerations arising from lease:
   a. Assignments/Subleases (see chart on p.1)
   b. Fixtures: Personal property or chattels that have been permanently attached to land:
      i. Common Law: Becomes property of landlord.
      ii. American courts: Look to objective intent of tenant, determined by: manner of attachment, damage from removal, fixture in context of property. *Sigrol Realty Corp. v. Valcich*, 11 N.Y.2d 668, 180 N.E.2d 904, 225 N.Y.S.2d 748 (1962).
      iii. Trade fixtures: Used to carry on a trade or business; tenant can remove but is responsible for any damage. Restatement of Property: all fixtures installed by T are trade fixtures.

LANDLORD'S RIGHTS / REMEDIES

1. Security deposit: L retains amount of posted deposit for T's costs and damages.
2. Rent acceleration clause: If T defaults on rent, all future rents become immediately due and payable.
3. Sue for unpaid rent: In the absence of an acceleration clause, L may only sue for the rental amount owed for the current lease period.
4. Eviction: If T materially breaches any lease term, including failure to pay rent timely; may evict by: ejectment, self-help (physical ouster), or summary proceedings.

DUTIES OF LANDLORD

1. Duty to Deliver Possession:
   a. Right to Possess: Breach if someone has superior right to possess at time of commencement of lease; T not required to move in
   b. Actual Possession: Under English Rule, L must deliver actual possession. *Dieffenbach v. McIntyre*, 208 Okla. 163, 254 P.2d 346 (1952); under American Rule (minority), L's not required to deliver. *Hannan v. Dusch*, 154 Va. 356, 153 S.E. 824 (1930).
2. Covenant of Quiet Enjoyment (implied): L promises that neither L nor third party will interfere with T's use and enjoyment of premises.
   a. Actual Eviction: Physical expulsion or exclusion from possession.
   b. Partial Eviction: Denial of possession for only part of the premises.
      i. Common Law: T's obligation to pay entire rent is suspended until possession of entire premises restored.
      ii. Restatement: T can abate rent or terminate lease and seek damages; cannot remain in possession and pay no rent.
   c. Constructive Eviction: L wrongfully performs or fails to perform some duty that substantially deprives T of use and enjoyment of premises.
      i. Common Law: L has no duty to repair premises unless L & T so agree; Statute/Case Law: L makes reasonable repairs. *Chambers v. N. River Line*, 179 N.C. 199, 102 S.E. 198 (1920).
3. Warranty of Fitness for Particular Purpose (implied):
   a. Common Law: In the absence of express lease provision, no warranty by L that premises would be fit for any purpose. *Anderson Drive-In Theatre Inc. v. Kirkpatrick*, 123 Ind. App. 388, 110 N.E.2d 506 (1953).
   b. Exceptions: Short-term lease of furnished residence and building under construction when rented. *Ingalls v. Hobbs*, 156 Mass. 348, 31 N.E. 286 (1892).
4. Warranty of Habitability (implied): L required to take all reasonable action to maintain premises in habitable condition, including duty to repair residential leases only; for commercial leases, implied warranty of suitability for intended commercial purpose. *Davidow v. Inwood North Professional Group*, 747 S.W.2d 373 (Tex. 1988).
5. Retaliatory eviction: L may not evict T, refuse to renew lease, terminate a periodic tenancy, or increase T's rent in retaliation for T's prior actions. *Edwards v. Habib*, 397 F.2d 687 (D.C. Cir. 1968).
   a. Not applicable to commercial leases.
   b. Tenant bears burden of demonstrating retaliatory motive of landlord.

LANDLORD'S TORT LIABILITIES

Generally, L not liable to T or third parties for injuries sustained on the premises.

1. Exceptions:
   a. Common Areas. *Johnson v. O'Brien*, 258 Minn. 502, 105 N.W.2d 244 (1960).
   b. Latent Defects: L fails to disclose.
   c. Negligent Repairs: Only if L voluntarily undertakes to make repair.

DUTIES OF TENANT

1. Duty to Pay Rent: T's obligation to pay rent is independent of L's duties; therefore T must continue to pay rent even if L fails to fulfill duties, unless warranty of habitability is breached.
2. Duty to Take Possession: No duty unless express or implied in lease.
3. Restrictions on use of leased premises:
   a. Cannot use property for illegal purpose
   b. Cannot commit waste (see "Doctrine of Waste" section under "Concurrent Estates").
4. Duty to Repair: No duty unless T expressly agrees; if premises completely destroyed, T might be obligated to rebuild.
5. Duty to Deliver Premises at End of Lease:
   a. T must give premises over timely or be treated as a holdover.
   b. Wrongful Abandonment: If T fails to pay rent and abandons the premises, L may:
      i. Accept the abandonment as a surrender and end the lease,
      ii. Leave premises vacant and sue for rent owed, or
      iii. Re-let premises to minimize T's damages.

TENANT'S RIGHTS / REMEDIES

1. Remain in possession, and
   a. Abate rent, or
   b. Suspend rent
2. Terminate lease, and
   a. Sue for damages, or
   b. Quit premises.

REAL COVENANTS & EQUITABLE SERVITUDES

EQUITABLE SERVITUDES

1. Generally, same as real covenants except that no privity is required;
2. Therefore, must be enforced in equity.
3. Creation: *Tulk v. Moxhay*, 2 Phillips 774, 41 Eng. Rep. 1143 (Ch. 1848).
   a. Express agreement.
   b. Implied:
      i. Implied Reciprocal Agreement.
      ii. Common Scheme.
      iii. Subdivision Plat.
      iv. California rule: will not be enforced unless in deed. *Werner v. Graham*, 181 Cal. 174, 183 P. 945 (Cal. 1919).

Real Covenants & Equitable Servitudes continues on page 3

REAL COVENANTS

1. Types of Real Covenants: Restrictive Covenants and Affirmative Covenants
2. Creation of Real Covenants:
   a. Intent: Promisors intend to bind their successors in interest, or covenant will only be enforced against original parties. *Moseley v. Bishop*, 470 N.E.2d 773 (Ind. App. 1984).
   b. Touch and Concern: Successor to burden will only be bound where the covenant has a connection to her use and enjoyment of the land. *Neponsit Property Owners' Assn. v. Emigrant Industrial Savings Bank*, 278 N.Y. 248, 15 N.E.2d 793 (1938).
   c. Privity of Estate:
      i. Horizontal (for burden to run): between original promisor and promisee.
      ii. Vertical (for benefit to run): between original parties and their assigns or successors.
   d. Must also comply with Statute of Frauds.
3. Scope of Real Covenants: Benefit to dominant estate and burden to servient estate.
4. Termination of Real Covenants: Not really termination, but burden or benefit will not run once horizontal/vertical privity is gone.

EASEMENTS

SCOPE OF EASEMENTS

1. Any change in use beyond the intent of the parties that created the easement is beyond the scope of the easement and not allowed.
2. Intent of parties is guiding principle.
3. Increases in frequency or intensity of use are generally permissible.
4. Scope may be determined from duration of easement, location of easement, or reasonable expectation of parties.

TRANSFER OF EASEMENTS

1. In Gross:
   a. Burden: Always transfers with land.
   b. Benefit: Generally transferable unless use as transferred creates unreasonable burden on servient estate.
2. Appurtenant:

   Note: No separate document is required to effectuate transfer, nor is notice of either required.

   a. Burden: Always transfers with land.
   b. Benefit: Always transfers with land.

TERMINATION OF EASEMENTS

Termination of easements can be made by:

- By Terms.
- Merger of Dominant and Servient Estates.
- Prescription.
- Forfeiture.
- Changed Conditions.
- Frustration of Purpose.
- Abandonment—requires intent and clear act.

CREATION OF EASEMENTS

1. Express Grant: Usually contained in a deed.
2. Deed: Owner of land may convey entire estate and reserve an easement for her own use, or to the benefit of a third party.
3. Donative Transfer: Created by gift deed or will; consideration not necessary unless intent is not clear.
4. Contract: Reciprocal easements are adequate consideration.
5. Estoppel: Easement is asserted in equity when land owner who permits certain use attempts to revoke that use at a later time.
6. Implication: In the absence of express agreement, intent of parties to create an easement can be implied from:
   a. Prior use requires that
      i. Dominant/servient estates were originally a single estate;
      ii. Prior use is permanent or long term, and not temporary;
      iii. Prior use is apparent and not concealed [*Romanchuk v. Plotkin*, 215 Minn. 156, 9 N.W.2d 421 (1943)]; and
      iv. Prior use is reasonably necessary to enjoy the property.
   b. Necessity requires either of the following:
      i. Unity of title followed by a severance;
      ii. Strict necessity, e.g., parcel is landlocked.
7. Prescription: Like adverse possession, use must be:
   a. Adverse—inconsistent with owner's use;
   b. Open/notorious—sufficient to put owner on notice;
   c. Continuous; and
   d. Uninterrupted for duration of statutory period.

TYPES OF EASEMENTS

1. Easement in Gross: Not attached to the land, will not transfer unless the owner of the land so intends.
2. Easement Appurtenant: Attached to the land, rights transfer to any new purchaser of the land.
   a. Dominant estate: Estate benefited, appurtenant easement transfers automatically when dominant estate is transferred.
   b. Servient estate: Estate burdened, need not be adjoining to dominant estate.
3. Negative Easements: Owner of easement has right to demand that the owner of the servient estate refrain from using land in a certain way.

FUTURE INTERESTS

TYPES OF FUTURE INTERESTS

1. In Grantor:
   a. Reversion.
   b. Possibility of reverter.
   c. Right of entry.
2. In Grantee:
   a. Executory Interest:
      i. Springing interest; shifting interest.
   b. Remainders:
      i. Vested:
         1. Indefeasibly,
         2. Subject to Open/Partial Divestment—class gifts.
      ii. Contingent:
         1. Subject to Condition Precedent,
         2. Unborn or Unascertained person.

RULE IN SHELLEY'S CASE

Example: Life estate in A, and remainder in "A's heirs" or the "heirs of A's body"

Effect: If the two estates are either both legal or both equitable, remainder is deemed to be in A, not A's heirs or the heirs of A's body

Doctrine of Merger: Where A has life estate and next vested estate, they merge to form a fee simple.

DOCTRINE OF WORTHIER TITLE

Example: O gives life estate in A, remainder in O's heirs; (future interest must be limited to heirs of grantor, and not issue or devise).

Effect: A will get a life estate and O has a reversion; O's heirs get nothing unless O dies within A's lifetime, at which point they get O's reversion.

RULE AGAINST PERPETUTITIES (RAP)

No interest is good unless it must vest, if at all, no later than 21 years (plus a period of gestation) after some life in being at interest creation.

1. Affected Interests: Contingent remainders, executory interests, vested remainders limited in favor of class of persons.
2. "Life in Being": Any life in existence at the time of the creation of the interest that is in any way connected to the interest.

Examples: Parent of class members, person named in instrument of conveyance, life tenant whose death creates interest.

3. "Within 21 Years": Satisfied if it can be shown that the interest vests during the measuring "life in being" plus 21 years (plus any period of gestation for the measuring life); time of death of measuring life is therefore relevant. *Lucas v. Hamm*, 56 Cal.2d 583, 364 P.2d 685 (1961).
4. Special RAP Cases:
   a. Unborn widow:
      i. Gift to issue is invalid.

Examples: O conveys property to son for life, then to son's widow for life, then to issue. Son could remarry a woman not yet born, and pre-decease her before she gives birth to other members of the class.

   b. Fertile octogenarian: *Jee v. Audley*, 29 Eng. Rep. 1186 (Ch. 1787).
      i. Gift to children is invalid

Example: T gives property to A for life, then to A's children "who attain the age of 25."

Example: A could have a child when he is 80 years old, and then die; the youngest child will not reach age 25 within 21 years of the death of A and the gift cannot vest to the entire class of children.

   c. Charitable transfers: RAP is wholly inapplicable to charitable transfers.

LAWS AFFECTING INTERESTS

DESCRIPTION OF PROPERTY

1. Metes and bounds.
2. Government survey.
3. Reference to plat/map.
4. Resolving inconsistencies:
   a. Natural monuments.
   b. Artificial monuments.
   c. References to adjacent tracts.
   d. Courses/directions.
   e. Distances.
   f. Area or quantity.
   g. Place names.

TYPES OF DEEDS

1. General Warranty Deed (contains six covenants of title):
   a. Covenant of Seisin: Promise by grantor who owns property to be conveyed.
   b. Covenant of Right to Convey: Promise grantor has power and legal ability to convey property.
   c. Covenant of Against Encumbrances: Promise property is free from encumbrances.
   d. Covenant of Quiet Enjoyment: Promise no third party with legal claim of superior title against grantee and that grantor will compensate grantee for losses incurred as a result.
   e. Covenant of Warranty: Promise grantor will defend against superior claims and will compensate grantee for losses incurred as a result.
   f. Covenant of Further Assurances: Promise grantor will do whatever is reasonably necessary to perfect title if title is defective.
2. Special Warranty Deed: Same covenants as general warranty, but only for the period of time that the grantor owned the property.
3. Quitclaim Deed: Contains no warranties and gives whatever interest in property grantor may have.

ZONING

1. Enacted pursuant to state police power for health, welfare, and safety of community.
2. Prevents certain use of property in favor of public good.
3. May be challenged on constitutional grounds or where benefit is primarily for private, and not public, interests.

NUISANCE

Owner of land may sue for interference with the use and enjoyment of her property. At common law, applied to noise, aesthetic harms, environmental changes, etc.

1. Private nuisance: substantial and unreasonable interference with the private use and enjoyment of another's land. *Hendricks v. Stalnaker*, 181 W.Va. 31, 380 S.E.2d 198 (1989).
   a. Interference must be substantial.
   b. Defendant's conduct must be intentional and unreasonable:
      i. Gravity of the harm outweighs utility, or
      ii. Utility outweighs harm, but harm is serious. *Boomer v. Atlantic Cement Co.*, 26 N.Y. 2d 219, 309 N.Y.S.2d 312, 257 N.E. 2d 870 (N.Y. 1970).
2. Public nuisance: harm to the community's use or enjoyment of public land.
3. Defense to a Nuisance Claim:
   a. Coming to the nuisance.
   b. Contributory negligence.
   c. Assumption of the risk.
4. Remedies for Nuisance:
   a. Enjoin D from acting, and
   b. Require D to pay.

THE REAL ESTATE CONTRACT

The sale of land is accompanied by a contract binding the buyer and seller to perform. Requires (must comply with Statute of Frauds):

1. Names of buyer and seller,
2. Description of realty to be sold,
3. Essential terms of the sale, and
4. Signature of party against whom enforcement is sought.

MORTGAGES

The purchase price is usually secured by the buyer from a third-party lender, which results in a lien on the property in favor of the lender.

1. Foreclosure: If the buyer defaults in repaying the lender, the property may be foreclosed upon and sold to repay the buyer's debts; the lender or one with a senior lien on the property will then be paid first out of the proceeds of the sale.
2. Equity of Redemption: Upon default, the buyer has the right to remedy the default and gain clear title to the land; some states limit the time in which the buyer may redeem after foreclosure.
3. Purchase Money Mortgage: When load funds are used in part to purchase property, the mortgage securing the loan is a purchase money mortgage.

THE REAL ESTATE CLOSING

At closing, seller conveys marketable title in exchange for the buyer's providing the purchase price, and the rights of the parties shift from sale contract to deed.

1. Marketable Title: All defects and encumbrances must be removed by the time of closing; any defect, including those that do not appear in the chain of title, may make the title unmarketable.
2. Equitable Conversion:
   a. Once buyer and seller have signed an enforceable contract (prior to closing, they enter into the contract for the sale of land) equity converts:
      i. Buyer's interest into interest in realty
      ii. Seller's interest into interest in personalty (the purchase price)
   b. Death of party: If buyer or seller dies before closing, converted rights pass to estate of either.
   c. Risk of loss: If property is destroyed, under the general rule buyer is now the owner of the property and will bear the loss.
3. Breach:
   a. Buyer's Remedies: Upon seller's failure to provide marketable title, buyer can demand specific performance, receive damages, or rescind contract.
   b. Seller's Remedies: Upon buyer's failure to pay the purchase price, seller can demand specific performance, receive damages, or rescind contract.

THE DEED

After closing, the duties of the buyer and seller are contained in the deed.

1. Formalities:
   a. Statute of Frauds:
      i. Must be in writing and signed by the grantor, and
      ii. Must describe property.
   b. Delivery of the Deed:
      i. Delivery is presumed where deed is in possession of grantee at time the issue arises; deed is recorded by grantor.
      i. If grantor retains deed in his possession and dies, no legal delivery.
      iii. Deposit with third party: Delivery effective if grantor intended to vest title in grantee and surrendered control to third party; delivery with conditions (no delivery unless); condition is certain to occur and is within control of the grantee.

EMINENT DOMAIN / TAKINGS

1. *Definitions:* A taking of private property for public use without just compensation, can be either direct or indirect (property is merely burdened); if government pays just compensation, taking is constitutional and therefore permissible.
2. "Public Use": Must be rationally related to accomplishing a public purpose or use results in a public benefit. *Hawaii Housing Authority v. Midkiff*, 467 U.S. 229 (1984).
3. "Just Compensation": Fair market value, valued at highest and best use, special value to owner is not relevant. *United States v. Fuller*, 409 U.S. 488 (1973).
4. Sovereign may not use its eminent domain power to take property of one private party for sole purpose of transferring it to another private party, even if first party is paid just compensation [*Kelo v. City of New London, Conn.*, 125 S.Ct. 2655 (2005)]. However, state may use its eminent domain power to transfer property from one private party to another if purpose of taking is future use by public, hence a city's exercise of eminent domain power in furtherance of economic development plan satisfied constitutional "public use" requirement [*Kelo v. City of New London, Conn.*, 125 S.Ct. 2655 (2005)].

RECORDATION

Grantee who can show that she received her interest in a deed executed earlier than a competing claimant will be recognized as the true owner. Exception: if subsequent purchase is a bona fide purchase (BFP).

1. Types of Recording Statutes:
   a. Pure Race: Whoever records first.
   b. Notice: Unrecorded conveyance is invalid against a BFP who has no notice, regardless of who records first.
   c. Race-Notice: Whoever records first, unless that person has notice of a prior grant.
2. Chain of Title: A title search can give notice of prior interests in the property at issue.
   a. Title Examination:
      i. Grantor/grantee index: Title is traced back through the seller in grantor's indices, and forward to each buyer through grantee indices.
      ii. Marketable title acts: Limits the title examiner's search by providing that chain of title need only be established within a certain range of years.

QUICK COURSE OUTLINE

PROPERTY

CONCURRENT ESTATES

RIGHTS OF CO-TENANTS BETWEEN THEMSELVES

1. Possession: Co-tenants are equally entitled to possession of the property and cannot exclude other co-tenants.
2. Contribution for expenses: Co-tenants in rightful possession of property bear the cost of maintenance and upkeep such as taxes, insurance, and ordinary repairs. *Barrow v. Barrow*, 527 So. 2d 1373 (Fla. 1988).
3. Right to lease property: A co-tenant may lease the property without the consent of the other co-tenants, but lessee takes subject to the rights of the nonconsenting co-tenants. *Carr v. Deking*, 52 Wash. App. 880, 765 P.2d 40 (1988).
4. Accounting: Co-tenant in possession is responsible for accounting of all rents and profits from third party lessees. *Georgen v. Maar*, 2 A.D.2d 276 [3d Dept. 1956], 153 N.Y.S.2d 826 (1956).
5. Ouster/Partition: Co-tenant takes affirmative actions to take sole possession and exclusive use of the property; co-tenant may file action for partition in court to divide property into individual tenancies, unless all co-tenants voluntarily agree to divide. *Penfield v. Jarvis*, 175 Conn. 463, 399 A.2d 1280 (1978).
6. Effect of will: Since a co-tenant's interest ceases at death, the co-tenant has no interest that can pass by will. *Huff v. Metz*, 676 So. 2d 264 (Miss. 1996).

DOCTRINE OF WASTE (TENANT'S DUTY TO REPAIR)

A tenant who is not the owner of land, or possesses the same interest in property at the same time as one or more co-tenants, is responsible to her co-tenants for any decrease in the value of the property through waste. *Kimbrough v. Reed*, 943 P.2d 1232 (Idaho 1997).

1. Permissive Waste: Tenant allows land to fall into disrepair; must preserve land and structures to a reasonable degree.
2. Voluntary (Affirmative) Waste: Tenant cannot use natural resources on land; use is permissible only for repair and maintenance, where permission is expressly given, or where land is only suitable for such use.
3. Ameliorative Waste: Tenant's use substantially changes the value of property, but the use increases the value of the land; may do it where the market value of future interests is not impaired, and change in character of neighborhood deprives the property of value in its current form.

COMMUNITY PROPERTY

1. *Example:* A husband and wife form a community, which is a separate entity that owns property for the benefit of the husband and wife; all property acquired during marriage is generally characterized as community property. Separate Property: Property acquired by gift, bequest, or devise during the marriage is characterized as separate property, belonging to the individual spouse who receives it.
2. Division of the Community:
   a. At Death: Community dissolves at death of one spouse; each spouse owns half an interest in each community asset.
   b. At Divorce: Community dissolves upon divorce and all community assets are owned by each spouse as tenants in common and may be divided according to settlement.

LICENSES & PROFITS

LICENSE

1. Bare revocable interest to use property for limited purpose and duration.
2. Irrevocable License: Cannot be revoked if consideration is given.

PROFITS

Right to come onto land solely to remove minerals or other value.

TYPES OF PROPERTY INTERESTS

INTERESTS IN THINGS

1. Wild Animals:
   a. Right to possess: Deprive them of natural liberty [*Pierson v. Post*, 3 Cai. R. 175 (N.Y. Sup. 1805).]:
      i. Actual physical possession.
      ii. Mortally wounding/continued pursuit.
      iii. Capture/netting.
2. Natural Gas and Oil:
   a. Right to possess: Whoever extracts first regardless of where.
3. Lost Property:
   a. *Definition*:
      i. Lost: Possessor can no longer find it.
      ii. Mislaid: Possessor voluntarily leaves it, but forgets where.
      iii. Abandoned: Possessor voluntarily relinquishes possession; ordinarily belongs to finder.
      iv. Treasure trove: Property hidden and found, owner unknown.
   b. General Rule: Prior possessor has superior rights to finder. *Armory v. Delamirie*, 1 Strange 525, 93 Eng. Rep. 664 (1722).
   c. Owner of Land *(Locus in Quo)*: Owner of land where lost property is found has superior rights to finder who is trespasser. *Favorite v. Miller*, 407 A.2d 974 (Conn. 1978).
4. Bailments/Borrowed Property:
   a. *Definition of Bailment*: Owner (bailor) entrusts goods to possession of another (bailee), who is in lawful possession of goods and has title against wrongdoers.
   b. Legal Relationship: Bailee is liable to bailor for negligent damage to goods, or conversion.

OTHER INTERESTS IN LAND

1. Easements: A nonpossessory interest entitling holder to some type of use or enjoyment of another person's land.
2. Covenants/Equitable Servitudes: A covenant is a type of servitude created by deed or contract and whose benefits or burdens "run with the land" to bind successors in interest. When the rules regarding real covenants are not met, the agreement may be enforced in equity as an equitable servitude.
3. Licenses: Owner grants permission to another to use the land.
4. Profits: An easement entitling holder to come onto the land in order to take something off it.

MISCELLANEOUS PROPERTY INTERESTS

1. Bona Fide Purchaser (BFP):
   a. *Definition*: One who takes possession:
      i. In good faith,
      ii. For valuable consideration, and
      iii. Without notice of any wrongful possession.

Types of Property Interests continues on page 2

LEGAL CONSIDERATIONS ARISING FROM LEASE

	SUBLET		ASSIGNMENT	
	Tenant (T1) transfers less than the entire remaining estate to transferee (T2)			
	Privity of Estate	Privity of Contract	Privity of Estate	Privity of Contract
T2 to Landlord (L)	NO	NO	YES	NO
Unless	1. T2 agrees with T1 to assume all lease provisions 2. T2 enters into separate agreement with L			
T1 to L	YES	YES	NO	YES
T2 to T1	T1 can be reimbursed by T2 for any rent paid to L under sublease		T1 can be reimbursed by T2 for any rent paid to L under assignment	

INTEREST OWNED	UNIQUE FEATURES	HOW TERMINATED
state in perpetuity, lasts forever	Highest estate recognized by law	Never terminated; perpetual
state in perpetuity, lasts forever	Terminates automatically on occurrence of an event; otherwise lasts forever	Occurrence or nonoccurrence of condition sometime in future, as set out in governing instrument
state in perpetuity, lasts forever	Doesn't terminate automatically; unless condition occurs, lasts forever	Grantor elects to terminate due to occurrence of condition
state for duration of owner's life	Assures that lands stay within a family from generation to generation by passing to owner's heirs	Owner's death
state with duration measured by life of another	Measuring life can be either land holder or another party	Measuring life ends
resent and future interests can be concurrent.		
qual right of possession of the whole by each o-tenant, regardless of the actual share owned; nay be freely conveyed	Modern Law: Any conveyance to two or more people creates a presumption of a tenancy in common	Partitioned through mutual agreement of co-tenants or judicial decree
qual right of possession of the whole by each o-tenant, regardless of the actual share owned; owever, cannot be freely conveyed (Right of Survivorship: once a co-tenant dies, remaining co-tenants take property free and clear of deceased co-tenant's interest)	**1.** Common Law: Any conveyance to two or more people creates a presumption of a joint tenancy **2.** Conveyance: If any co-tenant conveys interest, transferee takes as a tenant-in-common, while remaining co-tenants continue to hold in joint tenancy	Partitioned through mutual agreement of co-tenants or judicial decree
qual right of possession of the whole by each o-tenant, regardless of the actual share owned; nay be freely conveyed	Any conveyance to two or more people creates a presumption of a tenancy in common	Partitioned through mutual agreement of co-tenants or judicial decree
e form of duties owed between a landlord and the renter of the land.		
Right to occupy tenancy for fixed period (year, month, week, or day)	Automatically renews for a like period at the end of the preceding period	Notice must be given by either landlord or tenant a minimum of one whole period before last day of current period; death does not terminate
Right to occupy tenancy beginning on a fixed date and ending on a fixed date	Can also last for a period measured by the happening of an event or condition	Fixed end date arrives, or ending event takes place; no notice required
Right to occupy tenancy "at will" as long as both he landlord and tenant so desire	Law disfavors; some states have statutes requiring notice to terminate	May be terminated by either party without notice; death of either party can also terminate
Holdover tenant is treated as trespasser and evicted, or new periodic tenancy is imposed	Landlord has the right to elect either eviction or creation of new tenancy	If landlord chooses to evict, tenancy ends
ometime in the future.		
Balance of estate left after grantor transfers less than she has	May or may not become possessory in future; freely alienable, devisable, and descendible	Interest does not become possessory if prior estate given by grantor does not end
Balance of estate in fee simple absolute, left after grantor originally transfers less than she has	Landlord has the right to elect either eviction or creation of new tenancy	If landlord chooses to evict, prior tenancy ends
Balance of estate in fee simple absolute, left after grantor originally transfers less than she has	Does not go to grantor automatically; grantor must elect to enforce interest	If condition occurs and landlord chooses to enforce interest, prior tenancy ends
alance of estate in fee simple absolute, left after rantor originally transfers less than she has	**1.** Springing interest: Becomes possessory upon occurrence of a condition, if no present possessory estate exists in another transferee **2.** Shifting interest: Becomes possessory after divesting a present possessory freehold	If condition occurs, prior tenancy ends unless property is currently possessed and interest is springing (and therefore cannot divest an existing possessor)
An interest limited by the existence of a currently possessory estate created at the same time	**1.** Vested Remainders: Not subject to RAP, possessory right is certain **a.** Indefeasibly Vested: Born, ascertainable person **b.** Subject to Open/Partial Divestment: Class of persons, with at least one living member; interests divest in part as new class members are born; class closes when: **i.** Person who produces class members dies; or **ii.** Rule of Convenience: When any class member is entitled to demand possession of entitled shares; no outstanding present possessory estates/conditions precedent for any class member **2.** Contingent remainders: Subject to RAP, right to take is uncertain **a.** Subject to Condition Precedent: Words condition a person's right to take **b.** Unborn, unascertained persons	Remainder interest may never become possessory if outstanding, presently possessory estate continues to exist

Casenote™ Legal Briefs

PROPERTY

Keyed to Courses Using

Rabin, Kwall, Kwall, and Arnold's
Fundamentals of Modern Property Law
Sixth Edition

This publication is designed to provide accurate and authoritative information in regard to the subject matter covered. It is sold with the understanding that the publisher is not engaged in rendering legal, accounting, or other professional services. If legal advice or other expert assistance is required, the services of a competent professional person should be sought.

— From a Declaration of Principles adopted jointly
by a Committee of the American Bar Association
and a Committee of Publishers and Associates

www.wolterskluwerlb.com

Published by Wolters Kluwer Law & Business in New York.

Wolters Kluwer Law & Business serves customers worldwide with CCH, Aspen Publishers, and Kluwer Law International products.

To contact Customer Service, e-mail customer.service@wolterskluwer.com, call 1-800-234-1660, fax 1-800-901-9075, or mail correspondence to:

Wolters Kluwer Law & Business
Attn: Order Department
P.O. Box 990
Frederick, MD 21705

Printed in the United States of America.

1 2 3 4 5 6 7 8 9 0

ISBN 978-1-4548-0788-9

About Wolters Kluwer Law & Business

Wolters Kluwer Law & Business is a leading global provider of intelligent information and digital solutions for legal and business professionals in key specialty areas, and respected educational resources for professors and law students. Wolters Kluwer Law & Business connects legal and business professionals as well as those in the education market with timely, specialized authoritative content and information-enabled solutions to support success through productivity, accuracy and mobility.

Serving customers worldwide, Wolters Kluwer Law & Business products include those under the Aspen Publishers, CCH, Kluwer Law International, Loislaw, Best Case, ftwilliam.com and MediRegs family of products.

CCH products have been a trusted resource since 1913, and are highly regarded resources for legal, securities, antitrust and trade regulation, government contracting, banking, pension, payroll, employment and labor, and healthcare reimbursement and compliance professionals.

Aspen Publishers products provide essential information to attorneys, business professionals and law students. Written by preeminent authorities, the product line offers analytical and practical information in a range of specialty practice areas from securities law and intellectual property to mergers and acquisitions and pension/benefits. Aspen's trusted legal education resources provide professors and students with high-quality, up-to-date and effective resources for successful instruction and study in all areas of the law.

Kluwer Law International products provide the global business community with reliable international legal information in English. Legal practitioners, corporate counsel and business executives around the world rely on Kluwer Law journals, looseleafs, books, and electronic products for comprehensive information in many areas of international legal practice.

Loislaw is a comprehensive online legal research product providing legal content to law firm practitioners of various specializations. Loislaw provides attorneys with the ability to quickly and efficiently find the necessary legal information they need, when and where they need it, by facilitating access to primary law as well as state-specific law, records, forms and treatises.

Best Case Solutions is the leading bankruptcy software product to the bankruptcy industry. It provides software and workflow tools to flawlessly streamline petition preparation and the electronic filing process, while timely incorporating ever-changing court requirements.

ftwilliam.com offers employee benefits professionals the highest quality plan documents (retirement, welfare and non-qualified) and government forms (5500/PBGC, 1099 and IRS) software at highly competitive prices.

MediRegs products provide integrated health care compliance content and software solutions for professionals in healthcare, higher education and life sciences, including professionals in accounting, law and consulting.

Wolters Kluwer Law & Business, a division of Wolters Kluwer, is headquartered in New York. Wolters Kluwer is a market-leading global information services company focused on professionals.

Format for the Casenote Legal Brief

Nature of Case: This section identifies the form of action (e.g., breach of contract, negligence, battery), the type of proceeding (e.g., demurrer, appeal from trial court's jury instructions), or the relief sought (e.g., damages, injunction, criminal sanctions).

Fact Summary: This is included to refresh your memory and can be used as a quick reminder of the facts.

Rule of Law: Summarizes the general principle of law that the case illustrates. It may be used for instant recall of the court's holding and for classroom discussion or home review.

Facts: This section contains all relevant facts of the case, including the contentions of the parties and the lower court holdings. It is written in a logical order to give the student a clear understanding of the case. The plaintiff and defendant are identified by their proper names throughout and are always labeled with a (P) or (D).

Palsgraf v. Long Island R.R. Co.

Injured bystander (P) v. Railroad company (D)

N.Y. Ct. App., 248 N.Y. 339, 162 N.E. 99 (1928).

NATURE OF CASE: Appeal from judgment affirming verdict for plaintiff seeking damages for personal injury.

FACT SUMMARY: Helen Palsgraf (P) was injured on R.R.'s (D) train platform when R.R.'s (D) guard helped a passenger aboard a moving train, causing his package to fall on the tracks. The package contained fireworks which exploded, creating a shock that tipped a scale onto Palsgraf (P).

RULE OF LAW

The risk reasonably to be perceived defines the duty to be obeyed.

FACTS: Helen Palsgraf (P) purchased a ticket to Rockaway Beach from R.R. (D) and was waiting on the train platform. As she waited, two men ran to catch a train that was pulling out from the platform. The first man jumped aboard, but the second man, who appeared as if he might fall, was helped aboard by the guard on the train who had kept the door open so they could jump aboard. A guard on the platform also helped by pushing him onto the train. The man was carrying a package wrapped in newspaper. In the process, the man dropped his package, which fell on the tracks. The package contained fireworks and exploded. The shock of the explosion was apparently of great enough strength to tip over some scales at the other end of the platform, which fell on Palsgraf (P) and injured her. A jury awarded her damages, and R.R. (D) appealed.

ISSUE: Does the risk reasonably to be perceived define the duty to be obeyed?

HOLDING AND DECISION: (Cardozo, C.J.) Yes. The risk reasonably to be perceived defines the duty to be obeyed. If there is no foreseeable hazard to the injured party as the result of a seemingly innocent act, the act does not become a tort because it happened to be a wrong as to another. If the wrong was not willful, the plaintiff must show that the act as to her had such great and apparent possibilities of danger as to entitle her to protection. Negligence in the abstract is not enough upon which to base liability. Negligence is a relative concept, evolving out of the common law doctrine of trespass on the case. To establish liability, the defendant must owe a legal duty of reasonable care to the injured party. A cause of action in tort will lie where harm, though unintended, could have been averted or avoided by observance of such a duty. The scope of the duty is limited by the range of danger that a reasonable person could foresee. In this case, there was nothing to suggest from the appearance of the parcel or otherwise that the parcel contained fireworks. The guard could not reasonably have had any warning of a threat to Palsgraf (P), and R.R. (D) therefore cannot be held liable. Judgment is reversed in favor of R.R. (D).

DISSENT: (Andrews, J.) The concept that there is no negligence unless R.R. (D) owes a legal duty to take care as to Palsgraf (P) herself is too narrow. Everyone owes to the world at large the duty of refraining from those acts that may unreasonably threaten the safety of others. If the guard's action was negligent as to those nearby, it was also negligent as to those outside what might be termed the "danger zone." For Palsgraf (P) to recover, R.R.'s (D) negligence must have been the proximate cause of her injury, a question of fact for the jury.

ANALYSIS

The majority defined the limit of the defendant's liability in terms of the danger that a reasonable person in defendant's situation would have perceived. The dissent argued that the limitation should not be placed on liability, but rather on damages. Judge Andrews suggested that only injuries that would not have happened but for R.R.'s (D) negligence should be compensable. Both the majority and dissent recognized the policy-driven need to limit liability for negligent acts, seeking, in the words of Judge Andrews, to define a framework "that will be practical and in keeping with the general understanding of mankind." The Restatement (Second) of Torts has accepted Judge Cardozo's view.

Quicknotes

FORESEEABILITY A reasonable expectation that change is the probable result of certain acts or omissions.

NEGLIGENCE Conduct falling below the standard of care that a reasonable person would demonstrate under similar conditions.

PROXIMATE CAUSE The natural sequence of events without which an injury would not have been sustained.

Party ID: Quick identification of the relationship between the parties.

Concurrence/Dissent: All concurrences and dissents are briefed whenever they are included by the casebook editor.

Analysis: This last paragraph gives you a broad understanding of where the case "fits in" with other cases in the section of the book and with the entire course. It is a hornbook-style discussion indicating whether the case is a majority or minority opinion and comparing the principal case with other cases in the casebook. It may also provide analysis from restatements, uniform codes, and law review articles. The analysis will prove to be invaluable to classroom discussion.

Issue: The issue is a concise question that brings out the essence of the opinion as it relates to the section of the casebook in which the case appears. Both substantive and procedural issues are included if relevant to the decision.

Holding and Decision: This section offers a clear and in-depth discussion of the rule of the case and the court's rationale. It is written in easy-to-understand language and answers the issue presented by applying the law to the facts of the case. When relevant, it includes a thorough discussion of the exceptions to the case as listed by the court, any major cites to the other cases on point, and the names of the judges who wrote the decisions.

Quicknotes: Conveniently defines legal terms found in the case and summarizes the nature of any statutes, codes, or rules referred to in the text.

Note to Students

Wolters Kluwer Law & Business is proud to offer *Casenote Legal Briefs*—continuing thirty years of publishing America's best-selling legal briefs.

Casenote Legal Briefs are designed to help you save time when briefing assigned cases. Organized under convenient headings, they show you how to abstract the basic facts and holdings from the text of the actual opinions handed down by the courts. Used as part of a rigorous study regimen, they can help you spend more time analyzing and critiquing points of law than on copying bits and pieces of judicial opinions into your notebook or outline.

Casenote Legal Briefs should never be used as a substitute for assigned casebook readings. They work best when read as a follow-up to reviewing the underlying opinions themselves. Students who try to avoid reading and digesting the judicial opinions in their casebooks or online sources will end up shortchanging themselves in the long run. The ability to absorb, critique, and restate the dynamic and complex elements of case law decisions is crucial to your success in law school and beyond. It cannot be developed vicariously.

Casenote Legal Briefs represents but one of the many offerings in Legal Education's Study Aid Timeline, which includes:

- *Casenote Legal Briefs*
- *Emanuel Law Outlines*
- *Examples & Explanations* Series
- *Introduction to Law* Series
- Emanuel *Law in a Flash* Flash Cards
- Emanuel *CrunchTime* Series

Each of these series is designed to provide you with easy-to-understand explanations of complex points of law. Each volume offers guidance on the principles of legal analysis and, consulted regularly, will hone your ability to spot relevant issues. We have titles that will help you prepare for class, prepare for your exams, and enhance your general comprehension of the law along the way.

To find out more about Wolters Kluwer Law & Business's Study Aid publications, visit us online at *www.wolterskluwerlb.com* or email us at *legaledu@wolterskluwer.com.* We'll be happy to assist you.

Get this Casenote Legal Brief as an AspenLaw Studydesk eBook today!

By returning this form to Wolters Kluwer Law & Business, you will receive a complimentary eBook download of this Casenote Legal Brief and AspenLaw Studydesk productivity software.* Learn more about AspenLaw Studydesk today at *www.wolterskluwerlb.com.*

Name	**Phone** ( )
Address	**Apt. No.**
City **State**	**ZIP Code**
Law School	**Graduation Date** Month ________ Year ________

Cut out the UPC found on the lower left corner of the back cover of this book. Staple the UPC inside this box. Only the original UPC from the book cover will be accepted. (No photocopies or store stickers are allowed.)

Attach UPC inside this box.

Email (Print legibly or you may not get access!)
Title of this book (course subject)
ISBN of this book (10- or 13-digit number on the UPC)
Used with which casebook (provide author's name)

Mail the completed form to:

Wolters Kluwer Law & Business
Legal Education Division
130 Turner Street, Bldg 3, 4th Floor
Waltham, MA 02453-8901

* Upon receipt of this completed form, you will be emailed a code for the digital download of this book in AspenLaw Studydesk eBook format and a free copy of the software application, which is required to read the eBook.

For a full list of eBook study aids available for AspenLaw Studydesk software and other resources that will help you with your law school studies, visit *www.wolterskluwerlb.com.*

Make a photocopy of this form and your UPC for your records.

For detailed information on the use of the information you provide on this form, please see the PRIVACY POLICY at *www.wolterskluwerlb.com.*

How to Brief a Case

A. Decide on a Format and Stick to It

Structure is essential to a good brief. It enables you to arrange systematically the related parts that are scattered throughout most cases, thus making manageable and understandable what might otherwise seem to be an endless and unfathomable sea of information. There are, of course, an unlimited number of formats that can be utilized. However, it is best to find one that suits your needs and stick to it. Consistency breeds both efficiency and the security that when called upon you will know where to look in your brief for the information you are asked to give.

Any format, as long as it presents the essential elements of a case in an organized fashion, can be used. Experience, however, has led *Casenotes* to develop and utilize the following format because of its logical flow and universal applicability.

NATURE OF CASE: This is a brief statement of the legal character and procedural status of the case (e.g., "Appeal of a burglary conviction").

There are many different alternatives open to a litigant dissatisfied with a court ruling. The key to determining which one has been used is to discover *who is asking this court for what.*

This first entry in the brief should be kept as *short as possible.* Use the court's terminology if you understand it. But since jurisdictions vary as to the titles of pleadings, the best entry is the one that addresses who wants what in this proceeding, not the one that sounds most like the court's language.

RULE OF LAW: A statement of the general principle of law that the case illustrates (e.g., "An acceptance that varies any term of the offer is considered a rejection and counteroffer").

Determining the rule of law of a case is a procedure similar to determining the issue of the case. Avoid being fooled by red herrings; there may be a few rules of law mentioned in the case excerpt, but usually only one is *the* rule with which the casebook editor is concerned. The techniques used to locate the issue, described below, may also be utilized to find the rule of law. Generally, your best guide is simply the chapter heading. It is a clue to the point the casebook editor seeks to make and should be kept in mind when reading every case in the respective section.

FACTS: A synopsis of only the essential facts of the case, i.e., those bearing upon or leading up to the issue.

The facts entry should be a short statement of the events and transactions that led one party to initiate legal proceedings against another in the first place. While some cases conveniently state the salient facts at the beginning of the decision, in other instances they will have to be culled from hiding places throughout the text, even from concurring and dissenting opinions. Some of the "facts" will often be in dispute and should be so noted. Conflicting evidence may be briefly pointed up. "Hard" facts must be included. Both must be *relevant* in order to be listed in the facts entry. It is impossible to tell what is relevant until the entire case is read, as the ultimate determination of the rights and liabilities of the parties may turn on something buried deep in the opinion.

Generally, the facts entry should not be longer than three to five *short* sentences.

It is often helpful to identify the role played by a party in a given context. For example, in a construction contract case the identification of a party as the "contractor" or "builder" alleviates the need to tell that that party was the one who was supposed to have built the house.

It is always helpful, and a good general practice, to identify the "plaintiff" and the "defendant." This may seem elementary and uncomplicated, but, especially in view of the creative editing practiced by some casebook editors, it is sometimes a difficult or even impossible task. Bear in mind that the *party presently* seeking something from this court may not be the plaintiff, and that sometimes only the cross-claim of a defendant is treated in the excerpt. Confusing or misaligning the parties can ruin your analysis and understanding of the case.

ISSUE: A statement of the general legal question answered by or illustrated in the case. For clarity, the issue is best put in the form of a question capable of a "yes" or "no" answer. In reality, the issue is simply the Rule of Law put in the form of a question (e.g., "May an offer be accepted by performance?").

The major problem presented in discerning what is *the* issue in the case is that an opinion usually purports to raise and answer several questions. However, except for rare cases, only one such question is really the issue in the case. Collateral issues not necessary to the resolution of the matter in controversy are handled by the court by language known as *"obiter dictum"* or merely *"dictum."* While dicta may be included later in the brief, they have no place under the issue heading.

To find the issue, ask *who wants what* and then go on to ask *why did that party succeed or fail in getting it.* Once this is determined, the "why" should be turned into a question.

The complexity of the issues in the cases will vary, but in all cases a single-sentence question should sum up the issue. *In a few cases,* there will be two, or even more rarely, three issues of equal importance to the resolution of the case. Each should be expressed in a single-sentence question.

Since many issues are resolved by a court in coming to a final disposition of a case, the casebook editor will reproduce the portion of the opinion containing the issue or issues most relevant to the area of law under scrutiny. A noted law professor gave this advice: "Close the book; look at the title on the cover." Chances are, if it is Property, you need not concern yourself with whether, for example, the federal government's treatment of the plaintiff's land really raises a federal question sufficient to support jurisdiction on this ground in federal court.

The same rule applies to chapter headings designating sub-areas within the subjects. They tip you off as to what the text is designed to teach. The cases are arranged in a casebook to show a progression or development of the law, so that the preceding cases may also help.

It is also most important to remember to *read the notes and questions* at the end of a case to determine what the editors wanted you to have gleaned from it.

HOLDING AND DECISION: This section should succinctly explain the rationale of the court in arriving at its decision. In capsulizing the "reasoning" of the court, it should always include an application of the general rule or rules of law to the specific facts of the case. Hidden justifications come to light in this entry: the reasons for the state of the law, the public policies, the biases and prejudices, those considerations that influence the justices' thinking and, ultimately, the outcome of the case. At the end, there should be a short indication of the disposition or procedural resolution of the case (e.g., "Decision of the trial court for Mr. Smith (P) reversed").

The foregoing format is designed to help you "digest" the reams of case material with which you will be faced in your law school career. Once mastered by practice, it will place at your fingertips the information the authors of your casebooks have sought to impart to you in case-by-case illustration and analysis.

B. Be as Economical as Possible in Briefing Cases

Once armed with a format that encourages succinctness, it is as important to be economical with regard to the time spent on the actual reading of the case as it is to be economical in the writing of the brief itself. This does not mean "skimming" a case. Rather, it means reading the case with an "eye" trained to recognize into which "section" of your brief a particular passage or line fits and having a system for quickly and precisely marking the case so that the passages fitting any one particular part of the brief can be easily identified and brought together in a concise and accurate manner when the brief is actually written.

It is of no use to simply repeat everything in the opinion of the court; record only enough information to trigger your recollection of what the court said. Nevertheless, an accurate statement of the "law of the case," i.e., the legal principle applied to the facts, is absolutely essential to class preparation and to learning the law under the case method.

To that end, it is important to develop a "shorthand" that you can use to make marginal notations. These notations will tell you at a glance in which section of the brief you will be placing that particular passage or portion of the opinion.

Some students prefer to underline all the salient portions of the opinion (with a pencil or colored underliner marker), making marginal notations as they go along. Others prefer the color-coded method of underlining, utilizing different colors of markers to underline the salient portions of the case, each separate color being used to represent a different section of the brief. For example, blue underlining could be used for passages relating to the rule of law, yellow for those relating to the issue, and green for those relating to the holding and decision, etc. While it has its advocates, the color-coded method can be confusing and time-consuming (all that time spent on changing colored markers). Furthermore, it can interfere with the continuity and concentration many students deem essential to the reading of a case for maximum comprehension. In the end, however, it is a matter of personal preference and style. Just remember, whatever method you use, underlining must be used sparingly or its value is lost.

If you take the marginal notation route, an efficient and easy method is to go along underlining the key portions of the case and placing in the margin alongside them the following "markers" to indicate where a particular passage or line "belongs" in the brief you will write:

N (NATURE OF CASE)
RL (RULE OF LAW)
I (ISSUE)
HL (HOLDING AND DECISION, relates to the RULE OF LAW behind the decision)
HR (HOLDING AND DECISION, gives the RATIONALE or reasoning behind the decision)
HA (HOLDING AND DECISION, APPLIES the general principle(s) of law to the facts of the case to arrive at the decision)

Remember that a particular passage may well contain information necessary to more than one part of your brief, in which case you simply note that in the margin. If you are using the color-coded underlining method instead of marginal notation, simply make asterisks or checks in the margin next to the passage in question in the colors that indicate the additional sections of the brief where it might be utilized.

The economy of utilizing "shorthand" in marking cases for briefing can be maintained in the actual brief writing process itself by utilizing "law student shorthand" within the brief. There are many commonly used words and phrases for which abbreviations can be substituted in your briefs (and in your class notes also). You can develop abbreviations that are personal to you and which will save you a lot of time. A reference list of briefing abbreviations can be found on page xii of this book.

C. Use Both the Briefing Process and the Brief as a Learning Tool

Now that you have a format and the tools for briefing cases efficiently, the most important thing is to make the time spent in briefing profitable to you and to make the most advantageous use of the briefs you create. Of course, the briefs are invaluable for classroom reference when you are called upon to explain or analyze a particular case. However, they are also useful in reviewing for exams. A quick glance at the fact summary should bring the case to mind, and a rereading of the rule of law should enable you to go over the underlying legal concept in your mind, how it was applied in that particular case, and how it might apply in other factual settings.

As to the value to be derived from engaging in the briefing process itself, there is an immediate benefit that arises from being forced to sift through the essential facts and reasoning from the court's opinion and to succinctly express them in your own words in your brief. The process ensures that you understand the case and the point that it illustrates, and that means you will be ready to absorb further analysis and information brought forth in class. It also ensures you will have something to say when called upon in class. The briefing process helps develop a mental agility for getting to the *gist* of a case and for identifying, expounding on, and applying the legal concepts and issues found there. The briefing process is the mental process on which you must rely in taking law school examinations; it is also the mental process upon which a lawyer relies in serving his clients and in making his living.

Abbreviations for Briefs

acceptance .... acp
affirmed .... aff
answer .... ans
assumption of risk .... a/r
attorney .... atty
beyond a reasonable doubt .... b/r/d
bona fide purchaser .... BFP
breach of contract .... br/k
cause of action .... c/a
common law .... c/l
Constitution .... Con
constitutional .... con
contract .... K
contributory negligence .... c/n
cross x
cross-complaint .... x/c
cross-examination .... x/ex
cruel and unusual punishment .... c/u/p
defendant .... D
dismissed .... dis
double jeopardy .... d/j
due process .... d/p
equal protection .... e/p
equity .... eq
evidence .... ev
exclude .... exc
exclusionary rule .... exc/r
felony .... f/n
freedom of speech .... f/s
good faith .... g/f
habeas corpus .... h/c
hearsay .... hr
husband .... H
injunction .... inj
in loco parentis .... ILP
inter vivos .... I/v
joint tenancy .... j/t
judgment .... judgt
jurisdiction .... jur
last clear chance LCC
long-arm statute .... LAS
majority view .... maj
meeting of minds .... MOM
minority view .... min
Miranda rule .... Mir/r
Miranda warnings .... Mir/w
negligence .... neg
notice .... ntc
nuisance .... nus
obligation .... ob
obscene .... obs
offer .... O
offeree .... OE
offeror .... OR
ordinance .... ord
pain and suffering .... p/s
parol evidence .... p/e
plaintiff .... P
prima facie .... p/f
probable cause .... p/c
proximate cause .... px/c
real property .... r/p
reasonable doubt .... r/d
reasonable man .... r/m
rebuttable presumption .... rb/p
remanded .... rem
res ipsa loquitur .... RIL
respondeat superior .... r/s
Restatement .... RS
reversed .... rev
Rule Against Perpetuities .... RAP
search and seizure .... s/s
search warrant .... s/w
self-defense .... s/d
specific performance .... s/p
statute .... S
statute of frauds .... S/F
statute of limitations .... S/L
summary judgment .... s/j
tenancy at will .... t/w
tenancy in common .... t/c
tenant .... t
third party .... TP
third party beneficiary .... TPB
transferred intent .... TI
unconscionable .... uncon
unconstitutional .... unconst
undue influence .... u/e
Uniform Commercial Code .... UCC
unilateral .... uni
vendee .... VE
vendor .... VR
versus v
void for vagueness .... VFV
weight of authority .... w/a
weight of the evidence .... w/e
wife .... W
with .... w/
within .... w/i
without .... w/o
without prejudice .... w/o/p
wrongful death .... wr/d

Table of Cases

CHAPTER 1

The Right to Exclude Others from Private Property

Quick Reference Rules of Law

Jacque and Jacque v. Steenberg Homes, Inc.

Property owner (P) v. Company (D)

Wis. Sup. Ct., 563 N.W.2d 154 (1997).

NATURE OF CASE: Suit for intentional trespass to land.

FACT SUMMARY: The Jacques (P) brought suit against Steenberg Homes, Inc. (Steenberg) (D) claiming intentional trespass to their land when Steenberg (D) plowed a path across their field, over their protests, in order to deliver a mobile home.

RULE OF LAW

When nominal damages are awarded for an intentional trespass to land, punitive damages may also be awarded at the jury's discretion.

FACTS: Steenberg Homes (Steenberg) (D) was delivering a mobile home. It found the easiest route of delivery was through the Jacques' (P) land. Despite the Jacques' (P) protests, Steenberg (D) plowed a path through the Jacques' (P) field. The Jacques (P) sued Steenberg (D) for intentional trespass. At trial, Steenberg (D) conceded intentional trespass but argued that punitive damages could not be awarded since no compensatory damages had been awarded. Though the jury awarded $1 in nominal damages and $100,000 in punitive damages, the circuit court set aside the punitive damages award. The court of appeals affirmed and the Jacques (P) appealed.

ISSUE: When nominal damages are awarded for an intentional trespass to land, may punitive damages also be awarded at the jury's discretion?

HOLDING AND DECISION: (Bablitch, J.) Yes. When nominal damages are awarded for an intentional trespass to land, punitive damages may also be awarded at the jury's discretion. Steenberg (D) argued that punitive damages could not be awarded by the jury without an award of compensatory damages as a matter of law. The Jacques (P) argued that the rationale supporting the compensatory damage award requirement is not applicable when the wrongful act is an intentional trespass to land. This court agrees. The rationale for the requirement is that if the individual cannot show actual harm, society has little interest in having the unlawful, but harmless, conduct deterred and punitive damages are inappropriate. The issue of whether nominal damages can support a punitive damage award in intentional trespass to land cases is one of first impression. This court has recognized that in certain circumstances of trespass, the actual harm is not the damage to the land, but the loss of the individual's right to exclude others from his property, and has implied that the loss of this right may be punished by a large damage award despite the lack of measurable harm. Thus, the compensatory damages requirement should not apply when the tort supporting the award is intentional trespass to land. Next, we consider whether the $100,000 damage award was excessive. The court must consider three factors in determining whether a punitive damage award violates the Due Process Clause: (1) the degree of reprehensibility of the conduct; (2) the disparity between the harm suffered and the award; and (3) the difference between this remedy and the penalties authorized or imposed in comparable cases. Here the $100,000 award was not excessive. Steenberg's (D) intentional trespass demonstrated an indifference and reckless disregard for the law and for the rights of others. Moreover, such an award is necessary to deter similar conduct in the future. Reversed and remanded.

ANALYSIS

The Supreme Court has recognized the interest of a landowner in the right to exclude others from his land as one of the essential property rights. The law recognizes that harm occurs in every trespass to land by the nominal damage award, whether or not actual damages are sustained. The potential harm resulting from intentional trespass to land, which if repeated might ripen into prescription or adverse possession, may result in the owner's loss of property rights. Moreover, society's interest in deterring wrongdoing supports the conclusion in this case as well.

Quicknotes

COMPENSATORY DAMAGES Measure of damages necessary to compensate victim for actual injuries suffered.

PUNITIVE DAMAGES Damages exceeding the actual injury suffered for the purposes of punishment of the defendant, deterrence of the wrongful behavior or comfort to the plaintiff.

TRESPASS TO LAND Physical invasion of the plaintiff's property that is intended and caused by the defendant's conduct.

Intel Corporation v. Hamidi

Employer (P) v. Former employee (D)

Cal. Sup. Ct., 30 Cal. 4th 1342 (2003).

NATURE OF CASE: Appeal from injunction in action for trespass to chattels.

FACT SUMMARY: Hamidi (D) and his organization, Former and Current Employees of Intel (FACE-Intel) (D), mass-mailed e-mails which were critical of Intel Corporation (P) to thousands of Intel employees. Intel (P) claimed that this conduct constituted trespass to chattel because it intermeddled with its personal property (computers).

RULE OF LAW

Trespass to chattels does not encompass an electronic communication that neither damages a recipient computer system nor impairs its functioning.

FACTS: Hamidi (D), a former employee of Intel Corporation (P), formed an organization named Former and Current Employees of Intel (FACE-Intel) (D) to disseminate information and views critical of Intel's (P) employment and personnel policies and practices. Over a 21-month period, Hamidi (D), on behalf of FACE-Intel (D), sent six mass e-mails that criticized Intel (P) and invited recipients to go to FACE-Intel's (D) Web site, to as many as 35,000 employee addresses on Intel's (P) electronic mail system. Recipients could request to be removed from FACE-Intel's (D) mailing list. In sending the mass mailing, Hamidi did not breach Intel's (P) computer security. Despite Intel's (P) request that the e-mails cease, Hamidi (D) continued his mailings. Intel (P) sued Hamidi (D) and FACE-Intel (D) for trespass to chattels. The trial court granted summary judgment against Hamidi (D), permanently enjoining him from sending unsolicited e-mail to addresses on Intel's (P) computer systems. The appellate court affirmed, and the California Supreme Court granted review.

ISSUE: Does trespass to chattels encompass an electronic communication that neither damages a recipient computer system nor impairs its functioning?

HOLDING AND DECISION: (Werdegar, J.) No. Trespass to chattels does not encompass an electronic communication that neither damages a recipient computer system nor impairs its functioning. Such an electronic communication does not constitute actionable trespass to personal property because it does not interfere with the possessor's use or possession of, or any other protected interest in, the personal property itself. Under state law, and broader modern American law, trespass to chattels occurs where an intentional interference with the possession of personal property proximately causes actual injury. This is also the position of the Restatement (Second) of Torts, which requires actual injury for a trespass to chattels to be actionable. Notwithstanding that the relief sought is injunctive, rather than damages, a showing of injury is necessary since it would make little sense to issue an injunction without a showing of likely irreparable injury. Any consequential damages, such as loss of productivity, are not an injury to the company's interest in its computers. To prevail on this particular claim, Intel (P) would have to prove injury, whether actual or threatened, to its computer systems—as where the quantity of e-mail (spam) overloads a system and interferes with its functioning. Finally, an expansion of the law to cover the special case of computers is unwarranted. Computers, like telephones, are personal property, not realty, so that unwelcome content transmitted to or by that personalty does not constitute an injury to the property itself. Accordingly, trespass is not the appropriate tort for unwelcome communications that do not interfere with the functioning of the personal property, whether it is a telephone, a computer, or some other communication device. Reversed.

DISSENT: (Brown, J.) Intel (P) should not have to accommodate a continuing violation of its right to exclude Hamidi (D) from using Intel's (P) computers to transmit his messages. Contrary to the majority's reasoning, the requirement of actual injury matters in such cases only in claims for damages, not as to claims for injunctive relief. Even so, the record does show several forms of actual injury: economic loss, Intel's (P) impaired use of its computers, and appropriation and use of property paid for by Intel (P). A party has the right to prevent interference with its personal property. Authorities have disagreed, however, on how to remedy violations of that right when the chattel itself is not damaged. One court has found such violations actionable even without damage to the chattel, whereas other authorities permit a trespass-to-chattel action only if such violations are intentional. Section 218 of the Restatement (Second) of Torts also bars unauthorized use of personal property without permitting awards of nominal damages, in contrast to trespass actions involving land, which do permit nominal damages. The authorities agree that, like land, personal property is inviolable; that owners of personal property may prevent harmless interference; and that such prevention may occur via use of reasonable force. Several courts have enjoined uses of personal property that violated these principles. The majority's reasoning, however, ultimately rewards Hamidi (D) for outwitting Intel's (P) computer defenses—a path the law should not take. Moreover, Hamidi's (D) unlawful use of Intel's (P) property requires a remedy even if Hamidi (D) was not unjustly enriched by the use. As in *Buchanan Marine Inc. v. McCormack Sand Co.*, 743 F. Supp. 139 (E.D.N.Y. 1990), where an allegation of damage had no bearing on a request

Continued on next page.

for an injunction, in this case too the unlawful use of Intel's (P) property supports an injunction.

DISSENT: (Mosk, J.) Contrary to the majority, physical damage has not universally been a prerequisite for a trespass to chattels. It is appropriate to extend that cause of action to circumstances such as those found here—where Hamidi's (D) use of Intel's (P) computers clearly invades Intel's (P) right to exclude him from that use. One noted treatise even acknowledges application of the trespass tort to prevent unwanted e-mail from computer systems. The same authority (Dobbs) also notes that the necessary harm can be to some other interest besides the integrity of the personal property itself. In this case, the Restatement's preference for self-help in preventing harm to chattels clearly does not apply because the trespasses are electronic; Intel (P) tried self-help, and it did not work. Current law thus supports Intel's (P) request for an injunction. Even if this case presents a new question, though, the circumstances here require an extension of the law.

ANALYSIS

The court emphasized that its decision did not rest on any special immunity for e-mail communications, and noted that such communications could cause legally cognizable injury under other legal theories, such as interference with prospective economic relations, interference with contract, defamation, or intentional infliction of emotional distress. As the opinion makes clear, for conduct to amount to trespass to chattels, however, there must be injury to the chattel itself, or to some right in that property.

Quicknotes

TRESPASS TO CHATTELS Action for damages sustained as a result of defendant's unlawful interference with plaintiff's personal property.

CHAPTER 2

The Right to Exclude Others from Semi-Private Property: Free Speech Rights Versus Property Rights

Quick Reference Rules of Law

PAGE

1. **Exclusive Possession.** Real property rights are not absolute; and "necessity, private or public, may justify entry upon the lands of another." (State of New Jersey v. Shack and Tejeras) *6*

2. **Free Speech and Private Property.** The extent of free speech rights on private property depends on the nature of the use of the property, the extent of the public invitation to use that property, and the purpose of the speech activity in relation to the use of the property. (New Jersey Coalition Against War in the Middle East v. J.M.B Realty Corporation) *7*

State of New Jersey v. Shack and Tejeras

State (P) v. Aid workers (D)

N.J. Sup. Ct., 58 N.J. 297, 277 A.2d 369 (1971).

NATURE OF CASE: Appeal from a conviction of trespassing.

FACT SUMMARY: Tejeras (D) and Shack (D) entered upon private property against the orders of the owner of that property, to aid migrant farm workers employed and housed there.

RULE OF LAW

Real property rights are not absolute; and "necessity, private or public, may justify entry upon the lands of another."

FACTS: Tejeras (D) and Shack (D) worked with migrant farm workers. Tejeras (D) was a field worker for the Farm Workers Division of the Southwest Citizens Organization for Poverty Elimination (known as SCOPE), a nonprofit corporation funded by the Office of Economic Opportunity which provided for the "health services of the migrant farm worker." Shack (D) was a staff attorney with the Farm Workers Division of Camden Regional Legal Services, Inc. (known as CRLS), also a nonprofit corporation funded by the Office of Economic Opportunity which provided (along with other services) legal advice for, and representation of, migrant farm workers. Tejeras (D) and Shack (D), pursuant to their roles in SCOPE and CRLS, entered upon private property to aid migrant workers employed and housed there. When both Tejeras (D) and Shack (D) refused to leave the property at the owner's request, they were charged with trespassing under a New Jersey statute which provides that "any person who trespasses on any lands . . . after being forbidden so to trespass by the owner . . . is a disorderly person and shall be punished by a fine of not more than $50." After conviction for trespassing, Tejeras (D) and Shack (D) brought this appeal.

ISSUE: Does an owner of real property have the absolute right to exclude all others from that property?

HOLDING AND DECISION: (Weintraub, C.J.) No. Real property rights are not absolute; and "necessity, private or public, may justify entry upon the lands of another." This rule is based upon the basic rationale that "property rights serve human values. They are recognized to that end and are limited by it." Here, a central concern is the welfare of the migrant farm workers—a highly disadvantaged segment of society. Migrant farm workers, in general, are "outside of the mainstream of the communities in which they are housed and are unaware of their rights and opportunities, and of the services available to them." As such, here, the "necessity" of effective communication of legal rights and of providing medical services for the migrant farm workers justifies entry upon the private property. Of course, the owner of such property has the right to pursue his farming activities without interference, but, here, there is no legitimate need for the owner to exclude those attempting to assist the migrant farm workers. Furthermore, the migrant farm worker must be allowed to receive visitors of his choice, so long as there is no behavior harmful to others, and members of the press may not be denied access to any farm worker who wishes to see them. In any of these situations, since no possessory right of the farmer-employer-landowner has been invaded (i.e., since he has no right to exclude such persons), there can be no trespassing. Reversed and remanded.

ANALYSIS

Generally, the right to exclusive possession is considered "the oldest, most widely recognized right of private property in land." This case, though, illustrates the central limitation on the right to possession or use of private property—it may not be used to harm others. Here, the exclusion of Tejeras (D) and Shack (D) was, therefore, invalid because it would harm a very disadvantaged segment of society (the farm workers). Note that, under this principle, an owner of property, also, has no right to maintain a nuisance, to violate a building code, or to violate any "police power" laws (i.e., laws for the general public welfare).

Quicknotes

POSSESSORY RIGHT The right to possess particular real property to the exclusion of others.

TRESPASS TO LAND Physical invasion of the plaintiff's property that is intended and caused by the defendant's conduct.

New Jersey Coalition Against War in the Middle East v. J.M.B. Realty Corp.

Political group (P) v. Mall owner (D)

N.J. Sup. Ct., 138 N.J. 326, 650 A.2d 757 (1994).

NATURE OF CASE: Action to enjoin private property owners from banning political leafleting.

FACT SUMMARY: J.M.B. Realty (D), which owns several private indoor malls, banned the New Jersey Coalition Against the War in the Middle East (P) from passing out political leaflets in its malls.

RULE OF LAW

The extent of free speech rights on private property depends on the nature of the use of the property, the extent of the public invitation to use that property, and the purpose of the speech activity in relation to the use of the property.

FACTS: The New Jersey Coalition Against the War in the Middle East (Coalition) (P) sought to conduct a massive leafleting campaign in 1990 to seek support for their position that the United States should not be involved in the Gulf War. The Coalition (P) wanted to pass out their leaflets in ten large shopping center malls in New Jersey. Nine of the ten shopping centers had between 93 and 244 tenants, which included restaurants, department stores, banks, hair salons, theaters, doctor's offices, and many other specialty stores. In addition to these services, each of the malls also permitted and encouraged a variety of nonshopping, community activities. Most of these malls rejected the Coalition's (P) attempts to obtain permission to distribute leaflets at the malls. The Coalition (P) sought judicial relief, claiming that J.M.B. Realty Corp.'s (J.M.B.'s) (D) denial of permission violated their free speech rights under the First Amendment and the New Jersey Constitution.

ISSUE: Does the extent of free speech rights on private property depend on the nature of the use of the property, the extent of the public invitation to use that property, and the purpose of the speech activity in relation to the use of the property?

HOLDING AND DECISION: (Wilentz, C.J.) Yes. The extent of free speech rights on private property depends on the nature of the use of the property, the extent of the public invitation to use that property, and the purpose of the speech activity in relation to the use of the property. According to Supreme Court precedent, the First Amendment does not afford a general right to free speech in privately owned shopping centers. However, the New Jersey right to free speech has been held to confer some rights against interference from private property owners. The holding in *State v. Schmid*, 423 A.2d 615 (1980), determined that there are some free speech rights on private property provided that the use of the property and the nature of the speech meet certain criteria. The predominant characteristic of the use of large shopping center malls is their all-inclusiveness. People engage in all of the activities that previously took place in the public areas of towns and cities. Additionally, malls make an all-embracing invitation to the public and have significant nonretail uses. Given this invitation and wide range of use, J.M.B. (D) cannot deny all free speech rights. Historical records show that leafleting has not been a burden on retail locations. The speech interest at stake here goes to the central reason for free speech commentary regarding government actions. Therefore, J.M.B.'s (D) shopping centers must accommodate speech of this type, although they remain free to set reasonable time, place, and manner restrictions.

DISSENT: (Garibaldi, J.) The majority ignores the fact that the primary users of malls are shoppers and that mall owners are in business to sell goods. Under the majority's analysis, any time the public is invited onto large, privately owned property it becomes a place to congregate and the functional equivalent of a downtown.

ANALYSIS

This case represents the minority view. Only about five other states have maintained similar rights based upon their state constitutions. The majority went to great lengths to demonstrate that today's shopping malls are the equivalent of the town square and downtown business district of years ago. They seemed to feel that political groups would not be able to reach large amounts of people any other way.

Quicknotes

FREEDOM OF SPEECH The right to express oneself without governmental restrictions on the content of that expression.

STATE ACTION Actions brought pursuant to the Fourteenth Amendment claiming that the government violated the plaintiff's civil rights.

CHAPTER 3

Landlord-Tenant: The Right of Exclusive Physical Possession

Quick Reference Rules of Law

Beckett v. City of Paris Dry Goods Co.

Optometrist (P) v. Landlord (D)

Cal. Sup. Ct., 14 Cal. 2d 633, 96 P.2d 122 (1939).

NATURE OF CASE: Appeal from award of damages for unlawful eviction.

FACT SUMMARY: Paris Dry Goods Co. (Paris) (D) permitted Beckett (P) to operate an optometry office within Paris's (D) store under an agreement setting forth the usual leasehold provisions that did not specify the place for the shop; however, Beckett (P) occupied the same space until he was removed after a short notice.

RULE OF LAW

An agreement to permit the operation of a business in a store in an unspecified area is a lease where the parties act upon it so as to relate to a specific place and use the leasehold terminology in the writing.

FACTS: Beckett (P) was an optometrist who operated a shop in City of Paris Dry Goods Co.'s (Paris's) (D) store pursuant to an agreement whereby Beckett (P) was promised unspecified premises within the store in return for a percentage of gross receipts. There were provisions in this written agreement requiring delivery of the premises to Beckett (P) in good, tenantable condition and also against assignment. Beckett (P) operated his shop in the same several rooms for over two years until a dispute arose over Beckett's (P) obligation to deposit his receipts with Paris (D) for division between them. Beckett (P) was given a notice to vacate the premises and later his wares and equipment were removed therefrom by Paris (D). Beckett (P) recovered damages for wrongful eviction but was denied certain other damages, and both parties appealed.

ISSUE: Is an agreement to permit the operation of a business in a store in an unspecified area a lease where the parties act upon it so as to relate to a specific place and use the leasehold terminology in the writing?

HOLDING AND DECISION: (Edmonds, J.) Yes. The conduct of the parties shows an intention to create a lease. The written agreement is referred to in its text as a lease, the normal leasehold covenants are contained within and a restriction against "assignment" is included. Though no specific area is spelled out as the subject of the lease, the parties kept the same arrangement intact throughout as to the several rooms which Beckett (P) exclusively occupied. Where the parties act upon an agreement to permit the use of commercial space in such a way as to indicate that that specific place was intended and use the usual leasehold language, the agreement is a lease rather than a mere license. A mere license could have been terminated in the event Paris (D) intended to terminate this agreement, but a lease could not. Affirmed and damages award increased.

ANALYSIS

The caption or title on a document certainly does not conclusively control what it is. A so-called "lease" may in fact create a licensor-licensee relationship instead. Such a designation may often be evidence, however, of what intention the parties had with respect to the agreement. The conduct of the parties with respect to the transaction is also evidence, and is often more enlightening on the subject of the intent. In any case, it is the intent of the parties in contracting that controls such a situation.

Quicknotes

LEASE An agreement or contract that creates a relationship between a landlord and tenant (real property) or lessor and lessee (real or personal property).

LICENSE A right that is granted to a person allowing him or her to conduct an activity that without such permission he or she could not lawfully do, and which is unassignable and revocable at the will of the licensor.

Wenner and City of Phoenix v. Dayton-Hudson Corporation

City Treasurer and City (D) v. Department stores (P)

Ariz. Ct. App., 123 Ariz. 203, 598 P.2d 1022 (1979).

NATURE OF CASE: Challenge to municipal tax.

FACT SUMMARY: Dayton-Hudson Corporation (P) challenged a one percent privilege tax assessed by the City of Phoenix (D) on funds derived from the sublease of portions of its department stores.

RULE OF LAW

A license agreement is formed when a tenant does not have exclusive possession or any interest whatsoever in the premises being leased.

FACTS: Dayton-Hudson Corporation (Dayton) (P) operates department stores within the City of Phoenix (City) (D) and enters into agreements with other retailers to maintain certain departments within its stores. The agreements grant the retailer the exclusive right to operate the particular type of department and are restricted to such conduct. In consideration, the retailer pays Dayton (P) a percentage of gross receipts with a designated monthly minimum payment. The income derived from such agreements was assessed a 1 percent privilege tax by the City (D). Dayton (P) paid the tax under protest and was granted a hearing. After exhausting its administrative remedies, Dayton (P) brought suit in superior court. The trial court granted the City's (D) motion for summary judgment and awarded the City (D) $20,364.22 plus interest and costs. Dayton (P) appealed.

ISSUE: Is a license agreement formed when a tenant does not have exclusive possession or any interest whatsoever in the premises being leased?

HOLDING AND DECISION: (Donofrio, J.) Yes. A license agreement is formed when a tenant does not have exclusive possession or any interest whatsoever in the premises being leased. The Phoenix City Code § 14-2 imposes a tax equal to 1 percent of gross proceeds of sale or gross income from the business upon every person engaging in the leasing or renting for consideration the use or occupancy of real property. The City (D) contends that the agreement here is a lease and not a license as stated in the agreement. While section 5 of the agreement states that it is a license, this is not controlling. It must be determined whether the agreement as a whole is in accord with this intent. Under the agreement, Dayton (P) is obligated to furnish an agreeable amount of space in the store, which may be changed from time to time at Dayton's (P) direction. The retailer is not to receive any interest in the real property or exclusive possession of any portion thereof. The retailer has access to the premises only when the store is open to the public and may conduct business only at those times. The retailer is required to use Dayton's (P) trademark and trade name in conducting business. These factors indicate that the parties here intended to create a licensor-licensee relationship. Affirmed.

ANALYSIS

The Restatement (Second) of Property § 1.1 states that even where a tenant is subject to being moved from one location to another in a building this does not preclude formation of a lease agreement. In many cases, the terminology used in the agreement will govern.

Quicknotes

EXCLUSIVE POSSESSION Possession of property to the exclusion of all others; constitutes a requirement for the acquiring of property through adverse possession.

LEASE An agreement or contract that creates a relationship between a landlord and tenant (real property) or lessor and lessee (real or personal property).

LICENSE A right that is granted to a person allowing him or her to conduct an activity that without such permission he or she could not lawfully do, and which is unassignable and revocable at the will of the licensor.

REAL PROPERTY Land, an interest in land, or anything attached to the land that is incapable of being removed.

SUMMARY JUDGMENT Judgment rendered by a court in response to a motion made by one of the parties, claiming that the lack of a question of material fact in respect to an issue warrants disposition of the issue without consideration by the jury.

Smith v. McEnany

Landlord (P) v. Tenant (D)

Mass. Sup. Jud. Ct., 170 Mass. 26, 48 N.E. 781 (1897).

NATURE OF CASE: Appeal of judgment ruling an encroachment and eviction.

FACT SUMMARY: Smith (P) brought this action for the rental payment for a lot and shed, and the lessor, McEnany (D), asserted eviction as a complete defense because Smith (P) permitted the building of a structure that encroached onto the leasehold by some nine to 13 inches.

RULE OF LAW

The encroachment of a structure upon a portion of a leasehold constitutes an eviction and a defense to the entire rental payment otherwise due.

FACTS: Smith (P) leased certain premises to McEnany (D) consisting of a lot improved with a shed in which McEnany (D) stored wagons. Smith (P) owned an adjoining lot and permitted the building on that lot of a structure that encroached onto McEnany's (D) leasehold by somewhere between nine and 13 inches. McEnany (D) refused to make the rental payment alleging an eviction because of the encroachment, and Smith (P) brought this action for rent. The trial court ruled that the encroachment was an eviction and a good defense to the entire rental payment due. Smith (P) appealed.

ISSUE: Does the encroachment of a structure upon a portion of a leasehold constitute an eviction and a defense to the entire rental payment otherwise due?

HOLDING AND DECISION: (Holmes, J.) Yes. It is settled in this state as in England that a wrongful eviction of the tenant by the landlord from a part of the premises suspends the rent otherwise due under the lease. A landlord may not apportion his wrong and collect any partial payment. It is said by some authorities that the rent issues out of the land and is charged on every part of the land. Thus, a structure that encroaches upon part of a leasehold constitutes an eviction and is a defense to the entire rental payment otherwise due. Nonetheless, the lease remains in effect and the other obligations thereunder remain binding. Exceptions overruled.

ANALYSIS

This case typifies the "conveyance theory" of leases. The premises are conveyed, as in a sale, only with a reversion in the grantor-lessor at the end of the stated time. Some modern cases follow the "contract theory" that holds the obligations of rent and possession interdependent and damages are more readily apportionable under this theory.

Quicknotes

EVICTION The removal of a person from possession of property.

Echo Consulting Services, Inc. v. North Conway Bank

Tenant (P) v. Landlord (D)

N.H. Sup. Ct., 140 N.H. 566, 669 A.2d 227 (1995).

NATURE OF CASE: Suit claiming constructive eviction, partial actual eviction, breach of the implied covenant of quiet enjoyment, and breach of a lease agreement.

FACT SUMMARY: Echo Consulting Services, Inc. (P) brought suit against its landlord, North Conway Bank (Bank) (D), alleging constructive and actual eviction and breach of the covenant of quiet enjoyment as a result of a series of renovations undertaken by the Bank (D).

RULE OF LAW

The law implies a covenant of quiet enjoyment, which obligates the landlord to refrain from interfering with the tenant's possession of the premises during the period of the tenancy.

FACTS: Echo Consulting Services, Inc. (Echo) (P) leased premises on the downstairs floor of a building in Conway, along with "common right of access thereto." When North Conway Bank (Bank) (D) purchased the building from Echo's (P) prior landlord, it assumed the lease. The Bank (D) then underwent a series of renovations severely restricting access to Echo's (P) premises. Echo (P) brought suit against the Bank (D) claiming constructive eviction, partial actual eviction, breach of the implied covenant of quiet enjoyment, and breach of the lease agreement. The trial court denied all of Echo's (P) claims and Echo (P) appealed.

ISSUE: Does the law imply a covenant of quiet enjoyment, which obligates the landlord to refrain from interfering with the tenant's possession of the premises during the period of the tenancy?

HOLDING AND DECISION: (Brock, C.J.) Yes. The law implies a covenant of quiet enjoyment, which obligates the landlord to refrain from interfering with the tenant's possession of the premises during the period of the tenancy. There are various ways in which a landlord may breach this covenant, each giving rise to a different claim by the tenant. Partial actual eviction occurs where the landlord deprives the tenant of physical possession of some portion of the leased property, including denial of access to the leased premises. Since a landlord cannot apportion a tenant's rights under a lease, the Bank (D) cannot apportion Echo's (P) rights to choose which door to enter, if the lease gives Echo (P) a right to enter through two different doors. Echo (P), however, was not physically deprived of any portion of the property leased to it. The lease provides Echo (P) with the "common right of access." This means that Echo's (P) right of access was not exclusive, but in common with the landlord's (D). The finding that Echo (P) has access to its offices through at least one door at all times by the trial court is a determination that such access was reasonable. Constructive eviction occurs when the landlord deprives the tenant of the beneficial use or enjoyment of the property so that the action is tantamount to depriving the tenant of physical possession. The landlord (D) argued that a constructive eviction claim lies only where the premises are rendered unfit for occupancy, or the landlord permanently interferes with the tenant's beneficial use or enjoyment of the premises. The court does not agree. The landlord's conduct, and not his intent, is controlling. The relevant inquiry is the extent of the interference, i.e., whether it is substantial enough that it is equivalent to depriving the tenant of physical possession. Here the interference from the construction was "intermittent and temporary and did not substantially interfere or deprive Echo (P) of the use of the premises." Thus, it did not rise to the level of a constructive eviction. A breach of the covenant of quiet enjoyment occurs when the landlord substantially interferes with the tenant's beneficial use or enjoyment of the premises. Even if the interference is not substantial enough to rise to the level of a constructive eviction, the landlord may be liable for breach of the covenant, entitling the tenant to damages. The trial court concluded that the covenant only protects a tenant's possession against repossession by the landlord or one claiming superior title. This is an erroneous interpretation. The trial court's conclusion is reversed and remanded for further proceedings on this issue. Affirmed in part, reversed in part, and remanded.

ANALYSIS

Lease agreements are in essence contracts and must be construed in accordance with the general rules of contract interpretation. In determining the meaning of a disputed provision, the court looks to the entire agreement. The contract will be interpreted in accordance with its plain meaning, in the absence of ambiguity.

Quicknotes

CONSTRUCTIVE EVICTION An action whereby the landlord renders the property unsuitable for occupancy, either in whole or in part, so that the tenant is forced to leave the premises.

COVENANT OF QUIET ENJOYMENT A promise contained in a lease or a deed that the tenant or grantee will enjoy unimpaired use of the property.

EVICTION The removal of a person from possession of property.

LEASE AGREEMENT An agreement pursuant to which the owner of an interest in property relinquishes the right to possession to another.

CHAPTER 4

Implied Landlord's Duties and Implied Conditions to Tenant's Obligations

Quick Reference Rules of Law

Marini v. Ireland

Landlord (P) v. Tenant (D)

N.J. Sup. Ct., 56 N.J. 130, 265 A.2d 526 (1970).

NATURE OF CASE: Action to recover rent.

FACT SUMMARY: After Alice Ireland (D) leased certain resident premises from Joseph Marini (P), certain repairs became necessary and, when Marini (P) refused to make such repairs, Ireland (D) made them and offset the cost thereof against her rent.

RULE OF LAW

The implied covenant of habitability and livability fitness, which is found in every lease of residential premises, requires that the landlord maintain the leased premises in a livable condition "throughout the term of the lease" and, if the landlord fails, after timely and adequate notice of faulty conditions, to make repairs and replacements necessary to maintain the premises in a livable condition, the tenant may either (1) leave the premises with no further rent owing (i.e., "constructive eviction"), or (2) make the necessary repairs himself and deduct the cost thereof from future rents.

FACTS: Alice Ireland (D) leased certain residential premises from Joseph Marini (P), which consisted of four rooms and a bath to be used only for "dwelling purposes." After Ireland (D) moved in, it became necessary to make repairs on the toilet and she notified Joseph Marini (P) of this. Marini (P), however, failed to repair the toilet and, finally, Ireland (D) repaired it and offset the cost thereof against her rent. Thereupon, Marini (P) brought an action to recover such rent. As a defense to this action, Ireland (D) claims that the failure of the landlord to repair the toilet constituted a breach of the covenant of habitability and entitled her to self-help (i.e., to repair the toilet and offset the cost thereof against her rent).

ISSUE: When a landlord fails to make necessary repairs during the period of a lease of residential promises, does such failure constitute a violation of the covenant of habitability that entitles the tenant to self-help?

HOLDING AND DECISION: (Haneman, J.) Yes. The implied covenant of habitability and livability fitness, which is found in every lease of residential premises, requires that the landlord maintain the leased premises in a livable condition "throughout the term of the lease," and, if the landlord fails, after timely and adequate notice of faulty conditions, to make repairs and replacements necessary to maintain the premises in a livable condition, the tenant may either (1) leave the premises with no further rent owing (i.e., constructive eviction), or (2) make the necessary repairs himself and deduct the cost thereof from future rents. Of course, a covenant of habitability must be implied in every residential lease since the parties to such leases must have intended (even if they failed to express) that the premises were fit for habitation (i.e., their intended use). Furthermore, it is only fair to charge the landlord with the duty of warranting that a residential building is fit for that purpose at the inception of the term and will remain so during the term. As such, the landlord must have the duty to repair damage to vital facilities caused by "ordinary wear and tear during the term." Of course, where damage has been caused by maliciousness or by abnormal or unusual use, the tenant is liable for repair. Here, however, the improper functioning of the toilet was due to ordinary wear, and, as such, it was the duty of the landlord to repair it. When he failed to make necessary repairs, after notice and a reasonable time to do so, the tenant was entitled to make the repairs and deduct the cost thereof from her rent. Reversed and remanded.

ANALYSIS

This case illustrates the general rule that a warranty of habitability is implied in every residential lease (which includes the obligation to repair the premises throughout the lease period). The most common remedy for a breach of this warranty is the right of the tenant to refuse to pay rent or to vacate the premises with no further rent owing. Only a few states currently allow a tenant to repair and deduct the cost thereof from his rent payments. Some states, such as California, allow a tenant to repair and deduct but only for one month's rent. As such, this is a very limited remedy, since the cost of any repairs necessary to make premises habitable are usually great. Finally, it should be noted that the *Marini* case was expanded in *Berzito v. Gambins*, 63 N.J. 460 (1973), which held that a tenant can recover all or part of his rent paid during the term when the landlord has broken the implied covenant of habitability. Such remedy is not allowed in very many jurisdictions, though.

Quicknotes

CONSTRUCTIVE EVICTION An action whereby the landlord renders the property unsuitable for occupancy, either in whole or in part, so that the tenant is forced to leave the premises.

COVENANT OF HABITABILITY A warranty implied by a landlord that the premises are suitable, and will remain suitable, for habitation.

Knight v. Hallsthammar

Landlord (P) v. Tenant (D)

Cal. Sup. Ct., 29 Cal. 3d 46, 623 P.2d 268 (1981).

NATURE OF CASE: Appeals from judgments of eviction in unlawful detainer actions.

FACT SUMMARY: Knight (P) obtained unlawful detainer evictions of Hallsthammar and other tenants of his (D) upon their refusal to pay rent due to an alleged breach of the implied warranty of habitability by failing to correct problems relating to structural defects, insects, and rodents.

RULE OF LAW

A landlord's breach of the implied warranty of habitability of rented premises constitutes a defense to an unlawful detainer action even where the tenant remains in possession of the premises after the alleged breach.

FACTS: Knight (P) acquired title to a building with 30 units then occupied. Western Investment Properties (WIP) was hired to manage the building and promptly apprised the tenants of a substantial rent increase. WIP's officer informed the tenants that the only repairs planned were to common areas and vacated apartments. The tenants complained to the building manager about wall cracks, peeling paint, water leaks, heating and electrical problems, broken windows, rodents, and insects, but few and minor repairs resulted. The tenants then withheld rent, which brought about this unlawful detainer action. The tenants defended on the ground that Knight (P) had breached the implied warranty of habitability by failure to repair. Knight (P) countered with the assertion that this defense was not available to a tenant who, like Hallsthammar et al. (D), did not vacate the premises. The trial court so instructed the jury, and also instructed that Knight (P) was entitled to a reasonable time to repair. The jury reached no verdict as to some of the tenants, but as to Hallsthammar et al. (D) it found that the warranty defense was not available. Hallsthammar et al. (D) appealed, citing erroneous jury instructions.

ISSUE: Does a landlord's breach of an implied warranty of habitability constitute a defense to an unlawful detainer action even where the tenant remains in possession of the premises after the alleged breach?

HOLDING AND DECISION: (Bird, C.J.) Yes. This court has recognized the defense of the implied warranty of habitability and a public policy prohibiting waiver of that defense. This policy is consistent with California's statutory design in landlord and tenant relations. A landlord's breach of the implied warranty of habitability constitutes a defense to an unlawful detainer action even where the tenant remains in possession of the premises after the alleged breach. Furthermore, the knowledge of a tenant of such conditions of uninhabitability is dispositive of the landlord's duty to repair. Where a landlord has actual notice of the conditions in question, any duty to permit a reasonable time to repair has been met. Thus, the trial court's instructions to the jury were erroneous. Reversed.

DISSENT: (Clark, J.) Should a tenant be permitted to conclude his bargain with the landlord aware of the shortcomings of the premises and then later require improvements for the same amount of rent? The acceptance may constitute a waiver of the defense of the implied warranty of habitability. The payment of rent is dependent upon the fulfillment of the duty to repair, and nonpayment gives rise to an unlawful detainer action which cannot be defended on the ground of breach when the tenant is still in possession by agreement.

ANALYSIS

Generally in jurisdictions recognizing an implied warranty of habitability, a breach of the warranty entitles the tenant to withhold rent. The tenant, however, is liable for the reasonable rental value of the premises in its actual condition through the period of occupancy.

Quicknotes

IMPLIED WARRANTY OF HABITABILITY A warranty implied by a landlord that the premises are suitable, and will remain suitable, for habitation.

Wade v. Jobe

Landlord (P) v. Tenant (D)

Utah Sup. Ct., 818 P.2d 1006 (1991).

NATURE OF CASE: Suit to recover unpaid rent.

FACT SUMMARY: Jobe (D) refused to pay rent to Wade (P) on the basis that the house that she had leased was uninhabitable.

RULE OF LAW

There is a common law implied warranty of habitability in residential leases.

FACTS: Jobe (D) rented a house from Wade (P). Shortly after she took possession of the premises, she discovered numerous defects in the home, and a few days later she had no hot water. Investigation showed that the flame of the hot water heater had extinguished due to accumulated sewage and water in the basement, which also produced a foul odor throughout the house. These problems persisted until Jobe (D) notified Wade (P) that she would be withholding rent until the problem was permanently fixed. The situation did not improve and an inspection by the Ogden City Inspection Division revealed that the premises were unsafe for human occupancy. After Jobe (D) vacated the house, Wade (P) brought suit to recover unpaid rent. Jobe (D) filed a counterclaim, seeking an offset against rent owed because of the uninhabitable condition. Wade (P) was awarded judgment of unpaid rent of $770, the full rent due under the parties' agreement. Jobe (D) was denied any offsets and her counterclaim dismissed. Jobe (D) appealed.

ISSUE: Is there a common law implied warranty of habitability in residential leases?

HOLDING AND DECISION: (Durham, J.) Yes. There is a common law implied warranty of habitability in residential leases. The determination of whether a dwelling is habitable depends upon the facts of the particular case. This does not require that the landlord keep the premises in perfect condition, it does not prohibit minor housing code violations or other defects, and it does not make the landlord liable for defects caused by the tenant. The landlord must also be given a reasonable time to repair material defects before a breach can be shown. The general rule is that the warranty of habitability requires the landlord to maintain "bare living requirements," and that the premises are fit for human occupation. Substantial compliance with building and housing code standards generally serves as evidence of the landlord's satisfaction of his duty. In contrast, evidence of violations involving health or safety will sustain a tenant's claim for relief. The violation of a housing code is not necessary to establish a breach, so long as the claimed defect has an impact on the health or safety of the tenant. Here, Jobe (D) presented two city housing inspection reports detailing numerous code violations constituting a substantial hazard to the health and safety of the occupants. Jobe (D) testified that she repeatedly informed Wade (P) of the problems, and that he never did anything more than temporarily alleviate the problem. The trial court granted judgment for the landlord on the basis that Utah did not recognize the implied warranty of habitability for residential rental premises. This court now recognizes the warranty. Remanded for a determination of whether Wade (P) breached his duty.

ANALYSIS

The modern view of the residential lease as a contractual transaction provides that the tenant's obligation to pay rent is conditioned upon the landlord fulfilling any of his covenants, such as the duty to provide habitable premises. If the landlord breaches this duty, the tenant has the option of continuing to pay or withholding rent. If the tenant continues to pay full rent, he can later bring an affirmative action to establish the breach and receive reimbursement for excess rents paid.

Quicknotes

IMPLIED WARRANTY OF HABITABILITY A warranty implied by a landlord that the premises are suitable, and will remain suitable, for habitation.

LEASE An agreement or contract that creates a relationship between a landlord and tenant (real property) or lessor and lessee (real or personal property).

Davidow v. Inwood North Professional Group

Tenant (D) v. Landlord (P)

Tex. Sup. Ct., 747 S.W.2d 373 (1988).

NATURE OF CASE: Appeal from award of damages from breach of a lease agreement.

FACT SUMMARY: Inwood North Professional Group (P) leased medical office space to Dr. Davidow (D) that was basically unusable as a medical office.

RULE OF LAW

There is an implied warranty of suitability by the landlord in a commercial lease that the premises are suitable for their intended commercial purpose.

FACTS: Dr. Joseph Davidow (D) entered into a five-year lease agreement with Inwood North Professional Group (Inwood) (P). Inwood (P) was to provide Davidow (D) with medical office space. Additionally, the lease provided that Inwood (P) was required to furnish all repairs, utilities, maintenance, light fixtures, security, etc. Davidow (D) immediately began to experience problems: the roof leaked, cleaning and maintenance were not provided, heat and electricity were shut off, (Inwood (P) failed to pay the bills), rodents abounded, and the office was burglarized and vandalized. Davidow (D) moved out 14 months before the end of the lease term and stopped making rent payments. Inwood (P) sued Davidow (D) for unpaid rents. Davidow (D) answered with an affirmative defense that Inwood (P) breached its implied warranty that the office would be suitable for its intended use as a medical office, and that Davidow (D) was therefore relieved of his duty to pay rent. The trial court rendered judgment for Davidow (D). The court of appeals reversed, holding that Inwood's (P) covenant to maintain and repair the premises was independent of Davidow's (D) covenant to pay rent, and that the implied warranty of habitability for residential leases does not extend to commercial leases. Davidow (D) appealed.

ISSUE: Is there an implied warranty of suitability by the landlord in a commercial lease that the premises are suitable for their intended commercial purpose?

HOLDING AND DECISION: (Spears, J.) Yes. There is an implied warranty of suitability by the landlord in a commercial lease that the premises are suitable for their intended commercial purpose. The courts have been attempting to provide a more equitable and contemporary solution to landlord-tenant problems by easing the burden on tenants of the doctrine of independent lease covenants. The modern residential tenant seeks to lease a dwelling suitable for living purposes. The landlord usually has knowledge of any defects in the premises that may render the premises uninhabitable. Additionally, the landlord, as owner, should bear the cost of repairing the property. The court has previously recognized that an implied warranty of habitability extended to residential dwellers. Many of the same considerations apply to commercial tenants such as Davidow (D). A businessman cannot be expected to possess the expertise necessary to adequately inspect and repair the premises, and many commercial tenants lack the financial resources to hire inspectors and repairmen to assure the suitability of the premises. Therefore, such tenants rely on their landlord's greater abilities to inspect and repair the premises. Davidow (D) leased space from Inwood (P) for use as a medical office. Inwood (P) was aware of Davidow's (D) intended use. Davidow (D) was unable to use the space as intended because of Inwood's (P) acts and omissions. Therefore, Inwood (P) breached the implied duty of suitability. Reversed in part.

ANALYSIS

The court's holding suggests that there is little to distinguish between residential tenants and commercial tenants. Would the court's reasoning change if a large manufacturing corporation were the lessee? Doesn't such an entity lessee have equal ability as the lessor to inspect, repair, and bargain? Additionally, the corporation would likely be able to pass the costs of any repairs to the leased premises through to consumers buying its products.

Quicknotes

IMPLIED WARRANTY OF HABITABILITY A warranty implied by a landlord that the premises are suitable, and will remain suitable, for habitation.

LEASE AGREEMENT An agreement pursuant to which the owner of an interest in property relinquishes the right to possession to another for a specified consideration and for a definite time period.

CHAPTER 5

Landlord's Tort Liability for Personal Injuries

Quick Reference Rules of Law

Asper, Administratrix of the Estate of Joni Marie Asper v. Haffley

Tenant's administratrix (P) v. Landlord (D)

Pa. Super. Ct., 312 Pa. Super. 424, 458 A.2d 1364 (1983).

NATURE OF CASE: Appeal from decision granting judgment in personal injury action.

FACT SUMMARY: Asper (P) appealed from Haffley's (D) successful motion for summary judgment in Asper's (P) wrongful death action, contending that the issue of Haffley's (D) negligence based upon a dangerous condition of premises should have been submitted to the trier of fact.

RULE OF LAW

Where a plaintiff in a wrongful death action pleads facts sufficient to sustain a finding that a landlord has breached the implied warranty of habitability, he may proceed with an action for negligence against the landlord.

FACTS: Haffley (D) purchased the premises in question in 1972. He used it as a combination residence and office. He made certain structural alterations and rented the premises to Asper (P) in May 1976. In September 1976, a fire broke out and Asper's (P) daughter, Joni, was killed. Evidence indicated that the fire trapped Joni in her bedroom, and that she was unable to break through the storm windows installed by Haffley (D), which could not be opened from the inside. Asper (P) brought the present action, and Haffley (D) successfully moved for summary judgment, the court concluding that under the principles limiting landlord liability, Asper (P) had not alleged sufficient facts on which Haffley (D) could be held liable on a negligence theory. Asper (P) appealed.

ISSUE: Where a plaintiff in a wrongful death action pleads facts sufficient to sustain a finding that a landlord has breached an implied warranty of habitability may he then proceed with a negligence action against the landlord?

HOLDING AND DECISION: (Price, J.) Yes. Where a plaintiff in a wrongful death action pleads facts sufficient to sustain a finding that the landlord has breached the implied warranty of habitability, he may then proceed with an action for negligence action against the landlord. This jurisdiction has recognized that a landlord can be liable for physical harm caused by a dangerous condition of premises, if the condition violates an implied warranty of habitability. The facts presented in this case, and reasonable inferences that can be drawn from those facts, if proved, would support a finding of a dangerous condition of property in violation of the warranty of habitability. Thus, the question of Haffley's (D) negligence should have been submitted to the fact finder. Reversed and remanded.

CONCURRENCE: (Wieand, J.) Asper (P) should be allowed to proceed alternatively on a negligence action, or based on a violation of the warranty of habitability.

ANALYSIS

At least one state has imposed statutory strict liability on the part of lessors. See La. Civil Code Ann., art. 2695. One can argue that strict liability, the societal allocation of risk, need not be addressed in the commercial lease context.

Quicknotes

IMPLIED WARRANTY OF HABITABILITY A warranty implied by a landlord that the premises are suitable, and will remain suitable, for habitation.

SUMMARY JUDGMENT Judgment rendered by a court in response to a motion made by one of the parties, claiming that the lack of a question of material fact in respect to an issue warrants disposition of the issue without consideration by the jury.

WRONGFUL DEATH An action brought by the beneficiaries of a deceased person, claiming that the deceased's death was the result of wrongful conduct by the defendant.

Merrill v. Jansma

Rental home visitor (P) v. Landlord (D)

Wyo. Sup. Ct., 86 P.3d 270 (2004).

NATURE OF CASE: Negligence suit for personal injuries occurring on rental property.

FACT SUMMARY: Merrill fell on the unrepaired front steps of the mobile home rented by her daughter. Merrill then sued her daughter's landlord, Jansma, for negligence.

RULE OF LAW

A landlord owes a duty of care in cases involving personal injuries that occur on rental property.

FACTS: Merrill (P) fell and hurt her right shoulder when she walked up the front steps of the mobile home that her daughter rented from Jansma (D). A step had become loose after Merrill's (P) daughter started renting the home; the daughter had tried to fix the step herself and had told Jansma (D) that it needed repair. Although Jansma (D) did try to fix the step, it remained unrepaired when Merrill (P) stepped on it and fell. Merrill (P) sued Jansma (D) for negligence, alleging in part that Jansma (D) owed a duty of care to Merrill (P). Jansma (D) moved for summary judgment, arguing that she owed no duty of care under Wyoming law. The trial court granted Jansma's (D) motion for summary judgment, agreeing with Jansma (D) that she owed no duty of care to Merrill (P). Merrill (P) appealed.

ISSUE: Does a landlord owe a duty of care in cases involving personal injuries that occur on rental property?

HOLDING AND DECISION: (Kite, J.) Yes. A landlord owes a duty of care in cases involving personal injuries that occur on rental property. Traditionally, at common law landlords owed no duty of care in such circumstances. Courts, however, gradually recognized five exceptions to this traditional rule: (1) for defects on rented premises used to admit the public, (2) for defects resulting from a breach of a covenant to repair, (3) for negligent repairs, (4) for defects in common areas controlled by landlords, and (5) for defects that violate building or housing codes. An overwhelming majority of states eventually abandoned the common-law rule of landlord immunity altogether. Wyoming has until now remained in the minority of states still recognizing landlord immunity. Wyoming's most recent landlord-tenant statute, though, has created a duty of care for landlords where personal injuries occur on rental property. The statute does not expressly, literally state that it is abrogating the common-law rule of immunity, but it does create a previously unrecognized duty of care whose existence in the statute is beyond dispute. Accordingly, although the letter of the statute is silent on whether the legislature intended to abrogate the common law, the indisputable duty imposed by the statute also creates a new standard of care where personal injuries occur on rental property. Reversed and remanded.

ANALYSIS

This opinion illustrates an important point of statutory interpretation in addition to the substantive rule of property law. It is axiomatic that statutes must clearly evince a legislative intent to abrogate the common law. As *Merrill* shows, something less than an express statement of intent can suffice.

Quicknotes

DUTY OF CARE A principle of negligence requiring an individual to act in such a manner as to avoid injury to a person to whom he or she owes a duty.

INVITEE A person who enters upon another's property by an express or implied invitation, and to whom the owner of the property owes a duty of care to guard against injury from those hazards which are discoverable through the exercise of reasonable care.

LEGISLATIVE INTENT The legislature's motivation or rationale for promulgating a statute.

Peterson v. Superior Court of Riverside County

Injured guest (P) v. Court (D)

Cal. Sup. Ct., 10 Cal. 4th 1185 (1995).

NATURE OF CASE: Appeal from issuance of peremptory writ of mandate directing trial court to permit strict liability theory in personal injury action.

FACT SUMMARY: Peterson (P) sued proprietors of the Palm Springs Marquis Motel (D) on a theory of strict liability for injuries sustained when she slipped and fell in the bathtub.

RULE OF LAW

The proprietor of a hotel cannot be held strictly liable under a products liability theory in tort for injuries to guests caused by defects in the premises.

FACTS: Peterson (P), a guest at the Palm Springs Marquis Motel (D), slipped in the bathtub while taking a shower, sustaining serious head injuries. Peterson (P) filed suits against the owners of the hotel (D), the operator of the hotel (D), and the manufacturer of the bathtub (D). In addition to a cause of action for negligence, Peterson (P) brought a cause of action for strict liability in tort, asserting that the bathtub was so slippery and smooth that it was defective. Prior to trial, the operator of the hotel (D) filed a motion in limine to preclude Peterson (P) from bringing the strict liability action. The trial court granted the motion, but the court of appeal overruled and issued a peremptory writ to allow Peterson (P) to proceed on her strict liability claim. The California Supreme Court granted review to determine whether a hotel proprietor or a residential landlord can be held strictly liable in tort for injuries caused by defects in the premises.

ISSUE: Can the proprietor of a hotel be held strictly liable under a products liability theory in tort for injuries to guests caused by defects in the premises?

HOLDING AND DECISION: (George, J.) No. The proprietor of a hotel cannot be held strictly liable under a products liability theory in tort for injuries to guests caused by defects in the premises. A hotel owner differs significantly from a manufacturer or retailer of a product, and it would be unfair as a matter of principle, as well as from an economic standpoint, to hold the owner strictly liable. Although a tenant injured by a defect in the premises may bring a negligence action if the hotel owner breached its duty to exercise reasonable care, a tenant cannot reasonably expect that a proprietor would have eliminated in a rented dwelling defects of which the proprietor was unaware and which would not have been disclosed by a reasonable inspection. These principles apply to residential landlords as well. Therefore, *Becker v. IRM Corp.*, 38 Cal.3d 454 (1985), is overruled. Remanded.

ANALYSIS

Almost every state that has examined this issue has similarly refused to extend liability to landlords under strict liability for injuries caused by defects in leased premises. An injured party may still bring a strict liability case against the manufacturer of the product, or a negligence action against the proprietor or landlord, so a guilty party is by no means absolved of responsibility. Similar cases have arisen involving condominium associations; courts have generally held them to a standard similar to that applied to landlords and hotel proprietors.

Quicknotes

MOTION IN LIMINE Motion by one party brought prior to trial to exclude the potential introduction of prejudicial evidence.

NEGLIGENCE Conduct falling below the standard of care that a reasonable person would demonstrate under similar conditions.

PERSONAL INJURY Harm to an individual's person or body.

STRICT LIABILITY Liability for all injuries proximately caused by a party's conducting of certain inherently dangerous activities without regard to negligence or fault.

WRIT OF MANDATE The written order of a court directing a particular action.

Trentacost v. Brussel

Assaulted tenant (P) v. Landlord (D)

N.J. Sup. Ct., 82 N.J. 214, 412 A.2d 436 (1980).

NATURE OF CASE: Appeal from award of damages in personal injury case.

FACT SUMMARY: Brussel (D) appealed a damage award in favor of his tenant, Trentacost (P), for a criminal assault which occurred at the apartment building he owned, challenging the court's finding of liability for his alleged failure to prevent the criminal assault.

RULE OF LAW

A landlord's implied warranty of habitability obliges him to furnish reasonable safeguards to protect tenants from foreseeable criminal activity on the premises.

FACTS: Trentacost (P), a tenant in a building owned by Brussel (D), was assaulted at the top of the stairs leading to her apartment. Because the front door to the building had no padlock, her assailant gained easy access to the common areas of the complex, where the assault took place. Trentacost (P) brought suit against Brussel (D), claiming that the landlord had failed to secure the entrance to the common areas of the building. Trentacost (P) submitted evidence of criminal and other suspicious activity arising in the neighborhood, and within the building itself. It was disputed whether Brussel (D) had promised to padlock the front entrance. At the close of evidence, Trentacost (P) successfully moved to strike the defense of contributory negligence. The jury was instructed on an "enhanced risk" theory of liability, and returned a verdict in favor of Trentacost (P). Brussel's (D) motion for judgment notwithstanding the verdict was denied, and he refused to consent to an additur. Trentacost (P) was granted a new trial as to damages, and was awarded $25,000. The appellate division affirmed the judgment, and Brussel (D) appealed.

ISSUE: Does a landlord's implied warranty of habitability oblige him to furnish reasonable safeguards to protect tenants from foreseeable criminal activity on the premises?

HOLDING AND DECISION: (Pashman, J.) Yes. A landlord's implied warranty of habitability obliges him to furnish reasonable safeguards to protect tenants from foreseeable criminal activity on the premises. [The court first noted sufficient evidence was presented to affirm the judgment on the "enhancement of risk" theory of liability, noting that foreseeability of harm was the crucial factor in determining whether a duty existed to take measures to guard against criminal activity.] The implied warranty of habitability arises from the economic and social relationship between landlord and tenant, and extends to all "facilities vital to the use of the premises for residential purposes." The premises necessarily encompassed the common areas of multiple dwellings. By failing to secure the front entrance, Brussel (D) has breached his implied warranty, and his liability can be premised on this alternated theory of liability. Affirmed.

DISSENT IN PART: (Clifford, J.) The existence of a duty should not be premised solely on the landlord-tenant relationship, but should arise from the particular circumstances of the case. Today's decision creates what amounts to absolute liability, based solely on the landlord-tenant relationship.

ANALYSIS

Most courts that have expanded the scope of the landlord's liability, at the expense of the landlord's traditional immunity, have done so based on negligence rather than on strict liability. Courts have recently extended theories of premise liability to condominium associations and their directors. See *Frances T. v. Village Green Owners Association*, 42 Cal.3d 490 (1986).

Quicknotes

CONTRIBUTORY NEGLIGENCE Behavior on the part of an injured plaintiff that combines with the defendant's negligence, resulting in injury to the plaintiff.

IMPLIED WARRANTY OF HABITABILITY A warranty implied by a landlord that the premises are suitable, and will remain suitable, for habitation.

CHAPTER 6

Landlord's Motives in Selecting or Removing Tenants

Quick Reference Rules of Law

Kramarsky v. Stahl Management

State Human Rights Commissioner (P) v. Landlord (D)

N.Y. Sup. Ct., 92 Misc. 2d 1030, 401 N.Y.S.2d 943 (1977).

NATURE OF CASE: Appeal from grant of a temporary restraining order.

FACT SUMMARY: Kramarsky (P), commissioner of the State Division of Human Rights, represented Judith Pierce, a black, divorced female attorney who was denied the opportunity to rent an apartment by Stahl (D) who claimed that the denial was based on Pierce's being an attorney and not on racial or other grounds.

RULE OF LAW

A landlord may deny the rental of his premises to any person for any reason except race, color, creed, sex, national origin, or marital status.

FACTS: Pierce applied for tenancy in Stahl's (D) building and filled out an application form. On the form, under a heading of "Repairs and Remarks," Pierce marked down "Painting—New Rules." The form further revealed that she was an attorney. Stahl (D) denied the application and Pierce alleged in this action that the denial was due to the facts that she was black, female, and divorced. Stahl (D) denied these factors as motivations and claimed that Pierce's profession and the remarks on the application form indicated to him that she would have been "trouble . . . as a tenant." Pierce obtained a temporary restraining order (TRO) against Stahl's rental of the apartment except to her. Stahl (D) appealed, citing his rental of 30 percent of his units to blacks and 60 percent of them to unmarried persons as evidence of nondiscrimination.

ISSUE: May a landlord deny the rental of his premises to any person for any reason except race, color, creed, sex, national origin, or marital status?

HOLDING AND DECISION: (Greenfield, J.) Yes. Absent a supervening statutory proscription, a landlord is free to do what he wishes with his property and to rent or not rent to any person at his whim. The only restraint which the law recognizes is that he may not use race, creed, color, national origin, sex, or marital status as criteria. Any other criteria are permitted, including occupational ones. He may decide not to rent to singers because they are too noisy, or he may bar bald-headed men because he's heard they give wild parties. There is similarly nothing illegal about discriminating against lawyers as a group or against intelligent persons who are aware of their legal rights, in favor of those who are less likely to be "trouble" to him. Application is denied and the temporary restraining order is vacated.

ANALYSIS

This decision admits of the allowance of some very unfair practices. The arbitrary denial of a place to live can hurt persons who have not fallen into a category usually discriminated against as well as those always subjected to discrimination. It must be admitted though that, here, Pierce demonstrated a propensity to be a troublesome tenant from the onset of the transaction.

Marina Point, Ltd. v. Wolfson

Landlord (P) v. Parent tenant (D)

Cal. Sup. Ct., 30 Cal. 3d 721, 640 P.2d 115 (1982).

NATURE OF CASE: Appeal from order of eviction in unlawful detainer action.

FACT SUMMARY: Wolfson (D) appealed from a decision upholding the policy of Marina Point, Ltd. (P) that excluded families with children from their apartment complex, contending that the exclusion violated their rights under the state's Civil Rights Act, as well as their state and federal constitutional rights.

RULE OF LAW

The Unruh Civil Rights Act (Act) prohibits a landlord from refusing to rent its apartments to families solely on the basis that the family includes a minor child.

FACTS: Wolfson (D) rented an apartment at Marina Point, Ltd. (Marina) (P), an 846-unit complex. The one-year lease entered into provided that no minors could reside in the complex, but it was conceded that Marina (P) had a policy of renting to families with children as well as childless families. Marina (P) altered the policy, deciding to no longer rent to new families with children or to pregnant women. Approximately one year later, Wolfson (D) had a child. When Marina (P) learned of this fact, Wolfson (D) was told that his lease would not be renewed solely because of the child's presence. After negotiations broke down, Marina (P) brought the present unlawful detainer action. The trial court concluded that because children were "rowdier, noisier, more mischievous and more boisterous than adults" the exclusion of children from the complex proceeded from a reasonable economic motive and therefore did not violate Wolfson's (D) rights. From that decision, Wolfson (D) appealed.

ISSUE: May a landlord lawfully refuse to rent one of its apartments to a family solely on the basis that the family includes a minor child?

HOLDING AND DECISION: (Tobriner, J.) No. The Unruh Civil Rights Act prohibits a landlord from refusing to rent its apartments to families solely on the basis that the family includes a minor child. Precedent makes clear that the Act was designed not only to address only specific types of discrimination, but rather was intended to reach all arbitrary discrimination by business establishments. The statutory rights provided under the Act extend to "all persons," including minor children. The listing of possible bases of discrimination within the Act does not serve to exclude any listed bases from the scope of the Act, since the enumerated list is intended to be illustrative only, not restrictive. As a business establishment, Marina (P) falls within the purview of the Act. While Marina (P) clearly has a right to protect its establishment from the type of behavior attributed to children, it must do so by directly acting against those who are committing the behavior. To hold otherwise would promote the approval of wholesale discrimination against children. [The court found that Marina (P) did not constitute special purpose housing.] Reversed.

DISSENT: (Richardson, J.) The court has improperly phrased the question in such a manner so as to compel the conclusion reached in the present case.

ANALYSIS

The court reached none of the constitutional issues raised in the present case, resting its decision solely on statutory grounds, and the legislative history surrounding the Act. In some instances, the California Constitution affords more expansive rights under certain circumstances than does the U.S. Constitution. It is unlikely, therefore, that any decision concerning the scope of protection afforded individuals with children under circumstances such as those in the present case under the U.S. Constitution will be forthcoming until brought in another jurisdiction.

Quicknotes

DETAINER The unlawful withholding of real or personal property from an individual who is lawfully entitled to it.

United States of America v. Starrett City Associates

Federal government (P) v. Owner of apartment complex (D)

840 F.2d 1096 (2d Cir. 1988).

NATURE OF CASE: Appeal from grant of summary judgment and permanent injunction in housing discrimination case.

FACT SUMMARY: Starrett City Associates (Starrett) (D) appealed from a decision granting summary judgment and a permanent injunction in favor of the United States (Government) (P), preventing it from discriminating on the basis of race in the rental of apartments. Starrett (D) contended that its tenant selection procedures, designed to achieve racial integration, did not violate the Fair Housing Act (FHA).

RULE OF LAW

The FHA may prevent the use of rigid racial quotas of indefinite duration to maintain a fixed level of integration in public housing when such practices restrict minority access to public housing.

FACTS: Starrett (D) owned and operated Starrett City, the largest public housing complex in the nation. To prevent "white flight" and to maintain a racial balance of 64 percent white, 22 percent black, and 8 percent Hispanic, Starrett (D) adopted a selection proces whereby as vacancies arose, applicants of a similar race or national origin to those tenants departing were selected. It was undenied that this practice restricted minority access to the complex. The Government (P) brought suit against Starrett (D) alleging that the selection process discriminated on the basis of race, in violation of the FHA. The parties made cross-motions for summary judgment. The Government's (P) motion was granted and the court permanently enjoined the selection process which it determined had adversely impacted minority participation in the complex solely on the basis of race. From this decision, Starrett (D) appealed.

ISSUE: May the FHA prevent the use of rigid racial quotas of indefinite duration to maintain a fixed level of integration in public housing when such practices restrict minority access to public housing?

HOLDING AND DECISION: (Miner, J.) Yes. The FHA may prevent the use of rigid racial quotas of indefinite duration to maintain a fixed level of integration in public housing when such practices restrict minority access to public housing. Housing practices violative of the FHA include not only those motivated by racially discriminatory purposes, but also those that disproportionately affect minorities. Quotas bring the dual goals of the FHA—antidiscrimination and integration—into conflict. A racial classification is presumptively discriminating, but a race-conscious affirmative action plan does not necessarily violate federal constitutional or statutory law. Such plans must be temporary in nature and must terminate when a defined goal is reached. Access quotas which increase or ensure minority participation are generally upheld, while integration maintenance plans which restrict minority participation are of doubtful validity. Finally, quotas, when used, address the history of racial discrimination or imbalance. In the present case, Starrett's (D) selection process has as its only goal integration maintenance. There is no adequate explanation as to why it was in force for over fifteen years. Furthermore, the selection process redresses no prior discrimination or racial imbalance. In fact, it acts as a ceiling on minority access to Starrett's complex. Fear of "white flight" cannot justify the use of inflexible racial quotas in the present case. While race is not always an inappropriate factor, Starrett's (D) use of racial quotas in the present case is. Affirmed.

DISSENT: (Newman, J.) The FHA, which was promulgated to bar the perpetuation of segregation, was never designed or intended to apply to actions like Starrett's (D), which do not promote segregated housing, but rather maintain integrated housing.

ANALYSIS

Housing practices need not be motivated by a racially discriminatory purpose to be violative of the FHA; they may also be violative if they disproportionately affect minorities. Race-based factors, which are not motivated by a racially discriminating purpose, may not be violative of the FHA, even if they adversely affect minorities. A justifiable rental increase may decrease minority participation in a complex, but the increase, if not racially motivated, may not run afoul of the FHA.

Quicknotes

DISCRIMINATION Unequal treatment of a class of persons.

PERMANENT INJUNCTION A remedy imposed by the court ordering a party to cease the conduct of a specific activity until the final disposition of the cause of action.

SUMMARY JUDGMENT Judgment rendered by a court in response to a motion made by one of the parties, claiming that the lack of a question of material fact in respect to an issue warrants disposition of the issue without consideration by the jury.

CHAPTER 7

Assignments and Subleases

Quick Reference Rules of Law

PAGE

1. **Privity of Estate.** In the absence of the assumption by the assignee of the obligations of the lease, the liability of such an assignee to the lessor rests in privity of estate that is terminated by a new assignment. (A.D. Juilliard & Co. v. American Woolen Co.) *32*

2. **Transferred Leasehold Interest as Sublease.** If the parties clearly intend a sublease relationship, a transferred leasehold interest in real property is a sublease, instead of an assignment, such that equity should not prevent a forfeiture of the premises when the original lessee breaches the original lease agreement. (Abernathy v. Adous) *33*

3. **Withholding Consent.** Where a commercial lease does not expressly permit a lessor to withhold consent to an assignment of sublease, the lessor may withhold consent only when she has a good faith or reasonable objection to the assignment or sublease. (Newman v. Hinky Dinky Omaha-Lincoln, Inc.) *35*

4. **Refusing Consent of a Sublease or an Assignment.** Under New York law, if a lease requires a tenant to obtain prior written consent of a landlord to sublet or assign the premises, a landlord may refuse consent arbitrarily, unless there is a clause specifically stating that the landlord may not unreasonably withhold consent. (United States of America v. Epstein) *36*

A.D. Juilliard & Co. v. American Woolen Co.

Landlord (P) v. Lease assignee (D)

R.I. Sup. Ct., 69 R.I. 215, 32 A.2d 800 (1943).

NATURE OF CASE: Assumpsit for rent and taxes.

FACT SUMMARY: A.D. Juilliard & Co.'s (P) lease with its lessee contains a covenant to pay rent. The lessee's interest was subsequently assigned to American Woolen Co. (American) (D), who later assigned it to another. In its assignment, American (D) did not agree to assume the obligation to pay rent for the unexpired term.

RULE OF LAW

In the absence of the assumption by the assignee of the obligations of the lease, the liability of such an assignee to the lessor rests in privity of estate that is terminated by a new assignment.

FACTS: A.D. Juilliard & Co.'s (Julliard's) (P) predecessor in right leased certain premises. The lease contained a specific covenant by its lessee to pay rent. The lease did not provide that assignees should assume and be bound for the entire unexpired term by the covenant to pay rent. Several assignments of the lessee's interests subsequently occurred. The last three assignees were American Woolen Co. (Amercian) (D), Textile Realty Co., a subsidiary of American (D), and Reo Realty. In none of these assignments did the assignee agree to assume the obligation to pay rent for the unexpired term of the lease.

ISSUE: Is an assignee of a lease liable for the payment of the stipulated rent for the entire unexpired term even where he did not agree to assume such obligation and assigned the lease before the expiration of the term?

HOLDING AND DECISION: (Capotosto, J.) No. In the absence of the assumption by the assignee of the obligations of the lease, the liability of such an assignee to the lessor rests in privity of estate which is terminated by a new assignment of the lease by the assignee. Hence, American (D) cannot be liable for rent due after it assigned the lease to a third party. American (D) was virtually the lessee until the lease was assigned to Reo Realty. Juilliard (P) contends that the assignment to Reo Realty was colorable and hence did not terminate American's (D) liability. Where an assignee makes an assignment which, though proper in form, leaves him as a matter of fact in possession of the leased premises, the assignment is colorable and will not terminate his liability to the lessor for rent. Julliard (P) bases its contention of the small sum Reo Realty paid for the assignment. However, this fact is not enough to render the assignment to Reo Realty colorable so as to continue American's (D) liability to Juilliard (P). Exceptions overruled and case remitted for judgment.

ANALYSIS

The assignee of a leasehold is not liable for rents which accrued prior to his acquisition of the leasehold. However, he does take the premises subject to the burden of such rent and under the hazard of being dispossessed by the landlord and losing the term in the event the rent is not paid. A lessee who has assigned his term may recover from his assignee whatever he has been compelled to pay the lessor. However, a lessee, although compelled to pay rent to the lessor after having assigned his lease, cannot maintain an action against his assignee for rent falling due after the latter has assigned to a third person unless the assignee has expressly covenanted to pay the rent for the full unexpired term.

Quicknotes

ASSIGNEE A party to whom another party assigns his interest or rights.

ASSIGNMENT A transaction in which a party conveys his or her entire interest in property to another.

ASSUMPSIT An oral or written promise by one party to perform or pay another.

ASSUMPTION Act of acceptance or presumption of truth without proof of demonstration.

LEASE An agreement or contract that creates a relationship between a landlord and tenant (real property) or lessor and lessee (real or personal property).

LESSOR One who leases property to another, relinquishing the right to immediate possession of the property but retaining legal title.

PRIVITY OF ESTATE Common or successive relation to the same right in property.

Abernathy v. Adous

Original landlord (D) v. Sublessee (P)

Ark. Ct. App., 85 Ark. App. 242 (2004).

NATURE OF CASE: Suit for specific performance to require acceptance of rent payments.

FACT SUMMARY: Landowners leased property for use as a service station/convenience store. The original lessee then entered an agreement under which a third party would make payments to the original lessee in the exact amounts required by the original lessee's agreement with the landowners. A person with rights under the second agreement tried to make payments directly to the landowners, but they refused to accept the payments.

RULE OF LAW

If the parties clearly intend a sublease relationship, a transferred leasehold interest in real property is a sublease, instead of an assignment, such that equity should not prevent a forfeiture of the premises when the original lessee breaches the original lease agreement.

FACTS: The Abernathys (D) leased real property to Griffith Petroleum, Inc. (GPI) (D) for use as a service station/convenience store. Their written agreement specified a ten-year term and six consecutive five-year options to renew the agreement. Every month, GPI (D) would pay the Abernathys (D) the amount they owed their bank ($3,412.60), along with another $583.33, for a total monthly payment to the Abernathys (D) of $3,995.93. The agreement also required that GPI (D) would be in default if it missed a payment or became insolvent. No provision of the agreement prohibited GPI (D) from subleasing or assigning its rights to a third party. Four years and three months into its lease with the Abernathys (D), GPI (D) entered what they called a "sublease agreement" whose terms were expressly related to GPI's (D) original lease with the Abernathys (D): the term would be for the remainder of GPI's (D) ten-year agreement, along with the options for renewal, and the monthly payments were expressly equal to the $583.33 and the amount that the Abernathys (D) owed their bank for the property. Within a year after this second agreement, Adous (P) entered the second agreement as a subtenant and eventually became the only subtenant. At first, Adous (P) made payments to GPI (D), which then made its payments to the Abernathys (D). Approximately eight-and-a-half years into the original lease's ten-year term, however, GPI (D) failed to make its payments to the Abernathys (D). The Abernathys (D) sued GPI (D) and Adous (P), but withdrew their suit when they collected three months' rent from GPI (D) and Adous (P). GPI (D) then immediately failed to pay rent again, and Adous (P) tendered the payments due directly to the Abernathys (D), who refused to accept the payments. Adous (P) then sued the Abernathys and GPI (D), requesting an order directing either the Abernathys (D) or GPI (D) to accept Adous's (P) payments. One month after Adous (P) filed suit, the Abernathys (D) informed GPI (D) that they were terminating the original lease for GPI's (D) failure to pay rent and for GPI's (D) insolvency. The Abernathys (D) demanded that Adous (P) leave the property, but he stayed on it. Following a bench trial, the trial court ruled that Adous (P) was an assignee of the original lease who therefore enjoyed all the rights and responsibilities conferred upon GPI (D) by the original lease. Under the circumstances, the trial court ruled, ordering Adous (P) to forfeit the premises would be inequitable. The Abernathys (D) appealed.

ISSUE: If the parties clearly intend a sublease relationship, is a transferred leasehold interest in real property a sublease, instead of an assignment, such that equity should not prevent a forfeiture of the premises when the original lessee breaches the original lease agreement?

HOLDING AND DECISION: (Baker, J.) Yes. If the parties clearly intend a sublease relationship, a transferred leasehold interest in real property is a sublease, instead of an assignment, such that equity should not prevent a forfeiture of the premises when the original lessee breaches the original lease agreement. A sublease requires a termination of the right to possession when the original landlord terminates the original lease; an assignment confers privity of estate between the assignee and the original landlord that creates a landlord-tenant relationship between them. Arkansas courts decide whether a subsequent agreement is a sublease or an assignment by looking primarily to the parties' intent. Here, several factors show that GPI (D) and Adous (P) intended for their agreement to be a sublease: most important of all, they have consistently called their agreement a sublease; Adous (P) continued to pay rent, not directly to the Abernathys (D), but to GPI (D); and GPI (D) retained a right to repossess the premises if Adous (P) defaulted. These factors outweigh the factors that admittedly do support a finding of an assignment (the identical amounts of rent, Adous's (P) agreement to obey the original lease, and the application of the original lease's period of duration). Equity therefore permits a forfeiture of the premises in this case. As a sublessee, Adous (P) had no privity of estate with the Abernathys (D), and he could not overcome the fact of GPI's (D) insolvency even if he could make the company's rent payments to the Abernathys (D).

Continued on next page.

Since GPI's (D) insolvency was a triggering event for default under the original lease, it is therefore equitable to permit the Abernathys (D) to require Adous (D), who has no rights under the original lease, to forfeit the premises. Reversed and remanded.

DISSENT: (Robbins, J.) The distinction between a sublessee and an assignee is irrelevant, as is the absence of privity to whether equity should prevent a forfeiture in this case. The trial judge did not clearly err by finding forfeiture inequitable. The Abernathys (D) got the long-term lease they originally bargained for under an agreement in which they failed to prohibit GPI (D) from entering a sublease or assignment. Adous (P) has agreed to follow the original agreement and has made timely payments for almost four years. Given such facts, equity should prevent his forfeiture of the premises.

DISSENT: (Roaf, J.) The trial court correctly concluded that Adous (P) was an assignee of the original lease. Our supreme court has expressly rejected using a right of repossession to support a finding of a sublease. Further, the factors pointing toward an assignment here are at least as compelling as those suggesting a sublease. Different amounts of rent are necessary for finding a sublease. Moreover, the second agreement expressly incorporates the original lease between the Abernathys (D) and GPI (D)—an act that makes the second agreement an assignment under Arkansas law. In these circumstances, the trial judge did not clearly err by considering Adous (P) an assignee of the original lease.

ANALYSIS

This difficult case contains several disturbing tensions, one of which lies between GPI's (D) right to transfer its rights under the original lease and what would normally be the Abernathys' (D) right to choose with whom they enter contractual relationships. The majority considers it unfair to require the Abernathys (D) to have a contract with Adous (P). On the other hand, Judge Robbins, in dissent, would hold the Abernathys (D) responsible for an original lease that failed to prevent a sublease or assignment. As a matter of basic argumentation, the dissenters' responses to the majority's reasoning seem to seriously undermine the holdings in this case.

Quicknotes

ASSIGNEE A party to whom another party assigns his interest or rights.

EQUITY Fairness; justice; the determination of a matter consistent with principles of fairness and not in strict compliance with rules of law.

SPECIFIC PERFORMANCE An equitable remedy whereby the court requires the parties to perform their obligations pursuant to a contract.

SUBLEASE A transaction in which a tenant or lessee conveys an interest in the leased premises that is less than his own or retains a reversionary interest.

Newman v. Hinky Dinky Omaha-Lincoln, Inc.

Lessor (P) v. Supermarket owner (D)

Neb. Sup. Ct., 229 Neb. 382, 427 N.W.2d 50 (1988).

NATURE OF CASE: Appeal from judgment in forcible entry and detainer action.

FACT SUMMARY: Hinky Dinky Omaha-Lincoln, Inc. (Hinky Dinky) (D) appealed from a judgment of restitution of the premises in favor of Newman (P), alleging that as lessor, Newman (P) was required to demonstrate a commercially reasonable objection to an assignment of the lease or a subletting of the premises.

RULE OF LAW

Where a commercial lease does not expressly permit a lessor to withhold consent to an assignment of sublease, the lessor may withhold consent only when she has a good faith or reasonable objection to the assignment or sublease.

FACTS: Newman (P) leased real estate to ACS, which operated a supermarket on the premises. When ACS ceased its supermarket operations, it sought Newman's (P) consent to assign the lease to Nash Finch, and consent for Nash Finch to sublease the premises to Hinky Dinky Omaha-Lincoln, Inc. (Hinky-Dinky) (D). Newman (P) withheld her consent, and the assignment and sublease were executed without it. After notice to ACS, Nash Finch, and Hinky Dinky (D) (the latter then being in possession) that ACS was in default under the lease, Newman (P) served a "notice to quit" on Hinky Dinky (D) and filed a petition for restitution of the premises. Newman (P) successfully moved for summary judgment, the court determining that as a matter of law, Newman (P) as lessor could withhold consent for any reason. The court then granted Newman (P) a judgment for restitution of the premises. Hinky Dinky (D) appealed, arguing that Newman (P) could not unreasonably withhold her consent.

ISSUE: Can the lessor in a commercial lease situation withhold consent to an assignment of the lease or a sublease for any reason?

HOLDING AND DECISION: (Shanahan, J.) No. A lessor in a commercial lease situation cannot withhold consent to an assignment of the lease or a sublease for any reason. When a commercial lease does not expressly permit a lessor to withhold consent to an assignment, the lessor may withhold consent only when he has a good faith and reasonable objection to the assignment or sublease. One can withhold consent for any reason when the lease contains a freely negotiated provision giving the lessor an absolute right to withhold consent. Absent such a provision, there is a covenant of good faith and fair dealing implied in the lease, which requires the lessor to exercise the discretionary power to withhold consent only in good faith and in accordance with commercially reasonable standards. In the present case, the lease in question did not expressly permit Newman (P) to withhold consent to the assignment. Absent such permission, the question as to whether Newman (P) acted reasonably and in good faith is a question of material fact, which renders summary judgment premature. Reversed and remanded.

ANALYSIS

The case of *Kendall v. Ernest Pestana, Inc.*, 220 Cal. Rptr. 818 (1985), cites the aforementioned good faith and fair dealing requirement, which is implied in all contracts under California law. The implied covenant of good faith and fair dealing arises most often in the insurance bad faith context. California's statutory response to the *Kendall* decision was to pass Cal. Civil Code §§ 1195.010–1995.270, which codify the general rule of reasonableness but explicitly allow the parties to include within a lease a provision absolutely prohibiting assignments.

Quicknotes

ASSIGNMENT A transaction in which a party conveys his or her entire interest in property to another.

FORCIBLE ENTRY The entry onto real property of another through the use of violence in order to oust that person from possession.

LESSOR One who leases property to another, relinquishing the right to immediate possession of the property but retaining legal title.

SUBLEASE A transaction in which a tenant or lessee conveys an interest in the leased premises that is less than his own or retains a reversionary interest.

SUMMARY JUDGMENT Judgment rendered by a court in response to a motion made by one of the parties, claiming that the lack of a question of material fact in respect to an issue warrants disposition of the issue without consideration by the jury.

United States of America v. Epstein

Federal government (P) v. Private lessee (D)

27 F. Supp. 2d 404 (S.D.N.Y. 1998).

NATURE OF CASE: Action for eviction and back rent.

FACT SUMMARY: The Government (P) sought to terminate its lease to Epstein (D) on the basis that he sublet the building to Fisher (D) in violation of the lease agreement.

RULE OF LAW

Under New York law, if a lease requires a tenant to obtain prior written consent of a landlord to sublet or assign the premises, a landlord may refuse consent arbitrarily, unless there is a clause specifically stating that the landlord may not unreasonably withhold consent.

FACTS: The Government (P) seeks to evict Epstein (D) from a building formerly used as a residence by the Deputy Consul General of Iran. After diplomatic relations between Iran and the United States (P) were terminated, the Office of Foreign Missions (OFM) took possession of the building and leased it to Epstein (D), who sublet the building to Fisher (D) without the Government's (P) consent. Fisher (D) in turn sublet a portion of the building to other tenants. The Government (P) attempted to terminate the lease and brought this action to eject Epstein (D) and Fisher (D) from the building and seeking back rent.

ISSUE: Under New York law, if a lease requires a tenant to obtain prior written consent of a landlord to sublet or assign the premises, may a landlord refuse consent arbitrarily, unless there is a clause specifically stating that the landlord may not unreasonably withhold consent?

HOLDING AND DECISION: (Chin, J.) Yes. Under New York law, if a lease requires a tenant to obtain prior written consent of a landlord to sublet or assign the premises, a landlord may refuse consent arbitrarily, unless there is a clause specifically stating that the landlord may not unreasonably withhold consent. One issue here is whether OFM was entitled to refuse Epstein's (D) proposed sublet to Fisher (D) arbitrarily or whether it breached a duty of good faith and fair dealing implicit in the lease agreement by unreasonably refusing to consent to the sublease in writing. This depends on whether federal or New York law applies. Under New York law, if a lease requires a tenant to obtain prior written consent of a landlord to sublet or assign the premises, a landlord may refuse consent arbitrarily, unless there is a clause specifically stating that the landlord may not unreasonably withhold consent. Here the lease agreement required prior written consent of OFM to a sublet, but contained no provision prohibiting OFM from unreasonably withholding consent. Defendants argue that since the Government (P) is one of the parties, federal common law applies. Under federal common law, there is an implied covenant of good faith and fair dealing which prohibits OFM from withholding its consent unreasonably. Between federal contract principles and specific state landlord-tenant law, state law should be applied. Thus, the OFM was entitled to arbitrarily withhold its consent to Epstein's (D) request to sublet the premises.

ANALYSIS

Note that states differ with regard to the law on this subject. For example, California Civil Code §§ 1995.010–1995.270 provides that where a lease requires the landlord's consent for an assignment or sublease, but is silent as to the standard for withholding such consent, it is implied that such consent may not be unreasonably withheld.

Quicknotes

EVICTION The removal of a person from possession of property.

LEASE AGREEMENT An agreement pursuant to which the owner of an interest in property relinquishes the right to possession to another for a specified consideration and for a definite time period.

SUBLEASE A transaction in which a tenant or lessee conveys an interest in the leased premises that is less than his own or retains a reversionary interest.

CHAPTER 8

Tenant's Breach: Landlord's Remedies

Quick Reference Rules of Law

Reid v. Mutual of Omaha Insurance Co.

Landlord (P) v. Tenant (D)

Utah Sup. Ct., 776 P.2d 896 (1989).

NATURE OF CASE: Breach of lease.

FACT SUMMARY: The Reids (P) brought suit against Mutual of Omaha Insurance Co. (Mutual) (D) to recover unpaid rents owed pursuant to a lease agreement, which Mutual (D) breached when it vacated the premises.

RULE OF LAW

A landlord who is seeking to hold a breaching tenant liable for unpaid rents has an obligation to take commercially reasonable steps to mitigate its losses, meaning that the landlord must seek to relet the premises.

FACTS: Mutual of Omaha Insurance Co. (Mutual) (D) entered into a five-year lease agreement with the Reids (P) for office space at the monthly rate of $1,100. Soon after Mutual (D) took possession, another tenant, Intermountain, moved into the adjoining space. Mutual (D) made several complaints regarding Intermountain to the Reids (P). Mutual (D) felt that the Reids (P) did not adequately respond and vacated the premises. The Reids (P) brought suit, claiming Mutual (D) had breached the lease and was liable for monthly rental remaining on the lease. Mutual (D) counterclaimed, arguing that it had been constructively evicted. The trial court ruled in favor of the Reids (P) and Mutual (D) appealed, contending that the trial court erred in rejecting its claim of constructive eviction and in its calculation of damages.

ISSUE: Does a landlord who is seeking to hold a breaching tenant liable for unpaid rents have an obligation to take commercially reasonable steps to mitigate its losses, meaning that the landlord must seek to relet the premises?

HOLDING AND DECISION: (Zimmerman, J.) Yes. A landlord who is seeking to hold a breaching tenant liable for unpaid rents has an obligation to take commercially reasonable steps to mitigate its losses, meaning that the landlord must seek to relet the premises. Mutual (D) claimed that even if the constructive eviction claim were properly rejected, the Reids (P) were entitled only to nonpayment of rents as measured by those rents that came due between the date of Mutual's (D) last payment and the date of reletting to Intermountain. Mutual (D) argued that the trial court erred in including in the measure of damages the unpaid rents that accrued after the reletting. Mutual (D) relied upon the common-law doctrine of surrender and acceptance. Under that rule, when a tenant surrenders the premises to a landlord before the lease term expires and the landlord accepts such surrender, the tenant is relieved from the duty to pay rents accruing after the date of acceptance. On appeal, Mutual (D) had the burden of demonstrating that the trial court's finding on this point lacked adequate support under the clearly erroneous standard. Mutual (D) failed to meet its burden. While such conduct may be evidence of intent to accept the surrendered premises and terminate the lease, it is not conclusive. We affirm the trial court's finding that the Reid's (P) conduct constituted reletting without termination. Mutual (D) also contends that even if it were liable for some of the rents accrued after the premises had been relet, the trial court erred in fixing the amount. This poses the question of whether Utah law imposes a duty on landlords to mitigate damages by reletting premises after the tenant has wrongly vacated and defaulted on its promise to pay rent. This is an issue of first impression. Other jurisdictions are split on this question. The traditional rule is that landlords are not required to mitigate by reletting. The modern trend, however, has imposed by statute or judicial decision an obligation to relet, recognizing that leases are contractual in nature. The court finds more persuasive the modern rule on the basis that the economy benefits from a rule encouraging the reletting of premises, returning them to a productive use, rather than permitting them to sit idle while the landlord collects rents from the breaching tenant. This conclusion is also in accord with the current policy disfavoring contractual penalties. Damages recoverable under liquidated damages provisions are generally limited to an amount representing a reasonable estimation of what would be necessary to compensate the nonbreaching party for losses caused by the breach. Allowing a landlord to recover rents for idle property that it could have released is analogous to imposing a penalty upon the tenant. Thus, a landlord who is seeking to hold a breaching tenant liable for unpaid rents has an obligation to take commercially reasonable steps to mitigate its losses, meaning that the landlord must seek to relet the premises. Affirmed in part and reversed in part, and remanded.

ANALYSIS

The court here adopts the retained jurisdiction approach, allowing the landlord to obtain judgment soon after the tenant's breach; but rather than requiring the commencement of a new suit to collect future rents, it permits the court to retain jurisdiction over the parties and subject matter and enter new damage awards as they accrue. Thus, the damage awards will be based only on losses that have already accrued and will take into consideration

Continued on next page.

the landlord's mitigation efforts. Thus, the landlord will have an incentive to fulfill his duty to mitigate.

Quicknotes

CONSTRUCTIVE EVICTION An action whereby the landlord renders the property unsuitable for occupancy, either in whole or in part, so that the tenant is forced to leave the premises.

LEASE AGREEMENT An agreement pursuant to which the owner of an interest in property relinquishes the right to possession to another for a specified consideration and for a definite time period.

Isbey v. Crews

Lessor (P) v. Dialysis operator (D)

N.C. Ct. App., 55 N.C. App. 47, 284 S.E.2d 534 (1981).

NATURE OF CASE: Appeal from grant of summary judgment in action for breach of rental lease.

FACT SUMMARY: Crews (D) appealed from a decision granting Isbey (P) summary judgment in connection with Crews's (D) breach of a rental agreement, contending that Isbey (P) had unreasonably withheld his consent to a sublease on the premises and had failed to mitigate his damages.

RULE OF LAW

The burden is on the breaching party to a rental agreement to prove that the nonbreaching party has failed to exercise reasonable diligence in mitigating his damages.

FACTS: Isbey (P) and Crews (D) entered into a rental agreement whereby Crews (D) leased certain space from Isbey (P) to operate a dialysis unit. Monthly rental payments were $2,867.33. The lease provided that the premises could not be used for any activity other than a physician's office or as a dialysis unit without Isbey's (P) consent, and further could not be subleased without Isbey's (P) written consent. At the time Crews (D) vacated the premises in August 1980, all monthly payments as provided for in the rental agreement had been made. Isbey (P) refused Crews's (D) request for permission to sublease the premises to a company selling and distributing medical supplies. Isbey (P) brought suit for breach of the rental agreement, and upon motion for summary judgment, recovered $2,867.33, plus interest. Crews (D) appealed, contending that there was an issue of material fact presented because Isbey (P) had unreasonably withheld his consent to the proposed sublease, and further, because there was an issue as to whether Isbey (P) had properly mitigated his damages.

ISSUE: Is the burden on the breaching party to a rental agreement to prove that the nonbreaching party has failed to exercise reasonable diligence in mitigating his damages?

HOLDING AND DECISION: (Hedrick, J.) Yes. The burden is on the breaching party to a rental agreement to prove that the nonbreaching party has failed to exercise reasonable diligence in mitigating his damages. In the present case, the lease contains an express restraint which allows the landlord to unreasonably withhold his consent to a sublease. This court will not insert terms into a contract where the parties have omitted them, and a requirement that Isbey (P) not unreasonably withhold his consent will not be read into the rental agreement. In determining damages, the courts will attempt to place the nonbreaching party in the same position that he would have occupied had the contract been fully performed. Although a nonbreaching landlord had a duty to mitigate his damages, the burden of proving the failure to mitigate falls on the nonbreaching party, in this case Crews (D). Isbey (P) has presented evidence as to the damages resulting from the breach, which has not been controverted by any evidence presented by Crews (D). Summary judgment was proper. Affirmed.

ANALYSIS

The present case illustrates the tensions between the two competing concerns highlighted by Crews (D) in his appeal, the contradiction between allowing a landlord to unreasonably withhold consent while at the same time requiring him to mitigate his damages. Certainly there are limits, consonant with the original terms of the lease, under which a landlord should be required to relet the premises. In the present case, the business of selling and distributing medical supplies does not seem to be wholly disassociated with the business of Crews (D), the original tenant. It is difficult to discern how Crews (D) could have proven in the present case that Isbey (P) had failed to mitigate, since he could withhold consent to sublease at his will.

Quicknotes

SUBLEASE A transaction in which a tenant or lessee conveys an interest in the leased premises that is less than his own or retains a reversionary interest.

SUMMARY JUDGMENT Judgment rendered by a court in response to a motion made by one of the parties, claiming that the lack of a question of material fact in respect to an issue warrants disposition of the issue without consideration by the jury.

Ruud v. Larson

Lessor (P) v. Lessee (D)

N.D. Sup. Ct., 392 N.W.2d 62 (1986).

NATURE OF CASE: Appeal from judgment for damages following breach of a real estate lease.

FACT SUMMARY: Larson (D) appealed from a judgment awarding damages to Ruud (P) for their alleged breach of a real estate lease, contending that Ruud (P) had failed to make a good faith effort to sublease the property and mitigate their damages.

RULE OF LAW

A landlord may not condition his consent to a sublease, in mitigation of his damages, upon payment of all arrearages under the original lease.

FACTS: Larson (D) leased property from Ruud (P) in 1976. In 1982, Larson (D) failed to make monthly payments as required under the lease, and Ruud (P) brought suit for breach of the lease. Prior to trial, there was an agreement among counsel to withhold further proceedings because Larson's (D) company, Mid-State Oil Company, had filed bankruptcy. Larson (D) proposed a possible sublease of the property to Luna, agreeing to pay the tax arrearages due under the lease. Negotiations took place but were not concluded, and the sublease to Luna was never completed. Thereafter, Ruud (P) could not make further attempts to find a sublessee until Mid-State was determined in its bankruptcy proceedings to have no interest in the property. Although Ruud (P) did not hire a real estate agent, the evidence reflects that he made diligent attempts to relet the property, resulting in some 140 contacts with some 50 prospective tenants, but no sublease. The court awarded damages in favor of Ruud (P), making a specific finding that he had made good faith, diligent efforts to sublease the property and mitigate his damages. Larson (D) appealed, contending that Ruud (P) had not made a good faith effort to relet the premises and mitigate his damages, because the sublease to Luna was premised upon Larson's (D) payment of tax arrearages.

ISSUE: May a landlord condition his consent to a sublease, in mitigation of his damages, upon the payment of arrearages under the original lease?

HOLDING AND DECISION: (Gierke, J.) No. A landlord may not condition his consent to a sublease, in mitigation of his damages, upon the payment of arrearages under the original lease. Ruud (P) concedes this point, but correctly asserts that this principle has no application in the present case because Larson (D) agreed in the sublease negotiations to pay the arrearages as part of the sublease, and there is no evidence that Larson (D) ever requested that Ruud (P) consent to a sublease without requiring payment of the arrearages. The record reflects instead that Larson (D) made counter-proposals, which were not accepted, and that Larson (D) decided not to proceed with the sublease. Further, evidence that Ruud (P) did not employ a real estate agent to relet the premises and that he was seeking to secure a higher rental for the property, does not establish that he failed to make a good faith effort to relet the premises. The record is to the contrary, and Larson (D) has not established that the court's specific finding in this regard was clearly erroneous. Affirmed.

DISSENT: (Levine, J.) I disagree with the majority that if the breaching tenant reneges upon an agreement to pay arrearages, that the nonbreaching landlord may then make approval of a sublease contingent upon the payment of such arrearages.

ANALYSIS

Note that with 140 contacts with at least 50 prospective tenants, the reasonableness that Ruud (P) exhibited in attempting to sublease the premises, especially in light of the interference received from Mid-State's bankruptcy counsel, may have carried the day. Larson's rent was $700, while Ruud (P) attempted to sublease at $1200. While conceding that this was a reasonable rental for the property, an interesting question is raised as to whether in mitigation Larson (D) could have claimed credit for the entire $1200 rental had Ruud (P) been successful in renting the property.

Quicknotes

SUBLEASE A transaction in which a tenant or lessee conveys an interest in the leased premises that is less than his own or retains a reversionary interest.

Note: There are no principal cases in chapters 9 and 10 of the casebook.

CHAPTER 11

Modern Perpetuities Developments

Quick Reference Rules of Law

Abrams v. Templeton

Son's heirs (D) v. Daughter's heirs (P)

S.C. Ct. App., 320 S.C. 325, 465 S.E.2d 117 (1995).

NATURE OF CASE: Will contest arising from a will that violated the Rule Against perpetuities.

FACT SUMMARY: Heirs of a testator's daughter challenged the conveyance of 160 acres of real property to heirs of the testator's son.

RULE OF LAW

If a will purports to grant life estates to a testator's children, grandchildren, and great-grandchildren, fee title in the property does not revert back to the testator if she clearly intended for the remainder to vest in her great-grandchildren.

FACTS: In 1914, Mary Ann Taylor Ramage executed a will in which she left 130 acres of land to the five children of her daughter, Alma Templeton, who predeceased her. She also left a life estate in 160 acres to her husband, at whose death her son, Albert Ramage, would hold a life estate in the same property. The will provided further that, when Albert died, his children would inherit his life estate, and at their deaths their interests would be divided among their own children (i.e., Mary Ann's great-grandchildren). Albert had nine children, five of whom survived him and had children of their own; four of Albert's children died childless. The trial judge found that the will violated the Rule Against perpetuities and reformed the will as required by state statute to cure the perpetuities violation. In the process, the trial judge used the shares of the four children of Albert who died childless to increase the shares for the five children of his who did have children. The heirs of Mary Ann's grandchildren through Alma appealed; they sought to void the will outright for violating the Rule Against perpetuities or to take a portion of the 160 acres because, they argued, the life-estate shares of the four childless grandchildren reverted back to Mary Ann and thus should pass on in due part to the heirs in her daughter's line.

ISSUE: If a will purports to grant life estates to a testator's children, grandchildren, and great-grandchildren, does fee title in the property revert back to the testator if she clearly intended for the remainder to vest in her great-grandchildren?

HOLDING AND DECISION: (Hearn, J.) No. If a will purports to grant life estates to a testator's children, grandchildren, and great-grandchildren, fee title in the property does not revert back to the testator if she clearly intended for the remainder to vest in her great-grandchildren. Courts abhor forfeitures and intestacy and accordingly go to great lengths to find a will valid. It is true that the fee in a given parcel of land is always vested somewhere; the heirs on Alma's side of the family therefore correctly challenge the trial judge's reformation of the will that left as "floating" the four-ninths interest of the grandchildren who died childless. At the same time, because the trial judge also correctly concluded that Mary Ann intended for the 160 acres to stay on her son's side, and because intestacy is so disfavored, the proper result is for this court to further modify the will to effectuate the testator's intent. Affirmed as modified.

ANALYSIS

The *Abrams* court amply illustrates the contemporary trend to, as the court writes, "indulge every presumption in favor of the validity of the will." In this case, that indulgence meant that the Templeton heirs must lose—even though the court acknowledged that their arguments were technically correct.

Quicknotes

INTESTACY To die without leaving a valid testamentary instrument.

LIFE ESTATE An interest in land measured by the life of the tenant or a third party.

RULE AGAINST PERPETUITIES The doctrine that a future interest that is incapable of vesting within twenty-one years of lives in being at the time it is created is immediately void.

Symphony Space, Inc. v. Pergola Properties, Inc.

Lessee (P) v. Owner (D)

N.Y. Ct. App., 88 N.Y.2d 466, 669 N.E.2d 799 (1996).

NATURE OF CASE: Declaratory action.

FACT SUMMARY: Pergola Properties, Inc. (D) sought to exercise an option in a commercial lease to purchase property occupied by Symphony Space, Inc. (P).

RULE OF LAW

Options to purchase commercial property are not exempt from the prohibition on remote vesting under New York's Rule Against Perpetuities.

FACTS: Symphony Space, Inc. (Symphony) (P), a non-profit group devoted to the arts, rented a two-story building from Broadwest. The two entered into a transaction whereby Broadwest sold the building to Symphony (P) for the below-market price of $10,010 and leased back the commercial property for $1 a year. Symphony (P) also granted Broadwest an option to repurchase the building. In 1981, Broadwest sold and assigned its interest under the lease, option, mortgage and mortgage note to Pergola Properties, Inc. (Pergola) (D) for $4.8 million. Pergola (D) began a cooperation conversion of a portion of the property. Pergola (D) served Symphony (P) with notice that it was exercising the option clause due to Symphony's (P) alleged default on the mortgage note. Symphony (P) initiated this declaratory judgment proceeding and the trial court granted Symphony's (P) motion, concluding that the Rule Against Perpetuities (EPTL 9-1.1[b]) applied to the commercial option in the parties' agreement, that the option violated the Rule and that Symphony (P) was entitled to exercise its right to redeem the mortgage. The Appellate Division affirmed and certified the following question to this court: "Was the order of the Supreme Court, as affirmed by this court, properly made?"

ISSUE: Are options to purchase commercial property exempt from the prohibition on remote vesting under New York's Rule Against Perpetuities?

HOLDING AND DECISION: (Kaye, C.J.) No. Options to purchase commercial property are not exempt from the prohibition on remote vesting under New York's Rule Against Perpetuities. The rule states that, "No interest is good unless it must vest, if at all, not later than 21 years after some life in being at the creation of the interest." Pergola (D) offers three arguments for upholding the option. First, the statutory prohibition against remote vesting does not apply to commercial options. It is well settled in New York that the Rule Against remote vesting applies to options. Since the common-law rule prohibition applies to both commercial and noncommercial options, then EPTL 9-1.1(b) also applies to both. This option agreement is precisely the type of control over the future disposition of the property that the state law sought to prevent. The option grants the holder the absolute power to purchase the property at his whim and at a price far below market value. Second, Pergola (D) argues that the option here cannot be exercised beyond the statutory period. Pergola (D) claims that only the possible closing dates fall outside the permissible time frame. Where parties to a transaction are corporations and no measuring lives are stated in the instruments, the perpetuities period is simply 21 years. Third, Pergola (D) argues the court to adopt a "wait and see" approach to the Rule, meaning that an interest is valid if it actually vests during the perpetuities period. Here the option would survive under this approach since it was exercised within the 21-year limitation. This court, however, has long refused to adopt a wait and see approach to determine whether a perpetuities violation in fact occurs. Thus, the option agreement is invalid under EPTL 9-1.1(b). Affirmed.

ANALYSIS

Defendants also argued that the contract should be rescinded due to mutual mistake of fact on the basis that neither party realized the option violated the Rule Against Perpetuities. The court concludes that such mistake was simply a misunderstanding as to the applicable law and thus did not require undoing the transaction.

Quicknotes

RULE AGAINST PERPETUITIES The doctrine that a future interest that is incapable of vesting within twenty-one years of lives in being at the time it is created is immediately void.

CHAPTER 12

Life Estates and Associated Future Interests: The Doctrine of Waste

Quick Reference Rules of Law

Melms v. Pabst Brewing Company

Property owner (P) v. Life tenant (D)

Wis. Sup. Ct., 104 Wis. 7, 79 N.W. 738 (1899).

NATURE OF CASE: Action for waste.

FACT SUMMARY: Pabst Brewing Co. (Pabst) (D) was the owner of an estate for the life of another of certain land. Melms (P) was the owner of the remainder and claimed that Pabst (D) committed waste by destroying a house on the land.

RULE OF LAW

In the absence of any contract to use the property for a specified purpose, or to return it in the same condition in which it was received, a radical and permanent change of surrounding conditions must always be an important and sometimes controlling consideration upon the question whether a physical change in the use of the buildings constitutes waste.

FACTS: Pabst Brewing Co. (Pabst) (D) acquired Ms. Melms's life estate in a certain property. The house on the property was a large brick building built by Mr. Melms in 1864 and cost more than $20,000. Pabst (D) acquired the life estate when Mr. Melms died, leaving his estate in financial difficulties. Pabst (D) acquired full title to a brewery on adjacent land. The Melmses (P) are the owners of the residential property, subject to Pabst's (D) life estate. After Pabst (D) purchased the property, the general character of the surrounding neighborhood rapidly changed. Factories, railway tracks, and brewing buildings were built until the property in question became an isolated lot and building, standing 20 to 30 feet above street level. The residence became of no practical value and would not rent for enough to pay the taxes and insurance on it. Pabst (D) removed the house and graded down the property to street level. Melms (P) contended that these acts constituted waste.

ISSUE: Does a change in the nature of a building, though enhancing the value of the property, always constitute waste if the identity of the estate has been changed?

HOLDING AND DECISION: (Winslow, J.) No. The rule that any change in a building upon the premises constitutes waste has been greatly modified. While such a change may constitute technical waste, it will no longer be enjoined when it clearly appears that the change will be a meliorating one which actually improves the property rather than injuring it. Under ordinary circumstances the landlord or revisioner is entitled to receive the property in substantially the same condition as it was when the tenant received it. However, in the absence of any contract to use the property for a specified purpose or to return it in the same condition in which it was received, a radical and permanent change of the surrounding conditions, which deprives the property of its value and its usefulness as previously used, must always be an important, and sometimes controlling, consideration upon the question whether a physical change in the use of buildings constitutes waste. Here there was no contract. Pabst's (D) rights may continue for a number of years. The evidence shows that the property became valueless for the purpose of a residence, due to the change of the surrounding neighborhood. In light of these considerations, Pabst's (D) acts did not constitute waste. Affirmed.

ANALYSIS

The purpose of the doctrine of waste is the preservation of the property for the benefit of the owner of the future estate without permanent injury to it. As this case demonstrates, the law of waste is not unchanging. Hence, the same act may be waste in one part of the country while in another part it is considered a legitimate use of the land. The usages and customs of each community are important in the decision of whether a certain act constitutes waste.

Quicknotes

WASTE The mistreatment of another's property by someone in lawful possession.

Zauner v. Brewer

Devisee (P) v. Life tenant (D)

Conn. Sup. Ct., 220 Conn. 176, 596 A.2d 388 (1991).

NATURE OF CASE: Will construction suit.

FACT SUMMARY: Zauner (P), the remainderman, brought suit against Brewer (D), the life tenant, for immediate possession and fee simple title to a parcel of land on the basis that Brewer's (D) conduct constituted a surrender of the property and waste.

RULE OF LAW

A plaintiff may bring an action for permissive waste where the life tenant fails to make ordinary repairs.

FACTS: Zauner (P) is the wife and sole devisee on the testatrix's only son, John Barnett. Brewer (D) is the wife of testatrix's doctor and friend. The testatrix devised a 33-acre parcel of land to Brewer (D), the remainder to her son. Upon the testatrix's death, Brewer (D) entered into possession of the property. She subsequently purchased a home elsewhere and leased the property to a third party. Zauner (P) brought suit alleging that such conduct constituted a surrender of the property entitling her to immediate possession and fee simple title. She also alleged that Brewer (D) had committed waste by letting the property fall into disrepair and sought money damages and other appropriate equitable relief. Summary judgment was granted for Brewer (D) and Zauner (P) appealed.

ISSUE: May a plaintiff bring an action for permissive waste where the life tenant fails to make ordinary repairs?

HOLDING AND DECISION: (Glass, J.) Yes. A plaintiff may bring an action for permissive waste where the life tenant fails to make ordinary repairs. Zauner (P) first argued that the district court erred in concluding that no material issue of fact existed as to whether Brewer's (D) conduct constituted a surrender of the property within the meaning of the will provision. The term "surrender of the premises" as used in the will is not discernable from the language of the will alone and extrinsic evidence was necessary in determining the testatrix' true intention. Thus, the trial court should not have adjudicated that issue. Next, Zauner (P) argued that the trial court improperly concluded that no genuine issue of material fact existed as to whether the defendant committed actionable waste entitling Zauner (P) to damages. Brewer (D) contended that the claim of waste was not actionable because Zauner (P) failed to allege or produce evidence demonstrating Brewer's (D) conduct caused permanent and substantial injury to the property. Third, the statutory provision only authorizes equitable and not money damages. Defendant's reading of the statute would require the court to construe the word "injured" to require permanent and substantial injury to be actionable. Because this construction would absolve the tenant of her duty to make ordinary, reasonable repairs, we reject it. The life tenant is obligated to keep the land and the structures thereon as in good repair as they were when she took possession, except for ordinary wear and tear. The tenant has both the duty to make the ordinary repairs necessary to fix a presently existing condition that may impair the property substantially or permanently, and to make those ordinary repairs necessary to prevent the property from deteriorating to the point where such deterioration is permanent or substantial. In both circumstances, the tenant may be considered to have committed waste. Zauner (P) here established a sufficient basis to show that a genuine and material factual dispute existed as to whether the defendant committed permissive waste by neglecting to perform ordinary repairs. Reversed and remanded.

ANALYSIS

The court also concluded that both equitable and legal remedies were available to the plaintiff under the statute. Moreover, the Restatement, Property § 187, comment (a) indicates that the certainty of possession attendant to the possession of an indefeasible future interest in fee simple absolute entitles the owner to the maximum protection afforded by both equitable and legal remedies.

Quicknotes

LIFE TENANT An individual whose estate in real property is measured either by his own life or by that of another.

PERMISSIVE WASTE The mistreatment of another's property by someone in lawful possession by the failure to make ordinary repairs or maintenance.

REMAINDERMAN A person who has an interest in property to commence upon the termination of a present possessory interest.

McIntyre v. Scarbrough

Life tenant (D) v. Property owners (P)

Ga. Sup. Ct., 266 Ga. 824, 471 S.E.2d 199 (1996).

NATURE OF CASE: Petition to establish title and terminate a life estate.

FACT SUMMARY: The Scarbroughs (P) brought a petition to establish title and to terminate Ms. McIntyre's (D) interest in a portion of the land they purchased from her.

RULE OF LAW

A life tenant is entitled to the full use and enjoyment of the property if in such use he or she exercises the ordinary care of a prudent person for its preservation and protection and commits no acts which would permanently injure the remainder interest.

FACTS: The Scarbroughs (P) purchased a tract of land from McIntyre (D) by warranty deed, with the reservation of a life estate for McIntyre (D) of 1.2 acres of the land for her natural life. She was also to be responsible for the maintenance and upkeep of the property, all improvements thereon, and the payment of ad valorem taxes. The Scarbroughs (P) brought a petition to establish title and terminate the life estate and moved for summary judgment, claiming waste and violation of the warranty deed. The trial court first denied summary judgment, then reversed on the basis that McIntyre (D) failed to exercise ordinary care for the preservation of the property and thereby forfeited her interest to the remaindermen, who are entitled to immediate possession.

ISSUE: Is a life tenant entitled to the full use and enjoyment of the property if in such use he or she exercises the ordinary care of a prudent person for its preservation and protection and commits no acts which would permanently injure the remainder interest?

HOLDING AND DECISION: (Thompson, J.) Yes. A life tenant is entitled to the full use and enjoyment of the property if in such use he or she exercises the ordinary care of a prudent person for its preservation and protection and commits no acts which would permanently injure the remainder interest. This court has held that failure to pay burdens imposed by law on the property during the term constitutes such lack of ordinary care as a prudent person should exercise for its protection and preservation and would tend to divest the fee interest by subjecting it to sale. Here McIntyre (D) failed to pay the ad valorem property taxes on the tract for the years 1991–93 or the improvements for the years 1992–94, which was also a requirement of the warranty deed. Such failure results in forfeiture of the life estate as a matter of law. Affirmed.

DISSENT: (Benham, C.J.) The issue of waste is ordinarily one for the jury to decide. The question of whether McIntyre's (D) conduct with regard to the life estate was so egregiously wasteful as to warrant forfeiture of her interest in the property was inappropriate for summary judgment and should have been submitted to the jury.

ANALYSIS

The court here concluded that while the trial court too narrowly construed the definition of occupancy, it correctly determined that the life estate was terminated under the doctrine of waste. The trial court defined occupancy as "dwelling" in the subject premises. This court recognized that the term "occupy" is more expansive and encompasses those situations in which a person holds possession of property for use.

Quicknotes

LIFE ESTATE An interest in land measured by the life of the tenant or a third party.

LIFE TENANT An individual whose estate in real property is measured either by his own life or by that of another.

REMAINDER INTEREST An interest in land that remains after the termination of the immediately preceding estate.

CHAPTER **13**

Restraints on Alienation

Quick Reference Rules of Law

RTS Landfill, Inc. v. Appalachian Waste Systems, LLC

Property seller (P) v. Property buyer (D)

Ga. Ct. App., 267 Ga. App. 56, 598 S.E.2d 798 (2004).

NATURE OF CASE: Appeal from orders invalidating a preemptive right of first refusal.

FACT SUMMARY: RTS Landfill, Inc. (RTS) sold one of its divisions to Appalachian Waste Systems, LLC, which in turn tried to sell the business to a third party. RTS invoked its contractual preemptive right of first refusal and objected to the sale.

RULE OF LAW

A preemptive right of first refusal is not enforceable if it is unlimited in duration, requires a substantial discount from the sale price, and has no legitimate purpose for such a discount from what another party would pay for the property.

FACTS: RTS Landfill (RTS) (P) sold one of its divisions, Starr Sanitation (Starr), to Appalachian Waste Systems (Appalachian) (D). The asset purchase agreement for the sale provided that RTS (P) held a preemptive right to refuse future sales of Starr by Appalachian (D); the agreement specified no expiration date for RTS's (P) preemptive right and required Appalachian (D) to sell Starr back to RTS (P), if RTS so chose, for $500,000 less than a third party was willing to pay. Under this clause of the agreement, Appalachian (D) informed RTS (P) that a company had offered to buy a 20 percent interest in Starr for $2.5 million. RTS (P) objected to the notice, claiming that it did not give RTS (P) enough information to make an informed decision about the offer. [RTS (P) sued Appalachian (D), seeking damages and an injunction to block the 20 percent sale of Starr. Appalachian (D) counterclaimed for declaratory and injunctive relief, claiming in part that the preemptive right was unenforceable.] The trial judge declared the preemptive right unenforceable and granted Appalachian's (D) request for injunctive relief. RTS (P) appealed.

ISSUE: Is a preemptive right of first refusal enforceable if it is unlimited in duration, requires a substantial discount from the sale price, and has no legitimate purpose for such a discount from what another party would pay for the property?

HOLDING AND DECISION: (Mikell, J.) No. A preemptive right of first refusal is not enforceable if it is unlimited in duration, requires a substantial discount from the sale price, and has no legitimate purpose for such a discount from what another party would pay for the property. A preemptive right directly restrains alienation, and greatly interferes with it, when the right includes a right to purchase at a specific or reduced price. That rule from Georgia's law on transfers of real property applies here, in a case involving what is personal property under Georgia law, because restraints on alienation are also disfavored in this context. Precedent counsels further, however, that the test for determining the enforceability of a preemptive right should be flexible. Accordingly, the Court concludes that it must consider the right's duration, the purchase price, and parties' reason for agreeing to the preemptive right. Applying those factors here, the preemptive right is unreasonable because its duration is unlimited and it requires Appalachian (D) to sell Starr back to RTS (P) at $500,000 less than a third party would pay. Moreover, the record reveals no reason at all for the preemptive right in this case. Accordingly, it is not enforceable. Affirmed.

ANALYSIS

According to the Georgia Court of Appeals, the purchase agreement in *RTS Landfill* imposed an unreasonable restraint on Appalachian's (D) ability to resell Starr. Appalachian (D) presumably negotiated the agreement at arm's length and extensively with RTS Landfill (P)—complete with a barrage of reviewing attorneys on each side—and yet Appalachian (D) now may ignore a key term of the purchase agreement to which it knowingly agreed. Such a result squares more easily with the so-called "sanctity of contract" in a case of first impression, as this case is, but one can plausibly argue that cases like *RTS Landfill* ultimately encourage parties not to take their own agreements seriously—and perhaps even to negotiate in bad faith.

Quicknotes

ALIENATION Conveyance or transfer of property.

INJUNCTIVE RELIEF A court order issued as a remedy, requiring a person to do, or prohibiting that person from doing, a specific act.

PREEMPTIVE RIGHTS The right of existing shareholders to the first purchase of new issuances of stock in proportion to their share in ownership.

Ferrero Construction Company v. Dennis Rourke Corporation

Property owners (D) v. Right of first refusal holder (P)

Md. Ct. App., 311 Md. 560, 536 A.2d 1137 (1988).

NATURE OF CASE: Appeal from reversal of grant of summary judgment in action for specific performance.

FACT SUMMARY: Ferrero Construction Company (Ferrero) (D) appealed from a decision reversing a grant of summary judgment in his favor in Dennis Rourke Corporation's (Rourke) (P) action for specific performance, contending Rourke's (P) right of first refusal was violative of the Rule Against Perpetuities.

RULE OF LAW

The Rule Against Perpetuities applies to a right of first refusal to purchase an interest in property.

FACTS: Dennis Rourke Corporation (Rourke) (P) and Ferrero Construction Company (Ferrero) (D) entered into a contract for the purchase of two lots on Mercy Court. The contract contained a right of first refusal clause, granting Rourke (P) a first right of first refusal on the future sale of any of the seven remaining lots on Mercy Court. The purchase contract was never recorded. Three years later, Ferrero (D) notified Rourke (P) of an offer to purchase one of the remaining lots on Mercy Court. Rourke (P) responded immediately, indicating that it was exercising its right of first refusal and would purchase the lot on identical terms. Ferrero (D) then indicated it was rejecting both purchase offers. Rourke brought an action for specific performance, contending that Ferrero (D) was required to convey the lot to it by virtue of its right of first refusal. The trial court granted Ferrero's (D) motion for summary judgment, ruling that Rourke's (P) right of first refusal violated the Rule Against Perpetuities. The court later ruled that although there had been an offer and an acceptance regarding the lot, Ferrero's (D) offer was premised on a mistaken belief in the validity of the right of first refusal. Therefore the parties had not formed a contract. The appeals court reversed on the grounds that the Rule Against Perpetuities was inapplicable to the right of first refusal, and from that decision Ferrero (D) appealed.

ISSUE: Does the Rule Against Perpetuities apply to a right of first refusal to purchase an interest in property?

HOLDING AND DECISION: (Eldridge, J.) Yes. The Rule Against Perpetuities applies to a right of first refusal to purchase an interest in property. While recognizing that rights of first refusal are preemptive rights, this court notes that most jurisdictions hold that such rights are interests in property, and as such, have applied the Rule Against Perpetuities to these rights. The appeals court erred in assuming that an interest should not be subject to the Rule Against Perpetuities unless it constitutes a restraint on alienation because the rule is concerned not only with restraints on alienation, but also with restrictions that render title uncertain. Further, in our opinion, rights of first refusal do restrain the alienability of property. Rights of first refusal for a fixed price unquestionably inhibit alienability. Rights of first refusal to purchase at market value restrict sales in excess of market value. Finally, where, as here, the right of first refusal requires the holder of the right to purchase on identical terms with the bona fide third-party offer, restraint is evident since the preemptive effect of such a right will artificially depress the property's value. Where, as here, Rourke's (P) right is unrecorded, the necessity of locating the holder of the right serves to restrain alienation of the property. Since Rourke's (P) right of first refusal was of unlimited duration, the Rule Against Perpetuities was violated, and the right is thus unenforceable. [The court then held that Ferrero's (D) correspondence regarding the third-party offer would not constitute an offer to Rourke (P).] Reversed and remanded.

DISSENT: (Cole, J.) A right of first refusal does not hinder alienability, marketability, or the development of property. Thus, because the policies underlying the Rule Against Perpetuities are not furthered by its application in this case, and the right of first refusal does not constitute an unlawful restraint on alienation, I dissent.

ANALYSIS

The court in the present case appears to have blurred the lines between the preemptive rights, such as the right of first refusal, with options. The preemptive right of first refusal granted to Rourke (P) in the present case was designed to act as a shield and not as a sword. Rourke (P), by virtue of the right of first refusal clause, obtained the right to prevent the sale of the property to a third-party by simply matching the price. However, it is unclear why the trial court implicitly found that by virtue of this preemptive right, Ferrero (D) was required to convey the lot to Rourke (P).

Quicknotes

PREEMPTIVE RIGHTS The right of existing shareholders to the first purchase of new issuances of stock in proportion to their share in ownership.

RULE AGAINST PERPETUITIES The doctrine that a future interest that is incapable of vesting within twenty-one

Continued on next page.

years of lives in being at the time it is created is immediately void.

SPECIFIC PERFORMANCE An equitable remedy whereby the court requires the parties to perform their obligations pursuant to a contract.

SUMMARY JUDGMENT Judgment rendered by a court in response to a motion made by one of the parties, claiming that the lack of a question of material fact in respect to an issue warrants disposition of the issue without consideration by the jury.

Urquhart v. Teller and The Cinnabar Foundation

Purchasers (P) v. Property owners (D)

Mont. Sup. Ct., 288 Mont. 497, 958 P.2d 714 (1998).

NATURE OF CASE: Suit seeking specific performance of an option clause.

FACT SUMMARY: The Urquharts (P) sought to enforce an option in their Contract for Deed to purchase an additional ten acres of land reserved to the Tellers (D).

RULE OF LAW

A condition restraining alienation, when repugnant to the interest created, is void.

FACTS: Teller (D) entered into an agreement with Urquhart (P) to sell 270 of his 280 acres of land, reserving ten acres. In the contract for deed, there was a clause providing the Urquharts (P) with the option to purchase the ten acres, should the Tellers (D) wish to sell or in the event of their deaths. Teller (D) stated that this temporary option was intended to ensure that the property would not be divided should he or his wife die before the contract for deed was paid off. The Urquharts (P) claim this was intended to be an option exercisable upon the sale of the property or Teller's (D) death. Urquhart (P) later paid off the contract for deed and conveyed their interest in the 270 acres to the Urquhart Revocable Living Trust. The trust conveyed the property to Spring Creek Investments (Spring Creek) and purported to also assign the option, but agreed to exercise the option on behalf of Spring Creek in the event it was nonassignable. Teller (D) conveyed the ten-acre parcel to The Cinnabar Foundation (Cinnabar) (D) as a charitable gift. The Urquharts (P) filed suit seeking to enforce the option. Partial summary judgment was granted in favor of Teller (D), holding that the option, which it characterized as a preemptive right of first refusal, was limited to the duration of the contract for deed, constituted an unreasonable restraint on alienation and violated the Rule Against Perpetuities. The Urquharts (P) appealed.

ISSUE: Is a condition restraining alienation, when repugnant to the interest created, void?

HOLDING AND DECISION: (Leaphart, J.) Yes. A condition restraining alienation, when repugnant to the interest created, is void. The option provision here is actually a right of first refusal, triggered only by Teller's (D) choosing to sell or transfer the ten-acre parcel or upon his death. Urquhart (P) argued that the right of first refusal was triggered when Teller (D) transferred the property to Cinnabar (D). This court agrees that the right of first refusal was an unreasonable restraint on alienation and thus is void. Conditions to be considered in determining the reasonableness of a restraint on alienation are set forth in *Edgar v. Hunt*, 218 Mont. 30 (1985). First is the type of price set. If the price set is greatly disproportionate to the market value of the property, this supports a finding of unreasonableness. Second is the intent of the parties. Third is whether the restraint was entered into by mutual consent as a normal incident of an equal bargaining relationship or whether the parties intended to restrain alienation of the property. Here the market value of the property was grossly disproportionate to the option price. Moreover, while the Urquharts (P) did not appear to intend the right of first refusal to restrain the Tellers (D) from alienating their property, its enforcement at this time would either prevent Teller (D) from transferring the property or give the Urquharts (P) an unfair advantage. The Restatement's reasonableness factors also include whether the restraint is limited in duration, allows a variety of transfers, or is limited as to the number of persons to whom transfer is prohibited. Here the right was of potential perpetual duration and affected the alienability of the property in all types of transfers. Thus, the right of first refusal is an unreasonable restraint on alienation and is void. Affirmed.

ANALYSIS

Note that here the fair market value of the property to which the option applied was $400,000 at the time of the suit. The right of first refusal established the purchase price for the Urquharts (P), should they exercise the option, at $10,000.

Quicknotes

ALIENATION Conveyance or transfer of property.

MARKET VALUE The price of particular property or goods that a buyer would offer and a seller accept in the open market, following full disclosure.

SPECIFIC PERFORMANCE An equitable remedy whereby the court requires the parties to perform their obligations pursuant to a contract.

CHAPTER 14

Concurrent Estates: Creation

Quick Reference Rules of Law

Adamson v. Adamson and Hunt, and Adamson

Ex-wife (P) v. Former mother-in-law, seller, and ex-husband (D)

Or. Sup. Ct., 273 Or. 382, 541 P.2d 460 (1975).

NATURE OF CASE: Appeal from determination of equitable interests.

FACT SUMMARY: Margaret Adamson (P) was awarded a two-thirds interest in the property that was originally deeded to her husband, her mother-in-law, and herself.

RULE OF LAW

A conveyance to a husband and wife creates a tenancy by the entirety and creates a single interest between them.

FACTS: Margaret (P), her husband, Brian, and her mother-in-law, Inez (D), purchased an apartment building. The conveyance read "Brian Adamson and Margaret Adamson, husband and wife, and Inez Adamson." Subsequently, the marriage soured and the apartment was given to Margaret in the divorce decree, as far as there existed a community interest. Joel, Brian's father, received a conveyance from Inez (D) of her interest in the property. Margaret (P), just prior to the divorce and just prior to the expected birth of her child, signed her interest away to Joel. Suit was brought by Margaret (P) to determine the respective equitable interests. The trial court held that the deed to Joel was void as induced by fraud. It then determined Margaret's (P) interest at two-thirds and Joel's at one-third. Joel appealed.

ISSUE: Does a conveyance to a husband and wife create a single estate between them?

HOLDING AND DECISION: (Bryson, J.) Yes. A conveyance to a husband and wife creates a tenancy by the entirety and thereby reposes a single estate in them. As a result, the original conveyance created an undivided one-half interest in Inez (D) and an undivided one-half interest in Margaret (P) and Brian. Because the subsequent conveyance to Joel was void each party retained their original interests. Margaret (P) thus has an undivided one-half and Joel has an undivided one-half interest. Reversed.

ANALYSIS

The tenancy by the entirety is no longer recognized in many states. It was a common-law fiction that was based on the ancient view that the husband and wife were one legal entity. That entity was of course the husband. As times changed this underlying rationale became less and less palatable and the concept was phased out.

Quicknotes

EQUITABLE INTEREST A beneficiary's interest in a trust.

TENANCY BY THE ENTIRETY The ownership of property by a husband and wife whereby they hold undivided interests in the property with right of survivorship.

Margarite v. Ewald and Ewald

Wife's heir (P) v. Tenants in common (D)

Pa. Super. Ct., 252 Pa. Super. 244, 381 A.2d 480 (1977).

NATURE OF CASE: Appeal from judgment declaring title to real estate.

FACT SUMMARY: Margarite (P) was adjudged entitled to one-sixth interest in real property deeded to his deceased mother and stepfather as husband and wife along with a living third party "as tenants in common with the right of survivorship."

RULE OF LAW

Where interests in land are held by a married couple and a third party, intent to create a right of survivorship must be expressed with sufficient clarity to overcome a presumption that survivorship is not intended.

FACTS: John and Mary Ewald took title to certain real property by deed along with Joseph Ewald (D). The deed described John and Mary as husband and wife and recited that the three took title as "tenants in common with right of survivorship." Margarite (P) was the son of Mary Ewald by a previous marriage who obtained a declaratory judgment awarding him a one-sixth interest in the land, after the deaths of John and Mary. Joseph Ewald (D) sought to enforce the right of survivorship purported in the deed, and George Ewald (D) claimed an interest pursuant to John Ewald's will, leaving George his entire estate. George and Joseph Ewald (D) appealed.

ISSUE: Where interests in land are held by a married couple and a third party, must intent to create a right of survivorship be expressed with sufficient clarity to overcome a presumption that survivorship is not intended?

HOLDING AND DECISION: (Jacobs, J.) Yes. Where interests in land are held by a married couple and a third party, intent to create a right of survivorship must be expressed with sufficient clarity to overcome a presumption that survivorship is not intended. The terms in the deed are patently contradictory. The "right of survivorship" is not associated with a "tenancy in common." The use of the words "his wife" in the deed indicates intent to create a tenancy by the entireties, and thus John and Mary acquired a one-half interest, and Joseph Ewald (D) acquired a one-half interest. Upon Mary's death, John held the one-half interest with Joseph Ewald (D) in tenancy in common. While the words "with right of survivorship" appended to a valid joint tenancy satisfy this requirement, appending them to a tenancy in common does not. Vacated and remanded.

ANALYSIS

In the majority of jurisdictions, tenancy in common is presumed to be the status of any cotenancy, unless the conveying instrument clearly expresses the intention to create (1) a joint tenancy, and (2) the right of survivorship. (Cotenancy between married persons is tenancy by the entirety, passing at death to the survivor because of their marital status rather than because of the right of survivorship.)

Quicknotes

RIGHT OF SURVIVORSHIP Between two or more persons, such as in a joint tenancy relationship, the right to the property of a deceased passes to the survivor.

TENANCY IN COMMON An interest in property held by two or more people, each with equal right to its use and possession; interests may be partitioned, sold, conveyed, or devised.

Kurpiel v. Kurpiel

Ex-husband (P) v. Ex-wife (D)

N.Y. Sup. Ct., 50 Misc. 2d 604, 271 N.Y.S.2d 114 (1966).

NATURE OF CASE: Action for partition.

FACT SUMMARY: Jenny Kurpiel (D) contended no joint tenancy arose from words of conveyance that did not expressly state that the estate created was a joint tenancy.

RULE OF LAW

Words of conveyance, drafted by a lawyer, that indicated the estate is to be held jointly, are sufficient to create a joint tenancy.

FACTS: Jenny Kurpiel (D) obtained property under a conveyance that stated "to Joseph Kurpiel, Jenny Kurpiel and Edward Kurpiel . . . jointly and not as tenants in common." Following a divorce, Joseph (P) sued for partition of the property, contending it was held in joint tenancy. Jenny (D) and her son, Edward (D), opposed the partition, contending a tenancy by the entirety rather than a joint tenancy had been created.

ISSUE: Are words of conveyance indicating a joint estate sufficient to create a joint tenancy when drafted by a lawyer?

HOLDING AND DECISION: (Pittoni, J.) Yes. Words of conveyance, drafted by a lawyer, that indicate the estate is to be held jointly, are sufficient to create a joint tenancy. If the conveyance in this case had been drafted by a layperson, the conveyance would not be strictly construed. However, this deed was prepared by counsel and specifically intended to create a joint estate. Thus each held an undivided one-third joint tenancy interest, and the property may be partitioned. Plaintiff's motions granted and cross-motion denied.

ANALYSIS

The court in this case relied on the holding in *Jooss v. Fey*, 129 N.Y. 17 (1888), wherein the court held that the words "as joint tenants and not as tenants in common" created a joint tenancy. The court here said it did not matter that only the word "jointly" was used. The intent was clear and thus that concurrent estate was found to have been created.

Quicknotes

CONVEYANCE The transfer of property, or title to property, from one party to another party.

JOINT TENANCY An interest in property whereby a single interest is owned by two or more persons and created by a single instrument; joint tenants possess equal interests in the use of the entire property, and the last survivor is entitled to absolute ownership.

PARTITION The division of property held by co-owners, granting each, sole ownership of his or her share.

TENANCY IN COMMON An interest in property held by two or more people, each with equal right to its use and possession; interests may be partitioned, sold, conveyed, or devised.

S.S. Weems v. Frost National Bank of San Antonio

Estate heirs (P) v. Independent executor (D)

Tex. Ct. Civ. App., 301 S.W.2d 714 (1957).

NATURE OF CASE: Appeal from finding of no joint tenancy.

FACT SUMMARY: Weems (P) contended that a joint tenancy was created merely by the use of the words "to be held jointly" in the conveyance.

RULE OF LAW

A joint tenancy can be created only through the specific use of words of survivorship.

FACTS: Felder indicated in her will that her interest in gas royalties was to go to Weems (P) and others "jointly." Weems (P) sued, contending this language created a joint tenancy. The trial court rejected this and found a tenancy in common had been created. Weems (P) appealed.

ISSUE: Can a joint tenancy be created without words of survivorship?

HOLDING AND DECISION: (Fraser, J.) No. A joint tenancy cannot be created without express use of words of survivorship. In this case, the use of the word "jointly" was insufficient to create a joint tenancy estate. In the absence of words of survivorship, a tenancy in common is created and no survivorship rights are created. Affirmed.

ANALYSIS

At common law, words of concurrent estates, such as "to X and Y," were considered to presumptively create a joint tenancy. Over the years, this presumption changed as is reflected in the holding in this case. Today, a tenancy in common is presumed to be created in absence of specific language evidencing intent to create a joint tenancy.

Quicknotes

CONVEYANCE The transfer of property, or title to property, from one party to another party.

JOINT TENANCY An interest in property whereby a single interest is owned by two or more persons and created by a single instrument; joint tenants possess equal interests in the use of the entire property, and the last survivor is entitled to absolute ownership.

RIGHT OF SURVIVORSHIP Between two or more persons, such as in a joint tenancy relationship, the right to the property of a deceased passes to the survivor.

TENANCY IN COMMON An interest in property held by two or more people, each with equal right to its use and possession; interests may be partitioned, sold, conveyed, or devised.

CHAPTER 15

Concurrent Estates: Administration

Quick Reference Rules of Law

	PAGE
1. **Cotenancy.** When a cotenant out of possession makes a clear, unequivocal demand to use land that is in the exclusive possession of another cotenant, and that cotenant refuses to accommodate the other tenant's right to use the land, the tenant out of possession has established a claim for relief. (Gillmor v. Gillmor and Gillmor)	*64*
2. **Tenancy in Common.** The possession of a tenant in common is presumed to be the possession of all tenants until the one in possession communicates to the others the knowledge that he claims the exclusive right or title and there can be no holding adversely or ouster by the tenant in possession unless such adverse holding is communicated to the other cotenants. (Barrow v. Barrow)	*66*

Gillmor v. Gillmor and Gillmor

Ousted cotenant (P) v. Exclusive use cotenants (D)

Utah Sup. Ct., 694 P.2d 1037 (1984).

NATURE OF CASE: Suit for accounting and damages.

FACT SUMMARY: Florence Gillmor (P) sued Edward (D) Gillmor for an accounting and damages incurred as a result of his obstructing her from exercising her right to occupy land in which she owned an undivided interest.

RULE OF LAW

When a cotenant out of possession makes a clear, unequivocal demand to use land that is in the exclusive possession of another cotenant, and that cotenant refuses to accommodate the other tenant's right to use the land, the tenant out of possession has established a claim for relief.

FACTS: Two brothers owned the land in dispute and upon their death, their interests passed in equal shares to their children, Edward Gillmor (D) and Florence Gillmor (P), the parties to the present suit who became cotenants in the property. Florence (P) brought suit against Edward (D) for an accounting and damages for Edward's (D) exclusive use of the property since January 1, 1979 and for partition. The trial was divided into two phases to determine the damages for the time period January 1, 1979 to May 31, 1980 and then from June 1, 1980 to December 31, 1980. The trial court held that as to the first period, Edward (D) grazed his livestock to the exclusion of Florence's (P) livestock, and awarded damages of $21,544.91, one-half the rental value of the property. The court concluded likewise with respect to the second phase of the trial. Edward (D) appealed as to the second judgment, arguing that there was no evidence or finding on the issue of ouster and that the damages in any case were excessive.

ISSUE: When a cotenant out of possession makes a clear, unequivocal demand to use land that is in the exclusive possession of another cotenant, and that cotenant refuses to accommodate the other tenant's right to use the land, has the tenant out of possession established a claim for relief?

HOLDING AND DECISION: (Stewart, J.) Yes. When a cotenant out of possession makes a clear, unequivocal demand to use land that is in the exclusive possession of another cotenant, and that cotenant refuses to accommodate the other tenant's right to use the land, the tenant out of possession has established a claim for relief. A cotenant may sue for his share of rents and profits from common property if he has been ousted from possession of the common property. Edward (D) argued that the trial court did not find that he ousted Florence (P) from the property. While the trial court did not specifically use the term "ouster," it found that Edward (D) both exercised exclusive use and possession and excluded the plaintiff from use of the common properties. Mere exclusive use of commonly held properties is not sufficient. A tenant in common has the right to use and occupy the entire property held in cotenancy without liability to the other cotenants. However, when a cotenant ousts another cotenant or acts in a way to exclude the cotenant, he violates the cotenant's rights. To establish a right to share in the rents and profits from the common property, the cotenant must show that the other cotenant has used the property to "necessarily exclude his cotenant." This requires either an act of exclusion or use of such a nature that it prevents another cotenant from exercising his rights in the property. Here Florence (P) sought to graze livestock on the land and was prevented from doing so. Florence (P) sent Edward (D) a letter expressing her intent to graze her livestock on the property to the extent of her interest. Edward (D) refused to respond and continued grazing his livestock to the maximum capacity of the property. Thus, Florence (P) established a claim of relief. Edward (D) also argued that he is entitled to an offset for repairs made to the common property. When a cotenant in sole possession makes repairs or improvements to the common property without the consent of his fellow cotenants, he generally does not have a right to contribution. A cotenant may be required to contribute his pro rata share of expenses if the cotenant in possession acted in good faith, with the bona fide belief that he was the sole owner of the property, or if the repairs are necessary to preserve or protect the property. Where a cotenant out of possession seeks an accounting or damages, the cotenant in possession being held liable is entitled to recover reasonable expenditures for necessary repair and maintenance. Here the repairs were a necessary cost of grazing the livestock and should be deducted from the damage award. Affirmed in part, reversed in part, and remanded.

ANALYSIS

Under common law a cotenant receiving profits from the common estate was not obligated to compensate other cotenants. The Statute of Anne modified this rule, requiring a cotenant to account for rents received from third parties to his other cotenants. The modern majority rule is that a cotenant need not account for the rental value of his own

Continued on next page.

possession of the property to the other tenants, unless he is deemed an ouster.

■═■

Quicknotes

COTENANT A tenant possessing property with one or more persons jointly or whose interest is derived from a common grantor.

GOOD FAITH An honest intention to abstain from taking advantage of another.

OUSTER The unlawful dispossession of a party lawfully entitled to possession of real property.

PRO RATA In proportion.

TENANCY IN COMMON An interest in property held by two or more people, each with equal right to its use and possession; interests may be partitioned, sold, conveyed, or devised.

■═■

Barrow v. Barrow

Ex-wife (P) v. Ex-husband (D)

Fla. Sup. Ct., 527 So. 2d 1373 (1988).

NATURE OF CASE: Claim for rental value.

FACT SUMMARY: Donna Barrow (P) sought one-half the fair rental value of the marital residence for the time that her ex-husband, James Barrow (D), occupied the property following their separation.

RULE OF LAW

The possession of a tenant in common is presumed to be the possession of all tenants until the one in possession communicates to the others the knowledge that he claims the exclusive right or title and there can be no holding adversely or ouster by the tenant in possession unless such adverse holding is communicated to the other cotenants.

FACTS: James Barrow (D) owned title to and built a residence on land prior to his marriage to Donna (P). The property became their marital residence for the ten years that they were married. The final judgment for dissolution awarded Donna (P) an undivided one-half interest in the property as alimony. Donna (P) moved to Idaho immediately after separating from James (D). She initiated this proceeding seeking partition of the former marital residence. James (D) counterclaimed for one-half the amounts he expended for taxes, insurance, and other services necessary to maintain and improve the property. Donna (P) then sought one half the rental value for the period James (D) occupied the home after their divorce. The trial court concluded that Donna (P) was entitled to half the rental value under *Adkins v. Edwards*, 317 So. 2d 770 (Fla. App. 2 Dist. 1975), and James (D) was entitled to half the insurance premiums and property taxes. The district court affirmed. We granted review to resolve the conflict in case law.

ISSUE: Is the possession of a tenant in common presumed to be the possession of all tenants until the one in possession communicates to the others the knowledge that he claims the exclusive right or title and can there be no holding adversely or ouster by the tenant in possession unless such adverse holding is communicated to the other cotenants?

HOLDING AND DECISION: (Overton, J.) Yes. The possession of a tenant in common is presumed to be the possession of all tenants until the one in possession communicates to the others the knowledge that he claims the exclusive right or title and there can be no holding adversely or ouster by the tenant in possession unless such adverse holding is communicated to the other cotenants. In *Coggan v. Coggan*, 239 So. 2d 17 (Fla. 1970), this court stated that the possession of a tenant in common is presumed to be the possession of all cotenants until he manifests or communicates that he claims exclusive right or title to the property. In *Adkins v. Edwards*, the court distinguished this opinion on the basis that joint occupancy by the cotenants in *Coggan* was not effectively precluded. The reasoning of the court in *Adkins* is contrary to the rule initially approved by the court in *Bird v. Bird*, 15 Fla. 424 (1875). There we held that when one cotenant has exclusive possession of lands owned as a tenant in common with another, and uses such lands for his own benefit and does not receive rents or profits therefrom, the cotenant is not liable or accountable to the cotenant out of possession, unless such cotenant in exclusive possession holds adversely or as a result of ouster. Here there was no communication by James (D) to Donna (P) that he was holding the property exclusively and adversely to her interest. In addition, there is an exception that when a cotenant in possession seeks contribution for amounts expended in the improvement or preservation of the property, his claim may be offset by the value of his use of the property, which has exceeded his proportional share of ownership. Under this exception Donna (P) is entitled to claim the reasonable rental value as an offset against James's (D) claim for the costs of maintaining the property. Decision of the district court is quashed and the reasoning in *Adkins* disapproved. District court judgment reversed and court appeals court ordered to remand.

ANALYSIS

At common law, a cotenant deriving rents from the common estate was not obligated to reimburse the other cotenants for any profits he received therefrom. The Statute of Anne modified this rule, requiring a cotenant to account for rents received from third parties to his other cotenants. The modern majority rule is that a cotenant need not account for the rental value of his own possession of the property to the other tenants, unless he is deemed an ouster.

Quicknotes

OUSTER The unlawful dispossession of a party lawfully entitled to possession of real property.

PARTITION The division of property held by co-owners, granting each, sole ownership of his or her share.

TENANCY IN COMMON An interest in property held by two or more people, each with equal right to its use and possession; interests may be partitioned, sold, conveyed, or devised.

CHAPTER 16

Joint Tenancies: Termination (Severance)

Quick Reference Rules of Law

Harms v. Sprague

Joint tenant (P) v. Mortgage assignee (D)

Ill. Sup. Ct., 105 Ill. 2d 215, 473 N.E.2d 930 (1984).

NATURE OF CASE: Appeal of reversal of court order quieting title.

FACT SUMMARY: John Harms, deceased former joint tenant in property with William Harms (P) had executed a mortgage in favor of the predecessor in interest of Sprague (D) who claimed the mortgage survived John.

RULE OF LAW

A mortgage on a joint tenant's interest does not survive the mortgagor.

FACTS: William (P) and John Harms owned property in joint tenancy. John executed a mortgage favoring Simmons, who later assigned his interest to Sprague (D). After John died, William (P) contended that the mortgage had died with John and brought an action to quiet title. The trial court held that Sprague's (D) mortgage survived John's death and entered judgment in favor of Sprague (D). The appellate court reversed. Sprague (D) appealed.

ISSUE: Does a mortgage on a joint tenant's interest survive the mortgagor?

HOLDING AND DECISION: (Moran, J.) No. A mortgage on a joint tenant's interest does not survive the mortgagor. One requirement for joint tenancy is a unity of title. If a mortgage constituted a change in title, it would destroy this unity. However, this state recognizes that a mortgage will not constitute a change of title until foreclosure plus the running of any redemption period. Since a mortgage does not sever a joint tenancy, the entire estate of the decedent joint tenant passes to the survivor. This effects a nullification of any liens thereon. For this reason, Sprague's (D) interest was extinguished upon John's death. Affirmed.

ANALYSIS

An issue regarding both real property law and secured transaction law is the "lien" vs. "title" theories. As discussed in the case, mortgages have been seen as both transfers of title and mere encumbrances. It seems that most jurisdictions adhere to the lien theory.

Quicknotes

ACTION TO QUIET TITLE Equitable action to resolve conflicting claims to an interest in real property.

FORECLOSURE An action to recover the amount due on a mortgage of real property where the owner has failed to meet the mortgage obligations, terminating the owner's interest in the property which must then be sold to satisfy the debt.

JOINT TENANCY An interest in property whereby a single interest is owned by two or more persons and created by a single instrument; joint tenants possess equal interests in the use of the entire property, and the last survivor is entitled to absolute ownership.

LIEN A claim against the property of another in order to secure the payment of a debt.

REDEMPTION PERIOD The period during which a mortgagor has the right to reclaim forfeited property, following a default on mortgage payments, by the payment of the mortgage debt and any other interest, fees and costs.

Hutchinson National Bank v. Brown

Lender (P) v. Pledger (D)

Kan. Ct. App., 12 Kan. App. 2d 673, 753 P.2d 1299 (1988).

NATURE OF CASE: Appeal from judgment in declaratory relief action.

FACT SUMMARY: Hutchinson National Bank and Trust Co. (Bank) (P) appealed from a declaratory judgment in favor of Ida Brown (D), contending that Harry Brown's unilateral pledge of a certificate of deposit, held in joint tenancy, severed one of the four unities required for the continued existence of a joint tenancy in the certificate of deposit.

RULE OF LAW

A unilateral pledge of a certificate of deposit acts as a severance of a joint tenancy in the certificate of deposit.

FACTS: Harry Brown purchased a $15,000 certificate of deposit at Hutchinson National Bank and Trust Co. (Bank) (P). It was issued in his name and in the name of Ida Brown (D), who were husband and wife, as joint tenants. In 1984, his grandson, Dale Brown, applied for a $15,000 loan with the Bank (P). As security, Harry Brown agreed to pledge the certificate of deposit. Harry Brown died in 1985, and the Bank (P) continued to pay interest on the certificate of deposit to Ida Brown (D). In March of 1986, Dale Brown filed for bankruptcy. Shortly thereafter, the Bank (P) filed suit against Ida Brown (D) asking that it be allowed to apply the $15,000 certificate of deposit against the note of Dale Brown. Judgment was entered for Ida Brown (D), the court finding that the unilateral pledge of the certificate of deposit by Harry Brown did not sever the joint tenancy in the certificate of deposit. From that decision, the Bank (P) appealed.

ISSUE: Does a unilateral pledge of a certificate of deposit act as a severance of the joint tenancy interest in that certificate of deposit?

HOLDING AND DECISION: (Rulon, J.) Yes. A unilateral pledge of a certificate of deposit acts as a severance of the joint tenancy interest in the certificate of deposit. The creation and continued existence of the joint tenancy requires the co-existence of the four unities of time, title, interest, and possession. The joint tenancy may be terminated by operation of law upon the destruction of any one or more of the necessary unities. A pledge, by definition, is a bailment of personal property as security for a debt. A joint tenant has the right to sever his or her joint interest by mortgaging the joint tenancy interest. Once this is done, a tenancy in common results. A pledge acts as a severance of the joint tenancy interest because there is no legal distinction in the operative effect of a mortgage or a pledge. Thus, a unilateral pledge of the certificate of deposit by Harry Brown was a formal act which severed the unity of interest, creating a tenancy in common in the certificate of deposit. Reversed and remanded.

ANALYSIS

Note that the distinction between this case and the case of *Harms v. Sprague*, 473 N.E.2d 930 (1984). In that case, it was held that a joint tenancy in real property was not severed by a mortgage because unity of title was preserved. In the present case, the court, dealing with personal property, focused upon the unity of interest, and since in that jurisdiction a joint tenancy could be severed by way of a mortgage of the joint tenancy interest, it had no difficulty concluding that the pledge severed the joint tenancy interest in the certificate of deposit.

Quicknotes

DECLARATORY JUDGMENT A judgment of the court establishing the rights of the parties.

JOINT TENANCY An interest in property whereby a single interest is owned by two or more persons and created by a single instrument; joint tenants possess equal interests in the use of the entire property, and the last survivor is entitled to absolute ownership.

UNILATERAL One-sided; involving only one person.

UNITY OF TITLE Cotenants in a joint tenancy or tenancy by the entirety obtain their interest in the property under the same legal title.

Minonk State Bank v. Grassman

Administrator (P) v. Joint tenant (D)

Ill. Sup. Ct., 95 Ill. 2d 392, 447 N.E.2d 822 (1983).

NATURE OF CASE: Appeal from reversal of judgment in declaratory relief action.

FACT SUMMARY: Grassman (D) appealed from a decision reversing a trial court's decision that she was the sole surviving joint tenant in the disputed property, contending that the joint tenancy could not be severed by her act of conveying the property to herself.

RULE OF LAW

The right of survivorship in a joint tenancy property can be destroyed by a joint tenant's act of conveying the property to herself.

FACTS: The real property in dispute was conveyed to Grassman (D), Agnes Grassman, Gustav Grassman and Frieda Grassman, as joint tenants. Gustav and Frieda died. Then Grassman (D) executed and recorded a deed which conveyed the interest in the land from herself as grantor to herself as grantee, for the sole purpose of dissolving any and all rights of survivorship. Agnes Grassman had no knowledge of this conveyance. Upon the death of Agnes Grassman, the Bank (P), as administrator of her will, filed an action seeking a declaration that Agnes was the owner of an undivided one-half interest in the real property, and that Grassman (D) was a tenant-in-common with the decedent in the ownership of the property, and not a joint tenant with right of survivorship. The trial court disagreed, entering a judgment in favor of Grassman (D) that she was the sole surviving joint tenant of the disputed property. The appellate court, however, reversed, and from that decision Grassman (D) appealed, contending that her right of survivorship could not be destroyed by her act of conveying the property to herself.

ISSUE: Can a joint tenant's right of survivorship in joint tenancy property be destroyed by a joint tenant's act of conveying the property to herself?

HOLDING AND DECISION: (Goldenhersh, J.) Yes. The right of survivorship in a joint tenancy property can be destroyed by a joint tenant's act of conveying the property to herself. Grassman's (D) argument is that the courts are precluded from changing the common-law rule to the contrary by the "reception" statute, which specifically prohibits this court from changing the common law of England as it existed prior to the fourth year of James I, unless repealed by the General Assembly. The Bank (P), however, rightly argues that the reception statute amounted to an adoption of a system of law whose outstanding characteristic is its adaptability and capacity for growth. As such, we agree with the appellate court that it is necessary for the common law to keep pace with the modern rules for conveyances. The common-law rule that there must be a separate grantor and grantee was based on outmoded, obsolete considerations regarding the manner in which land transfers were effectuated and recorded, such as livery of seisin. Under modern conveyance laws, a conveyance like the one executed and recorded by Grassman (D) poses no problems. Although in some circumstances it may be that the parties to a joint tenancy might not be able to rely upon the relationship that led them to originally acquire the property, we are not presented with such a situation here. Affirmed.

ANALYSIS

There has been considerable discussion regarding the effect of a lease on the continued existence of a joint tenancy. There is authority for a novel proposition of law referred to as conditional severance, where the joint tenancy is severed during the term of the lease, but revived if upon termination of the lease both of the joint tenants are still living. Note also an approach entitled temporary or partial severance, under which the joint tenancy survives, but the surviving joint tenant's interest remains subject to the lease. See Comment, "The Consequences of a Lease to a Third Party Made by One Joint Tenant," 66 *Cal. L. Rev.* 69 (1978).

Quicknotes

CONVEYANCE The transfer of property, or title to property, from one party to another party.

GRANTOR Conveyor of property or settlor of a trust.

JOINT TENANCY An interest in property whereby a single interest is owned by two or more persons and created by a single instrument; joint tenants possess equal interests in the use of the entire property, and the last survivor is entitled to absolute ownership.

RIGHT OF SURVIVORSHIP Between two or more persons, such as in a joint tenancy relationship, the right to the property of a deceased passes to the survivor.

CHAPTER 17

Marital Property

Quick Reference Rules of Law

O'Brien v. O'Brien

Physician ex-husband (P) v. Ex-wife (D)

N.Y. Ct. App., 489 N.E.2d 712 (1985).

NATURE OF CASE: Review of property division ordered pursuant to marital dissolution.

FACT SUMMARY: The divorcing wife (D) of Dr. O'Brien (P) claimed a marital property interest in his medical license.

RULE OF LAW

A professional license may constitute marital property.

FACTS: While the O'Briens were married, the husband (P) attended medical school full-time. Ms. O'Brien (D) worked and contributed most of the funds to maintain the household and the husband's (P) studies. Not long after Dr. O'Brien (P) obtained his license to practice, he filed for divorce. The trial court held Dr. O'Brien's (P) license to be marital property and awarded Ms. O'Brien (D) 40 percent of the present value of Dr. O'Brien's (P) expected lifetime earnings. The appellate division reversed, holding that a professional license was not marital property. Ms. O'Brien (D) appealed.

ISSUE: May a professional license constitute marital property?

HOLDING AND DECISION: (Simons, J.) Yes. A professional license may constitute marital property. New York's Equitable Distribution Law is not bound by traditional concepts of property. It provides that spouses have an equitable claim to things of value arising out of the marital relationship, whether or not such things of value fit into the common law notion of property. In fact, one of the reasons for the adoption of the law was the realization that application of traditional property concepts had led to inequities upon dissolution of a marriage. Here, Dr. O'Brien's (P) professional license constitutes the most valuable marital asset, and an equitable division of its value was proper. Reversed.

CONCURRENCE: (Meyer, J.) A court needs to be able to retain jurisdiction to modify an award of this nature in the event that circumstances force the licensed former spouse into a less remunerative situation than originally anticipated.

ANALYSIS

Whether a professional license is "property" has been a hotly debated topic during the 1980s. This is because it has some attributes of traditional property but not all. Like property, it has value that can be measured. Unlike property, it cannot be alienated and becomes nonexistent upon the licensee's death or loss of license.

Quicknotes

MARITAL PROPERTY Property accumulated by a married couple during the term of their marriage.

Simmons v. Simmons

Husband (P) v. Wife (D)

Conn. Sup. Ct., 244 Conn. 158, 708 A.2d 949 (1998).

NATURE OF CASE: Appeal from marital property distribution.

FACT SUMMARY: The trial court decided that Mr. Simmons's (P) medical degree was not property subject to equitable distribution and Ms. Simmons (D) appealed.

RULE OF LAW

An advanced degree is properly classified as an expectancy rather than a presently existing property interest.

FACTS: After completing medical school, Mr. Simmons (P) sued for dissolution of marriage. Until Mr. Simmons (P) started medical school, both spouses pursued their educational goals and worked to support their family. After Mr. Simmons (P) entered medical school, Ms. Simmons (D) worked to support the family, but did not make any direct financial contributions to Mr. Simmons's (P) medical school education. Ms. Simmons (D) alleged that Mr. Simmons's (P) medical degree was property subject to equitable distribution, and presented evidence that the degree's present value was $3.1 million. Accordingly, Ms. Simmons (D) sought over $1.5 million as her share. The trial court disagreed and denied alimony to both parties. Ms. Simmons (D) appealed.

ISSUE: Is an advanced degree properly classified as an expectancy rather than a presently existing property interest?

HOLDING AND DECISION: (Callahan, J.) Yes. An advanced degree is properly classified as an expectancy rather than a presently existing property interest. Under the applicable statute, while "property" is defined broadly, the scope of the definition is not without limits. Whether the interest is distributable in a marital dissolution depends on whether it is a presently existing property interest or a mere expectancy. Contrary to Ms. Simmons's (D) argument, a medical degree is not like a vested pension interest—which is considered distributable property. That is because an advanced degree entails no presently existing, enforceable right to receive any particular income in the future. It represents nothing more than an opportunity for the degree holder, through his or her own efforts, in the absence of any contingency that might limit or frustrate those efforts, to earn income in the future. Therefore, an advanced degree is not subject to equitable distribution, and that conclusion is supported by the great weight of authority and the fact that an advanced degree has no inherent value extrinsic to the recipient. However, there are other ways to compensate Ms. Simmons (D) without subjecting the degree to classification as property—such as through an award of alimony. Thus, sound public policy would dictate an award of alimony in this case since Ms. Simmons (D) had become the sole source of support of the family in order to help Mr. Simmons (P) complete his degree and because various factors indicate that she has foregone earning as much income as she might have if she had not become the family's sole source of support. The trial court abused its discretion in not awarding alimony. Reversed in part and remanded.

ANALYSIS

By awarding alimony, which would be reviewable by a family court upon changed circumstances of the parties, the court avoided sentencing Mr. Simmons (P) to a life of involuntary servitude that would otherwise be attributed to his degree if it were characterized as property rather than an expectancy. As the court points out, Mr. Simmons (P) could become disabled, die or fail his medical boards and be precluded from the practice of medicine. He could choose an alternative career either within medicine or in an unrelated field or a career as a medical missionary, earning only a subsistence income. An award of alimony will allow the court to consider these changes if and when they occur.

Quicknotes

ALIMONY Allowances (usually monetary) which husband or wife by court order pays other spouse for maintenance while they are separated, or after they are divorced (permanent alimony), or temporarily, pending a suit for divorce (pendente lite).

DISSOLUTION The termination of a marriage.

EQUITABLE DISTRIBUTION The means by which a court distributes all assets acquired during a marriage by the spouses equitably upon dissolution.

CHAPTER 18

Express Easements: Classification and Manner of Creation

Quick Reference Rules of Law

Northwest Realty Co. v. Jacobs

Landowner (P) v. Transferee (D)

S.D. Sup. Ct., 273 N.W.2d 141 (1978).

NATURE OF CASE: Appeal from grant of injunction requiring removal of fill.

FACT SUMMARY: One Smith executed a deed granting an unclear interest in land to Iowa Ditch Co., and Smith's successor transferred Smith's reserved interest to Jacobs (D), who filled part of the land, while Northwest Realty Co. (P) sought removal of the fill claiming title in fee to the property by a purported transfer thereof by the directors of Iowa Ditch.

RULE OF LAW

A deed of an interest in land without an exact description of the location of transferred property and containing restriction as to the kind of use to which the property must be put transfers an easement rather than a fee simple title.

FACTS: In 1898, one Smith granted to Iowa Ditch "A Strip of land not exceeding forty (40) feet in width . . . to be used as a right of way for an irrigation ditch." Smith took in return the sum of $50 and was issued three shares of Iowa Ditch stock. Smith's successor, Phillips, transferred the shares and Smith's reserved interest to Jacobs (D). Jacobs (D) filled in part of the ditch that was built and paved it for use as an automobile dealership lot. In 1973, the directors of Iowa Ditch dissolved the corporation and issued quitclaim deeds to stockholders who owned property adjacent to the ditch. Pursuant to the directors' deed, Northwest Realty Co. (Northwest) (P), an adjacent landowner grantee, brought suit seeking an order to have Jacobs (D) remove the fill dirt from the ditch, while Jacobs (D) counterclaimed for an order quieting their title as against Northwest (P). The trial court held that Northwest (P) held a fee simple interest, and Jacobs (D) appealed.

ISSUE: Does a deed of interest in land, without an exact description of the transferred property and containing a restriction as to the kind of use to which the property must be put, transfer an easement rather than a fee simple title?

HOLDING AND DECISION: (Zastrow, J.) Yes. The real question here is whether deed from Smith to Iowa Ditch conveyed a fee simple or a right-of-way easement. This determination requires consideration of the amount of consideration, the particularity of the deed description, the limitation on the use of the property, the purpose of the parties, the wording of the deed, who paid the taxes, and how the parties have treated the land. Considering these factors, here, a right-of-way easement only was created by the deed. A deed of an interest in land without an exact description of the transferred property containing a restriction as to the kind of use to which the property must be put transfers an easement rather than a fee simple title. The description is somewhat indefinite here, and the use of the land was to be for a right of way in this case. The other factors mentioned similarly lead to this conclusion. Reversed.

ANALYSIS

It is not necessary that the exact physical location of an easement be properly described in a deed of easement. Any convenient location in view of the intent of the parties will suffice. The grant of a fee simple absolutely requires an exact description and will fail for lacking such description. Here, the court construed the instrument to be a deed of easement because a right of which was expressly mentioned as part of the grant, whereas without such mention it could have failed entirely.

Quicknotes

DEED A signed writing transferring title to real property from one person to another.

EASEMENT The right to utilize a portion of another's real property for a specific use.

FEE SIMPLE An estate in land characterized by ownership of the entire property for an unlimited duration and by absolute power over distribution.

RIGHT OF WAY The right of a party to pass over the property of another.

Greaves v. McGee

Lessee (D) v. Property owners (P)

Ala. Sup. Ct., 492 So. 2d 307 (1986).

NATURE OF CASE: Appeal of order establishing mineral rights in certain real estate.

FACT SUMMARY: The McGees (P) contended that their predecessors had conveyed only an easement in certain real estate, not fee simple title.

RULE OF LAW

A conveyance intended to grant only an easement shall be so construed.

FACTS: The Yorks had title to certain property. In 1928, they conveyed to the County of Lamar, Alabama, all title to "a right of way for public road twenty feet in width," followed by a description of the property. The conveyance went on to note that it covered the existing road and any road built in the future. Years later, the McGees (P), successors in interest to the Yorks, brought a declaratory relief action seeking a declaration that they had title to any mineral rights appurtenant to the deeded land. The trial court held that the conveyance had been of an easement only and entered judgment in favor of the McGees (P). An appeal was taken.

ISSUE: Shall a conveyance intended to grant only an easement be so construed?

HOLDING AND DECISION: (Houston, J.) Yes. A conveyance intended to grant only an easement shall be so construed. It is a fundamental precept of property law that courts should construe instruments so as to give effect to the intent of the parties. The primary manner by which a court should attempt to ascertain the intention of the parties is by looking at the entire instrument. The court should then look first to the circumstances surrounding the execution of the instrument and then to the subsequent acts of the parties. Here an examination of the entire document clearly demonstrated that the parties to the 1928 conveyance intended the conveyance to be an easement. The document speaks of conveyance of a "right of way," which is a classic example of easement language. No counterbalancing language indicating conveyance of a fee can be found, so the trial court correctly held that the Yorks retained title to the land in question. Affirmed.

ANALYSIS

An easement is a particular type of interest in property, this being a right of ingress and egress, and the right to make improvements pertaining to such ingress and egress. This right is served from possessory rights. Easements can be created by express conveyance, prescription, or operation of law.

Quicknotes

CONVEYANCE The transfer of property, or title to property, from one party to another party.

EASEMENT The right to utilize a portion of another's real property for a specific use.

Hurst v. Baker

Easement holders (P) v. Property owner (D)

Ohio Ct. App., 1997 WL 215767 (1997).

NATURE OF CASE: Action to quiet title in an easement.

FACT SUMMARY: Hurst (P) sought to quiet title in a twenty-foot wide roadway running through their land.

RULE OF LAW

The transfer of a fee simple interest in property is presumed to be conveyed in the absence of clear language indicating intent to transfer a lesser interest by the parties.

FACTS: Ninety-four acres of land were conveyed to John and Effie Lowks in 1912. Soon thereafter a portion of that tract was conveyed to William Lowks. The deed provided for an easement in a 20-foot wide road running through John and Effie's land. William Lowks died nine years later and his land was transferred several times until it was owned by Baker (D). The road was described as a "roadway in common" in later conveyances including the one to Baker (D). The Hursts (P) also acquired their property through mesne conveyances from the original master tract. The remainder of the master tract was later conveyed, excepting from the legal description the 40 acres and road. Later deeds, including the one to Hurst (P), provided that "a roadway 20 feet in width" running through the property was excepted from the conveyance. The Hursts (P) commenced this action asserting fee simple interest in the roadway and seeking to quiet title thereto. Baker (D) claimed the road was an easement to be used in common by the owners of both tracts. The court concluded that Baker (D) was the fee simple owner of the roadway. A second hearing was held to determine the parties' respective interests in the roadway. Hurst (P) was determined to have the responsibility for maintaining the roadway and Baker (D) was instructed that they could not farm the 54-acre tract in any manner that would interfere with the ingress and egress to the back 40-acre tract. The parties appealed.

ISSUE: Is the transfer of a fee simple interest in property presumed to be conveyed in the absence of clear language indicating intent to transfer a lesser interest by the parties?

HOLDING AND DECISION: (Stephenson, J.) Yes. The transfer of a fee simple interest in property is presumed to be conveyed in the absence of clear language indicating intent to transfer a lesser interest by the parties. Hurst (P) argued that the lower court erroneously ruled in favor of Baker (D) and that Hurst (P) is in fact the fee simple owner of the roadway. This court agrees. The result here is governed by the original deed from John and Effie to William Lowks in which a fee simple interest in the roadway was granted. It is the intent of the parties to the original instrument that will control its interpretation. If that intent is clear from the language of the deed, then it will be given effect despite rules of construction. The language of the deed is sufficiently clear to conclude that a fee interest in the disputed roadway was conveyed to William and continued in the chain of title to the Bakers (D). There was no dispute that a fee interest was created in the 40 acres. The legal description of the property states that a road was "also" included in the grant. This implies that the roadway was "equal in weight" to the interest preceding it. Since the 40 acres was conveyed in fee simple, it follows that so was the roadway. Instruments such as deeds must be construed in favor of the grantee in order to detract as little as possible from the extent of the grant. This requires the court to construe the deed as granting a fee simple interest rather than a mere easement. In addition, deeds must be construed as conveying the grantor's entire interest in the land described unless a clear limitation is placed on such interest. In the absence of language regarding the use or purpose of the grant or limiting the estate conveyed, a transfer of a strip of land is construed as transferring an estate in fee. Reversed and remanded.

ANALYSIS

The court states that the lower court erred in applying the technical rules of construction in concluding the roadway was merely an easement. Such rules of construction are not invoked where the express language of the instrument is unambiguous.

Quicknotes

ACTION TO QUIET TITLE Equitable action to resolve conflicting claims to an interest in real property.

CONVEYANCE The transfer of property, or title to property, from one party to another party.

DEED A signed writing transferring title to real property from one person to another.

EASEMENT The right to utilize a portion of another's real property for a specific use.

FEE SIMPLE An estate in land characterized by ownership of the entire property for an unlimited duration and by absolute power over distribution.

CHAPTER 19

Express Easements: Interpretation and Extent

Quick Reference Rules of Law

Brown v. Voss

Easement grantee (P) v. Easement grantor (D)

Wash. Sup. Ct., 715 P.2d 514 (1986).

NATURE OF CASE: Appeal from denial of injunctive relief.

FACT SUMMARY: The court of appeals held that an easement granted for the benefit of one dominant estate could be used for two dominant estates where no increased burden to the servient estate is shown.

RULE OF LAW

If an easement is appurtenant to a particular parcel of land, any extension thereof to other parcels is a misuse of the easement unless the servient estate does not overburden it.

FACTS: In 1952, Voss (D) granted an easement to Brown (P) to allow ingress and egress to Voss's (D) property. Brown (P) subsequently obtained title to a third parcel and attempted to use the easement to gain access thereto. Brown (P) sued to establish the right to so use the easement, yet Voss (D) sought an injunction to forbid such use. The trial court denied the injunction, the court of appeals reversed, and Voss (D) appealed.

ISSUE: If an easement is appurtenant to a particular parcel of land, is any extension thereof to other parcels a misuse of the easement, unless the easement is not overburdened?

HOLDING AND DECISION: (Brachtenbach, J.) Yes. If an easement is appurtenant to a particular parcel of land, any extension thereof to other parcels is a misuse of the easement, unless the use does not overburden the easement. The easement received no greater use as a result of Brown's (P) acquisition of the second parcel. Brown (P) reasonably developed his property, and thus the injunction was correctly denied. Reversed.

DISSENT: (Dore, J.) Any extension of this easement is a misuse. Thus, injunctive relief should have been granted.

ANALYSIS

This case illustrates that while the law of easements can be traced back to common law, it is subject to judicial interpretation. Here, the reasonableness of the development, in the eyes of the court, served as the basis for denying the injunction.

Quicknotes

DOMINANT ESTATE Property that benefits from the use of an easement on other property.

EASEMENT The right to utilize a portion of another's real property for a specific use.

INJUNCTIVE RELIEF A court order issued as a remedy, requiring a person to do, or prohibiting that person from doing, a specific act.

SERVIENT ESTATE Property that is burdened in some aspect for the benefit of a dominant estate.

M.P.M. Builders, LLC v. Dwyer

Landowner (P) v. Easement holder (D)

Mass. Sup. Jud. Ct., 809 N.E.2d 1053 (2004).

NATURE OF CASE: Suit for declaratory relief.

FACT SUMMARY: A landowner sought to relocate an easement without the easement holder's consent.

RULE OF LAW

Within certain general limits, a landowner can unilaterally relocate an easement on its property.

FACTS: Dwyer (D) bought a parcel of land in 1941. His deed to the property also conveyed an easement to him across adjoining land owned by M.P.M. Builders (M.P.M.) (P). Silent on whether the easement could be relocated, Dwyer's (D) deed did specify the easement's location. M.P.M. (P) sought to develop its adjoining property in 2002. To accommodate those plans, M.P.M. (P) offered to construct, entirely at its own expense, two new easements to Dwyer's (D) property, both of which would have continued to grant Dwyer (D) unrestricted access to his parcel. Dwyer (D) refused the offer. M.P.M. (P) sued for a declaratory judgment that it could unilaterally relocate Dwyer's (D) easements. The trial judge ruled that current law required him to deny M.P.M.'s (P) motion for summary judgment and to enter summary judgment instead for Dwyer (D). M.P.M. (P) appealed.

ISSUE: Can a landowner unilaterally relocate an easement on its property?

HOLDING AND DECISION: (Cowin, J.) Yes. Within certain general limits, a landowner can unilaterally relocate an easement on its property. The trial judge correctly applied existing law to permit the dominant tenant, in this case Dwyer (D), to block the development efforts of a servient tenant, in this case M.P.M. (P). The court concludes, however, that recent developments in this area of the law require the adoption of a new rule that permits servient tenants to unilaterally relocate easements if the proposed relocations meet certain conditions. Specifically, the court adopts § 4.8(3) of the Restatement (Third) of Property (Servitudes). Section 4.8(3) permits a servient tenant to relocate an easement, without the dominant tenant's consent, but only if the relocation does not significantly lessen the dominant tenant's use of the easement, increase the dominant tenant's burdens in using the easement, or frustrate the original reason for the easement. Contrary to Dwyer's (D) arguments, this rule will not devalue or render property interests intolerably uncertain; indeed, the conditions recognized under § 4.8(3) strive to ensure that values of easements will remain the same. As for Dwyer's (D) predicted rise in litigation, any increase should level off over time as owners and easement holders better identify their respective rights and responsibilities in this context. In this particular case, though, the record is not sufficiently developed to allow review of M.P.M.'s (P) compliance with the new standard. Accordingly, the case should be returned to the Land Court for further proceedings. Vacated and remanded.

ANALYSIS

Unlike the potentially harsh common-law rule, § 4.8(3) permits a flexible analysis that accommodates the interests of both sides in easement-relocation disputes. The watchword in the analysis is "reasonable," which means that, as Dwyer (D) predicted, the judicial system probably will be burdened with a rise in such disputes until more solid principles emerge via case-by-case adjudications.

Quicknotes

DOMINANT ESTATE Property that benefits from the use of an easement on other property.

EASEMENT The right to utilize a portion of another's real property for a specific use.

SERVIENT ESTATE Property that is burdened in some aspect for the benefit of a dominant estate.

Hayes v. Aquia Marina, Inc.

Landowner (P) v. Easement holder (D)

Va. Sup. Ct., 243 Va. 255, 414 S.E.2d 820 (1992).

NATURE OF CASE: Chancery suit to enjoin proposed expanded use of an easement.

FACT SUMMARY: Hayes (P), owner of the servient estate, brought suit against Aquia Marina, Inc. (D), owner of the dominant estate, seeking to enjoin its proposed expansion.

RULE OF LAW

When an easement is created by grant or reservation and the instrument creating the easement does not limit the use to be made of it, the easement may be used for any purpose to which the dominant estate may then, or in the future, reasonably be devoted.

FACTS: The parties' predecessors in title entered into a written agreement to establish a certain roadway or right of way beginning at the state highway and ending at the property division line between the dominant and servient estates. By 1959, three residential buildings, a wooden pier and ten boat slips were located on the dominant estate. In 1961, the current marina was constructed, consisting of 84 boat slips, a public boat launch and a gas dock. In 1989, the county granted a permit to expand the marina by increasing the number of boat slips to 280. Hayes (P) brought suit against Aquia Marina, Inc. (D) alleging that the proposed expansion of the marina would overburden the easement across his lands. The cause was referred to a commissioner in chancery who filed a report. The trial court overruled all Hayes's (P) exceptions to the report and confirmed the report in all respects. Hayes (P) appealed.

ISSUE: When an easement is created by grant or reservation and the instrument creating the easement does not limit the use to be made of it, may the easement be used for any purpose to which the dominant estate may then, or in the future, reasonably be devoted?

HOLDING AND DECISION: (Stephenson, J.) Yes. When an easement is created by grant or reservation and the instrument creating the easement does not limit the use to be made of it, the easement may be used for any purpose to which the dominant estate may then, or in the future, reasonably be devoted. Thus, an easement created by a general grant or reservation, without words limiting it to any particular use of the dominant estate, is not affected by any reasonable change in the use of the dominant estate. However, no use may be made of the easement that is different from that established at the time it was created, and which imposes an additional burden on the servient estate. Hayes (P) argued that the easement agreement refers to a "private roadway," meaning the parties intended to limit the use to domestic purposes. When the agreement is read as a whole, however, that phrase was intended to differentiate between that portion of the easement which could be taken for use as part of the state highway from that which could not. The phrase was thus descriptive, not restrictive, and created no terms of limitation upon the easement's use. The record also supports the conclusion that the operation of a marina is a use to which the dominant estate could reasonably be devoted. Hayes (P) also argued that the proposed expansion would impose an additional and unreasonable burden on the easement. Hayes (P) has the burden of proving this allegation. On appeal, a decree confirming the commissioner's report is presumed correct unless plainly wrong. Here the trial court's conclusion is amply supported by the record and law. Affirmed.

ANALYSIS

Hayes (P) also contested the defendant's right to pave the easement. While the owner of an easement has the duty to maintain it, he also has the right to make reasonable improvements, provided that such improvements do not unreasonably increase the burden on the servient estate.

Quicknotes

DOMINANT ESTATE Property that benefits from the use of an easement on other property.

EASEMENT The right to utilize a portion of another's real property for a specific use.

ENJOIN The ordering of a party to cease the conduct of a specific activity.

SERVIENT ESTATE Property that is burdened in some aspect for the benefit of a dominant estate.

CHAPTER **20**

Express Easements: Succession

Quick Reference Rules of Law

Nelson v. Johnson

Easement holder (P) v. Landowner (D)

Idaho Sup. Ct., 679 P.2d 662 (1984).

NATURE OF CASE: Appeal of order declaring the existence of an easement.

FACT SUMMARY: Nelson's (P) predecessor created a water rights easement on land to which the Johnsons (D) eventually succeeded, to which Nelson (P) claimed he had succeeded in interest.

RULE OF LAW

An easement created to benefit the use of certain land will be presumed to run with the land.

FACTS: The Wakes owned certain land, part of which was used for farming and part for cattle ranching. In 1956 the two interests were divided. An easement was created in the farm's water source for use by the owner of the cattle ranch. Nelson (P) eventually succeeded in interest to the ranch, and the Johnsons (D) to the farm. In 1979 the Johnsons (D) barred Nelson (P) from access to their water. Nelson (P) brought an action to have the easement declared valid. The trial court held that the easement was valid, and Johnson (D) appealed.

ISSUE: Will an easement created to benefit the use of certain land be presumed to run with the land?

HOLDING AND DECISION: (Huntley, J.) Yes. An easement created to benefit the use of certain land will be presumed to run with the land. When the parties to the creation of an easement intend that the easement is to benefit the use of the dominant estate as opposed to the estate's owner personally, the easement will run with any assignment of the dominant estate. Here, it seems clear that the easement was created to facilitate the use of the cattle ranch and as such, should be seen as benefitting the land and not anyone personally. It therefore remained incident to the ranch as it passed from owner to owner. Affirmed.

ANALYSIS

The type of easement described here is called an "appurtenant" easement. This is opposed to an easement "in gross," which is personal in nature. An easement in gross can be assigned. However, a specific assignment is required; it does not automatically pass with title to the dominant estate.

Quicknotes

DOMINANT ESTATE Property that benefits from the use of an easement on other property.

EASEMENT The right to utilize a portion of another's real property for a specific use.

WATER RIGHTS The right to reduce water naturally flowing to possession for private use.

Burcky v. Knowles

Easement holder (P) v. Landowner (D)

N.H. Sup. Ct., 413 A.2d 585 (1980).

NATURE OF CASE: Appeal of order declaring the nonexistence of an easement.

FACT SUMMARY: The Burckys' (P) predecessor had reserved an easement across land deeded to the Knowleses' (D) predecessor without using words of inheritance in the deed.

RULE OF LAW

Words of inheritance are unnecessary for an easement to pass from grantor to grantee.

FACTS: Garland owned certain property. In 1934, he conveyed a portion to the Knowleses' (D) predecessor, reserving to himself an easement to pass through the property so that his livestock could cross to grazing areas beyond the deeded property. No words of inheritance or assignment were used with respect to the easement. The Burckys (P) succeeded to Garland's interest in the portion of the property not conveyed in 1934. They brought an action seeking a declaration that the easement was valid. The trial court, based on the lack of inheritance language, held that the easement was personal to Garland. It thus declared that no easement existed. The Burckys (P) appealed.

ISSUE: Are words of inheritance necessary for an easement to pass from grantor to grantee?

HOLDING AND DECISION: (Bois, J.) No. Words of inheritance are not necessary for an easement to pass from grantor to grantee. An easement created to benefit the owner of property in his capacity as owner is called an appurtenant easement, and runs from grantor to grantee automatically. An easement benefitting a person apart from in his capacity as owner of property is called an easement in gross, and does not run with the land. With respect to an appurtenant easement, its characteristic of running with the land exists irrespective of any words of succession or inheritance that might or might not be contained in the deed. Here, it is clear that the easement reserved by Garland was intended to facilitate his beneficial use of the property he reserved. This being so, the lack of words of succession in his deed to the Burckys' (P) predecessor is irrelevant. Reversed.

ANALYSIS

The law tends to favor easements appurtenant over easements in gross. Generally speaking, in close cases courts will find an easement to run with the land. The main determining factor remains the intent of the original grantor. If an intention for an easement in gross is manifest, it will be so found.

Quicknotes

DEED A signed writing transferring title to real property from one person to another.

EASEMENT The right to utilize a portion of another's real property for a specific use.

GRANTOR Conveyor of property or settlor of a trust.

Crane v. Crane

Unincorporated association (P) v. Landowners (D)

Utah Sup. Ct., 683 P.2d 1062 (1984).

NATURE OF CASE: Appeal of order declaring the existence of an easement.

FACT SUMMARY: The Water Hollow Grazing Assn. (P) claimed succession to an easement in gross that had been created across the Cranes' (D) property.

RULE OF LAW

An easement in gross may in some circumstances be assignable.

FACTS: The Water Hollow Grazing Association (Association) (P) was an unincorporated association of twelve cattle ranchers. Predecessors thereto had obtained a prescriptive easement across land owned by the Cranes (D). The Association (P) and its constituent members brought an action against the Cranes (D) to have the easement declared valid. The trial court so held, and the Cranes (D) appealed.

ISSUE: May an easement in gross in some circumstances be assignable?

HOLDING AND DECISION: (Oaks, J.) Yes. An easement in gross in some circumstances may be assignable. Generally, an easement in gross is personal to its holder, and may not be devised or assigned. However, courts have begun to make an exception to this rule when the easement is of a commercial nature rather than for personal satisfaction. Examples include easements for telephone lines and electric power lines. This court believes this exception to be good policy, and adopts it here. The easement claimed by the Association (P) is of a purely commercial nature, and consequently the Association (P) and its constituent members could succeed to it. Affirmed.

ANALYSIS

One essential requirement of an appurtenant easement is land, which it can attach. The nature of such an easement requires that it be adjacent to the servient estate. In this particular case, no plaintiff owned land adjacent to the Cranes' (D) property. Consequently, their easement of necessity was in gross.

Quicknotes

ASSIGNABLE Capable of being transferred or conveyed.

DEVISE The conferring of a gift of real or personal property by means of a testamentary instrument.

EASEMENT IN GROSS A right to use the land of another that is specific to a particular individual and that expires upon the death of that person.

O'Donovan v. McIntosh v. Huggins

Developer (P) v. Landowner (D)

Me. Sup. Jud. Ct., 728 A.2d 681 (1999).

NATURE OF CASE: Suit for declaratory judgment regarding the transferability of an easement.

FACT SUMMARY: O'Donovan (P) sued McIntosh (D) and Huggins (D) seeking a declaratory judgment concerning his right to purchase and sell an easement.

RULE OF LAW

An easement in gross is assignable when the parties so intend.

FACTS: McIntosh (D) purchased real property adjacent to the Fish parcel as well as an option on the Fish parcel. He optioned both properties to Casco Partners for development of a multiple-lot subdivision. When that option lapsed, McIntosh (D) conveyed the original property to Huggins (D) by warranty deed, and retained a right of way and easement across the property that would allow access to, and the development of, the Fish parcel. The deed incorporated by reference a side agreement that it would be binding on subsequent owners and in which Huggins (D) agreed not to actively oppose any application for development permits for the Fish parcel. O'Donovan (P) entered into a purchase and sale agreement with the owners of the Fish parcel, and with McIntosh (D) for the easement. After the planning board suspended his subdivision proposal over a dispute regarding the transferability of the easement, O'Donovan (P) brought suit against McIntosh (D) and Huggins (D) seeking a declaratory judgment concerning his rights to purchase and sell the easement. The court concluded the easement was not assignable. O'Donovan (P) appealed.

ISSUE: Is an easement in gross assignable when the parties so intend?

HOLDING AND DECISION: (Dana, J.) Yes. An easement in gross is assignable when the parties so intend. An easement is a right of use over the property of another. Easements are of two types: in gross and appurtenant. An easement appurtenant is created to benefit the dominant tenement and runs with the land. To be appurtenant, the easement must be attached to or related to a dominant estate of the grantor. Since McIntosh (D) owned no dominant estate to which the easement could be appurtenant, this is an easement in gross. The easement here is assignable because the parties clearly expressed that intent in the deed. While an easement in gross is generally not assignable, it may be assignable in certain circumstances, especially where to hold otherwise would frustrate the parties' express intent. Judgment vacated and remanded.

DISSENT: (Wathen, C.J.) While the intent of the parties is relevant in determining whether an easement is appurtenant or in gross, it is well settled that an easement in gross is personal and not assignable.

ANALYSIS

The court bases its conclusion here on the general policy that the law favors alienability.

Quicknotes

ASSIGNABLE Capable of being transferred or conveyed.

DECLARATORY JUDGMENT A judgment of the court establishing the rights of the parties.

DEED A signed writing transferring title to real property from one person to another.

DOMINANT ESTATE Property that benefits from the use of an easement on other property.

EASEMENT IN GROSS A right to use the land of another that is specific to a particular individual and that expires upon the death of that person.

CHAPTER 21

Express Easements: Termination and Extinguishment

Quick Reference Rules of Law

Wetmore v. The Ladies of Loretto, Wheaton

Seller (P) v. Easement holder (D)

Ill. Ct. App., 220 N.E.2d 491 (1966).

NATURE OF CASE: Action by grantor to enjoin grantee's use of express easement.

FACT SUMMARY: After conveying parcel of land and express easement over his own property to The Ladies of Loretto, Wheaton (Loretto) (D), Wetmore (P), objected to extension of the easement by Loretto (D) for the benefit of a second parcel he had sold it.

RULE OF LAW

Although an extension of an easement appurtenant to one tract of land to another tract of land is a misuse, the owner of the servient tenement will be denied injunctive relief where the misuse is of a trivial and inconsequential nature.

FACTS: Wetmore (P), who owned 80 acres of land, sold 10 acres of this tract to The Ladies of Loretto, Wheaton (D), a nonprofit home for nuns. Loretto (D) built a mansion, pool, garden, and various outbuildings on the tract. Because the parcel was landlocked, Wetmore (P) granted to Loretto (D) an express easement east over his property, and through an existing driveway which ran by his house, to Hawthorne Lane and then north along this lane. Loretto (D), wishing to have access west of its parcel, to a public road, purchased from Wetmore (P) a forty-acre land parcel, which, but for a 33-foot strip, also conveyed to them by Wetmore (P), was also landlocked. In return, Wetmore (P) agreed to build a new road over the 33-foot strip, but was unsuccessful in his negotiating for a surrender of the express easement appurtenant to the 10-acre tract that ran by his house and over his driveway, to Hawthorne Lane. Loretto (D) did, however, promise to divert the bulk of its traffic from the express easement to the 33-foot strip. Loretto (D) then constructed a new House of Studies, part of which was on the 10-acre parcel and part on the 40-acre one. Although Loretto (D) had succeeded in reducing the amount of traffic over the easement from 50 vehicles daily to just five per day, Wetmore (P) objected to use of the easement to provide access to the 40-acre parcel, and sought an injunction. Wetmore (P) also stopped drivers on Hawthorne Lane, told them they were trespassers, and directed them to turn back.

ISSUE: Will a court of equity restrain every extension of an easement appurtenant to one tract of land to another tract?

HOLDING AND DECISION: (Davis, J.) No. While every extension of the use of an easement to an additional tract is a misuse, and not just those which change the burden on the servient estate, equitable remedies are not always available to the servient tenement owner. An injunction has been granted, or the easement held extinguished, only in cases where it was impossible to sever or distinguish between the authorized and unauthorized use of the servient tenement. Here, however, the new building was separate and distinct from the other buildings on the 10-acre tract. Furthermore, unlike in those cases where equitable relief was granted, Wetmore (P) had control over the extension. Wetmore (P) had made the conveyance of the 40 acres with full knowledge that Loretto (D) intended to use the land for purposes other than as a roadway to the public road on the west, and that Loretto (D) refused to surrender its easement benefiting the 10-acre tract. Finally, and most important, Loretto (D) had succeeded in greatly reducing the traffic over the easement. Accordingly, although the extension is a technical misuse, it is too trivial and inconsequential a misuse to justify the issuance of an injunction. The benefit to be obtained here does not warrant the hardship imposed. Nor is Wetmore (P) entitled to punitive damages for the extension was not done willfully, wantonly, or with malice or oppression. Wetmore (P) will be restrained from interfering with Loretto's (D) use of the easement. Reversed and remanded.

ANALYSIS

Where the use of the easement for the nondominant estate is only incidental, and not substantial, an injunction will not ordinarily issue. An injunction is, however, the appropriate remedy where the use is substantial, and it is possible to, in some way, restrict use of the easement just for the benefit of the dominant estate. But where unauthorized use cannot be prevented by injunction, most courts hold that the easement, as a result of the misuse, has been extinguished.

Quicknotes

EASEMENT The right to utilize a portion of another's real property for a specific use.

PUNITIVE DAMAGES Damages exceeding the actual injury suffered for the purposes of punishment of the defendant, deterrence of the wrongful behavior or comfort to the plaintiff.

Pavlick v. Consolidation Coal Co.

Landowners (P) v. Easement holders (D)

456 F.2d 378 (6th Cir. 1972).

NATURE OF CASE: Action for declaration of rights under contract granting an easement.

FACT SUMMARY: Consolidation Coal Co. (Consolidation) (D), although ready to transport coal, failed to do so, and Pavlick (P) invoked the defeasement clause in contract granting Consolidation (D) an easement over his property.

RULE OF LAW

An easement may be terminated by a contingency, or neglect of an obligation, the occurrence of which is expressly provided for in a contract, if neither the contract taken as a whole nor the parties' subsequent conduct suggests a contrary intention.

FACTS: The Wellmans, Pavlick's (P) predecessors in title, granted to Pittsburgh Consolidation Coal (D) for a consideration of $995, a right of way over their land. The contract recited, in a defeasance clause, that the easement would terminate if, for a period of one year, the easement was not used "for the purposes . . . of constructing, maintaining, operating, altering, repairing, replacing, and removing . . . for the transportation of coal slurry." Pittsburgh's successor in title, Consolidation Coal Co. (Consolidation) (D), negotiated with Pavlick (P), who had acquired the Wellmans' property for 15 one-year extensions of the contract and defeasance clause. Pavlick (P) refused to grant any more extensions claiming that since Consolidation (D), notwithstanding its readiness to do so, had failed to transport coal for a year, and had forfeited its right to the easement as provided for by the contract.

ISSUE: May an easement be defeated by a minor violation if such contingency is covered by an express agreement?

HOLDING AND DECISION: (Edwards, J.) Yes. Even though termination of an easement will work a hardship on the holder, if defeasance is unambiguously covered by a defeasance clause, it will be honored. Here, the purpose of the easement was for the "transportation of coal slurry." Since the language is clear, there is no need to turn to rules of construction. Secondly, the contract taken as a whole supports giving literal effect to the harshness of the defeasance clause. For one, the meagerness of the consideration ($995) is appropriate for the contract's rigid pro-grantor terms. Finally, Consolidation (P) had 15 occasions on which to negotiate but failed to obtain a dropping of the defeasance clause. The easement is terminated. Vacated and remanded.

DISSENT: (McCree, J.) The easement was granted for seven purposes, and not just one: it was maintained and ready for coal slurry transportation. Neither, evidence of settlement negotiations nor consideration paid is relevant to the issue at hand.

ANALYSIS

Courts are generally more apt to find a termination of an easement than other interests. This is because termination enhances the marketability and use of the servient tenement. Defeasance clauses, or other formal agreements, will be readily invoked and upheld notwithstanding difficulties inherent in their interpretation.

Quicknotes

SERVIENT ESTATE Property that is burdened in some aspect for the benefit of a dominant estate.

Mueller v. Hoblyn

Landowner (D) v. Easement holder (P)

Wy. Sup. Ct., 887 P.2d 500 (1994).

NATURE OF CASE: Action to quiet title to an easement.

FACT SUMMARY: Hoblyn (P), the owner of a right of way easement of Mueller's (D) property, brought suit to quiet title to an easement that Mueller (D) claimed was terminated through adverse possession.

RULE OF LAW

To extinguish an easement over the servient tenement, the servient tenement owner must demonstrate a visible, notorious and continuous adverse and hostile use of the land that is inconsistent with the use made and rights held by the easement holder.

FACTS: The Englemans owned a single undivided tract of property. They conveyed a parcel of land to REB along with an easement to provide access to Yellowstone Road via a private roadway across their property. The Englemans later transferred title to the property to Mueller (D). REB sold a parcel of property that eventually was conveyed to Hoblyn (P), including the easement in the Mueller's (D) property. Hoblyn (P) experienced difficulties using the dirt driveway to access his property. A survey disclosed that the route of the dirt driveway did not correspond with the easement. Hoblyn (P) requested permission to use the easement from Mueller (D), who refused. Hoblyn (P) filed suit to quiet title to the easement. The district court held that Mueller's (D) drilling of a water-well within the easement boundaries constituted a termination of the easement by adverse possession. The parties appealed.

ISSUE: To extinguish an easement over the servient tenement, must the servient tenement owner demonstrate a visible, notorious and continuous adverse and hostile use of the land that is inconsistent with the use made and rights held by the easement holder?

HOLDING AND DECISION: (Taylor, J.) Yes. To extinguish an easement over the servient tenement, the servient tenement owner must demonstrate a visible, notorious and continuous adverse and hostile use of the land that is inconsistent with the use made and rights held by the easement holder. The owner of the servient estate retains all incidents of ownership in the land that are not in contradiction to the rights of the easement holder. For example, where a right of way easement exists over a certain portion of the servient estate, the servient estate owner is permitted to use that easement in any way not to interfere with the easement owner's right to do so. Here Mueller (D) argues that the entire easement has been extinguished under several theories. The Hoblyns (P), on the other hand, argue that their rights could not be terminated until they made a demand on Mueller (D) to use the land. This court concludes that the easement has not been terminated by operation of law. Here the initial easement granted by the Englemans provided for unlimited use for ingress and egress. The later subdivision of the property did not create an additional burden on the easement since its use remained the same. Though the degree of the burden was increased, the easement was not terminated. Easements may be terminated by abandonment. This occurs where one person intentionally relinquishes rights or property to another by conduct indicating intent to surrender the right to use the land as authorized by the easement. Here there is no evidence of intentional relinquishment on the part of Hoblyn (P). Mueller (D) argues that use of the dirt driveway terminated the easement. This is incorrect. Abandonment requires more than nonuse of an easement, for however long the period of nonuse, but the intent to abandon must be proved and may be inferred only from strong and convincing evidence. Here the nonuse of the easement for twenty-seven years did not disclose an affirmative and unequivocal intent to abandon the easement. The use of the alternative route also does not establish intent to abandon the easement. Detrimental reliance may also result in the abandonment of an easement. Here Mueller (D) failed to make a showing of conduct on the part of the Hoblyns (P) or their predecessors in interest that he unreasonably relied upon to his detriment. Last, adverse possession for the ten-year statutory period may result in the termination of the easement. There is a distinction between adverse possession of land and adverse possession of an easement. To extinguish an easement over the servient tenement, the servient tenement owner must demonstrate a visible, notorious and continuous adverse and hostile use of the land that is inconsistent with the use made and rights held by the easement holder, not merely possession that is inconsistent with another's claim of title. Termination of an easement by adverse possession is not favored by the law. No portion of the easement here was terminated by adverse possession. Since the easement has never been developed through use, the period of adverse possession did not commence until Hoblyn (P) demanded that the easement be opened and Mueller (D) refused. Affirmed in part and reversed in part.

DISSENT: (Thomas, J.) The court ignores a narrow exception to the general rule that an easement created by grant may be extinguished through adverse possession. Where an easement has not been definitively located, it is

Continued on next page.

not extinguished by adverse possession because the owner of the easement had no occasion to assert the right of way during the prescriptive period. Such easements may not be extinguished through adverse possession absent a demand by the owner that the easement be opened and a refusal by the party in adverse possession.

ANALYSIS

Here Mueller (D) had fenced in the property, used the land for cultivation of crops and drilled a water-well. The court concludes that this did not constitute adverse possession since such uses were not inconsistent with the rights of the owners of the dominant estates. The owners of the dominant estates had the right to demand the easement be cleared when they desired to use it.

Quicknotes

ACTION TO QUIET TITLE Equitable action to resolve conflicting claims to an interest in real property.

ADVERSE POSSESSION A means of acquiring title to real property by remaining in actual, open, continuous, exclusive possession of the property for the statutory period.

DOMINANT ESTATE Property that benefits from the use of an easement on other property.

EASEMENT The right to utilize a portion of another's real property for a specific use.

RIGHT OF WAY The right of a party to pass over the property of another.

SERVIENT ESTATE Property that is burdened in some aspect for the benefit of a dominant estate.

TERMINATION OF EASEMENT (BY ABANDONMENT) Conduct on the part of the user of an easement demonstrating an intent to abandon the easement and not to reclaim it.

CHAPTER 22

Non-Express Easements

Quick Reference Rules of Law

Hillside Development Company v. Fields

Landowner (P) v. Easement holder (D)

Mo. Ct. App., 928 S.W.2d 886 (1996).

NATURE OF CASE: Suit for ejectment and trespass.

FACT SUMMARY: Hillside Development Company (P) brought suit against Fields (D) for trespass and ejectment on the basis of his use of a driveway providing access to his house.

RULE OF LAW

In determining whether a visible easement exists, the court must consider whether the easement is reasonably necessary to the full enjoyment of the dominant estate.

FACTS: The parties' property once constituted a single tract belonging to Nelson. Nelson constructed a house on the tract now owned by Fields (D). The only public road providing access to the house was located on the north side of the property. The house was designed with a basement garage on the north side of the house, the driveway circling around the front and far side of the house in order to reach the garage. When Nelson died, the property was left to the Shriners Hospital who sold most of the land to Hillside Development Company (Hillside) (P), including nearly all of the land on which the driveway was located. The title documents expressly reserve an ingress/egress easement for the use of the retained house; however, the easement did not correspond with the driveway. Hillside (P) filed suit against Fields (D) for trespass and ejectment. Fields (D) counterclaimed seeking a declaratory judgment that he had an implied easement across the disputed portion of the driveway. The trial court denied Fields's (D) summary judgment motion and entered judgment for Hillside (D) for ejectment and trespass. Fields (D) appealed.

ISSUE: In determining whether a visible easement exists, must the court consider whether the easement is reasonably necessary to the full enjoyment of the dominant estate?

HOLDING AND DECISION: (Stith, J.) Yes. In determining whether a visible easement exists, the court must consider whether the easement is reasonably necessary to the full enjoyment of the dominant estate. The issue is whether Fields (D) obtained an implied easement for use of the driveway to his home. Hillside (P) claims he is precluded from doing so on the basis that he was aware of the encroachment as documented on the title report and that the express right of way easement did not extend across the disputed portion of the driveway. This argument is erroneous. Neither the lack of an express easement for the driveway nor the existence of an express ingress-egress easement negates the existence of an implied easement from pre-existing use, also known as a "visible easement." Missouri courts invoke a four-prong test for the establishment of a visible easement: (1) unity of common ownership followed by separation of title into dominant and servient estates; (2) the purported easement must have been arranged by the common owner so as to constitute an open, obvious and visible benefit to the claimant's property and burden to the servient estate; (3) the purported easement must have been used long enough prior to separation of title and under such circumstances to show that the arrangement was intended to be permanent; and (4) the purported easement must be reasonably necessary for the full beneficial use and enjoyment of the dominant estate. The first factor was established through Nelson's and the Shriners' common ownership. The second factor was satisfied since the driveway was constructed at the time the house was built and constituted an open, obvious and visible benefit to Fields's (D) property. The third prong is satisfied since the house and driveway had been used for 17 years prior to the separation of title. With respect to the fourth factor, the proponent of the easement need only show what is reasonable, not what it is absolutely necessary. In similar situations, courts of this state have held that a garage specifically constructed for use by the dominant estate at a time prior to separation of title is reasonably necessary for the full beneficial use and enjoyment of the premises. Here Fields (D) would not have full enjoyment of his estate without the recognition of a visible easement. Thus use of the driveway is reasonably necessary for Fields's (D) full beneficial use and enjoyment of the premises. Reversed and remanded.

ANALYSIS

Note the distinction between an easement by necessity and a visible easement. An easement by necessity does not arise in the absence of absolute necessity for the easement, such as the property being landlocked.

Quicknotes

DOMINANT ESTATE Property that benefits from the use of an easement on other property.

EASEMENT The right to utilize a portion of another's real property for a specific use.

EJECTMENT An action to oust someone in unlawful possession of real property and to restore possession to the party lawfully entitled to it.

MOTION FOR SUMMARY JUDGMENT Judgment rendered by a court in response to a motion by one of the parties, claiming that the lack of a question of material fact in

Continued on next page.

respect to an issue warrants disposition of the issue without consideration by the jury.

SERVIENT ESTATE Property that is burdened in some aspect for the benefit of a dominant estate.

TRESPASS TO LAND Physical invasion of the plaintiff's property that is intended and caused by the defendant's conduct.

Ward v. Slavecek

Easement seeker (P) v. Fence builder (D)

Tex. Ct. Civil App., 466 S.W.2d 91 (1971).

NATURE OF CASE: Action to establish an implied easement.

FACT SUMMARY: Ward (P) sought to establish an implied easement on and over driveway to her garage, although she had other adequate means of access to the garage.

RULE OF LAW

An implied easement will arise only where the easement is of strict necessity to the use of the dominant estate.

FACTS: Ward (P) and Slavecek (D), who owned adjacent lots, could trace their title to a common predecessor. The common owner had built a driveway down the division line between the two lots to a garage which was later to be located on Ward's (P) lot. Slavecek (D) built a garage on her lot. Although the driveway was used in common for 42 years, Slavecek (D) built a fence along the division line which also divided the driveway in half. Ward (P) was unable to use the driveway as access to her garage, although an alley in back of her lot had been occasionally used by her for access. Ward (P) sought to have declared in her favor an easement by implication on and over the driveway.

ISSUE: Will an implied easement be found if it is not of strict necessity to the use of the dominant estate?

HOLDING AND DECISION: (Wilson, J.) No. An implied easement will only be found where the party of the dominant estate who seeks to establish it proves that it is of strict necessity to the use of his property. Such is clearly not the case here. Without the driveway, Ward (P) still has perfectly adequate access to her driveway since she can use the alley, and has done so in the past. No implied easement will be established here as a matter of law. Affirmed.

ANALYSIS

The easement here, although termed as an easement by implication, may be more precisely categorized as an easement by necessity. The only cases where the easement by necessity is sought to be proved are generally those where a parcel of realty has become landlocked. Most courts, in accord with the instant case, require not only a common grantor, but that the easement be of strict necessity to the use of enjoyment of the dominant estate. A minority only requires a showing of "reasonable necessity." Under the latter approach, there are more cases in which the easement is recognized. Easements by necessity can be argued for drainage, sewers, etc., as well as for access pursuant to the minority rule.

Quicknotes

DOMINANT ESTATE Property that benefits from the use of an easement on other property.

IMPLIED EASEMENT An easement that is not expressly stated in a deed, but which is inferred upon conveyance, that a portion of one parcel had been used to benefit the other parcel and that upon sale the buyer of the benefited parcel could reasonably expect such benefits to continue.

Epstein Family Partnership; Levitz Furniture Corp. v. Kmart Corp.

Easement holders v. Landowner

13 F.3d 762 (3d Cir. 1994).

NATURE OF CASE: Appeal from order permanently enjoining construction.

FACT SUMMARY: Kmart was permanently enjoined from constructing certain barriers and traffic control devices on its property and from removing a sign installed and maintained by Levitz on the basis that Levitz had an implied easement in Kmart's property.

RULE OF LAW

An easement by implication arises when the parties intend to create an easement at the time the property is severed, but neglect to include it in a written agreement.

FACTS: Epstein holds an easement for ingress and egress over Kmart's property. The district court permanently enjoined Kmart from constructing certain barriers and traffic control devices on its property as well as only from removing a sign on its property that was erected by Epstein's tenant, Levitz Furniture. The court found that Levitz had an implied easement or, in the alternative, an easement by estoppel. Kmart was also enjoined from future violations of the easements. Kmart appealed.

ISSUE: Does an easement by implication arise when the parties intend to create an easement at the time the property is severed, but neglect to include it in a written agreement?

HOLDING AND DECISION: (Hutchinson, J.) Yes. An easement by implication arises when the parties intend to create an easement at the time the property is severed, but neglect to include it in a written agreement. The proper test in Pennsylvania for the existence of an easement by implication is an issue for debate. Some courts involve the traditional test, others the Restatement test, and others a hybrid approach. The court need not select among the competing tests since they provide but a surrogate for determining the intent of the parties at the time the estates were severed. The issue is whether the parties intended a permanent encumbrance on the servient estate. Here the facts do not indicate the parties' intent to provide expressly for easements on other portions of the estate. Additionally, the requirement that these be permanent is lacking. At the time of severance, the Epsteins expressly provided for the ingress-egress easement but did not mention the sign. The omission of a particular right from an express grant of others relating to the same property weighs against any inference of an intent to make the unmentioned grant. Moreover, the proponent of the easement must show that its use indicates a permanent arrangement. The presumption that a road sign was a permanent encumbrance on the servient estate was erroneous. The parties may, nevertheless, intend a permanent encumbrance when the nature of the contested use or object does not raise a presumption of permanency. This requires the court to look to the interests of the parties to see whether they intended to create a permanent encumbrance. Permanency must be determined with respect to the object, not the user's interest in the object. Here Levitz was a tenant who had the right to erect exterior signs with the written permission of the lessor. When a lease terminates, tenants usually take their signs with them. The facts here indicate that the owners did not intend a permanent encumbrance for a sign in the location in which Levitz maintains it. Reversed.

ANALYSIS

In Pennsylvania, courts presume the permanency of the easement from the type of user unless the attendant circumstances indicate otherwise. This presumption generally applies in the cases of sewer lines and sewage treatment services.

Quicknotes

ENCUMBRANCE An interest in property that operates as a claim or lien against its title making it potentially unmarketable.

IMPLIED EASEMENT An easement that is not expressly stated in a deed, but which is inferred upon conveyance, that a portion of one parcel had been used to benefit the other parcel and that upon sale the buyer of the benefited parcel could reasonably expect such benefits to continue.

LEASE An agreement or contract that creates a relationship between a landlord and tenant (real property) or lessor and lessee (real or personal property).

LESSOR One who leases property to another, relinquishing the right to immediate possession of the property but retaining legal title.

SERVIENT ESTATE Property that is burdened in some aspect for the benefit of a dominant estate.

CHAPTER 23

Creation and Validity

Quick Reference Rules of Law

Nahrstedt v. Lakeside Village Condominium Association

Condominium owner (P) v. Homeowners' association (D)

Cal. Sup. Ct., 8 Cal. 4th 361, 878 P.2d 1275 Cal. Rptr. 2d 63 (1994).

NATURE OF CASE: Review of reversal of dismissal of claim for declaratory judgment and damages.

FACT SUMMARY: The trial court dismissed Nahrstedt's (P) complaint alleging that use restrictions forbidding the keeping of cats in her condominium were unreasonable.

RULE OF LAW

Common interest development use restrictions contained in a project's recorded declaration are enforceable unless unreasonable.

FACTS: Nahrstedt (P) bought a condominium and moved in with her three cats. When the Lakeside Village Condominium Association (Lakeside) (D) learned of the presence of the cats, it assessed fines against Nahrstedt (P) for violating a use restriction that the project's developer had included in the recorded declaration of the covenants, conditions and restrictions. Nahrstedt (P) sued for declaratory judgment and damages, alleging that the condominium use restrictions were unreasonable because they restricted the use of her unit. The trial court sustained Lakeside's (D) demurrer and dismissed. The court of appeals reversed and Lakeside (D) appealed.

ISSUE: Are common interest development use restrictions contained in a project's recorded declaration enforceable unless unreasonable?

HOLDING AND DECISION: (Kennard, J.) Yes. Common interest development use restrictions contained in a project's recorded declaration are enforceable unless unreasonable. Courts accord presumptive validity to recorded use restrictions to promote stability and predictability. When an association determines that a homeowner violated a use restriction, it must do so in good faith and not in an arbitrary or capricious manner. Here, Nahrstedt's (P) allegations, even if true, were insufficient to show that the pet restriction's harmful effects substantially outweighed its benefits to the condominium development as a whole or that it violated public policy. Reversed.

DISSENT: (Arabian, J.) The pet restriction is patently arbitrary and unreasonable.

ANALYSIS

The court here explained that giving deference to use restrictions protects the general expectations of all condominium owners. In a common interest development, individual property rights are subordinated to the collective judgment of the owners' association. Each unit owner must give up a little freedom of choice when using facilities in common.

Quicknotes

ARBITRARY AND CAPRICIOUS Standard imposed in reviewing the decision of an agency or court that the decision was made in disregard of the facts or law.

USE RESTRICTION A restriction on the right to utilize one's personal or real property.

Hill v. Community of Damien

Neighbors (P) v. Group home (D)

N.M. Sup. Ct., 121 N.M. 353, 911 P.2d 861 (1996).

NATURE OF CASE: Review of order enforcing restrictive covenant upon real estate.

FACT SUMMARY: Local residents contended that Community of Damien of Molokai (D) violated a covenant limiting use to a single-family residence on premises it occupied by operating a group home for persons with AIDS.

RULE OF LAW

A restrictive covenant limiting the use of a residence to single-family occupancy does not prohibit the use of the residence as a group home.

FACTS: A certain real estate development contained, on all homes in the development, a restrictive covenant that mandated use of the homes as single-family dwellings exclusively. Community of Damien of Molokai (Community) (D) began operating at the property a group home for persons with AIDS. Hill (P) and other neighbors (P) brought suit to enforce the covenant. The trial court entered an order enforcing the covenant, and the Community (D) appealed.

ISSUE: Does a restrictive covenant limiting the use of a residence to single-family occupancy prohibit the use of the residence as a group home?

HOLDING AND DECISION: (Frost, J.) No. A restrictive covenant limiting the use of a residence to single-family occupancy does not prohibit the use of the residence as a group home. There are two reasons why such a covenant does not create the limitation advanced by Hill (P). First, this court does not accept the notion that a use as a single-family residence solely means occupancy by persons related by blood or adoption. The local zoning law defines "family" as, among other things, "any group of not more than five unrelated persons living together in a dwelling." Moreover, federal policy favors including small group homes as "families," as the federal government has expressed a strong policy toward breaking down barriers preventing persons with disabilities from living together, and including a small group of persons with similar disabilities living together advances this policy. The second reason why the covenant must fail in this instance is that the interpretation advanced here violates the Fair Housing Act. Section 3604(f)(1) prohibits discrimination in housing against those with disabilities; HIV infection has been classified as a disability, so the covenant here, if applied to the Community (D), would violate the Federal Fair Housing Act (FHA). For these reasons, this court finds that the covenant does not apply as against the Community (D). Reversed.

ANALYSIS

Restrictive covenants such as the one at issue here are fairly common around the nation. Because of this, there has been a good deal of litigation regarding what exactly a family is. As the current opinion shows, courts have deviated considerably from the traditional notions of a family in deciding these types of cases.

Quicknotes

RESTRICTIVE COVENANT A promise contained in a deed to limit the uses to which the property will be made.

Franklin v. Spadafora

Condominium owner (P) v. Trustee of condominium association (D)

Mass. Sup. Jud. Ct., 388 Mass. 764, 447 N.E.2d 1244 (1983).

NATURE OF CASE: Appeal of order dismissing challenge to condominium bylaw.

FACT SUMMARY: A condominium complex adopted a bylaw limiting ownership to no more than two units per any individual.

RULE OF LAW

A condominium bylaw restricting ownership to no more than two units per any individual is valid.

FACTS: Franklin (P) owned six units at the Melrose Towers Condominiums. In 1980, the owners of the units adopted a Homeowners' Association (D) bylaw limiting ownership to no more than two units per any individual. Persons who already owned more than two units were permitted to retain ownership under a grandfather provision. When Franklin (P) attempted to purchase another unit, he was informed by the Homeowners' Association (D) that the sale was against the bylaws. Franklin (P) went ahead with the transaction and sued for an injunction against enforcement of the bylaw. The trial court held the bylaw valid, dismissed the action, and declared the deed a nullity. Franklin (P) appealed.

ISSUE: Is a condominium bylaw restricting ownership to no more than two units per any individual valid?

HOLDING AND DECISION: (Nolan, J.) Yes. A condominium bylaw restricting ownership to no more than two units per any individual is valid. Reasonable restraints on alienation are permissible. Factors tending to support such restraints are as follows: (1) the one imposing the restraint has an interest in the property; (2) the restraint is of limited duration; (3) the restraint serves a worthwhile purpose; (4) the restraint will not often be evoked; and (5) the number of persons affected is small. Here, the Homeowners' Association (D) obviously has an interest in the property. The duration is potentially unlimited but may be revoked at any time. The bylaw serves the purpose of encouraging owner occupancy, which is perceived as enhancing the value of the property. This is a worthwhile purpose. As most owners approved of the bylaw, it stands to reason that most will not try to violate it, so it should not be often invoked. Finally, although it is unclear as to how many owners will be affected by the bylaw, this will of necessity be small in comparison to all persons who might purchase a unit. Consequently, the bylaw does not constitute an unreasonable restraint on alienation. On the constitutional level, no "suspect classification" is involved, so the restriction will be valid if rationally related to its objective, which this court has no trouble agreeing is the case. Affirmed.

ANALYSIS

Over the years, constitutional attacks have often been made to covenants relating to property. For the most part, state action necessary to involve the Constitution has been found to be absent. The best known exception to this rule is *Shelley v. Kraemer*, 334 U.S. 1 (1948). There, the Supreme Court held judicial enforcement of a racially restrictive covenant to be the state action necessary to implicate the Constitution.

Quicknotes

ALIENATION Conveyance or transfer of property.

SUSPECT CLASSIFICATION A class of persons that have historically been subject to discriminatory treatment; statutes drawing a distinction between persons based on a suspect classification, i.e., race, nationality or alienage, are subject to a strict scrutiny standard of review.

CHAPTER 24–25

Enforcement and Running of Covenants

Quick Reference Rules of Law

Runyon v. Paley

Property owner v. Condominium builder

N.C. Sup. Ct., 331 N.C. 293 (1992).

NATURE OF CASE: Review of dismissal of case to enjoin construction of condominiums.

FACT SUMMARY: After a property conveyance, Paley (D) sought to develop a parcel of land in violation of restrictions in the deed, and Runyon (P) sought to enforce those restrictions.

RULE OF LAW

A restrictive covenant may be enforced, so long as a subsequent taker has notice, on the theory of equitable servitude.

FACTS: In 1937, Ruth Gaskins aquired a four-acre tract of land, bounded on one side by Pamlico Sound, and on the other side by Silver Lake. One and a half acres of sound-front property were conveyed by Gaskins to Runyon (P) in 1954. In 1960, Runyon (P) reconveyed the one-and-a-half-acre tract, together with a second tract of one-eighth acre, to Gaskins. By separate deed in 1960, Gaskins conveyed to Runyon (P) a lake-front lot and a 15-foot-wide strip of land that runs to the shore of Pamlico Sound from the road separating the lake-front and sound-front lots. The 15-foot-wide strip was part of the one-and-a-half-acre parcel reconveyed to Gaskins by Runyon (P). The deed to the strip was not recorded for some 15 days. The day after the conveyance of the strip, Gaskins conveyed the remainder of the one-and-a-half-acre parcel to Doward Brugh. The deed contained a restriction against building apartments or more than two residences on the parcel. Prior to the conveyance to the Brughs, Gaskins constructed a residence on a lake-front lot, across from the parcel conveyed to the Brughs. She retained the land until her death in 1961. Williams (P), Gaskins's daughter, acquired the land. By mesne conveyances, Paley (D) acquired the property of the Brughs. Paley (D) entered into a partnership with Midgett Realty to construct condominiums on the property. Runyon (P) and Williams (P) brought suit to enjoin the use of the property in this manner, alleging the restrictive covenants were for their benefit and were still in force. Paley's (D) motion to dismiss for failure to state a claim was granted. Runyon (D) appealed.

ISSUE: May a covenant be enforced, so long as a subsequent taker has notice, on the theory of equitable servitude?

HOLDING AND DECISION: (Meyer, J.) Yes. A restrictive covenant may be enforced, so long as a subsequent taker has notice of the restrictions, on the theory of equitable servitude. A subsequent purchaser of property burdened by a restrictive covenant must have notice in the chain of title for the restriction to be enforceable. So long as this notice exists, the restriction may be enforced by any holder of property that was intended to benefit from the restriction. Here, Runyon (P) took the parcel prior to the creation of the restrictive covenant. On this basis, no assumption can be made that this parcel was intended to benefit by the restrictive covenant in question. Furthermore, even if the deed of the strip of land were sufficient to show that Runyon (P) was intended to benefit from restrictions on the adjoining parcel, Runyon (P) failed to record the transaction in time. On the other hand, Williams (P) is the successor in the parcel owned by Gaskins. Clearly, the restrictive covenant was for the benefit of the parcel on which Gaskins lived. The only reasonable inference is that her successor be entitled to receive the benefit as well. Williams (P) is entitled to enforce the restrictions under a theory of equitable servitude. The court affirms the dismissal of Runyon's (P) claim and reverses the dismissal of Williams's (P) claim.

ANALYSIS

An equitable servitude is never labeled as such in a document. Instead, it will take the form of a covenant. Since the requirements for both are often met, a plaintiff must choose to either enforce on a covenant theory at law or on an equitable servitude theory in equity. Part of the consideration is that damages are generally not available in equity. Another consideration is that privity is not required in the case of equitable servitudes; possession of the land is what matters, not an interest in the land.

Quicknotes

CONVEYANCE The transfer of property, or title to property, from one party to another party.

DEED A signed writing transferring title to real property from one person to another.

EQUITABLE SERVITUDE Land use restriction enforceable in equity.

MESNE Intermediate; intervening.

RESTRICTIVE COVENANT A promise contained in a deed to limit the uses to which the property will be made.

Davidson Bros., Inc. v. D. Katz & Sons, Inc.

Store owner (P) v. Prospective competitor (D)

N.J. Sup. Ct., 121 N.J. 196, 579 A.2d 288 (1990).

NATURE OF CASE: Appeal from grant of summary judgment in action to enforce a restrictive covenant.

FACT SUMMARY: Having included in a deed a restrictive covenant that the property being conveyed would not be used as a supermarket, Davidson Bros., Inc. (P), the grantor, sought to enforce the covenant against the New Brunswick Housing Authority (D), a subsequent purchaser with actual notice of the covenant.

RULE OF LAW

A noncompetition covenant will be enforced if the covenant is "reasonable."

FACTS: Davidson Bros., Inc. (P), the owner of two grocery stores, one on George Street and the other two miles away on Elizabeth Street, decided to close down the George Street store that was operating at a loss and sell the property to D. Katz & Sons, Inc. (D). The deed conveying the property contained a restrictive covenant not to operate a supermarket on the premises for a period of 40 years, presumably to protect business at the Elizabeth Street store from competition. When residents complained that the closure of the store left them without a nearby supermarket, the local Housing Authority (D) purchased the George Street site from D. Katz & Sons, Inc. (D), and agreed to lease it to another supermarket chain. The Housing Authority (D) had actual notice of the noncompetition covenant contained in the deed. Davidson Bros. (P) sued to enforce the covenant by injunction. The Housing Authority (D) et al. contended that the covenant interfered with the public's interest and therefore should not be enforced. [The text does not include the trial court's ruling.] The appellate court ruled that the burden ran with the property but should not be enforced because the covenant did not produce a countervailing benefit to the Elizabeth Street store to justify the burden. Davidson Bros. (P) appealed.

ISSUE: Will a noncompetition covenant be enforced if the covenant is "reasonable"?

HOLDING AND DECISION: (Garibaldi, J.) Yes. A noncompetition covenant will be enforced if the covenant is "reasonable." Some courts employ a "touch and concern" rule that requires that the covenant touch and concern both the burdened and the benefited property in order to run with the land. Covenants not to compete do touch and concern the land. But the "touch and concern" test is only one factor to consider in making the ultimate determination as to the reasonableness of the covenant. Courts should consider eight other "reasonableness" factors as well: (1) the intention of the parties when the covenant was executed; (2) if consideration was paid in exchange for the covenant; (3) whether the covenant clearly and expressly set forth the restrictions; (4) whether the covenant was in writing and recorded; (5) whether the covenant was reasonable concerning area, time or duration; (6) whether the covenant imposed an unreasonable restraint on trade; (7) whether the covenant interfered with the public interest; and (8) whether changed circumstances now make the covenant unreasonable. In this case, there is not enough evidence to determine whether the covenant not to compete was reasonable, and what type of remedy is appropriate. Summary judgment, however, must be denied because of the fact-sensitive nature of the reasonableness analysis. The trial court must thoroughly analyze each of the eight factors in order to determine whether the covenant was reasonable at the time it was enacted and, if so, whether it now interferes with the public interest. Reversed and remanded.

CONCURRENCE: (Pollock, J.) "Changed circumstances" and the "public interest" should not affect the enforceability of a covenant. The only issue on remand should be whether the appropriate remedy is damages or an injunction. An award of damages to Davidson Bros. (P) would compensate it for the breach of the covenant while at the same time allowing residents convenient access to a supermarket on Elizabeth Street.

ANALYSIS

Where changed circumstances makes enforcement of a covenant inequitable, courts may refuse to do so. The doctrine of changed circumstances may be applied to refuse enforcement when (1) the hardship which enforcement at the present time will impose on the covenantor (or his successor) has substantially increased since the time of the covenant due to unforeseen circumstances and (2) the benefit which enforcement will give to the covenantee has substantially decreased. The emphasis is on the change in circumstances since the enactment of the covenant. By itself, mere lapse of time, or hardship on the covenantor, would be insufficient to make a covenant unenforceable under the doctrine.

Quicknotes

RESTRICTIVE COVENANT A promise contained in a deed to limit the uses to which the property will be made.

Continued on next page.

SUMMARY JUDGMENT Judgment rendered by a court in response to a motion made by one of the parties, claiming that the lack of a question of material fact in respect to an issue warrants disposition of the issue without consideration by the jury.

TOUCH AND CONCERN The requirement, in order for a covenant to be binding upon successors, that the covenant enhance the use or value of the benefited party.

Eagle Enterprises, Inc. v. Gross

Covenantor (P) v. Covenantee (D)

N.Y. Ct. App., 39 N.Y.2d 505, 384 N.Y.S.2d 717, 349 N.E.2d 816 (1976).

NATURE OF CASE: Appeal in an action for goods sold and delivered.

FACT SUMMARY: Both Eagle Enterprises, Inc. (Eagle) (P) and Gross (D) succeeded to parcels of land burdened by covenants whereby Gross (D) had to pay for water to be supplied annually by Eagle (P).

RULE OF LAW

An affirmative covenant will not run with the land unless it "touches and concerns" the land; nor will it run when the covenant either creates an undue restriction on alienation or a burden in perpetuity.

FACTS: Orchid Hill Realtors (Orchid Hill) conveyed property in its subdivision to the Baums. The deed provided that Orchid Hill would provide the property with water for six months annually for which the Baums would pay $35. The deed expressly stated that this covenant would run with the land and bind all successive takers. Gross (D) succeeded to the Baums interest by a deed making no mention of the covenant to purchase water. Accordingly, Gross (D) refused to accept or pay for it, especially because he (D) had since constructed his own water supply. Eagle Enterprises, Inc. (Eagle) (P), the successor to Orchid Hill, brought this action to collect the fee specified in the covenant. Although the lower courts ruled for Eagle (P), finding that the covenant "ran with the land," the appellate division reversed, holding that the covenant failed to "touch and concern" the land, was an undue restriction on alienation, and a burden in perpetuity. Eagle (P) appealed.

ISSUE: Will affirmative covenants run with the land when they fail to "touch and concern" the land, or when they either create an undue restraint on alienation or a burden in perpetuity?

HOLDING AND DECISION: (Gabrielli, J.) No. Affirmative covenants will not run with the land when they fail to "touch and concern" the land, or when they either create an undue restraint on alienation or a burden in perpetuity. But this covenant to supply water for six months fails to touch and concern the land, since the record shows that no landowners would be deprived of water without it, nor that the price of water would be prohibitive without this service. In fact, this obligation to receive water more closely resembles a contractual promise rather than an interest attaching to the property. Also, the covenant creates a burden in perpetuity to all future owners, regardless of how they choose to use the land. Affirmed.

ANALYSIS

If the covenant affects the quality or value of the property, or has some impact on its use, it is said to touch and concern the land. There is no mechanical test for "touch and concern." The following are examples: (1) a promise restricting use of the land; (2) a promise to pay rent, taxes, or insurance; (3) a promise to repair, maintain, improve, or cultivate the land.

Quicknotes

AFFIRMATIVE COVENANT A written promise to do a particular activity.

TOUCH AND CONCERN The requirement, in order for a covenant to be binding upon successors, that the covenant enhances the use or value of the benefited party.

CHAPTER 26

Defenses to the Enforcement of Covenants

Quick Reference Rules of Law

Chevy Chase Village v. Jaggers

Municipal corporation (P) v. Physician homeowner (D)

Md. Ct. App., 261 Md. 309, 275 A.2d 167 (1971).

NATURE OF CASE: Suit seeking injunctive relief.

FACT SUMMARY: Chevy Chase Village (P) argued that a restriction against nonresidential land use precluded Jaggers (D) from occupying space in his former residence and using it as an office.

RULE OF LAW

Acquiescence in minor deviations from a general plan of development does not render a restrictive covenant unenforceable on the ground that changing circumstances in the neighborhood have undermined the purposes of the covenant.

FACTS: Deed provisions provided that lots in Chevy Chase Village (P) were restricted to residential uses only. Dr. Jaggers (D) practiced medicine for 20 years from an office in his home, and during this period no objection was raised. Several other doctors in the village also operated practices from their homes, and a few other exceptions to the nonresidential use prohibition also went unchecked. When, however, Dr. Jaggers (D) decided to move out of the village but to retain the office he had maintained in the home, Chevy Chase Village (P) sued to enjoin him from violating the covenant against nonresidential uses. In defense of the suit, Jaggers (D) alleged that, by tolerating several nonresidential uses, the village had abandoned the original plan of development. He also argued a lack of evidence to establish a uniform plan of development, that Chevy Chase Village (P) was guilty of laches, and that the hardship which the injunction would cause him outweighed any injury which would be caused by his retaining his office in his former home. The lower court denied the injunction, and Chevy Chase Village (P) appealed.

ISSUE: Do minimal deviations from a plan of development constitute sufficient abandonment of that plan to render unenforceable any covenants entered into pursuant to it?

HOLDING AND DECISION: (Digges, J.) No. Acquiescence in minor deviations from a general plan is insufficient to render a restrictive covenant unenforceable on the ground that changed neighborhood circumstances have undermined the purposes of the covenant. In this case the few nonresidential land-uses that the village tolerated did not constitute an abandonment of the original plan of development since they did not detract from the effort to preserve a residential atmosphere. The argument that no general plan of development has been established by the evidence is inappropriate since no such plan need be present when, as in the present case, a restrictive covenant has been imposed by the grantor of a single tract who retains property adjacent to that devised. Jaggers's (D) arguments that Chevy Chase Village (P) is guilty of laches and that the hardship to his neighbors resulting from his maintenance of the office is minimal compared to the harm to him in having to relocate are both unsupported by the evidence. Therefore, Chevy Chase Village (P) is entitled to the injunction that it seeks. Reversed and remanded.

ANALYSIS

The argument that abandonment of a general plan or scheme of development has occurred will succeed only rarely. To sustain such a contention, it is usually necessary to demonstrate deviations which are numerous and significant. Courts realize that over prolonged periods of time the needs of a community require that it accommodate some land uses that are inconsistent with its original plan. Thus, it is only when changed circumstances such as would indicate an unwillingness to sustain the objectives of the original plan are present that abandonment will be deemed to have occurred.

Quicknotes

INJUNCTIVE RELIEF A court order issued as a remedy, requiring a person to do, or prohibiting that person from doing, a specific act.

LACHES An equitable defense against the enforcement of rights that have been neglected for a long period of time.

RESTRICTIVE COVENANT A promise contained in a deed to limit the uses to which the property will be made.

City of Bowie v. MIE Properties, Inc.

Municipality-covenantee (P) v. Property owner-successor covenantor (D)

Md. Ct. App., 398 Md. 657, 922 A.2d 509 (2007).

NATURE OF CASE: Appeal from reversal of judgment upholding the continued validity of real property restrictive covenants.

FACT SUMMARY: The City of Bowie (City) (P), a covenantee, contended that restrictive covenants limiting the use of land were valid and that MIE Properties, Inc.'s (MIE's) (D) use of the land violated the covenants.

RULE OF LAW

The proper legal standard for determining the continuing validity of a restrictive covenant is whether, after the passage of a reasonable period of time, the continuing validity of the covenant cannot further the purpose for which it was formed in light of changed relevant circumstances.

FACTS: The City of Bowie (City) (P), as covenantee, had entered into restrictive covenants limiting the permissible use of land now owned by MIE Properties, Inc. (MIE) (D), as successor covenantor. At the same time the covenants were entered into, the City (P) entered into an Annexation Agreement that contemplated the property being developed as a "science and technology, research and office park." At some point, MIE (D) leased the property to a dance studio, and the City (P) brought a declaratory judgment seeking judgment that such use contravened the covenants. MIE (D) counterclaimed, asserting that the covenants were no longer valid given changes in circumstances, but the City (P) maintained that the property could be, and was, being developed in accord with the covenants. The trial court, determining that there was a theoretical possibility that the land could be developed as foreseen when the covenants were entered into, ruled that the covenants were valid and enforceable, and entered judgment for the City (P). The state's intermediate court, finding that the appropriate standard was whether there was a reasonable probability that the parties would be able to achieve the covenants' goals within a reasonable period of time, reversed, and the state's highest court granted review.

ISSUE: Is the proper legal standard for determining the continuing validity of a restrictive covenant whether, after the passage of a reasonable period of time, the continuing validity of the covenant cannot further the purpose for which it was formed in light of changed relevant circumstances?

HOLDING AND DECISION: (Harrell, J.) Yes. The proper legal standard for determining the continuing validity of a restrictive covenant is whether, after the passage of a reasonable period of time, the continuing validity of the covenant cannot further the purpose for which it was formed in light of changed relevant circumstances. This standard is an objective one that links the result to objective factors outside of the property owner's control. Unlike the trial court, the intermediate appellate court misconceived the operation of the rule of reasonable construction of restrictive covenants by subjecting every aspect of such covenants, including their validity, to a reasonableness inquiry. Thus, the intermediate appellate court applied a rule meant to ascertain the intent of the parties to a covenant to determine its continuing validity by evaluating the reasonable chances of accomplishing its purpose. Applying the correct standard, a key factor in determining whether the covenant is still valid is whether there has been a "radical change" in the neighborhood that causes the restrictions to outlive their usefulness. Another factor is one of comparative hardship, but that factor has not been raised here. Focusing on the "radical change" factor leads to the conclusion that there had not been a radical change in the neighborhood over a reasonable period of time—which, unless specified in the covenant, tends to be a relatively generous portion of time, given the enduring nature of real property. Reversed

ANALYSIS

MIE (D) also claimed that the imposition of the covenants constituted a sort of illegal contract zoning by a municipality. The court rejected this argument, finding that contrary to MIE's (D) argument, restrictive covenants may be more restrictive than the zoning classification imposed by the zoning authority, since the point of restrictive covenants is to enable controls on property that are independent of zoning. Thus, as long as a covenant is as or more restrictive than the underlying zoning classification, zoning goals are not frustrated.

Quicknotes

DECLARATORY JUDGMENT A judgment of the court establishing the rights of the parties.

RESTRICTIVE COVENANT A promise contained in a deed to limit the uses to which the property will be made.

Orange and Rockland Utilities, Inc. v. Philwood Estates, Inc.

Restricted landowners (P) v. Adjoining landowner (D)

N.Y. Ct. App., 52 N.Y.2d 253, 418 N.E.2d 1310 (1981).

NATURE OF CASE: Appeal from extinguishment of easement.

FACT SUMMARY: Orange and Rockland Utilities, Inc. (Orange and Rockland) (P), which succeeded to a parcel on the Neversink River subject to a restrictive covenant limiting use to operation of a hydroelectric plant, sued Philwood Estates, Inc. (D), successor to adjacent property, and sought to extinguish an easement after the city condemned Orange and Rockland's (P) riparian rights.

RULE OF LAW

When a restrictive covenant, if enforced, renders the burdened land valueless, a court may equitably extinguish the covenant.

FACTS: Bradford sold a parcel on the east bank of the Neversink River along with a separate parcel on the west bank to Crane. Bradford retained hunting and fishing rights on both parcels and restricted the use of the west bank property to operation of a hydroelectric plant. He also retained a tract contiguous to the west bank. Orange and Rockland Utilities, Inc. (Orange and Rockland) (P) succeeded to the restricted west bank land, and Philwood Estates, Inc. (Philwood) (D) succeeded to the tract contiguous to it. The city condemned Orange and Rockland's (P) riparian rights in the Neversink River. Orange and Rockland (P) brought suit against Philwood (D), alleging (1) that the restriction was personal to Bradford and did not run with the land, and (2) that, in the alternative, the restriction should be extinguished under § 1951 of the Real Property Actions and Proceedings Law due to changed conditions. The Special Term dismissed, but the appellate division reversed and held that while the covenant was not personal and did descend to Orange and Rockland (P), it should be extinguished under the statute. Philwood (D) sought damages for the extinguishment of the restriction, but was denied. The court of appeals granted review.

ISSUE: When a restrictive covenant, if enforced, renders the burdened land valueless, may a court equitably extinguish the covenant?

HOLDING AND DECISION: (Meyer, J.) Yes. The city's condemnation of Orange and Rockland's (P) riparian rights in the Neversink River rendered that parcel useless. Except for the privileges of taking measures to avoid liability for injuries to hunters and fishermen under Philwood's (D) easement and of paying taxes on the property, that land became valueless to Orange and Rockland (P). When a restrictive covenant, if enforced, renders the burdened land valueless, a court may equitably extinguish the covenant. The Real Property Actions and Proceedings Law § 1951 authorizes this result where "changed conditions" prevail. The appellate division was correct in ruling that the restriction was not personal to Bradford, but ran with the land. The parties so intended, the covenant touches and concerns the land and the parties were in privity of estate. However, since Philwood (D) had an opportunity to prove alleged injury to fishing and hunting rights, the order should be modified inasmuch as it erroneously granted Philwood (D) the right to later show damages arising from the extinguishment. Except as modified, affirmed.

ANALYSIS

Generally, the "changed circumstances" defense, or statutory right to extinguishment, turns on a balance between the hardship on the burdened land and the benefit to the benefitted land. While the degree of benefit and hardship requisite is not uniform state to state, it is clear that a substantial tip on the balance scale is necessary.

Quicknotes

EASEMENT The right to utilize a portion of another's real property for a specific use.

RESTRICTIVE COVENANT A promise contained in a deed to limit the uses to which the property will be made.

RIPARIAN RIGHT The right of an owner of real property to the use of water naturally flowing through his land.

CHAPTER 27

Common Interest Communities

Quick Reference Rules of Law

PAGE

1. **Associational Standing.** A homeowners' association has standing to file suit to enforce a restrictive covenant that runs with the land. (Westmoreland Association, Inc. v. West Cutter Estates, Ltd.) *116*

2. **Amending Covenants.** (1) A modification clause of a subdivision's covenants that permits changes or modifications to the covenants permits the addition of an entirely new covenant where the effect of the new covenant is not unreasonable or unduly burdensome on the lot owners. (2) Even in the absence of an express covenant mandating payment of assessments, a homeowners association that is a common interest community has the implied power to levy assessments against lot owners in a subdivision to raise the funds necessary to maintain the common areas of the subdivision. (Evergreen Highlands Association v. West) *117*

3. **Restrictive Covenants.** A condominium association need not provide an adversary proceeding to a unit owner before enforcing restrictive covenants in formal litigation. (Majestic View Condo. Assn., Inc. v. Bolotin) *119*

4. **Restrictive Covenants.** A homeowners' association does not waive the right to enforce a restrictive covenant if failures to enforce the covenant have not substantially affected the covenant's value. (Raintree of Albemarle Homeowners Association, Inc. v. Jones) *120*

Westmoreland Association, Inc. v. West Cutter Estates, Ltd.

Homeowners' association (P) v. Real estate developer (D)

N.Y. Sup. Ct. App. Div., 579 N.Y.S.2d 413, 174 A.D.2d 144 (1992).

NATURE OF CASE: Suit to permanently enjoin construction of homes that would violate restrictive covenants.

FACT SUMMARY: The restrictive covenants of record for a residential area required that every home in the area be built at least 20 feet from the front line of the home's property. A real estate developer received a permit to build three homes in the area only 15 feet behind the homes' respective front lines, and the homeowners' association sued the developer to permanently enjoin construction of the homes.

RULE OF LAW

A homeowners' association has standing to file suit to enforce a restrictive covenant that runs with the land.

FACTS: Private restrictive covenants governed all lots in the residential area of Westmoreland, which was near the border of Queens and Nassau Counties in New York. The covenants appeared in a 1924 deed in the chain of title for West Cutter Estates, Ltd. (West Cutter) (D) for the six lots that West Cutter (D) owned in Westmoreland. The homeowners' association for Westmoreland, Westmoreland Association Inc. (Association) (P), represented members who resided in or owned property in Westmoreland; according to its certificate of incorporation, the Association (P) fulfilled a main purpose of "tak[ing] all lawful action to maintain and enforce" Westmoreland's recorded covenants and restrictions. One restriction required that each home in the area be built at least 20 feet behind the lot line for the property. West Cutter (D) obtained a permit to build three homes in the area only 15 feet from their respective properties' lot lines. The Association (P) sued West Cutter (D) for a permanent injunction prohibiting construction of the homes. West Cutter (D) defended, in part, by arguing that the Association (P) had no standing to sue because it had no privity of estate as to the covenants. [The trial court held that the Association (P) did have standing and permanently enjoined West Cutter (D) from building the three homes in violation of the covenants. West Cutter (D) appealed.]

ISSUE: Does a homeowners' association have standing to file suit to enforce a restrictive covenant that runs with the land?

HOLDING AND DECISION: (Kunzeman, J.) Yes. A homeowners' association has standing to file suit to enforce a restrictive covenant that runs with the land. Traditionally, a covenant is enforceable by one who benefits from it if it is a real covenant—that is, one that was intended to run with the land, that touches or concerns the land, and that has privity of estate between the benefiting and burdened parties. This narrow rule would defeat the Association's (P) standing. New York has gradually adopted a more relaxed approach to associational standing that recognizes the economic and practical realities of contemporary litigation. An association, for example, was specifically held to have privity in one case based on its representative status. In the context of associational standing itself, our highest court has noted the benefit of spreading litigation expenses through several owners who have a common interest. Associational standing is limited, though, by consideration of four factors: whether the association can take an adversarial position in a case, whether its size and composition make it representative of the affected community, whether the reviewed decision will adversely affect the represented group, and whether all residents and owners in an area can be members in the association. Under these standards, the Association (P) in this case does have standing even though it does not satisfy the strict technical requirement of privity of estate. Affirmed.

ANALYSIS

The relatively relaxed, even welcoming concept of associational standing as seen in *Westmoreland Association* should be contrasted with the far more rigorous demands of Article III standing that applies in federal courts. See, e.g., *Lujan v. Defenders of Wildlife*, 504 U.S. 555 (1992). In the context of associational standing in state courts, pragmatic concerns can carry more weight than they do where standing implicates a federal court's subject-matter jurisdiction to hear a case at all.

Quicknotes

PRIVITY OF ESTATE Common or successive relation to the same right in property.

RESTRICTIVE COVENANT A promise contained in a deed to limit the uses to which the property will be made.

STANDING The right to commence suit against another party because of a personal stake in the resolution of the controversy.

Evergreen Highlands Association v. West

Homeowners association (D) v. Homeowner (P)

Colo. Sup. Ct., 73 P.3d 1 (2003).

NATURE OF CASE: Appeal from reversal of judgment that a homeowners association has authority to amend a subdivision's covenants to permit for mandatory assessments.

FACT SUMMARY: West (P) claimed that Evergreen Highlands Association (Association) (D), the homeowners association for the Evergreen Highlands Subdivision (Evergreen Highlands), did not have the power to amend its covenants to allow for assessments for maintaining common areas. The Association (D) counterclaimed that it had implied power to make such assessments.

RULE OF LAW

(1) A modification clause of a subdivision's covenants that permits changes or modifications to the covenants permits the addition of an entirely new covenant where the effect of the new covenant is not unreasonable or unduly burdensome on the lot owners.

(2) Even in the absence of an express covenant mandating payment of assessments, a homeowners association that is a common interest community has the implied power to levy assessments against lot owners in a subdivision to raise the funds necessary to maintain the common areas of the subdivision.

FACTS: Evergreen Highlands Association (Association) (D), the homeowners association for the Evergreen Highlands Subdivision (Evergreen Highlands) was incorporated to maintain the subdivision's common areas and facilities, enforce the subdivision's covenants, pay taxes on the common areas, and determine annual fees. Evergreen Highlands had a 22-acre park area open to all residents of the subdivision. Protective covenants for Evergreen Highlands did not require lot owners to be members of or pay dues to the Association (D), which had title to the park. Initially, the Association (D) relied on voluntary assessments from lot owners to pay for maintenance and improvements to the park. Article 13 of the original Evergreen Highlands covenants provided that a majority (75 percent) of lot owners could modify the covenants—"change or modify any one or more of said restrictions. . . . " Pursuant to the article, the required majority voted to add a new article that required all lot owners to be members of and pay assessments to the Association (D), and permitted the Association (D) to impose liens on the property of any owners who failed to pay their assessment. West (P) had purchased his lot when membership in the Association (D), and payment of assessments, was voluntary. He did not vote for the new article that made membership and assessments mandatory, and he refused to pay his lot assessment of $50 per year. When the Association (D) threatened to record a lien against his property, he filed suit challenging the validity of the amendment. The Association (D) counterclaimed for a declaratory judgment that it had the implied power to collect assessments from all lot owners in the subdivision, and sought damages from West (P) for breach of the implied contract. The trial court ruled in favor of the Association (D) on the ground that the amendment was valid and binding. The intermediate court of appeals reversed, finding that the terms "change" or "modify" did not permit the addition of new covenants, but applied only to existing covenants. The state's highest court granted certiorari.

ISSUE:

(1) Does a modification clause of a subdivision's covenants that permits changes or modifications to the covenants permit the addition of an entirely new covenant where the effect of the new covenant is not unreasonable or unduly burdensome on the lot owners?

(2) Even in the absence of an express covenant mandating payment of assessments, does a homeowners association that is a common interest community have the implied power to levy assessments against lot owners in a subdivision to raise the funds necessary to maintain the common areas of the subdivision?

HOLDING AND DECISION: (Rice, J.)

(1) Yes. A modification clause of a subdivision's covenants that permits changes or modifications to the covenants permits the addition of an entirely new covenant where the effect of the new covenant is not unreasonable or unduly burdensome on the lot owners. Some courts faced with nearly identical fact patterns have held that the modification clause does not permit the addition of a new covenant, whereas others have permitted the addition of a new covenant. The distinction between these cases does not turn on how narrowly or broadly the particular modification clause is written, but rather on the differing factual scenarios and severity of consequences that the cases present. In those cases where courts disallowed the amendment of the covenants, the impact on the objecting lot owner was far more substantial and unforeseeable than the impact of the amendment at issue in this case. Those cases that permitted amendments did so where the amendment's purpose was to impose mandatory assessments on

Continued on next page.

lot owners for the purpose of maintaining common elements of a subdivision. That line of cases (the *Zito* line), *Zito v. Gerken*, 225 Ill. App. 3d 79, 587 N.E.2d 1048 (1992), is more applicable here. Moreover, the amendment in this case was changed according to the modification clause of the original Evergreen Highlands covenants, of which West (P) had notice when he purchased his property. Finally, at $50 per year, the mandatory assessment is neither unreasonable nor burdensome. To the contrary, the existence of a well-maintained park immediately adjacent to West's (P) lot undoubtedly enhances his property value. The amendment was valid and binding on all lot owners in Evergreen Highlands. Reversed as to this issue.

(2) Yes. Even in the absence of an express covenant mandating payment of assessments, a homeowners association that is a common interest community has the implied power to levy assessments against lot owners in a subdivision to raise the funds necessary to maintain the common areas of the subdivision. This is a question of first impression in this state. Most other jurisdictions hold that homeowners associations have the implied power to levy dues or assessments even in the absence of express authority. The latest version of the Restatement of Property (Servitudes) reflects this approach, but refers to "common-interest" communities. West (P) argues that the implied power to mandate assessments can only be imputed to such communities, which are defined as residential communities in which there exists a mandatory obligation or servitude imposed on individual owners to pay for common elements of the community. He therefore argues that because the original covenants did not impose such servitude, Evergreen Highlands is not a common interest community. This argument is rejected because West (P) incorrectly assumes that the obligation or servitude had to be expressed in the covenants or in his deed. Instead, such obligation need only arise from the "declarations," which are defined as "any recorded instruments however denominated." The declarations in effect for Evergreen Highlands at the time West (P) bought his property included the covenants; a plat that noted the park would be conveyed to the Association (D); the Association's (D) articles of incorporation, which stated the Association's (D) purpose; and the deed whereby the developer quit-claimed his ownership in the park to the Association (D). These declarations were sufficient to create a common interest community by implication, and the Association (D) had the implicit power to levy assessments against lot owners for the purpose of maintaining and operating the common area. Reversed and remanded.

ANALYSIS

The Restatement (Third) § 6.10(2) provides that amendments to covenants that do not apply uniformly to similar lots and amendments that treat members unfairly are not effective without approval of the members whose interests would be adversely affected. Here, the court seems to conclude that the assessments were fair and treated all members of Evergreen Highlands alike. Had this not been the case, West's (P) action would have been significantly stronger.

Quicknotes

LIEN A claim against the property of another in order to secure the payment of a debt.

Majestic View Condo. Assn., Inc. v. Bolotin

Condominium association (P) v. Condominium owner (D)

Fla. Dist. Ct. App., 429 So. 2d 438 (1983).

NATURE OF CASE: Suit for an injunction requiring compliance with a Declaration of Condominium on the keeping of pets.

FACT SUMMARY: A condominium community expressly restricted pet ownership to one dog or cat under 25 pounds per owner. An owner in the community acquired two large dogs in violation of the restriction.

RULE OF LAW

A condominium association need not provide an adversary proceeding to a unit owner before enforcing restrictive covenants in formal litigation.

FACTS: Majestic View Condominium Inc.'s Number One Declaration of Condominium restricted the pet ownership of all condominium owners in the community to one dog or cat of up to twenty-five pounds. Bolotin (D) acquired a dog that grew to exceed 25 pounds, and then he acquired a second large dog. His dogs became nuisances in the community, and the Majestic View Condo. Assn. (Association) (P) intervened. The Association (P) asked Bolotin (D) several times, in writing, to comply with the pet restriction. Bolotin (D) refused, and the Association (D) filed suit for injunctive relief. The trial court upheld the pet restriction and denied Bolotin's (D) counterclaim for arbitrary enforcement of the restriction. Even so, the trial judge entered judgment for Bolotin (D), apparently because the judge reasoned that the Association (D) owed Bolotin (D) an informal adversary proceeding before it sued him. The Association (P) appealed.

ISSUE: Must a condominium association provide an adversary proceeding to a unit owner before enforcing restrictive covenants in formal litigation?

HOLDING AND DECISION: (Dell, J.) No. A condominium association need not provide an adversary proceeding to a unit owner before enforcing restrictive covenants in formal litigation. The Association (P) complied with each of the three steps required by law: it gave him actual or constructive notice of the pet restriction, reasonably demanded his compliance with the restriction, and satisfied constitutional due process when it began this litigation. Nothing in these requirements compelled the Association (P) to offer Bolotin (D) a separate adversary proceeding before suing him. The trial court therefore erred in denying the Association's (P) request to enforce its covenants and in entering judgment for Bolotin (D). Reversed.

ANALYSIS

As the court notes, the seminal case of *Hidden Harbor Estates, Inc. v. Norman*, 309 So. 2d 180 (Fla. Dist. Ct. App. 1975), supports the pet restriction at issue in *Majestic View*. In exchange for the benefits of community residential standards, members of common-interest communities must in turn accept more restrictive policies than they could find if they lived outside those communities.

Quicknotes

INJUNCTIVE RELIEF A court order issued as a remedy, requiring a person to do, or prohibiting that person from doing, a specific act.

RESTRICTIVE COVENANT A promise contained in a deed to limit the uses to which the property will be made.

Raintree of Albemarle Homeowners Association, Inc. v. Jones

Homeowners' association (P) v. Homeowner (D)

Va. Sup. Ct., 243 Va. 155, 413 S.E.2d 340 (1992).

NATURE OF CASE: Suit to prohibit homeowners from keeping a tow truck on their property.

FACT SUMMARY: A restrictive covenant prohibited the outdoor parking of trucks overnight in a subdivision. Two homeowners in the subdivision regularly parked a tow truck on their property outdoors overnight, and the homeowners' association sought to bar the practice as a violation of the covenant.

RULE OF LAW

A homeowners' association does not waive the right to enforce a restrictive covenant if failures to enforce the covenant have not substantially affected the covenant's value.

FACTS: A restrictive covenant for the Raintree subdivision prohibited owners from keeping school buses, commercial vehicles, or habitable motor vehicles on their property except inside a garage. The covenant further restricted any outdoor, overnight parking of any trucks in the subdivision. Charles and Glenda Jones (D) started parking a tow truck on their property, and the Raintree of Albemarle Homeowners Association, Inc. (Association) (P) asked them to stop that use of their property. Mr. Jones (D) refused. Two other property owners in the Raintree subdivision occasionally parked trucks on their properties, but the Association (P) did not try to enforce the covenant against them. The Association (P) filed suit for an injunction requiring only the Joneses (D) to comply with the covenant. As to the tow truck, the chancellor [i.e., the trial judge] concluded that the Association (P) had waived its right to enforce the covenant because of its failures to enforce it against the other two owners in addition to the Joneses who occasionally parked trucks in the subdivision. The Association (P) appealed, and the Joneses (D) cross-appealed [on issues not discussed at length in the casebook excerpt].

ISSUE: Does a homeowners' association waive the right to enforce a restrictive covenant if failures to enforce the covenant have not substantially affected the covenant's value?

HOLDING AND DECISION: (Hassell, J.) No. A homeowners' association does not waive the right to enforce a restrictive covenant if failures to enforce the covenant have not substantially affected the covenant's value. A homeowners' association waives its right to enforce restrictive covenants only if no substantial value is left in the restriction at issue. Here, the Association's (P) decision not to enforce the covenant against the other two owners besides the Joneses (D) did not substantially affect the covenant's value. The trial court therefore erred. Reversed.

ANALYSIS

It is important to note that the Association's (P) stated rationale for not enforcing the covenant against the other two owners besides the Joneses (D) fails to conform to the covenant's terms. The Association's (P) president testified that no action was taken against the other two owners because the Association (P) deemed their trucks not to be "commercial" vehicles within the meaning of the covenant. The covenant, however, expressly forbids overnight, outdoor parking of any trucks—a contradiction suggesting that the Association (P) really was arbitrarily enforcing the covenant against the Joneses (D). In this Virginia case, though, the key consideration was only whether such enforcement practices had appreciably reduced the covenant's value.

Quicknotes

RESTRICTIVE COVENANT A promise contained in a deed to limit the uses to which the property will be made.

WAIVER The intentional or voluntary forfeiture of a recognized right.

CHAPTER 28

Nuisance

Quick Reference Rules of Law

	PAGE
1. **Nuisance and Injunctions.** Although the rule in New York is that a nuisance will be enjoined even when there is a marked disparity shown in economic consequence between the effect of the injunction and the effect of the nuisance, an injunction should not be applied if the result is to close down a plant. Permanent damages may be awarded as an alternative. (Boomer v. Atlantic Cement Co.)	*122*
2. **Nuisance and Indemnification.** A pre-existing lawful enterprise may become a nuisance by reason of subsequent development of an area, but a party wishing that nuisance abated must indemnify the operator of the enterprise for the costs of going out of business or relocating. (Spur Industries, Inc. v. Del E. Webb Development Co.)	*123*
3. **Landowner's Right to Access of Sunlight.** An action brought by a landowner claiming unreasonable obstruction of his access to sunlight is maintainable under private nuisance law. (Prah v. Maretti)	*124*

Boomer v. Atlantic Cement Co.

Land owners (P) v. Cement plant (D)

N.Y. Ct. App., 26 N.Y.2d 219, 309 N.Y.S.2d 312, 257 N.E.2d 870, (1970).

NATURE OF CASE: Action to enjoin maintenance of nuisance and for damages.

FACT SUMMARY: Trial court refused to issue injunction that would close down a cement plant, but awarded permanent damages instead.

RULE OF LAW

Although the rule in New York is that a nuisance will be enjoined even when there is a marked disparity shown in economic consequence between the effect of the injunction and the effect of the nuisance, an injunction should not be applied if the result is to close down a plant. Permanent damages may be awarded as an alternative.

FACTS: A group of land owners (P), complaining of injury to their property from dirt, smoke, and vibration emanating from a neighboring cement plant (D), brought an action to enjoin the continued operation of the plant and for damages. The trial court held that the plant constituted a nuisance, found substantial damage but, because an injunction would shut down the plant's operation, refused to issue one. Permanent damages of $185,000 were awarded the group of land owners (P) instead.

ISSUE: Where the issuance of an injunction to enjoin the maintenance of a business would shut down a business, may permanent damages be issued as an alternative?

HOLDING AND DECISION: (Bergan, J.) Yes. Damages may be awarded as an alternative to an injunction in nuisance cases. Another alternative would be to grant the injunction but postpone its effect to a specified future date to give opportunity for technical advances to permit the company (D) to eliminate the nuisance. However, there is no assurance that any significant technical improvement would occur. Moreover, the problem is universal, and can only be solved by an industrywide effort. Permanent damages would themselves be a spur to conduct more research. Future owners of this land would not be able to recover additional damages, since the award is to the land. Reversed and remanded.

DISSENT: (Jasen, J.) The majority approach is licensing a continuing wrong. Furthermore, permanent damages alleviate the need for more research, and decrease incentive.

ANALYSIS

The reasoning advanced here has been carried one step further by other courts. In *Pennsylvania Coal Co. v. Sanderson*, 113 Pa. St. 126, 6 A. 453 (1886), a suit for damages was frowned upon by the Supreme Court which said, "To encourage the development of the great natural resources of a country, trifling inconveniences to particular persons must sometimes give way to the necessities of a great community."

Quicknotes

NUISANCE An unlawful use of property that interferes with the lawful use of another's property.

Spur Industries, Inc. v. Del E. Webb Development Co.

Cattle feeding operation (D) v. Housing developer (P)

Ariz. Sup. Ct., 108 Ariz. 178, 494 P.2d 700 (1972).

NATURE OF CASE: Suit seeking a permanent injunction.

FACT SUMMARY: Del E. Webb Development Co. (P) claimed that the cattle feedlots operated by Spur Industries, Inc. (D) constituted a nuisance which should be abated.

RULE OF LAW

A pre-existing lawful enterprise may become a nuisance by reason of subsequent development of an area, but a party wishing that nuisance abated must indemnify the operator of the enterprise for the costs of going out of business or relocating.

FACTS: Spur Industries, Inc. (Spur) (D), or its predecessors, had operated cattle feedlots in Maricopa County, Arizona, for some years prior to the time that Del E. Webb Development Co. (Webb) (P) commenced construction of a community of retirement homes to the north of the Spur (D) property. As Webb's (P) construction extended southward toward the Spur (D) operation, the problem of noxious odors and flies attracted by the feedlots became more acute, and Webb (P) encountered increasing sales resistance. Eventually, Webb (P) filed suit to enjoin the Spur (D) operation, alleging that it constituted a public nuisance. The trial court agreed, and Spur (D) appealed, arguing that it should not be required to cease operations, and that, if required to shut down, it should be indemnified by Webb (P).

ISSUE:

(1) May a pre-existing lawful enterprise become an enjoinable nuisance by reason of conditions that subsequently develop in a region?

(2) If such an enterprise is enjoined from further operations, is it entitled to be indemnified by the party obtaining the injunction?

HOLDING AND DECISION: (Cameron, Vice C.J.)

(1) Yes. A pre-existing lawful enterprise may become a nuisance by reason of subsequent development of the region in which it is located. State law provides that any condition that constitutes a breeding ground for flies or vermin is injurious to the public health and is therefore an abatable public nuisance. In this case, then, Spur (D) must be enjoined from operating its feedlots.

(2) Yes. A party who "comes to the nuisance" must indemnify a pre-existing lawful enterprise if it is enjoined from further operation. Until Webb (P) erected its residential community, the Spur (D) operation was not a nuisance to anyone. Accordingly, although Spur's (D) activities may be enjoined, Webb (P) must indemnify Spur (D) for its costs in either relocating or going out of business. Remanded.

ANALYSIS

The result of this case accords with the reasoning employed by modern, enlightened courts in dealing with nuisances. The operator of a nuisance imposes an externality upon the parties affected thereby. Those parties may simultaneously impose an externality upon the operator of the nuisance by interfering with his lawful enterprise. In such a situation, the most economically efficient solution is one which requires one party to be compensated for his economic loss, while permitting the other party to continue his desired conduct. This result may be accomplished by permitting the operator of the nuisance to pay, in the form of damages to affected parties, for the privilege of continuing to operate. Or, it may be accomplished as it was in this case, by letting the complaining party pay for the privilege of enjoining the nuisance by indemnifying the operator of the nuisance for the economic loss which he suffers as a result of the injunction.

Quicknotes

INDEMNIFY Securing against potential injury; compensation for injury suffered.

NUISANCE An unlawful use of property that interferes with the lawful use of another's property.

PERMANENT INJUNCTION A remedy imposed by the court ordering a party to cease the conduct of a specific activity until the final disposition of the cause of action.

Prah v. Maretti

Homeowners (P) v. Builder of obstructing home (D)

Wis. Sup. Ct., 108 Wis. 2d 223, 321 N.W.2d 182 (1982).

NATURE OF CASE: Action to enjoin construction of a residence and seeking damages.

FACT SUMMARY: Plaintiff, owner of a solar heated residence, brought suit against his neighbor, claiming that his proposed construction of a residence interfered with his access to an unobstructed path for sunlight across the neighbor's property, seeking injunctive relief and damages.

RULE OF LAW

An action brought by a landowner claiming unreasonable obstruction of his access to sunlight is maintainable under private nuisance law.

FACTS: Plaintiff, owner of a solar heated residence, brought suit against his neighbor, claiming that his proposed construction of a residence interfered with his access to an unobstructed path for sunlight across the neighbor's property, seeking injunctive relief and damages. The circuit court denied plaintiff's motion for injunctive relief and entered summary judgment in favor of defendant.

ISSUE: Is an action brought by a landowner claiming unreasonable obstruction of his access to sunlight maintainable under private nuisance law?

HOLDING AND DECISION: (Abrahamson, J.) Yes. An action brought by a landowner claiming unreasonable obstruction of his access to sunlight is maintainable under private nuisance law. First it must be determined whether the complaint states a claim for relief based on common-law private nuisance. When a landowner's use of his or her property unreasonably interferes with another's enjoyment of his or her property, such use constitutes a private nuisance. The Restatement (Second) of Torts § 821D defines private nuisance as "a nontrespassory invasion of another's interest in the private use and enjoyment of land." Although defendant's obstruction of plaintiff's access to sunlight appears to fall within this definition, defendant claims he has a right to develop his property in accordance with statutes, ordinances and covenants without regard to whether he blocks his neighbor's access to sunlight. While courts have declined to recognize easements to light and air across adjacent property, many jurisdictions protect landowners from malicious obstructions of access to light under the common-law private nuisance doctrine. This jurisdiction has recognized "spite fences" as an actionable private nuisance. The policy considerations which limited broader protection for a landowner's access to sunlight are now obsolete. Thus, recognition of a nuisance claim for unreasonable obstruction of access to sunlight will not prevent land development or unduly hinder the use of adjoining land. The dispositive question is whether the conduct complained of is unreasonable. Here the plaintiff has stated a claim for relief. Reversed and remanded.

DISSENT: (Callow, J.) A landowner has the right to use his property within the limits of ordinances, statutes and restrictions of record. The facts of this case do not give rise to a cause of action for private nuisance.

ANALYSIS

American courts have not been as receptive as English courts in recognizing a landowner's right to access to sunlight. At English common law, a landowner could acquire such right through express agreement or the doctrine of "ancient lights." The doctrine of ancient lights permitted a landowner to continue to receive unobstructed access to sunlight across adjacent property, if the landowner had previously received such sunlight for a prescribed time period. While American courts honor express easements for access to sunlight, they will not find that such easements are created or acquired by prescription or implication.

Quicknotes

INJUNCTIVE RELIEF A court order issued as a remedy, requiring a person to do, or prohibiting that person from doing, a specific act.

PRIVATE NUISANCE An unlawful use of property interfering with the enjoyment of the private rights of an individual or a small number of persons.

CHAPTER 29

Governmental Power to Take Property: The "Public Use" Requirement

Quick Reference Rules of Law

Hawaii Housing Authority v. Midkiff

State agency (D) v. Landowners (P)

467 U.S. 229 (1984).

NATURE OF CASE: Appeal from reversal of judgment upholding the constitutionality of state condemnation legislation, and from the enjoining of that legislation.

FACT SUMMARY: The Hawaii Land Reform Act of 1967 created a mechanism for redistribution of lands by condemnation of residential tracts and transferring ownership of the condemned fees simple to existing lessees, with the goal of remedying the social and economic ills resulting from a land oligopoly on the Hawaiian Islands.

RULE OF LAW

Redistribution of fees simple to correct deficiencies in the market attributable to land oligopoly is a rational exercise of the eminent domain power.

FACTS: The Hawaii Housing Authority (HHA) (D) was authorized by the Hawaii Land Reform Act of 1967 to condemn residential tracts for resale to existing lessees as part of a plan to remedy the social and economic ills resulting from a land oligopoly on the Hawaiian Islands. The legislature had concluded that concentrated land ownership, whereby 47 percent of the land was in the hands of only 72 private owners, was responsible for skewing the State's residential fee simple market, inflating land prices, and injuring the public tranquility and welfare. Accordingly, the legislature intended to compel the large landowners to break up their estates, by requiring the large landowners to sell the lands they were leasing to homeowners. By using the condemnation mechanism, the legislature sought to reduce the federal tax consequences for the landowners. The landowners brought suit in district court, which held that the Act's goals were within the bounds of the State's police powers and that the means the legislature had chosen to serve those goals were not arbitrary, capricious, or selected in bad faith. The court of appeals reversed, finding the legislation to be unconstitutional, on the basis that it found that the legislation was a naked taking of private land from one party and a transfer to another private party, and enjoined enforcement. The HHA (D) appealed, and the U.S. Supreme Court granted certiorari.

ISSUE: Is redistribution of fees simple to correct deficiencies in the market attributable to land oligopoly a rational exercise of the eminent domain power?

HOLDING AND DECISION: (O'Connor, J.) Yes. Redistribution of fees simple to correct deficiencies in the market is a rational exercise of the eminent domain power. Where land is taken from one private party and transferred to another private party through the State's eminent domain powers, with due compensation, such a taking is constitutional if there is a justifying public purpose. Precedent in this area holds that the "public use" requirement is coterminous with the State's police powers. Here, the State legislature had determined that the deficiencies in the real estate market were attributable to the land oligopoly. Regulating oligopoly and the evils associated with it is a classic exercise of a State's police powers. Thus, Hawaii had a proper public purpose in enacting the legislation. Moreover, the Act's approach to correcting the land oligopoly problem was rational and comprehensive. Accordingly, the Fifth Amendment does not prohibit Hawaii from taking property, with just compensation, from lessors and transferring it to lessees in order to reduce the concentration of private ownership of fees simple in the State. The exercise of the eminent domain power was rationally related to a legitimate public purpose and was therefore constitutional. Reversed and remanded.

ANALYSIS

The Court here found that the government itself did not have to use the land to legitimize its taking. Only the taking's purpose, not its mechanics, must pass constitutional scrutiny. Judicial deference was also due to the findings of the state legislature.

Quicknotes

EMINENT DOMAIN The governmental power to take private property for public use so long as just compensation is paid therefore.

FIFTH AMENDMENT Provides that no person shall be compelled to serve as a witness against himself, or be subject to trial for the same offense twice, or be deprived of life, liberty, or property without due process of law.

County of Wayne v. Hathcock

County (P) v. Landowners (D)

Mich. Sup. Ct., 684 N.W.2d 765 (2004).

NATURE OF CASE: Condemnation action.

FACT SUMMARY: A Michigan county condemned nineteen parcels of land solely for the ultimate purpose of rejuvenating the local economy.

RULE OF LAW

A government taking of private property for the purpose of economic development does not satisfy the public-use requirement of Article 10, Section 2 of the Michigan Constitution.

FACTS: In conjunction with local airport improvements, Wayne County (County) (P) planned to develop 1,300 acres into a state-of-the-art center for business and technology; the planned development was called the Pinnacle Project (Project). The County (P) estimated that the Project would create 30,000 jobs and generate $350 million in tax revenues while broadening the make-up of the area's tax base. After acquiring more than 1,000 acres for the Project, the County (P) decided to acquire the remaining land, 19 parcels, through eminent domain; the County (P) would then transfer the parcels to other private owners to participate in the planned development. The parcels' owners (D) resisted, but the trial court upheld the County's (P) finding that the condemnation was necessary. The court of appeals affirmed, and the landowners (D) appealed to the Michigan Supreme Court.

ISSUE: Does a government taking of private property for the purpose of economic development satisfy the public-use requirement of Article 10, Section 2 of the Michigan Constitution?

HOLDING AND DECISION: (Young, J.) No. A government taking of private property for the purpose of economic development does not satisfy the public-use requirement of Article 10, Section 2 of the Michigan Constitution. The condemnation of the 19 parcels here is not consistent with the term "public use" as it was understood in 1963 when the Michigan Constitution was ratified. Forced transfers of private property comply with Michigan's public-use requirement when they exhibit one of three characteristics: where extreme public necessity requires the transfer, where public oversight continues after the transfer, and where publicly significant considerations justify the transfer. As exercised in the Pinnacle Project, the use of eminent domain in this case fulfills none of these criteria. The only support for the condemnation here lies in the "economic benefit" rationale of *Poletown Neighborhood Council v. Detroit,* 304 N.W.2d 455 (Mich. 1981). That rationale, however, which is based on vague notions of private owners voluntarily contributing to the general economic health, eviscerates the public-use requirement of Article 10, Section 2 of the Michigan Constitution. Accordingly, *Poletown* is hereby overruled, and the condemnations in this case therefore violate the state constitutional requirement of a public use. Reversed.

CONCURRENCE AND DISSENT: (Weaver, J.) Regardless of the County's (P) laudable goals, these condemnations plainly would result in transferring property to private owners who will be under no public oversight. Furthermore, the condemnations would not seek to correct blight or other adverse effects on the public welfare. This case therefore presents a straightforward violation of Michigan's public-use requirement.

ANALYSIS

When read with *Kelo v. City of New London,* 545 U.S. 469 (2005), *Hathcock* illustrates a fundamental aspect of federalism. It is always possible for state law to provide greater protections than those afforded under federal law. Justice Stevens's majority opinion in *Kelo* explicitly recognizes that principle in the eminent-domain context. Students also should note a potentially important factual difference between *Hathcock* and *Kelo*: the chronically depressed economic conditions faced by the municipality in *Kelo* seem much more onerous than those that Wayne County (P) sought to remedy in *Hathcock.* Even if *Hathcock* were decided under *Kelo's* statement of the federal standard, then, the proposed takings likely still would not satisfy the Federal Constitution's public-use requirement, either.

Quicknotes

CONDEMNATION The taking of private property for public use so long as just compensation is paid therefore.

EMINENT DOMAIN The governmental power to take private property for public use so long as just compensation is paid therefore.

PUBLIC USE Basis for governmental taking of property pursuant to its power of eminent domain so that property taken may be utilized for the benefit of the public at large.

Kelo v. City of New London

Landowners (P) v. Municipality (D)

545 U.S. 469 (2005).

NATURE OF CASE: Suit challenging a city's proposed taking of private properties to promote the city's planned economic revitalization.

FACT SUMMARY: A city adopted a development plan designed to revitalize the local economy. To implement its plan, the city sought to condemn 15 properties owned by nine private landowners who refused to sell their properties to the city.

RULE OF LAW

A city's proposed taking of private property for general economic development qualifies as a public use consistent with the Takings Clause of the Fifth Amendment to the U.S. Constitution.

FACTS: In 1990, a Connecticut state agency officially designated the City of New London (City or New London) (D) as a "distressed municipality." New London's (D) economy worsened in 1996 when the federal government closed a facility that employed 1,500 people. The City's (D) unemployment rate almost doubled that for the rest of the state, and its population had dwindled to its lowest level in almost eighty years. State and local officials therefore targeted New London (D) for economic revitalization. Eventually a development plan focused on a 90-acre area known as Fort Trumbull as the center of the City's (D) revitalization efforts. The drafters designed the development plan to coincide with the expected arrival of a major company, Pfizer Inc., and to rejuvenate the local economy with jobs, tax revenue, and a generalized momentum for future growth and recreational activities. Most landowners in the Fort Trumbull area agreed to sell their properties to the City (D). Nine owners, however, refused to sell their 15 properties. The City (D) condemned the 15 properties purely because they were within the area designated for development; the City (D) never alleged that the properties were in any degree of substandard condition. [Susette Kelo (P) and the other eight resisting owners sued the City (D) in state court, where the trial judge permanently enjoined the City (D) from taking 11 of the contested properties but permitted the taking of the other four properties. Both sides appealed to the Connecticut Supreme Court, which held that all 15 properties could properly be taken by New London (D). Applying state statute, the state's highest court held that the proposed taking was for a public use that satisfied both state and federal constitutional requirements. Kelo (P) and her fellow landowners petitioned the U.S. Supreme Court for further review.]

ISSUE: Does a city's proposed taking of private property for general economic development qualify as a public use consistent with the Takings Clause of the Fifth Amendment to the U.S. Constitution?

HOLDING AND DECISION: (Stevens, J.) Yes. A city's proposed taking of private property for general economic development qualifies as a public use consistent with the Takings Clause of the Fifth Amendment to the U.S. Constitution. A government may not take private property merely to transfer it to another private owner; conversely, private property may be taken if the taking is legitimately for "use by the public." Neither of these general propositions controls this case, though, because the question here narrows to whether a proposed taking for general economic development serves a "public purpose," which is the broader reading of "public use" that this Court has consistently used for more than a century. The Court upheld the redevelopment plan at issue in *Berman v. Parker*, 348 U.S. 26 (1954), because creating a "better balanced, more attractive community" was a valid public purpose. Similarly, in *Hawaii Housing Authority v. Midkiff*, 467 U.S. 229 (1984), the Court upheld a state statute that took fee title from lessors and vested title in lessees to more broadly distribute land ownership in the affected area. Thus, under the appropriately deferential standard of review, New London's (D) proposed takings here do meet the public use requirement imposed by the Takings Clause. Kelo's (P) objection that economic development confuses the distinction between public and private use contradicts precedent; public use often benefits specific private owners, too. Finally, Kelo's (P) objection that nothing would stop a city from transferring land from one private owner to another specific private owner for a public purpose presents issues that are not before the Court in this case. Accordingly, this Court's takings jurisprudence provides no basis for preventing the City of New London (D) from taking the 15 properties in the Fort Trumbull area. Affirmed.

CONCURRENCE: (Kennedy, J.) Rational-basis review under the Public Use Clause should invalidate a taking clearly designed primarily to favor a specific private party where only minor or pretextual benefits will accrue to the public. Some cases might justify a higher standard of review to justify takings, but this is not such a case, given the City's several safeguards in formulating its proposed development plan.

DISSENT: (O'Connor, J.) The Court has abandoned one of the Constitution's most basic restraints on governments by removing any distinction between public and

Continued on next page.

private uses. To define the proper distinction, this Court's role is to decide the matter for itself instead of blindly deferring to legislative determinations, as the majority does today. Properly considered under judicial standards, takings for economic development are not consistent with the Takings Clause. The takings in *Berman* and *Midkiff* differed from the takings here because those takings directly benefited the public by immediately removing harmful uses. In sharp contrast, the uses of the homes by Kelo (P) and the other landowners here are not inherently harmful. The definition of public use, then, now means much more than it has ever meant in earlier cases. The Takings Clause's requirement that takings be "for public use" is effectively meaningless now because the phrase no longer reasonably excludes any takings. In these circumstances, the City's deliberative process is irrelevant because the new standard of wholesale deference to legislative bodies means that takings resulting from less-stringent processes must also be upheld. These conditions will benefit citizens who already have more resources and more political influence—a situation that flouts what was supposed to be the American commitment to just, impartial government.

DISSENT: (Thomas, J.) The text of the Constitution permits takings of private property for public use, not for public necessity. Justice O'Connor therefore correctly argues that this Court cannot abridge specifically enumerated constitutional liberties guaranteed by the Takings Clause. But the majority's error today is far more fundamental: as originally understood, and as this Court long ago forgot, the Takings Clause imposes real restraints on the power of eminent domain. The Court certainly does not owe effectively complete deference to legislative determinations of public use, just as such deference is not appropriate when reviewing legislative definitions of other constitutional provisions. This deferential standard is particularly inappropriate when compared to the searching review extended to, for example, grants of welfare benefits or warrants for mere searches of homes. Such a standard of review only ensures that those who already have more resources will more easily victimize the weak, which in most cases will regrettably equate with the black landowners most often affected by urban renewal projects.

ANALYSIS

Despite the public outcry that greeted the *Kelo* decision, the majority opinion has too much support in precedent, specifically in *Berman* and *Midkiff,* to fit naïve definitions of judicial activism. At the same time, Justice O'Connor's distinction between the inherently harmful uses in *Berman* and *Midkiff* and what she sees as the inherently harmless uses in *Kelo* seems to impose something like the higher standard hinted at in Justice Kennedy's concurrence. For Justice O'Connor, New London's (D) chronic and deepening economic demise does not qualify as a harm caused by the affected private ownership itself that would, for her, justify a taking.

Quicknotes

EMINENT DOMAIN The governmental power to take private property for public use so long as just compensation is paid therefore.

PUBLIC USE Basis for governmental taking of property pursuant to its power of eminent domain so that property taken may be utilized for the benefit of the public at large.

TAKINGS CLAUSE Provision of the Fifth Amendment to the United States Constitution prohibiting the government from taking private property for public use without providing just compensation therefore.

CHAPTER 30

Zoning and Land Use Regulation

Quick Reference Rules of Law

Village of Euclid v. Ambler Realty Co.

Municipal corporation (D) v. Landowner (P)

272 U.S. 365 (1926).

NATURE OF CASE: Action claiming a zoning ordinance is an unconstitutional violation of due process and equal protection rights. [The procedural posture of the case is not indicated in the casebook extract.]

FACT SUMMARY: Village of Euclid (D) zoned property of Ambler Realty (P) in a manner which materially reduced its potential value, which Ambler Realty (P) claimed was an unconstitutional violation of due process and equal protection.

RULE OF LAW

A zoning ordinance is not unconstitutional as a deprivation of property without due process or equal protection where it results in a diminution of value in the property zoned but otherwise is neither arbitrary nor capricious and has some substantial relation to the public health, safety, morals, or general welfare.

FACTS: Ambler Realty (P) was the owner of 68 acres in the village of Euclid (D). Though surrounded primarily by residential neighborhoods, the 68 acres also was bounded by a major thoroughfare, Euclid Avenue, to the south and a railroad to the north. Euclid (D) instituted a zoning ordinance that placed use, height, and area restrictions on land, including Ambler Realty's (P) property. As a result of this zoning, the value of Ambler Realty's (P) property declined from $10,000 per acre for industrial use to $2,500 per acre, and from $150 per front foot to $50 per front foot, when restricted to residential use. Ambler Realty (P) brought suit claiming that the ordinance constituted a violation of the Constitution's due process and equal protection provisions. The U.S. Supreme Court granted certiorari. [The procedural posture of the case is not indicated in the casebook extract.]

ISSUE: Is a zoning ordinance unconstitutional as a deprivation of property without due process or equal protection where it results in a diminution of value in the property zoned but otherwise is neither arbitrary nor capricious and has some substantial relation to the public health, safety, morals, or general welfare?

HOLDING AND DECISION: (Sutherland, J.) No. A zoning ordinance is not unconstitutional as a deprivation of property without due process or equal protection where it results in a diminution of value in the property zoned but otherwise is neither arbitrary nor capricious and has some substantial relation to the public health, safety, morals, or general welfare. Zoning ordinances, and all similar laws and regulations, must find their justification in some aspect of the police power, asserted for the public welfare. Until recent years, urban life was comparatively simple; but with the great increase and concentration of population, problems have developed that require new restrictions on the use and occupation of private lands in urban communities. There is no serious difference of opinion on the state power to avoid the nuisances which industry may cause in a residential area. As for residential regulation, many considerations point toward their validity, as they encourage the health and safety of the community. Segregation of residential business and industrial buildings makes it easier to provide appropriate fire apparatus, for example, or to prevent street accidents. Further, it is often observed that the construction of one type of building, such as apartment buildings, destroys an area for other types, such as detached residential housing. These reasons are sufficiently cogent to preclude a determination that the zoning ordinance is clearly arbitrary and unreasonable, having no substantial relation to the public health, safety, morals, or general welfare. The ordinance, therefore, is not unconstitutional and must be upheld. [The procedural result of this case is not indicated in the casebook extract.]

ANALYSIS

Village of Euclid v. Ambler Realty is the landmark Supreme Court decision on zoning ordinances as valid exercises of the police power. Essentially, any zoning ordinance that is tied to public health, safety, morals, or welfare will be upheld unless clearly arbitrary and unreasonable. So-called *Euclidian* Zoning, which resulted from this decision, usually consists in the division of areas into zones, in which building use, height, and area are regulated in a manner designed to guarantee homogeneity of building patterns. All too often, however, zoning operates not so much to protect the public interest as to protect the vested interests in a community. Building restrictions may all too easily be used as an economic sanction by which social segregation is perpetuated. (Barring low-cost housing keeps out economically deprived segment of the population.) Note, however, that *Euclid* did not foreclose the possibility that government land-use regulations may constitute a "taking" which requires compensation. In *Pennsylvania Coal Co. v. Mahon*, 260 U.S. 393 (1922), the U.S. Supreme Court held that an anti-mining restriction, which totally destroyed the interest of the party who owned only the mineral rights, constituted a taking as to that person for which compensation had to be paid. In the *Mahon* case, the diminution in value of the party's property was total, and was thus clearly a "taking."

Continued on next page.

Quicknotes

POLICE POWER The power of a government to impose restrictions on the rights of private persons, as long as those restrictions are reasonably related to the promotion and protection of public health, safety, morals, and the general welfare.

PUBLIC WELFARE The well-being of the general community.

TAKING A governmental action that substantially deprives an owner of the use and enjoyment of his or her property, requiring compensation.

ZONING ORDINANCE A statute that divides land into defined areas and which regulates the form and use of buildings and structures within those areas.

Western Land Equities, Inc. v. City of Logan

Property owner-developer (P) v. Municipality (D)

Utah Sup. Ct., 617 P.2d 388 (1980).

NATURE OF CASE: Appeal from judgment estopping enforcement of a zoning change that would retroactively prohibit a previously permitted use.

FACT SUMMARY: Western Land Equities, Inc. (Western) (P) owned land in the City of Logan (City) (D) that was in a zone that permitted single-family dwellings, with the plan of developing a subdivision of such housing. After the planning commission rejected Western's (P) project, and the City (D) amended the zoning ordinance to prohibit Western's (P) proposed use, Western (P) sued, claiming it had a vested right to develop the land in accord with the zoning in effect when it proposed the project.

RULE OF LAW

A zoning law may not be retroactively applied to prohibit a previously permitted use where an applicant's proposal meets the zoning requirements in existence at the time of the application, the applicant proceeds with reasonable diligence, and there is no compelling, countervailing public interest.

FACTS: Western Land Equities, Inc. (Western) (P) owned land in the City of Logan (City) (D) that was in an M-1 zone, a manufacturing zone that permitted single-family dwellings. Western (P) planned to develop a subdivision of such housing. The City's (D) planning commission, however, went on record opposing subdivisions in M-1 zones and rejected Western's (P) plan. Western (P) unsuccessfully appealed that decision to the municipal council. A few months later, the City (D) amended its zoning ordinance to prohibit Western's (P) proposed use, and Western (P) sued, claiming it had a vested right to develop the land in accord with the zoning in effect when it proposed the project and that the City (D) was estopped from withholding approval of the project. The trial court granted judgment for Western (P). The state's highest court granted review.

ISSUE: May a zoning law be retroactively applied to prohibit a previously permitted use where an applicant's proposal meets the zoning requirements in existence at the time of the application, the applicant proceeds with reasonable diligence, and there is no compelling, countervailing public interest?

HOLDING AND DECISION: (Stewart, J.) No. A zoning law may not be retroactively applied to prohibit a previously permitted use where an applicant's proposal meets the zoning requirements in existence at the time of the application, the applicant proceeds with reasonable diligence, and there is no compelling, countervailing public interest. The date of application for a building permit fixes the applicable zoning laws and that application may not be denied on the basis of a subsequently-enacted zoning ordinance. Here, Western (P) substantially complied with procedural requirements, and the trial court applied zoning estoppel to estop the City (D) from withholding approval of the proposed subdivision. Under zoning estoppel, a government entity is estopped from exercising its zoning powers to prohibit a proposed land use when a property owner, relying reasonably and in good faith on some governmental act or omission, has made a substantial change in position or incurred such extensive obligations or expenses that it would be highly inequitable to deprive the owner of his right to complete his proposed development. The trial court erred in applying this approach, because Western's (P) "substantial compliance" with procedural requirements by itself did not justify estoppel of the City's (D) enforcement of a new zoning ordinance, since the costs Western (P) incurred were not that extensive. Western (P) spent $1,335 for a boundary survey and $890 for a preliminary subdivision plat—and the boundary survey retains value regardless of whether the project is approved or not. The expenditure of $890 is not significant in relation to the size of the parcel and the proposed plan. The better approach is one that engenders predictability for landowners while protecting important public interests that may legitimately require interference with planned private development. The rule enunciated accommodates those competing interests. Under that rule, if a city or county has initiated proceedings to amend its zoning ordinances, a landowner who subsequently makes application for a permit is not entitled to rely on the original zoning classification. Applying this rule here, at the time of Western's (P) application, zoning law permitted the proposed use, and Western (P) had even received encouragement from city officials. Additionally, the reasons given by the City (D) for changing the zoning ordinance were not sufficiently compelling to overcome the presumption that an applicant for a building permit or subdivision approval is entitled to affirmative official action if he meets the zoning requirements in force at the time of his application. Affirmed.

ANALYSIS

The majority rule is that an applicant for a building permit or subdivision approval does not acquire any vested right under existing zoning regulations prior to the issuance of the permit or official approval of a proposed subdivision, and, generally, denial of an application may be based on subsequently-enacted zoning regulations. The court in this

Continued on next page.

case was of the view that the majority rule fails to strike a proper balance between public and private interests and opens the area to so many variables as to result in unnecessary litigation and economic waste, and sometimes subjects landowners to even calamitous expense because of changing city councils or zoning boards or their dilatory action.

Quicknotes

ZONING ORDINANCE A statute that divides land into defined areas and which regulates the form and use of buildings and structures within those areas.

Maryland Reclamation Associates, Inc. v. Harford County

Landowner (P) v. County (D)

Md. Ct. App., 994 A.2d 842 (2010).

NATURE OF CASE: Appeal in zoning law matter seeking the application of zoning estoppel. [The procedural posture of the case is not indicated in the casebook extract.]

FACT SUMMARY: Maryland Reclamation Associates (MRA) (P), which had sought approval to operate a rubble landfill, contended, inter alia, that zoning estoppel should be applied to estop Harford County (County) (D) from applying an amendment to its zoning code that would render MRA's (P) property ineligible for use as a rubble landfill.

RULE OF LAW

Zoning estoppel should not be applied where a landowner cannot prove substantial reliance on government action.

FACTS: Maryland Reclamation Associates (MRA) (P) owned a 68-acre tract of land in Harford County (County) (D) that it wished to use as a rubble landfill. The County (D) had included the land in its Solid Waste Management Plan (SWMP), subject to certain conditions, and a state agency had issued an environmental permit for the site, all prior to the County (D) reversing course and adopting a zoning code amendment that would subject all rubble landfills (not just MRA's (P)) to new conditions and that would require use variances for them. MRA (P) contended that zoning estoppel should apply to estop the County (D) from applying the amended zoning code in a way that would render MRA's (P) property ineligible for use as a rubble landfill. The case went before the state's highest court, which granted review. One of the other issues the court ruled on was that MRA (P) did not have a vested right to develop the land as a rubble landfill because, contrary to the requirement of vested-rights precedents, it did not have a valid local land-use permit. The court further held that the County's (D) zoning amendment was not arbitrary or capricious, since it was based on widespread opposition to landfill projects in general, not just to MRA's (P) proposed landfill in particular. [The precise procedural posture of the case is not indicated in the casebook extract.]

ISSUE: Should zoning estoppel be applied where a landowner cannot prove substantial reliance on government action?

HOLDING AND DECISION: (Adkins, J.) No. Zoning estoppel should not be applied where a landowner cannot prove substantial reliance on government action. There is a need for the doctrine of zoning estoppel as zoning and permitting processes become increasingly complex and highly regulated. On the one hand, developers may expend a great deal of money before even breaking ground, and on the other hand, a government's responsibilities to its citizens cannot be ignored. Zoning estoppel can play a role in balancing the legitimate interests and rights of landowners wishing to develop against equally legitimate environmental and community concerns. While landowners must be aware that, to a limited extent, the local government may shift course in its zoning decisions, so that the land developer should not incur significant expense without final permitting, there may be cases where a developer's good faith reliance on government action in the pre-construction stage is so extensive and expensive that zoning estoppel is an appropriate doctrine to apply. The key elements of zoning estoppel are good faith by the owner, substantial reliance, and government action that has led to such reliance. Good faith focuses on the land owner's mental attitude and honest intentions, in a way that the owner does not accelerate development or increase investment in an effort to establish substantial reliance or prevent rezoning. Substantial reliance typically entitles an owner to relief if the owner has changed her position beyond a certain set degree or amount. Courts generally differ in what that set amount is. Here, the application of zoning estoppel is not warranted. First, zoning estoppel must be applied, if at all, sparingly and with utmost caution and only in those situations creating great inequity or oppression. Therefore, the burden of proof is on the landowner. If a developer "has good reason to believe, before or while acting to his detriment, that the official's mind may soon change, estoppel may not be justified." In other words, the owner must prove that she lacked knowledge of those facts that would have put her on sufficient notice that she should not rely on the government action in question. Here, MRA (P) was on notice that there was a very real possibility that its landfill would not be approved. First, the parcel's inclusion in the SWMP was achieved by a fragile majority of the County Council, and that many more steps would have to be taken before final approval. Second, there was strong public opposition to the landfill by hundreds of individuals at the public hearings. Third, the membership of the County Council changed. Fourth, the closing on MRA's (P) purchase of the parcel would not be the definitive milemarker of zoning estoppel, since the mere purchase of land by itself generally is insufficient to constitute "substantial reliance." To hold otherwise would mean that a purchaser could lock in the zoning of any parcel simply by the act of purchasing property and asking for a permit. MRA's (P) other attempts to prove substantial reliance also must be rejected. MRA (P) asserts that it spent $325,000 on engineering fees, but it does not specify when, and there is insufficient evidence that those fees were incurred in good faith reliance on the results of any public hearings. Such bald

Continued on next page.

assertions are insufficient to meet MRA's (P) burden of proof. For these reasons, MRA (P) has failed to prove zoning estoppel. [The procedural results of the court's holding are not included in the Casebook extract.]

ANALYSIS

In most states in which zoning estoppel is most often invoked and allowed fall into four factual categories: (1) reliance on a validly issued permit; (2) reliance on the probability of issuance of a permit; (3) reliance on an erroneously issued permit; or (4) reliance on the non-enforcement of a zoning violation. Such reliance requires good faith on the landowner's part, and, typically, requires some physical construction to establish the substantiality of the reliance.

Van Sicklen v. Browne

Landowner (P) v. Government official (D)

Cal. Ct. App., 92 Cal. Rptr. 786 (1971).

NATURE OF CASE: Appeal from judgment sustaining a city planning commission's denial of a conditional use permit.

FACT SUMMARY: Van Sicklen (P) contended that his application for a use permit to construct an automobile service station on property that complied with minimum width, frontage and area requirements was erroneously denied, in part because the denial represented an invalid attempt to regulate economic competition through zoning laws.

RULE OF LAW

Overconcentration of a conditionally permitted use is a sufficient basis for denying a conditional use permit, even where such denial has some impact on economic competition.

FACTS: Van Sicklen (P) applied for a use permit to construct an automobile service station on property that complied with minimum width, frontage and area requirements. The planning commission denied the application, finding that approval would oversaturate the neighborhood with service stations and set a precedent that would make it difficult to deny applicants on other street corners; there was no demonstrated need for an additional service station in the neighborhood; if approved, the station would be too close to a residential area, without logically being at the intersection of two heavily traveled major streets; and, approval on the basis of a future freeway location was premature. The city's zoning ordinance expressly provided that automobile service stations could be permitted if their location conformed to the objectives of the master plan. Van Sicklen (P) argued that the denial was arbitrary and was a prohibited attempt to regulate economic competition through zoning laws. The trial court sustained the planning commission, and the state's intermediate appellate court granted review.

ISSUE: Is overconcentration of a conditionally permitted use a sufficient basis for denying a conditional use permit, even where such denial has some impact on economic competition?

HOLDING AND DECISION: (Molinari, J.) Yes. Overconcentration of a conditionally permitted use is a sufficient basis for denying a conditional use permit, even where such denial has some impact on economic competition. Because the zoning ordinance expressly provides that automobile service stations may be permitted in conformance with the master plan, the planning commission has considerable discretion in determining whether the proposed use serves the master plan's key objectives. The planning commission's findings and determination were a legitimate, non-arbitrary, non-capricious exercise of its discretionary power. Given the specifically stated purposes of both the zoning ordinance and the master plan, it could not have been the legislative intent that use permits for service stations would be granted for any number of service stations so long as each parcel met the minimum width, frontage and area requirements. As to Van Sicklen's (P) contention that the city denied the use permit for economic rather than planning considerations resulting in an invalid attempt to regulate competition through zoning laws, although a municipality may not use zoning powers to regulate economic competition, it is also recognized that all zoning and land use decisions will have some economic impact. Provided that the primary purpose of the zoning ordinance is not to regulate economic competition, but to serve a valid objective pursuant to a city's police powers, such ordinance is not invalid even though it might have an indirect impact on economic competition. The intensity of land use is a well-recognized and valid zoning concern that relates to health and safety factors. Regarding service stations, for example, it is a valid public health safety concern that such uses store and use highly flammable, explosive products, so that an increase in the concentration of such stations in small areas increases the dangers to the public. Affirmed.

ANALYSIS

The traditional purpose of the conditional use permit is to enable a municipality to exercise some measure of control over the extent of certain uses, such as service stations, which, although desirable in limited numbers, could have a detrimental effect on the community in large numbers.

Quicknotes

POLICE POWER The power of a government to impose restrictions on the rights of private persons, so long as those restrictions are reasonably related to the promotion and protection of public health, safety, morals, and the general welfare.

ZONING ORDINANCE A statute that divides land into defined areas and which regulates the form and use of buildings and structures within those areas.

CHAPTER 31–32

Takings: Physical, Regulatory and Exactions

Quick Reference Rules of Law

Loretto v. Teleprompter Manhattan CATV Corp.

Landlord (P) v. Cable company (D)

458 U.S. 419 (1982).

NATURE OF CASE: Appeal from denial of damages for taking of property without just compensation.

FACT SUMMARY: The trial court held that Teleprompter's (D) governmentally approved installation of cable television equipment on Loretto's (P) building without her permission did not constitute a "taking" of property.

RULE OF LAW

A permanent physical occupation authorized by the government is a taking without regard to the public interests it may serve.

FACTS: Teleprompter (D) installed its cable television equipment on a building subsequently purchased by Loretto (P). The equipment was permanently fastened to the building and was placed there under authority of the previous owner and the state. Loretto (P) sued, contending this constituted a taking of property without due process. The trial court held that this was not a taking, as cable television served an important public interest. Loretto (P) appealed from entry of summary judgment, and the court of appeals affirmed, upholding the constitutionality of the state statute granting permission to Teleprompter (D). The U.S. Supreme Court granted certiorari.

ISSUE: Is a permanent physical occupation of property authorized by government a taking regardless of the interests served?

HOLDING AND DECISION: (Marshall, J.) Yes. A permanent physical occupation authorized by the government is a taking without regard to the public interest served. Although substantial regulation of use is not necessarily a compensable taking, an actual physical occupation, no matter how slight, must be considered to be a taking and requires just compensation. Reversed and remanded.

DISSENT: (Blackmun, J.) Contrary to established precedent, the Court announces a per se taking test arising out of physical occupation.

ANALYSIS

The Court distinguished *Loretto* from *Penn Central Transportation Co. v. New York City*, 438 U.S. 104 (1978), based on the fact in that case no actual physical occupation occurred. The state merely prohibited an intended use rather than actually entering the property, and no compensable taking was found.

Quicknotes

TAKING A governmental action that substantially deprives an owner of the use and enjoyment of his property, requiring compensation.

Yee v. City of Escondido

Mobile home park owners (P) v. City (D)

503 U.S. 519 (1992).

NATURE OF CASE: Appeal from a defense judgment in an action for damages resulting from a regulatory taking.

FACT SUMMARY: The Yees (P), owners of two mobile home parks, brought this suit for damages alleging that a state law, in conjunction with a local rent control ordinance, deprived them of all use and occupancy of their real property amounting to a physical taking of that property.

RULE OF LAW

States have broad power to regulate housing conditions in general and the landlord-tenant relationship in particular without paying compensation for all economic injuries that such regulation entails.

FACTS: The Yees (P) owned two mobile home parks in Escondido, California. The state enacted a Mobile home Residency Law, limiting the bases upon which a park owner may terminate a mobile home owner's tenancy. While a rental agreement was in effect, the park owner generally could not require the removal of a mobile home when it was sold. This law was enacted to protect mobile home owners because mobile homes are largely immobile as a practical matter. After Escondido (D) enacted a mobile home rent control ordinance, the Yees (P) brought suit, alleging that the ordinance, in conjunction with the state's Mobile home Residency Law, deprived them of all use and occupancy of their real property, amounting to a physical occupation of that property. They requested damages, a declaration that the ordinance was unconstitutional, and an injunction barring its enforcement.

ISSUE: Do states have broad power to regulate housing conditions in general and the landlord-tenant relationship in particular without paying compensation for all economic injuries that such regulation entails?

HOLDING AND DECISION: (O'Connor, J.) Yes. States have broad power to regulate housing conditions in general and the landlord-tenant relationship in particular without paying compensation for all economic injuries that such regulation entails. No government has required any physical invasion of the Yees' (P) property. On their face, the state and local laws at issue here merely regulate the Yees' (P) use of their land by regulating the relationship between landlord and tenant. Ordinary rent control often transfers wealth from landlords to tenants by reducing the landlords' income and the tenants' monthly payments. The ordinance does not require the Yees (P) to submit to the physical occupation of their land. Mere regulation of an owner's use of his or her property does not amount to a per se taking. Affirmed.

ANALYSIS

The Takings Clause of the Fifth Amendment to the U.S. Constitution provides: "[N]or shall private property be taken for public use without just compensation." Where the government authorizes a physical occupation of property, the Takings Clause generally requires compensation. But where the use of property is regulated, compensation is required only if the regulation has unfairly singled out the property owner to bear a burden that should be borne by the public as a whole.

Quicknotes

FIFTH AMENDMENT Provides that no person shall be compelled to serve as a witness against himself, or be subject to trial for the same offense twice, or be deprived of life, liberty, or property without due process of law.

INJUNCTION A remedy imposed by the court ordering a party to cease the conduct of a specific activity.

Pennsylvania Coal Co. v. Mahon

Coal company (D) v. Property owner (P)

260 U.S. 393 (1922).

NATURE OF CASE: Appeal from the granting of an injunction.

FACT SUMMARY: Mahon (P) desired to prevent the exercise of the mineral rights which the Pennsylvania Coal Co. (D) reserved in a deed transferring certain surface property to Mahon (P).

RULE OF LAW

Private property may be regulated pursuant to the police power of the state to protect public health, safety, or morals; but if such regulation goes so far as to destroy or appropriate a property right, it becomes a "taking" under the Fifth and Fourteenth Amendments, requiring just compensation therefor.

FACTS: In 1878, Pennsylvania Coal Co. (Coal Co.) (D) transferred certain real property to Mahon (P) by a deed in which the Coal Co. (D) reserved the mineral rights on the property and Mahon (P) waived all rights to object to or receive damages for the removal of such minerals. In 1921, the Pennsylvania legislature enacted the "Kohler Act," which forbade the mining of coal in such a way as to cause the subsidence of any human habitation. When the Coal Co. (D) decided to exercise its mineral rights pursuant to the deed, Mahon (P) instituted an action for an injunction on the grounds that the mining would violate the Kohler Act by causing the subsidence of his home. From a decree granting the injunction, the Coal Co. (D) appealed, contending that such an application of the statute would constitute a taking without compensation contrary to due process.

ISSUE: Will an exercise of the police power be upheld if it, in effect, provides for the destruction or appropriation of a private property right?

HOLDING AND DECISION: (Holmes, J.) No. Private property may be regulated pursuant to the police power of the state to protect public health, safety, or morals; but if such regulation goes so far as to destroy or appropriate a property right, it becomes a "taking" under the Fifth and Fourteenth Amendments, requiring just compensation therefor. It is well established, of course, that some property rights must yield to the public interest and the police power. Here, however, the limited public interest in protecting Mahon's (P) surface rights does not justify the total destruction of the mineral rights which the Coal Co. (D) reserved in its deed to Mahon (P). As such, the Kohler Act is unconstitutional insofar as it fails to provide for compensation for the taking of the Coal Co.'s (D) property rights. The decree which was based upon it is accordingly reversed.

DISSENT: (Brandeis, J.) No taking occurred here. Rather, the state merely exercised the police power to prevent a noxious use of property. The property remains in the possession of the owners.

ANALYSIS

This case illustrates the minority rule. Generally, when a landowner conveys to someone else a right to take minerals underneath the surface of his land, the grantee owes the grantor-landowner the duty to support the surface in its natural state (i.e., without any buildings). Furthermore, generally, ownership of land carries with it the right to have the land supported in its natural state by adjoining land (i.e., the right to have the support of the land undisturbed by excavation on adjoining land). Under this general rule, if an adjoining landowner excavates in such a manner as to cause subsidence on one's own land, he is "absolutely liable" for such subsidence. If, however, there is a structure on the land which subsides "and the land would not have subsided but for such structure," the adjoining landowner is not liable as a matter of law (i.e., he is not "absolutely liable"), but he may be liable for negligent excavation.

Quicknotes

FIFTH AMENDMENT Provides that no person shall be compelled to serve as a witness against himself, or be subject to trial for the same offense twice, or be deprived of life, liberty, or property without due process of law.

FOURTEENTH AMENDMENT Declares that no state shall make or enforce any law that shall abridge the privileges and immunities of citizens of the United States. No state shall deny to any person within its jurisdiction the equal protection of the laws.

INJUNCTIVE RELIEF A court order issued as a remedy, requiring a person to do, or prohibiting that person from doing, a specific act.

KOHLER ACT Legislation passed in 1921 that prohibited the mining of coal that would cause the caving in, collapse, or subsidence of a number of specific structures or public facilities.

TAKING A governmental action that substantially deprives an owner of the use and enjoyment of his property, requiring compensation.

Penn Central Transportation Co. v. City of New York

Railroad (P) v. Property owner (D)

438 U.S. 104 (1978).

NATURE OF CASE: Action claiming that a statute effected a "taking" of property without just compensation in violation of the Fifth and Fourteenth Amendments of the Constitution.

FACT SUMMARY: Because Penn Central Transportation Co.'s (P) terminal was declared a "landmark" under New York's Landmark Preservation Law, restrictions were placed on the use and alteration of the terminal site.

RULE OF LAW

A landmark preservation statute that restricts the exploitation of sites determined to be "landmarks" does not effect a "taking" of the property so designated for a public use within the meaning of the Fifth Amendment.

FACTS: New York City's Landmark Preservation Law provided for a commission to designate a building as a "landmark" and allowed the property owner to seek judicial review of the decision. Although it opposed designation of its Grand Central Terminal as a "landmark," Penn Central (P) did not seek such judicial review of the designation decision nor of the subsequent decision disallowing construction of a multi-story office building over the terminal. The building project was part of a lease agreement with Union General Properties (UGP) under which UGP was to construct the office building and lease it for $3,000,000 a year, also paying $1,000,000 during construction thereof. Claiming that failure to permit construction of the building called for in this 50-year lease agreement had severely restricted the use of its property, Penn Central (P) brought suit in state court. They argued that the application of the Landmark Law had "taken" their property without just compensation in violation of the Fifth and Fourteenth Amendments and arbitrarily deprived them of property without due process of law. Although the trial court granted relief, the court of appeals reversed, finding that there had been no "taking" because the property was not transferred to the control of the City of New York (D), but was simply subject to restrictions on its exploitation. It was also held that no denial of due process had occurred because the same use of the terminal which was presently going on could continue, there had been no showing that a reasonable return on the investment in the terminal could not be realized by continuing such use, and the fact that development rights above the terminal were specifically made transferrable, by the Landmark Law, to other property in the vicinity owned by Penn Central (P) provided significant compensation for any loss of use of the air rights above the terminal itself. From that decision, Penn Central (P) appealed.

ISSUE: If an owner is restricted in the exploitation of his property because it had been designated as a "landmark" under a landmark preservation statute, has there been a "taking" of his property for a public use within the meaning of the Fifth Amendment?

HOLDING AND DECISION: (Brennan, J.) No. The fact that an owner's use or exploitation of his property has been restricted by a landmark preservation statute because it has been designated a "landmark" does not mean that there has been a "taking" of his property for a public use within the meaning of the Fifth Amendment. It is untenable to suggest that a "taking" is established by simply showing that Penn Central (P) has been denied the ability to exploit a property interest that they heretofore had believed was available for development. Nor can diminution in property value, standing alone, establish a "taking." If that were the case, zoning laws could never be upheld. The argument that landmark laws, per se, constitute something akin to discriminatory or "reverse spot" zoning, arbitrarily singling out particular parcels for different and less favorable treatment than neighboring ones, is not compelling. In this case, the landmark legislation involves a comprehensive plan to preserve structures of historic or aesthetic interest wherever they might be found. The decision to designate property as a "landmark" might be somewhat subjective, but it is not arbitrary or unprincipled. Like zoning laws, the Landmark Law may impact more severely on some property owners than others in attempting to promote the general welfare, but that does not in and of itself mean that it "effects" a "taking." In any event, it is not true that Penn Central (P) is solely burdened and unbenefited, the preservation of landmarks being of benefit to all the citizens of New York City both economically and in improving the quality of life in the city as a whole. Nor is this a case where the government has appropriated part of Penn Central's (P) property for its own use, the restrictions on use of the air space above the terminal being akin to the constitutionally valid zoning law which prohibits, for "aesthetic" reasons, two or more adult theatres within a specified area. Here, the basic inquiry is whether or not there has been interference of such magnitude with Penn Central's (P) property as to require an exercise of eminent domain and compensation to sustain it. In that it does not prevent Penn Central (P) from continuing to make reasonable beneficial use of the terminal, the law does not interfere with what must be regarded as Penn Central's (P) primary expectation concerning the use of the parcel. Furthermore, Penn Central's (P) right to the air space above the terminal has not been totally denied. Other plans to build above the terminal might be approved if they harmonized

Continued on next page.

with its character. Most importantly, however, the right to exploit the air space above the terminal is transferrable to other local parcels on which the desired office building could be constructed. This scheme lessens the severity of impact of the law on the property in question and thereby prevents it from effecting a "taking" under the Fifth Amendment. Affirmed.

ANALYSIS

Many jurisdictions now have what is called "historic zoning" legislation, which obligates owners of historic buildings to preserve and maintain the exterior appearance. Although this imposes a direct financial burden instead of simply limiting use of the property, such laws have consistently been upheld.

Quicknotes

FIFTH AMENDMENT Provides that no person shall be compelled to serve as a witness against himself, or be subject to trial for the same offense twice, or be deprived of life, liberty, or property without due process of law.

PUBLIC USE Basis for governmental taking of property pursuant to its power of eminent domain so that property taken may be utilized for the benefit of the public at large.

TAKING A governmental action that substantially deprives an owner of the use and enjoyment of his property, requiring compensation.

ZONING Municipal statutory scheme dividing an area into districts in order to regulate the use or building of structures within those districts.

Lucas v. South Carolina Coastal Council

Beachfront property owner (P) v. State (D)

505 U.S. 1003 (1992).

NATURE OF CASE: Appeal from reversal of award of damages in action for compensation under the Takings Clause.

FACT SUMMARY: After Lucas (P) invested $975,000 in two beachfront lots, South Carolina (D) enacted a statute prohibiting construction on the barrier islands where the lots were located, entitling him, he contended, to compensation under the Takings Clause.

RULE OF LAW

The state must compensate a landowner when a regulatory action denies an owner economically viable use of his land, unless the prohibited use of the land constitutes a nuisance under state common law.

FACTS: Lucas (P) purchased two residential lots for $975,000 on the Isle of Palms, a barrier island off the coast of South Carolina, on which he planned to build single-family homes. The Isle of Palms development, of which Lucas (P) was a co-owner, was located on highly unstable ground, prone to flooding and erosion. At the time of purchase, the state, county and town had not imposed any restrictions on residential use of the property. However, two years after Lucas's (P) purchase, but before he began construction, South Carolina (D) enacted the Beachfront Management Act, in an attempt to counteract the critical erosion of South Carolina beaches. The Act prohibited, without exception, the construction of any habitable improvements seaward of a baseline connecting historical points of erosion on the Isle of Palms. Lucas's (P) lots were located within the restricted area. He filed suit against South Carolina (D), contending that the Act's ban on construction amounted to a taking of his property without just compensation. He conceded that the Act was a lawful exercise of South Carolina's (D) police power but claimed that the Act rendered his property valueless, entitling him to compensation. The trial court agreed and ordered South Carolina (D) to pay $1,232,387. The Supreme Court of South Carolina reversed, ruling that when an otherwise valid regulation respecting the use of property is designed to prevent public harm, as this Act was, no compensation was owed. Lucas (P) appealed, and the U.S. Supreme Court granted certiorari.

ISSUE: Must the state compensate a landowner when a regulatory action denies an owner economically viable use of his land?

HOLDING AND DECISION: (Scalia, J.) Yes. The state must compensate a landowner when a regulatory action denies an owner economically valuable use of his land, unless the prohibited use of the land constitutes a nuisance under state common law. Traditionally, compensation has been required for two separate categories of regulatory actions: (1) those that cause a physical invasion of private property and (2) those that deprive a landowner of all economically beneficial or productive use of land. However, there is also a long line of cases denying compensation to owners whose property is regulated to prevent a public harm, the seminal case being *Mugler v. Kansas*, 123 U.S. 623 (1887), in which a law prohibiting the manufacture of alcoholic beverages was sustained against a taking claim brought by a brewery owner. Under this line of cases, regulation of "harmful or noxious uses" of property was allowed to affect property values without obligating the government to pay compensation. This early focus on noxious uses later evolved into the Court's contemporary analysis that finds no taking if a land-use regulation substantially advances a legitimate state interest. Whether the regulation prevents a harmful use can no longer be the basis for an exception from the rule that total regulatory taking must be compensated; if it were, no compensation would ever be necessary, since most regulations may be described as mitigating some harm, depending on the observer's point of view. Instead, a better test is that confiscatory regulations, i.e., those that prohibit all economically beneficial use of land, may not be enacted without compensation, unless the regulation serves to prohibit a purpose that was already unlawful under existing nuisance and property law. In this case, the Act rendered Lucas's (P) lots valueless by requiring that they remain in their natural state. Therefore, South Carolina (D) must either identify the relevant common-law principles of nuisance and property that would prohibit construction on Lucas's (P) beachfront property or compensate him for the value of his property. Reversed and remanded.

CONCURRENCE: (Kennedy, J.) The trial court's finding that Lucas's (P) land had been deprived of all beneficial use is highly questionable. Furthermore, the nuisance exception should not be the sole justification for severe restrictions when the state's unique concerns for fragile land systems are involved.

DISSENT: (Blackmun, J.) This Court has consistently upheld regulations that prohibit an owner from using his property in a way that is harmful to the public. Lucas (P) never challenged the legislature's findings that a building ban was necessary to protect property and life and, therefore, the lower court correctly found no taking. Now, with this case, the majority has created a new rule and an exception, based on the trial court's finding that the property had lost all economic value. Furthermore, the majority

Continued on next page.

alters the traditional rule that the plaintiff challenge the constitutionality of an ordinance, by requiring the state to convince the courts that its legislative judgments are correct. Finally, the majority decides that it will permit a state to regulate all economic value only if the state prohibits uses that would not be permitted under state common law, notwithstanding that the Court has previously and explicitly rejected any consideration of a nuisance when evaluating a taking. There is no reason to believe the majority's claim that new interpretation of old common-law nuisance doctrine will be any more objective or value-free than reliance on legislative judgments of what constitutes a harm.

DISSENT: (Stevens, J.) The majority's categorical rule that total regulatory takings must be compensated is an unsound and unwise addition to the law, unsupported by prior decisions, and its exception to that rule is too rigid and too narrow. Because the majority's new rule only applies to total regulatory takings, it arbitrarily awards compensation to a landowner whose property is diminished by 100 percent, while denying compensation to one who suffers a 95 percent diminishment. Furthermore, the Court's holding effectively freezes a state's traditional common law, making it immune to legislative revision.

ANALYSIS

Note the central debate in *Lucas* is actually over who should have the authority to allocate loss. *Lucas* allocates the authority to decide which regulations will require compensation to the state judiciary, rather than to the state legislature. *Lucas* implies that the state's ability to completely extinguish the value of a parcel of land gives it too much power and potential for excessive legislative regulation, necessitating an independent judicial determination of what constitutes a nuisance. Although *Lucas* was the most closely watched land use case of 1991 (over 50 amicus briefs were filed), its impact may turn out to be relatively slight since its fact pattern is relatively rare.

Quicknotes

NUISANCE An unlawful use of property that interferes with the lawful use of another's property.

TAKINGS CLAUSE Provision of the Fifth Amendment to the United States Constitution, prohibiting the government from taking private property for public use without providing just compensation therefor.

Palazzolo v. Rhode Island

Developer (P) v. State (D)

533 U.S. 606 (2001).

NATURE OF CASE: Appeal from state supreme court judgment rejecting a takings claim in an inverse condemnation action.

FACT SUMMARY: Palazzolo (P) brought an inverse condemnation suit against the State of Rhode Island (D) after his development proposals for a parcel of waterfront property were rejected.

RULE OF LAW

A purchaser or successive title holder of land is not barred from bringing a regulatory takings claim by the mere fact that the title was acquired after the effective date of the state regulation alleged to effect the taking.

FACTS: Palazzolo (P) owned a waterfront parcel of land, almost all of which was designated as coastal wetlands prior to his acquisition of the land. After his development proposals for a residential subdivision were rejected, he filed suit in state court claiming the State of Rhode Island's (D) application of its wetlands regulations constituted a taking in violation of the Fifth Amendment's Takings Clause. The Rhode Island Supreme Court rejected the claim that Palazzolo (P) was denied all economically beneficial use of the property since the uplands portion of the property could still be developed. The state court also ruled that because the regulation predated Palazzolo's (P) ownership of the property, he was precluded from bringing a takings claim challenging the regulation. Finally, the court also held that the case was not ripe for adjudication. Palazzolo (P) appealed, and the U.S. Supreme Court granted certiorari.

ISSUE: Is a purchaser or successive title holder of land barred from bringing a regulatory takings claim by the mere fact that the title was acquired after the effective date of the state regulation alleged to effect the taking?

HOLDING AND DECISION: (Kennedy, J.) No. A purchaser or successive title holder of land is not barred from bringing a regulatory takings claim by the mere fact that the title was acquired after the effective date of the state regulation alleged to effect the taking. The state court was correct in deciding that all economically viable use of the property was not deprived, because the uplands portion of the property could still be developed. The state court erred, however, in determining that the case was not ripe for adjudication. Finally, the state court also was incorrect that postenactment purchasers can never challenge a regulation under the Takings Clause. The State's (D) sweeping rule, that a purchaser or a successive title holder is deemed to have notice of an earlier-enacted restriction and is barred from claiming that it effects a taking would absolve the State of its obligation to defend any action restricting land use, no matter how extreme or unreasonable. A State would be allowed, in effect, to put an expiration date on the Takings Clause. This ought not to be the rule. Future generations, too, have a right to challenge unreasonable limitations on the use and value of land. The State's notice justification does not take into account the effect on owners at the time of enactment, who are prejudiced as well. Should an owner attempt to challenge a new regulation, but not survive the process of ripening his or her claim (which, as this case demonstrates, will often take years), under the State's (D) rule the right to compensation may not be asserted by an heir or successor, and so may not be asserted at all. The State's (D) rule also would work a critical alteration to the nature of property, as the newly regulated landowner is stripped of the ability to transfer the interest which was possessed prior to the regulation. The State (D) may not by this means secure a windfall for itself. The rule is, furthermore, capricious in effect. The young owner contrasted with the older owner, the owner with the resources to hold contrasted with the owner with the need to sell, would be in different positions. The Takings Clause is not so quixotic. A blanket rule that purchasers with notice have no compensation right when a claim becomes ripe is too blunt an instrument to accord with the duty to compensate for what is taken. Thus, on remand, the court must address the merits of Palazzolo's (P) *Penn Central Transportation Co. v. City of New York*, 438 U.S. 104 (1978), claim. Affirmed in part, reversed in part, and remanded.

CONCURRENCE: (O'Connor, J.) *Penn Central* still controls. Under that analysis interference with investment-backed expectations is one of a number of factors that a court must examine. The regulatory scheme at the time the property is acquired also shapes the reasonableness of the claimant's expectations.

CONCURRENCE: (Scalia, J.) The investment-backed expectations the law will take into account on remand do not include the assumed validity of a restriction that in fact deprives property of so much of its value that it is an unconstitutional taking.

CONCURRENCE AND DISSENT: (Stevens, J.) Palazzolo (P) is the wrong person to be bringing this action; if anyone is to be compensated it is the owner of the property at the time the regulations were adopted.

Continued on next page.

DISSENT: (Ginsburg, J.) The Rhode Island Supreme Court was correct in finding that the claim was not ripe for several reasons including that Palazzolo (P) had not sought permission for development of the upland portion of the property only.

DISSENT: (Breyer, J.) As Justice O'Connor says in her concurrence, the simple fact that property has changed hands (e.g., by inheritance) does not always and automatically bar a takings claim, nor is the fact that one acquires the subject property after a regulatory law has been enacted dispositive of the issue, although that is a relevant factor.

ANALYSIS

The Court here did away with the prior rule under *Lucas v. South Carolina Coastal Council*, 505 U.S. 100. (1992) and *Penn Central* that a purchaser or successive title holder was deemed to have notice of an earlier-enacted restriction and was barred from bringing a takings claim. The Court also held that a state does not avoid the duty to compensate based on a "token interest." So long as a landowner is permitted to build a substantial residence on the parcel, then it is not deemed to constitute a deprivation of all economic value.

Quicknotes

FIFTH AMENDMENT Provides that no person shall be compelled to serve as a witness against himself, or be subject to trial for the same offense twice, or be deprived of life, liberty, or property without due process of law.

NOTICE Communication of information to a person by an authorized person or an otherwise proper source.

INVERSE CONDEMNATION The taking of private property for public use so as to impair or decrease the value of property near or adjacent to, but not a part of, the property taken.

TAKING A governmental action that substantially deprives an owner of the use and enjoyment of his or her property, requiring compensation.

Tahoe-Sierra Preservation Council, Inc. v. Tahoe Regional Planning Agency

Landowners (P) v. Regional planning agency (D)

535 U.S. 302 (2002).

NATURE OF CASE: Appeal from reversal of judgment finding a per se taking of property.

FACT SUMMARY: Tahoe Regional Planning Agency (TRPA) (D) imposed two moratoria, totaling 32 months, on development in the Lake Tahoe Basin while formulating a comprehensive land-use plan for the area. Landowners (P) affected by the moratoria filed suit, claiming that TRPA's (D) actions constituted a taking of their property without just compensation in violation of the Takings Clause.

RULE OF LAW

A moratorium on development imposed during the process of devising a comprehensive land-use plan does not constitute a per se taking of property requiring compensation under the Takings Clause.

FACTS: Tahoe Regional Planning Agency (TRPA) (D) imposed two moratoria, one, from 1981 to 1983, and a more restrictive one, from 1983 to 1984, totaling 32 months, on development in the Lake Tahoe region while formulating a comprehensive land-use plan of environmentally sound growth for the area. The moratoria were triggered by the increased pollution of Lake Tahoe from accelerating development of the area. During the moratoria, virtually all development was prohibited. Landowners (P) affected by the moratoria filed suit, claiming that TRPA's (D) actions constituted a taking of their property without just compensation in violation of the Takings Clause. The district court found a taking, but the court of appeals reversed. The U.S. Supreme Court granted certiorari.

ISSUE: Does a moratorium on development imposed during the process of devising a comprehensive land-use plan constitute a per se taking of property requiring compensation under the Takings Clause?

HOLDING AND DECISION: (Stevens, J.) No. A moratorium on development imposed during the process of devising a comprehensive land-use plan does not constitute a per se taking of property requiring compensation under the Takings Clause. The attack on the moratoria is only facial. The landowners contend that the mere enactment of a temporary regulation that, while in effect, denies a property owner of all viable economic use of the property gives rise to an unqualified constitutional obligation to compensate for the value of the property's use during that period. The landowners want a categorical rule, but the Court's cases do not support such a rule. The answer to any given case depends on the particular circumstances of the case, and the circumstances in this case are best analyzed within the framework of *Penn Central Transp. Co. v. New York* (1978). The long-standing distinction between physical and regulatory takings makes it inappropriate to treat precedent from one as controlling on the other. The landowners (P) in this case rely on *First English Evangelical Lutheran Church of Glendale v. County of Los Angeles*, 482 U.S. 304 (1987) and *Lucas v. South Carolina Coastal Council*, 505 U.S. 1003 (1992)—both regulatory takings cases—to argue for a categorical rule that whenever the government imposes a deprivation of all economically viable use of property, no matter how brief, it effects a taking. In *First English*, the Court addressed the separate remedial question of how compensation is measured once a regulatory taking is established, but not the different and prior question whether the temporary regulation was in fact a taking. Nor is *Lucas* dispositive of the question presented. Its categorical rule—requiring compensation when a regulation permanently deprives an owner of "all economically beneficial uses" of his land—does not answer the question whether a regulation prohibiting any economic use of land for 32 months must be compensated. The landowners (P) attempt to bring this case under the rule in *Lucas* by focusing exclusively on the property during the moratoria is unavailing. This Court has consistently rejected such an approach to the "denominator" question. To sever a 32-month segment from the remainder of each fee simple estate and then ask whether that segment has been taken in its entirety would ignore *Penn Central*'s admonition to focus on "the parcel as a whole." Both dimensions of a real property interest—the metes and bounds describing its geographic dimensions and the term of years describing its temporal aspect—must be considered when viewing the interest in its entirety. A permanent deprivation of all use is a taking of the parcel as a whole, but a temporary restriction causing a diminution in value is not, for the property will recover value when the prohibition is lifted. *Lucas* was carved out for the "extraordinary case" in which a regulation permanently deprives property of all use; the default rule remains that a fact specific inquiry is required in the regulatory taking context. Nevertheless, the Court will consider the landowners' (P) argument that the interest in protecting property owners from bearing public burdens "which, in all fairness and justice, should be borne by the public as a whole," justifies creating a new categorical rule. "Fairness and justice" will not be better served by a categorical rule that any deprivation of all economic use, no matter how brief, constitutes a compensable taking. That

Continued on next page.

rule would apply to numerous normal delays—in obtaining building permits, variances, zoning changes, etc.—and would require changes in practices that have long been considered permissible exercises of the police power. Such an important change in the law should be the product of legislative rulemaking, not adjudication. More importantly, the better approach to a temporary regulatory taking claim requires careful examination and weighing of all the relevant circumstances—only one of which is the length of the delay. A narrower rule excluding normal delays in processing permits, or covering only delays of more than a year, would have a less severe impact on prevailing practices, but would still impose serious constraints on the planning process. Moratoria are an essential tool of successful development. The interest in informed decision-making counsels against adopting a per se rule that would treat such interim measures as takings—regardless of the planners' good faith, the landowners' reasonable expectations, or the moratorium's actual impact on property values. The financial constraints of compensating property owners during a moratorium may force officials to rush through the planning process or abandon the practice altogether. And the interest in protecting the decisional process is even stronger when an agency is developing a regional plan than when it is considering a permit for a single parcel. Here, TRPA (D) obtained the benefit of comments and criticisms from interested parties during its deliberations, but a categorical rule tied to the deliberations' length would likely create added pressure on decision makers to quickly resolve land-use questions, disadvantaging landowners and interest groups less organized or familiar with the planning process. Moreover, with a temporary development ban, there is less risk that individual landowners will be singled out to bear a special burden that should be shared by the public as a whole. It may be true that a moratorium lasting more than one year should be viewed with special skepticism, but the district court found that the instant delay was not unreasonable. The restriction's duration is one factor for a court to consider in appraising regulatory takings claims, but with respect to that factor, the temptation to adopt per se rules in either direction must be resisted. Affirmed.

DISSENT: (Rehnquist, C.J.) The relevant time frame here is not, as the majority indicates, 32 months, but rather it is six years because the 1984 Regional Plan that was implemented after the moratoria were lifted also denied landowners (P) all use of their property until 1987, thus extending the period from 1981 to 1987. Neither the takings clause nor the Court's precedent, supports a distinction between "temporary" and "permanent" prohibitions. Such a distinction is tenuous—here, the "temporary" prohibition lasted six years, whereas the "permanent" prohibition in *Lucas* lasted only two years. Using this distinction, the government only has to label its prohibition "temporary" in order avoid compensation. Such a designation would not preclude the government from repeatedly extending the "temporary" prohibition into a long-term ban on all development. Even if a practical distinction between temporary and permanent deprivations were plausible, to treat the two differently in terms of takings law would be at odds with the justification for the *Lucas* rule. The *Lucas* rule is derived from the fact that a total deprivation of use is, from the landowner's point of view, the equivalent of a physical appropriation. Because the rationale for the *Lucas* rule applies just as strongly in this case, the "temporary" denial of all viable use of land for six years is a taking. The majority is concerned that applying *Lucas* here would compel a finding that many traditional, short-term, land-use planning devices are takings. However, the Court has recognized that property rights are enjoyed under an implied limitation. When a regulation merely delays a final land use decision, there are other background principles of state property law that prevent the delay from being deemed a taking, as in the case of normal delays in obtaining building permits, changes in zoning ordinances, variances, and the like. Thus, the short-term delays attendant to zoning and permit regimes are a longstanding feature of state property law and part of a landowner's reasonable investment-backed expectations. But a moratorium prohibiting all economic use for a period of six years is not one of the longstanding, implied limitations of state property law. As is the case with most governmental action that furthers the public interest, here the preservation of Lake Tahoe should be borne by the public at large and not just by a few landowners, and the moratoria constitute a taking that requires compensation.

DISSENT: (Thomas, J.) The majority's conclusion that the temporary moratorium at issue here was not a taking because it was not a "taking of 'the parcel as a whole.'" This position was rejected in the context of *temporal* deprivations of property by *First English*, which held that temporary and permanent takings "are not different in kind" when a landowner is deprived of all beneficial use of his land. Thus, a total deprivation of the use of a so-called "temporal slice" of property is compensable under the Takings Clause unless background principles of state property law prevent it from being deemed a taking. Regulations prohibiting all productive uses of property are subject to *Lucas*'s per se rule regardless of whether the property retains theoretical useful life and value, if and when, the "temporary" moratorium is lifted. Such potential future value, which the majority assures will be recovered upon lifting the moratorium, bears on the amount of compensation due and not on whether there was a taking in the first place.

ANALYSIS

With this case, the majority of the Court seems to have adopted the approach recommended by Justice O'Connor's concurring opinion in *Palazzolo v. Rhode Island,* 533

Continued on next page.

U.S. 606 (2001)—namely, an ad hoc approach that evaluates the circumstances of each case using the *Penn Central* framework—and rejected a categorical rule for all regulatory takings cases. The majority also seemed to resolve the "denominator" issue that had hitherto been unsettled in takings jurisprudence.

Quicknotes

LAND-USE PLAN General plan for real estate, including local zoning ordinances or real estate development scheme.

PER SE An activity that is so inherently obvious that it is unnecessary to examine its underlying validity. By itself; not requiring additional evidence for proof.

TAKING A governmental action that substantially deprives an owner of the use and enjoyment of his property, requiring compensation.

Dolan v. City of Tigard

Waterfront property owner (P) v. City (D)

512 U.S. 374 (1994).

NATURE OF CASE: Review of an appeal upholding the denial of a variance to local zoning provisions.

FACT SUMMARY: The City of Tigard (D) required an easement for a public bike path and flood control area as a condition to issuing a permit for property redevelopment.

RULE OF LAW

A conditional grant of a building permit is constitutional, only if a reasonable relationship exists between the exactions demanded by the city's permit and a legitimate state interest.

FACTS: Dolan (P) owned a business near a creek, and she wanted to expand the business on her property. The City of Tigard (City) (D) required that 15 percent of land on each parcel be left as open space and that any development in or near the 100-year creek floodplain be accompanied by a land dedication sufficient to develop a vegetation greenway in the floodplain to minimize flood damage. The City (D) also required that new developments dedicate a pedestrian/bike path to promote alternative transportation. The City (D) made certain findings that the bike path might reduce traffic congestion. The City (D) also found that impervious surfaces, such as cement pavement, increased the risk of severe flooding along Fanno Creek. Dolan (P) sought a variance to the required dedications of a greenway and bike path along the creek and was denied. She appealed to the Land Use Board of Appeals, which upheld the Commission findings. The court of appeals affirmed.

ISSUE: Must a reasonable relationship exist between the exactions demanded by the city's permit and a legitimate state interest for a conditional building permit to be constitutional?

HOLDING AND DECISION: (Rehnquist, C.J.) Yes. A conditional grant of a building permit is constitutional only if a reasonable relationship exists between the exactions demanded by the city's permit and a legitimate state interest. The primary purpose of the Takings Clause is to prohibit government from forcing some people to bear public burdens that, in all fairness, should be borne by the public as a whole. On the other hand, land-use planning has been upheld as a necessary incident to government activity designed to protect the larger interests of the public. However, land-use regulation must not exact an overly burdensome economic cost. If a city is going to exact dedications of property as a condition to issuing a building permit for a development, then the exaction must show the required relationship to the impact of the development. Here, it is hard to see how recreational visitors using a floodplain easement are sufficiently related to the City's (D) legitimate interest in reducing flooding problems. The City (D) has not shown that it considered other alternatives in reducing the flooding problem. And as to the bicycle path, the City (D) has made no showing of how much traffic will be reduced by the required exaction of such a path. Dolan (P) lost the ability to control access to her property. Reversed and remanded.

DISSENT: (Stevens, J.) Previously, the Court has required that the analysis focus on the impact of city regulation on the entire parcel of private property. Here, the parcel has been divided into discrete segments to see if rights are abrogated along one sliver. The restrictions in this case do not unreasonably impair the value or use of Dolan's (P) property.

ANALYSIS

Many cities require "impact" fees to be paid for new developments. After this decision, the Supreme Court upheld fees that were arguably no more closely related to the governmental purpose than the exactions in *Dolan*. But the Supreme Court felt that exactions of physical interest in private property are the most invasive, thus requiring "heightened scrutiny."

Quicknotes

EASEMENT The right to utilize a portion of another's real property for a specific use.

TAKINGS CLAUSE Provision of the Fifth Amendment to the United States Constitution prohibiting the government from taking private property for public use without providing just compensation therefor.

CHAPTER 33

Exclusion, Discrimination, Equal Protection and Due Process

Quick Reference Rules of Law

Village of Arlington Heights v. Metropolitan Housing Development Corp.

Municipality (D) v. Developer (P)

429 U.S. 252 (1977).

NATURE OF CASE: Challenge to a zoning ordinance.

FACT SUMMARY: The Village of Arlington Heights's (D) zoning ordinance prevented construction of low- and moderate-income housing.

RULE OF LAW

Unless one of the grounds for a zoning decision involves racial discrimination, a zoning ordinance that has an indirect adverse impact on minorities is not unconstitutional.

FACTS: Village of Arlington Heights (Village) (D) was almost exclusively zoned for single-family residences. Metropolitan Housing Development Corp. (P) (MHDC) wanted to build low- and moderate-income cluster housing on a 15-acre tract at the outskirts of the Village (D). Three public hearings were held to determine whether the area should be rezoned for multi-unit residences. A number of speakers raised racial issues since the development would be approximately 40 percent black in order to qualify for federal funds. The Village (D) focused on reduction in neighboring property value and the need for a buffer zone as grounds for denying the rezoning request. The Village (D) was almost 100 percent white and no other suitable site for such housing was available in the Village (D). MHDC (P) brought an action in federal court alleging that the denial was racially discriminatory, violating the Fourteenth Amendment and the Fair Housing Act of 1968. Both the district court and the court of appeals found that the Village (D) had no racial motive in its action; the ordinances had been adopted many years earlier; other rezoning requests had been denied for similar reasons. It was held that the incidental impact of the ordinance was racially discriminatory and that this was sufficient to constitute a Fourteenth Amendment violation.

ISSUE: Must there be a racially discriminatory motive before a zoning ordinance can be deemed violative of the Fourteenth Amendment?

HOLDING AND DECISION: (Powell, J.) Yes. No Fourteenth Amendment violation may be found merely because an ordinance has a discriminatory effect. There must be a showing that there was some racially discriminatory motive behind its adoption. It need not be the principal motive or even an important one, but it must be present. The motive may be inferred from the conduct, speech or other circumstantial evidence. Here, there was no discriminatory motive found and the evidence bears this out. The ordinance is valid. The allegation that the ordinance violated the Fair Housing Act was not considered below, and we remand for consideration of this issue. Reversed and remanded.

ANALYSIS

Where the impact of official action bears more heavily on one race than another, it is an indication (but no more) that there may be a racially discriminatory motive. *Washington v. Davis*, 426 U.S. at 242 (1976). This, however, is a mere starting point. There must be some reasonably clear pattern, unexplainable on any other ground but race, to establish that apparently neutral legislation is racially motivated. *Yick Wo v. Hopkins*, 118 U.S. 356 (1886).

Quicknotes

CIRCUMSTANTIAL EVIDENCE Evidence that, though not directly observed, supports the inference of principal facts.

ZONING ORDINANCE A statute that divides land into defined areas and which regulates the form and use of buildings and structures within those areas.

City of Cleburne, Texas v. Cleburne Living Center, Inc.

Municipality (D) v. Group home for the mentally disabled (P)

473 U.S. 432 (1985).

NATURE OF CASE: Appeal of order enjoining enforcement of zoning ordinance.

FACT SUMMARY: In reviewing a local ordinance that regulated group housing of the feeble-minded, the court of appeals imposed a heightened-scrutiny standard of review and found the ordinance to deny equal protection.

RULE OF LAW

Mental retardation is not a suspect or quasi-suspect classification requiring heightened judicial scrutiny.

FACTS: The City of Cleburne, Texas (City) (D) had zoned certain portions of the city to permit group housing. Certain types of such housing required a special use permit. One such use was group housing of the "insane" or "feeble-minded." The Cleburne Living Center, Inc. (Center) (P) applied for such a use. Citing neighbors' fears and concerns about occupants' interactions with an adjacent junior high school, the permit was denied. The Center (P) sued, contending that the ordinance denied equal protection. The district court entered judgment in favor of the City (D). The Fifth Circuit reversed, finding retardation to be a quasi-suspect class and that the City (D) therefore had to justify the ordinance under a heightened-scrutiny standard of review. The City (D) obtained review in the U.S. Supreme Court.

ISSUE: Is mental retardation a suspect or quasi-suspect classification requiring heightened judicial scrutiny?

HOLDING AND DECISION: (White, J.) No. Mental retardation is not a suspect or quasi-suspect classification requiring heightened judicial scrutiny. Generally speaking, governmental regulation is presumptively valid, and must only be shown to be rationally related to a legitimate governmental objective to be valid. Certain classifications, such as race or national origin, are presumed to bear no relation to legitimate governmental interests, so strict scrutiny requiring the showing of a compelling interest will be imposed. Gender is a classification that does sometimes further governmental interests but usually does not, and an intermediate level of scrutiny, which requires substantial relation to important governmental interests, is required. Here, the court of appeals placed mental retardation into this latter category. This was improper. Mental retardation has several characteristics that make it appropriate for governmental regulation. First, persons so affected do have a reduced ability to cope with and function in the world. Second, the retarded do have differing ability levels. As a consequence of this, regulating how they are treated is a legitimate governmental activity. In light of this, heightened scrutiny is not appropriate. [The Court went on to hold that, under the rational basis standard of review, the regulation was not valid. The Court ruled that differing treatment accorded the retarded in this case from other group living arrangements in the City (D) was based on irrational fear and prejudice, not legitimate policy considerations.] Affirmed in part, vacated in part, and remanded.

CONCURRENCE AND DISSENT: (Marshall, J.) The Court says it imposes only a rational basis test. However, under traditional rational basis scrutiny, the regulation would certainly have been valid. The Court has in fact imposed heightened scrutiny, but has failed to so articulate.

ANALYSIS

The Court's equal protection analysis has become more complicated in recent years. Formerly, a strict dichotomy existed: strict scrutiny and rational basis. In 1973, the Court adopted intermediate review to apply to gender. Further complicating matters is the present case. In years past, a regulation would always survive rational basis review; here it did not. The Court appears to have toughened its rational basis review, without so stating.

Quicknotes

HEIGHTENED SCRUTINY A purposefully vague judicial description of all levels of scrutiny more exacting than minimal scrutiny.

STRICT SCRUTINY The method by which courts determine the constitutionality of a law, when a law affects a fundamental right. Under the test, the legislature must have had a compelling interest to enact the law and measures prescribed by the law must be the least restrictive means possible to accomplish its goal.

ZONING ORDINANCE A statute that divides land into defined areas and which regulates the form and use of buildings and structures within those areas.

Bay Area Addiction Research and Treatment, Inc. v. City of Antioch

Methadone clinic (P) v. City (D)

179 F.3d 725 (9th Cir. 1999).

NATURE OF CASE: Suit under the Americans with Disabilities Act and the Rehabilitation Act.

FACT SUMMARY: Bay Area Addiction Research and Treatment, Inc. (BAART) (P) brought suit against the City of Antioch (D) claiming its passing of a municipal ordinance precluding the operation of methadone clinics within 500 feet of residential areas was in violation of the Americans with Disabilities Act and the Rehabilitation Act among others.

RULE OF LAW

Title II of the Americans with Disabilities Act and § 504 of the Rehabilitation Act apply to zoning ordinances.

FACTS: In 1998 Bay Area Addiction Research and Treatment, Inc. (BAART) (P) tried to relocate its methadone clinic to the City of Antioch (D). After BAART (P) was notified that the proposed location could be used for the clinic, the city council enacted an urgency ordinance prohibiting the operation of methadone clinics within 500 feet of residential areas, precluding the use of the proposed site. BAART (P) brought suit against Antioch (D) under the Americans with Disabilities Act. The district court denied BAART's (P) motion for a preliminary injunction enjoining the urgency ordinance. BAART (P) appealed, arguing that the district court applied the wrong legal test to its Americans with Disabilities Act and Rehabilitation Act claims and misjudged the irreparability of harm it would suffer if an injunction did not issue.

ISSUE: Do Title II of the Americans with Disabilities Act and § 504 of the Rehabilitation Act apply to zoning ordinances?

HOLDING AND DECISION: (Tashima, J.) Yes. Title II of the Americans with Disabilities Act and § 504 of the Rehabilitation Act apply to zoning ordinances. Section 12132 of the Americans with Disabilities Act prohibits discrimination on the basis of disability by public entities, providing that no individual shall "be excluded from participation in or be denied the benefits of the services, programs, or activities of a public entity." Antioch (D) argued that zoning is not such a service, program or activity and therefore § 12132 does not apply. This is erroneous. The Rehabilitation Act defines "program or activity" as "all of the operations of" a local government. Because these two statutes are to be interpreted consistently, both apply to zoning. This does not end the inquiry. Section 12131 defines the class of individuals entitled to its protection and includes a test that evaluates the risk posed by an individual. An individual who poses a significant risk to the health or safety of others that cannot be ameliorated by means of a reasonable modification is not a qualified individual under § 12131. The district court should have used the significant risk test to analyze the threat posed here by BAART (P). The district court abused its discretion in applying an erroneous legal standard to determine whether to grant BAART's (P) motion for a preliminary injunction. To obtain a preliminary injunction, BAART (P) must demonstrate either both probable success on the merits and irreparable injury or serious questions are raised and the balance of hardships tips in its favor. These questions must be resolved on remand. Since the ordinance facially discriminates on the basis of BAART's (P) disability in violation of § 12132, to establish a likelihood of success on the merits, BAART (P) must show that it is likely that it does not pose a significant risk to the health or safety of the community. Reversed and remanded.

ANALYSIS

In determining whether an individual poses a significant risk under the test set forth here, the court must first inquire whether a reasonable modification exists that would eliminate the risk. If so, then the individual is qualified for purposes of the Americans with Disabilities Act. If not, the court never need reach the issue of whether there exists a reasonable modification. It is not enough for purposes of the statute that the individual poses a hypothetical or presumed risk, but he or she must pose a significant risk of a serious nature.

Quicknotes

AMERICANS WITH DISABILITIES ACT (ADA) Prohibits discrimination in employment, housing, transportation and other services on the basis of an individual's physical or mental disabilities.

IRREPARABLE INJURY Such harm that because it is either too great, too small or of a continuing character that it cannot be properly compensated in damages, and the remedy for which is typically injunctive relief.

CHAPTER 34

Religious Land Uses

Quick Reference Rules of Law

Messiah Baptist Church v. County of Jefferson, State of Colorado

Property owner (P) v. County government (D)

859 F.2d 820 (10th Cir. 1988).

NATURE OF CASE: Appeal of summary judgment dismissing action for damages for civil rights violation.

FACT SUMMARY: The County of Jefferson, Colorado (D) enacted a zoning ordinance which had the effect of prohibiting the use of buildings as houses of worship.

RULE OF LAW

A local government may enact a zoning plan which has the effect of prohibiting the use of buildings as houses of worship.

FACTS: In 1974, Messiah Baptist Church (Church) (P) purchased certain improved property zoned for certain agricultural uses. The Church (P) applied for a permit to erect a building to be used as a church, along with administrative offices. This was denied. In 1976, the ordinance was changed to allow church uses by special-use permit, subject to County of Jefferson, Colorado (County) (D) approval. In 1978, the Church (P) again applied for a permit, this time to erect a rather extensive church and administrative complex. Citing concerns with access problems, erosion hazards, and inadequate local fire protection, the permit was denied. The Church (P) brought an action under 42 U.S.C. § 1983, seeking damages for violation of constitutional rights. The district court granted summary judgment dismissing the County (D), and the Church (P) appealed.

ISSUE: May a local government enact a zoning plan which has the effect of prohibiting the use of buildings as houses of worship?

HOLDING AND DECISION: (Brorby, J.) Yes. A local government may enact a zoning plan which has the effect of prohibiting the use of buildings as houses of worship. Under due process analysis, a zoning ordinance will be declared unconstitutional only if it is clearly arbitrary and not substantially related to public health, safety, morals, or welfare. The reasons cited by the County (D) here all fall well within these criteria, and the due process argument must fail. More problematic is the Church's (P) contention that the ordinance interferes with the Free Exercise Clause of the First Amendment. The initial inquiry in this area is whether the challenged regulation attempts to regulate belief or conduct. Only the latter case can be valid, and the regulation here does in fact have the effect of regulating, at most, religious conduct. When religious conduct is regulated, such regulation will be upheld if it does not unduly burden conduct which is not integrally related to belief. While a house of worship is no doubt integral to most religion, there is no evidence here that erection of a church on the site in question is integral to any tenant of the Church's (P) belief system. The regulation does not prohibit church erection in toto, but only in selected zones. Therefore, the conclusion must be that the regulation does not proscribe conduct integral to the Church's (P) belief system, and that it therefore does not run afoul of the Free Exercise Clause. Affirmed.

ANALYSIS

The Free Exercise Clause comes into conflict with state power in a variety of contexts, only one of which is land use. Historically, the Supreme Court has tended to favor the clause over governmental attempts to regulate. In recent years, however, the pattern has been reversed. Examples include Employment Division, State of *Oregon v. Smith*, 494 U.S. 872 (1990), and *Goldman v. Weinberger*, 475 U.S. 503 (1986). *Smith* involved a First Amendment challenge to a state law prohibiting the use of peyote, and *Goldman* involved a challenge to military dress regulations that had the effect of prohibiting religious headwear. In both cases the challenges were rejected.

Quicknotes

DUE PROCESS The constitutional mandate requiring the courts to protect and enforce individuals' rights and liberties consistent with prevailing principles of fairness and justice and prohibiting the federal and state governments from such activities that deprive its citizens of life, liberty, or property interest.

FREE EXERCISE CLAUSE The guarantee of the First Amendment to the United States Constitution prohibiting Congress from enacting laws regarding the establishment of religion or prohibiting the free exercise thereof.

SUMMARY JUDGMENT Judgment rendered by a court in response to a motion made by one of the parties, claiming that the lack of a question of material fact in respect to an issue warrants disposition of the issue without consideration by the jury.

ZONING ORDINANCE A statute that divides land into defined areas and which regulates the form and use of buildings and structures within those areas.

Civil Liberties for Urban Believers v. City of Chicago

Religious association (P) v. Municipality (D)

342 F.3d 752 (7th Cir. 2003).

NATURE OF CASE: Suit challenging a municipal zoning ordinance.

FACT SUMMARY: An association of churches challenged a municipal zoning ordinance for alleged violations of the U.S. Constitution and the federal Religious Land Use and Institutionalized Persons Act.

RULE OF LAW

The Chicago Zoning Ordinance does not substantially burden religious exercise in violation of the Religious Land Use and Institutionalized Persons Act or violate the free exercise, freedom of speech, freedom of assembly, equal protection, or procedural due process guarantees of the U.S. Constitution.

FACTS: Chicago's Zoning Ordinance (CZO) specifies R, B, C, and M zones regulating residential, business, commercial, and manufacturing land uses in the City (D). Most land available for development in Chicago lies in R zones, in which churches are permitted uses as of right. The CZO considers churches to be special uses in all B and C1, C2, C3, and C5 zones, however, and the process of acquiring approval for a special use from the zoning board can cost almost $5,000. Churches can locate in C4 or M zones only if the Chicago City Council first votes to, in effect, rezone such areas to permit church use. Civil Liberties for Urban Believers (CLUB) (P), an unincorporated association of churches, challenged these restrictions. CLUB (P) alleged that the restrictions violated the requirement of the Religious Land Use and Institutionalized Persons Act that restrictions substantially burdening religious exercise must advance a compelling government interest through the least restrictive means. CLUB (P) alleged further that the CZO violated the free exercise, free speech, and free assembly guarantees of the First Amendment, as well as the equal protection and procedural due process guarantees of the Fourteenth Amendment. The trial judge granted summary judgment for the City (D) on all counts. CLUB (P) appealed.

ISSUE: Does the Chicago Zoning Ordinance substantially burden religious exercise in violation of the Religious Land Use and Institutionalized Persons Act or violate the free exercise, freedom of speech, freedom of assembly, equal protection, or procedural due process guarantees of the U.S. Constitution?

HOLDING AND DECISION: (Bauer, J.) No. The Chicago Zoning Ordinance does not substantially burden religious exercise in violation of the Religious Land Use and Institutionalized Persons Act (RLUIPA) or violate the free exercise, freedom of speech, freedom of assembly, equal protection, or procedural due process guarantees of the U.S. Constitution. A violation of the RLUIPA requires a threshold showing that the government's restriction "substantially burdens" religious exercise. In this context, "substantially burdens" refers to a restriction that renders religious exercise effectively impracticable. The facts of this case do not show a substantial burden; instead, the record shows only that the religious land uses in Chicago must abide by the same standards with which all other uses in the City must comply. CLUB's (P) constitutional claims fare no better. The CZO does not merit heightened scrutiny under the Free Exercise Clause because the ordinance is facially neutral as to religious uses and because the hybrid rights supposedly buttressing CLUB's (P) free exercise claim are meritless. Likewise, the CZO does not warrant strict scrutiny under the Equal Protection Clause because any burden on religious exercise here is both incidental and insubstantial. Under the appropriate standard of review, rational basis, the CZO complies with the Equal Protection Clause because it rationally advances the City's (D) legitimate interest in regulating land use. Finally, CLUB's (P) procedural due process claim summarily fails because, asserting only a failure to follow state-mandated procedures, the claim belongs in state court. Affirmed.

ANALYSIS

CLUB's (P) free exercise challenge in the land-use context fails under the ostensibly unrelated rule announced in *Employment Division v. Smith*, 494 U.S. 872 (1990). Under *Smith*, the CZO does not violate the Free Exercise Clause because an incidental limitation on isolated religious exercises does not prohibit "[t]he government's ability to enforce generally applicable," facially neutral standards.

Quicknotes

DUE PROCESS CLAUSE Clauses, found in the Fifth and Fourteenth Amendments to the United States Constitution, providing that no person shall be deprived of "life, liberty, or property, without due process of law."

FREE EXERCISE CLAUSE The guarantee of the First Amendment to the United States Constitution prohibiting Congress from enacting laws regarding the establishment of religion or prohibiting the free exercise thereof.

ZONING ORDINANCE A statute that divides land into defined areas and which regulates the form and use of buildings and structures within those areas.

CHAPTER **35–36**

Water Rights and the Public Trust Doctrine

Quick Reference Rules of Law

PAGE

1. **Groundwater Rights.** A possessor of land who withdraws ground water from the land and uses it for a beneficial purpose is not liable for interference with the use of water by another, unless the withdrawal causes unreasonable harm. (State v. Michels Pipeline Construction, Inc.) *162*

2. **Groundwater Rights.** The law of capture allows a landowner to pump as much groundwater as he chooses, without liability to neighbors who claim the pumping has depleted their wells. (Sipriano v. Great Spring Waters of America, Inc.) *163*

3. **The Public Trust Doctrine.** The environmental impact of traditional water diversion must be taken into account in deciding whether to continue such diversion. (National Audubon Society v. Superior Court) *164*

4. **The Public Trust Doctrine.** The common-law public trust doctrine is authority for water allocation determinations separate and independent from statutory authority, so that an agency that renders water allocation consistent with the scope and purposes of that doctrine does not exceed its statutory authority. (In the Matter of the Water Use Permit Applications (The Waiahole Ditch Case)) *165*

State v. Michels Pipeline Construction, Inc.

State (P) v. Corporation (D)

Wis. Sup. Ct., 217 N.W.2d 339 (1974).

NATURE OF CASE: Appeal from judgment granting a demurrer in an action concerning rights in underground water.

FACT SUMMARY: When Michels Pipeline Construction Inc.'s (Michels) (D) construction of a sewer caused some local wells to dry up, the State (P) brought suit, seeking an order that Michels (D) conduct construction so as not to adversely affect area residents.

RULE OF LAW

A possessor of land who withdraws ground water from the land and uses it for a beneficial purpose is not liable for interference with the use of water by another, unless the withdrawal causes unreasonable harm.

FACTS: Michels Pipeline Construction, Inc. (Michels) (D) contracted to construct a sewer in Milwaukee County (D). To facilitate tunneling for the sewer, Michels (D) had to pump water from local wells to dewater the soil. This action lowered the ground water table from which area residents drew water for private wells. The State of Wisconsin (P) filed a complaint, seeking an order that Michels (D) and the County (D) conduct construction of the sewer so as not to create a nuisance and to take action to eliminate the hardship and adverse effect imposed upon the citizens. The trial court sustained Michels's (D) demurrer on the basis that in Wisconsin (P), there was no cause of action on the part of an injured person concerning his water table. The State (P) appealed.

ISSUE: Is a possessor of land, who withdraws ground water from the land and uses it for a beneficial purpose liable for interference with the use of water by another, unless the withdrawal causes unreasonable harm?

HOLDING AND DECISION: (Wilkie, J.) No. A possessor of land who withdraws ground water from the land and uses it for a beneficial purpose is not liable for interference with the use of water by another, unless the withdrawal causes unreasonable harm. This rule preserves the basic expression of a rule of nonliability to use ground water beneath the land. The formulation of the exception to this basic rule recognizes that there is usually enough water for all users so that apportionment is not necessary but that the problem is who shall bear the costs necessitated by a lowering of the water table by a large user. Whereas the common-law rule placed the burden of making improvements on each user, the proposed "reasonable use" rule gives protection to existing wells if the water withdrawal is taken off the land for use elsewhere but not if the water is used for beneficial purposes on the overlying land. Such a rule places the matter of cost on the same rational basis as the rule applicable to surface streams, the reasonableness of placing the burden on one party or the other. In adopting the stated rule, the order of the trial court sustaining the demurrer is overruled here. Reversed and remanded.

ANALYSIS

The court adopted proposed § 858A of the Restatement (Second) of Torts. In arriving at this decision, the court examined and rejected the common-law rule, the reasonable use rule, and the rule of correlative rights. The court here also overruled its prior decision in *Huber v. Merkel*, 94 N.W. 354 (1903), which established that there is no cause of action for interference with ground water.

Quicknotes

DEMURRER The assertion that the opposing party's pleadings are insufficient and the demurring party should not be made to answer.

NUISANCE An unlawful use of property, that interferes with the lawful use of another's property.

Sipriano v. Great Spring Waters of America, Inc.

Landowners (P) v. Bottled water company (D)

Tex. Sup. Ct., 1 S.W.3d 75 (1999).

NATURE OF CASE: Appeal from affirmance of summary judgment for defendant in action for negligent draining of wells.

FACT SUMMARY: Relying on the common-law rule of capture, which had been the law of the state for over 90 years, the trial court granted summary judgment against landowners who sued a bottled-water company for negligently draining their water wells.

RULE OF LAW

The law of capture allows a landowner to pump as much groundwater as he chooses, without liability to neighbors who claim the pumping has depleted their wells.

FACTS: Landowners (P) sued a bottled-water company (D) for negligently draining their water wells. The trial court granted summary judgment against landowners (P) based on the common-law rule of capture, which had been state law for over 90 years. That rule provides, with some quite limited exceptions, that a landowner may pump as much groundwater as the landowner chooses without liability to neighbors whose wells are depleted as a consequence. The court of appeals affirmed, and the state's highest court granted review.

ISSUE: Does the law of capture allow a landowner to pump as much groundwater as he chooses, without liability to neighbors who claim the pumping has depleted their wells?

HOLDING AND DECISION: (Enoch, J.) Yes. The law of capture allows a landowner to pump as much groundwater as he chooses, without liability to neighbors who claim the pumping has depleted their wells. The key exception to that long-standing rule is that a landowner may not maliciously take water for the sole purpose of injuring the neighbor, or willfully or wantonly waste it. The proposed rule of reasonable use constitutes a sweeping change in the law that is not appropriate at this time. In any event, such a change must come from the state legislature, which has the duty to regulate the state's natural resources, and groundwater in particular. Because the legislature has made recent efforts to regulate groundwater, it is inappropriate for the court to insert itself into the regulatory mix by substituting the rule of reasonable use for the current rule of capture. Affirmed.

CONCURRENCE: (Hecht, J.) Texas is the only remaining state adhering to the law of capture. The legislature's chosen method of groundwater regulation and management is being used only minimally, and what hampers groundwater management is precisely the rule of capture, which should be abandoned, as there are no principled reasons for retaining it. Even though there surely would be disruption from abandoning the current rule, the cost of such disruption must be weighed against the danger that the State's water supply will be threatened due to a lack of reasoned water planning. Nonetheless, because the legislature has recently put in place a groundwater management scheme, that scheme should be given a chance to work, so that, for now, the rule of capture should not be disrupted.

ANALYSIS

The rule of reasonable use limits the common-law right of landowners to take water from a common well by imposing liability on those who take "unreasonably" to their neighbors' detriment.

Quicknotes

COMMON LAW A body of law developed through the judicial decisions of the courts as opposed to the legislative process.

NEGLIGENCE Conduct falling below the standard of care that a reasonable person would demonstrate under similar conditions.

National Audubon Society v. Superior Court

Environmental group (P) v. Municipality (D)

Cal. Sup. Ct., 33 Cal. 3d 419, 658 P.2d 709 (1983).

NATURE OF CASE: Appeal of order dismissing challenge to water allocation system.

FACT SUMMARY: The National Audubon Society (P) contended that the environmental impact of traditional water diversion had to be taken into account in deciding whether to continue such diversion.

RULE OF LAW

The environmental impact of traditional water diversion must be taken into account in deciding whether to continue such diversion.

FACTS: Mono Lake, situated in the central-eastern portion of California, had originally been fed by five streams. The lake, which is saline, contained plentiful brine shrimp which constituted an important food source for migrating birds. Also, two islands were used as rookeries by migrating gulls. In the mid-twentieth century, agencies of the City of Los Angeles obtained permission from state authorities to divert water from these streams to service the city's water needs. The level of Mono Lake began to fall, triggering numerous adverse impacts on the local environment. A suit was brought by the National Audubon Society (Society) (P) to halt the diversions, on the theory that the lake was a public trust that the state was obligated to protect. The trial court dismissed, holding the public trust doctrine inapplicable to water diversion. The California Supreme Court granted the Society's (P) petition for mandate.

ISSUE: Must the environmental impact of traditional water diversion be taken into account in deciding whether to continue such diversion?

HOLDING AND DECISION: (Broussard, J.) Yes. The environmental impact of traditional water diversion must be taken into account in deciding whether to continue such diversion. The public trust doctrine, whose antecedents go back to Roman times, states that government holds all navigable waterways and the lands underneath them as trustee for the benefit of the people. The scope of the trust includes all navigable waterways, of which Mono Lake is an example. It also includes the tributaries of such waterways, which include the diverted streams at issue here. As trustee, the government must weigh the competing interests of various segments of the public in deciding how waters under its public trust jurisdiction will be utilized. In the context of Mono Lake, the competing interests of Los Angeles in its water supply must be weighed against the interests of the public in general in maintaining the unique ecological balance of the Mono Lake region. The 1940 agreement between the state and the city did not take into account the public trust aspect of the doctrine of the tributaries; the interests of Los Angeles were the only factors taken into account. As the state has a duty to consider the public trust in its allocation of the state's water resources, the trial court's holding to the contrary cannot stand. Reversed.

ANALYSIS

The instant case represents a rather expansive example of the public trust doctrine. As stated in the case, the doctrine covers navigable waters. The court here stated, without much analysis, that non-navigable tributaries thereof were also part of the public trust. This has not been recognized in most jurisdictions.

Quicknotes

PUBLIC TRUST DOCTRINE The government holds lands that are submerged beneath the water, or that are capable of being submerged, in trust for the public's benefit.

In the Matter of the Water Use Permit Applications (The Waiahole Ditch Case)

[Parties not identified.]

Hawaii Sup. Ct., 9 P.3d 409 (2000).

NATURE OF CASE: Appeal from a commission's final decision and order in a contested case over waters collected by a major irrigation infrastructure.

FACT SUMMARY: When a major irrigation infrastructure on Oahu Island, known as the Waiahole Ditch System, was no longer being used to divert waters from the island's windward (wet) side to its leeward (dry) side for agricultural purposes, the Commission on Water Resource Management (the Commission) held a combined contested case hearing involving 25 parties and issued a final decision and order (D & O) that relied heavily on the public trust doctrine.

RULE OF LAW

The common-law public trust doctrine is authority for water allocation determinations separate and independent from statutory authority, so that an agency that renders water allocation consistent with the scope and purposes of that doctrine does not exceed its statutory authority.

FACTS: The Oahu Sugar Company, Ltd. (OSCo) had a ditch system built on Oahu Island that supplied the island's leeward (dry) side with water diverted from its windward (wet) side. This ditch system, known as the Waiahole Ditch System, irrigated OSCo's sugar plantation for around 80 years. Diversions by the ditch system reduced the flows in several windward streams, specifically, Waiahole, Waianu, Waikane, and Kahana streams, affecting the natural environment and human communities dependent upon them. Diminished flows impaired native stream life and may have contributed to the decline in the greater Kane'ohe Bay ecosystem, including the offshore fisheries. A few years before OSCo ceased operations, the Commission on Water Resource Management (the Commission) designated the five aquifer systems of the windward part of Oahu as ground water management areas, effectively requiring existing users of Waiahole Ditch water to apply for water use permits within one year. The Waiahole Irrigation Company (WIC), the operator of the ditch system, filed a combined water use permit application for the existing users of ditch water. Then OSCo announced that it would end its sugar operations, signaling the imminent availability of the ditch water used by OSCo and raising the question of its future allocation. Afterward, numerous state, county and municipal governments, as well as private parties, filed competing claims to reserve or draw water from the Waiahole Ditch. These competing claims were mediated and an interim agreement was reached that required surplus ditch waters to be returned to the windward streams. The interim restoration of windward stream flows had an immediate apparent positive effect on the stream ecology. The Commission then held a contested case hearing involving 25 parties, issued final findings of fact (FOFs), conclusions of law (COLs), and a decision and order (D & O). In issuing the D & O, the Commission focused particularly on the "public trust doctrine" and identified the island's windward groundwater and streams, and the Kane'ohe Bay ecosystem as part of the public trust res, subject to review under the state's Water Code (Code). The state's highest court reviewed the D & O.

ISSUE: Is the common-law public trust doctrine authority for water allocation determinations separate and independent from statutory authority, so that an agency that renders water allocation consistent with the scope and purposes of that doctrine does not exceed its statutory authority?

HOLDING AND DECISION: (Nakayama, J.) Yes. The common-law public trust doctrine is authority for water allocation determinations separate and independent from statutory authority, so that an agency that renders water allocation consistent with the scope and purposes of that doctrine does not exceed its statutory authority. Historically, it has long been held in the United States that the government holds certain lands, waters, and resources in trust for the public. In this state, it has long been held that the people of the state hold the absolute rights to all its navigable waters and the soils thereunder. These waters and soils are held in trust for the public uses of navigation and as resources unto themselves. Additionally, pursuant to the state's constitution, the state enacted the State Water Code. The enactment of the Code did not signal the legislature's intent to supplant the common-law public trust doctrine, which, in any event, by its very nature prevents its legislative abrogation. Most importantly, the public trust doctrine has been elevated to the level of a constitutional mandate. The state constitution requires the state to protect and conserve all natural resources, including water, which are held in trust for the public. Thus, the public trust doctrine is a fundamental principle of constitutional law in the state. Other states' courts, without the benefit of such constitutional provisions, have decided that the public trust doctrine exists independently of any statutory protections supplied by the legislature. Such a view is even more compelling given the constitutional stature of the doctrine in this state. Given that the doctrine has

Continued on next page.

validity independent of any statute, the next questions that must be resolved are what are the scope and the substance of the trust, and what powers and duties does the doctrine confer on the state. In this state, the trust encompasses all the water resources of the state, without exception or distinction, and such a view is supported by the legislative history. Moreover, it is an unpersuasive argument that the sovereign reservation does not extend to groundwater. Common-law distinctions between ground waters and surface waters are no longer scientifically supported, and water is a critical resource regardless of whether it is found above or below the ground. Given the ultimate value of water to the ancient Hawaiians, it is inescapable that the sovereign reservation was intended to guarantee public rights to all water, regardless of its immediate source. For all these reasons, there is no exception to the public trust doctrine for ground waters; the doctrine applies to all water resources, ground and surface, navigable and consumptive. This broad scope of the trust fixes the trust's purposes. Not only is the purpose to preserve the public rights of navigation, commerce and fishing, or even recreational uses such as bathing, swimming, boating and scenic viewing, but the purpose is also resource protection. Thus, the maintenance of waters in their natural state constitutes a distinct "use" under the water resources trust, and does not constitute "waste." Although the public trust may allow grants of private interests in trust resources under certain circumstances, this in no way means that private commercial use is among the public purposes protected by the trust. The purpose of the public trust has never been understood to safeguard rights of exclusive use for private commercial gain. In fact, such an interpretation would eviscerate the trust's basic purpose. The trust's scope and purpose define the state's powers and duties under the trust. These are to maintain (protect) the purity and flow of the state's waters and to put those waters to reasonable and beneficial uses, which requires equitable and maximum beneficial allocation of water resources. The duty to protect the waters includes the protection of the waters from irrevocable transfer to private parties and to maintain their availability and existence for present and future generations. These two goals are not mutually exclusive. "Protection" is consonant with assuring the "highest economic and social benefits" of the resource. Thus, the goal is not maximum consumptive use, but rather the most equitable, reasonable, and beneficial allocation of state water resources that recognizes resource protection as a "use." The continuing authority of the state over its water resources precludes any grant or assertion of vested rights to use water to the detriment of public trust purposes. This authority empowers the state to revisit prior diversions and allocations, even those made with due consideration of their effect on the public trust. The state also bears an affirmative duty to take the public trust into account in the planning and allocation of water resources, and to protect public trust uses whenever feasible. This could lead to the public trust having to accommodate offstream diversions inconsistent with the mandate of protection, e.g., for agricultural uses. Although offstream uses are not precluded, what is required is that all uses, offstream or instream, public or private, promote the best economic and social interests of the public. Accommodation of both instream and offstream uses, where feasible, is preferable but resource allocation decisions must be made on an ongoing basis, and it is not prudent to designate absolute priorities between broad categories of uses under the water resources trust. Contrary to the Commission's conclusion that the trust establishes resource protection as "a categorical imperative and the precondition to all subsequent considerations," the Commission inevitably must weigh competing public and private water uses on a case-by-case basis, according to any appropriate standards provided by law. Insofar as the public trust, by nature and definition, establishes use consistent with trust purposes as the norm, the Commission's conclusion that it effectively prescribes a "higher level of scrutiny" for private commercial uses such as those proposed in this case is affirmed. In practical terms, this means that the burden ultimately lies with those seeking or approving such uses to justify them in light of the purposes protected by the trust. Because the Commission is the guardian of the public trust's rights, it is required to conduct planning, decision-making, and regulation from a global, long-term perspective. While the Commission has largely rendered its decision within the framework of this mandate, there are a few matters to which the Commission must give further consideration to on remand. Affirmed in part, vacated in part, and remanded.

DISSENT: (Ramil, J.) The majority errs in characterizing the public trust doctrine as separate and distinct from statutory mandates, and, therefore, errs in assigning "superior claims" status to "public instream uses" and "native Hawaiian and traditional and customary rights" on the basis of that doctrine. The legislative history merely shows that the legislature and framers of the state's constitution viewed the public trust simply as a fiduciary duty imposed on the state to "protect, control and regulate the use of Hawaii's water resources for the benefit of its people." Accordingly, the Commission exceeded its statutory authority in relying on the public trust doctrine as a separate and distinct authority for prioritizing particular water uses.

ANALYSIS

The court in this case clearly eschews the view of the public trust doctrine as one where the "public interest" advanced by the trust is the sum of competing private interests and the rhetorical distinction between public trust and private gain is a false dichotomy. Under such a view, the public trust must recognize enduring public

Continued on next page.

rights in trust resources separate and apart from, and superior to, the prevailing private interests in the resources at any given time.

Quicknotes

PUBLIC TRUST DOCTRINE The government holds lands that are submerged beneath the water, or that are capable of being submerged, in trust for the public's benefit.

CHAPTER 37

Environmentally Sensitive lands

Quick Reference Rules of Laws

PAGE

1. **Constructive Taking.** A zoning ordinance that regulates the development of land for non-indigenous, non-natural uses does not constitute an unconstitutional constructive taking of the land where the ordinance is designed to prevent harm to public rights and resources, notwithstanding that the ordinance's restrictions may cause loss of economic value to the landowner by preventing the owner from changing the character of the land. (Just v. Marinette County) *170*

2. **Denial of Development.** A denial of development pursuant to a land use regulation does not constitute an unconstitutional taking or inverse condemnation where: the development, if approved, would constitute a public nuisance; the state holds title to part of the land under the public trust doctrine, thus diminishing the owner's reasonable investment-backed expectations; and the owner may develop part of the land for a modest return on investment. (Palazzolo v. Rhode Island) *172*

Just v. Marinette County

Landowner (P) v. County (D)

Wisc. Sup. Ct., 201 N.W.2d 761 (1972).

NATURE OF CASE: Appeal in action claiming a constructive taking of property and unconstitutionality of a shoreland zoning regulation. [The precise procedural posture of this case is not indicated in the casebook extract.]

FACT SUMMARY: The Justs (P), who owned swamp wetlands adjacent to a navigable lake, contended that Marinette County's (D) shoreland zoning regulation, prohibiting the filling of the land without a conditional use permit, constituted a constructive taking of their property and was unconstitutional.

RULE OF LAW

A zoning ordinance that regulates the development of land for non-indigenous, non-natural uses does not constitute an unconstitutional constructive taking of the land where the ordinance is designed to prevent harm to public rights and resources, notwithstanding that the ordinance's restrictions may cause loss of economic value to the landowner by preventing the owner from changing the character of the land.

FACTS: Pursuant to state statute, Marinette County (County) (D) enacted a shoreland zoning ordinance that regulated lands within 1,000 feet of the normal high-water elevation of navigable lakes, ponds, or flowages and 300 feet from a navigable river or stream. The fundamental purpose of the ordinance was to protect navigable waters and the public rights therein from the degradation and deterioration which results from uncontrolled use and development of shorelands. One of the districts established by the ordinance was a conservancy district that encompassed wetlands. In such a district, a conditional use permit was required for filling more than 500 square feet of any wetland contiguous to navigable waters. The ordinance provided a fine for failure to obtain a required permit. Prior to the passage of the ordinance, the Justs (P) purchased land along the shore of a navigable lake. The land was designated as swamps or marshes, and came within the ordinance's definition of wetlands and was included in a conservancy district. Six months after the ordinance became effective the Justs (P) hauled over 1,000 square yards of sand onto their property and, in violation of the ordinance, filled an area on the property without the required conditional use permit. The Justs (P) brought suit, claiming that the ordinance's conservancy district provisions and the wetlands-filling restrictions constituted an unconstitutional constructive taking of their property because the ordinance caused a severe depreciation in their property's value, as the land would be worth a great deal more if it could be filled and developed. The state's highest court granted review in the case. [The precise procedural posture of this case is not indicated in the casebook extract.]

ISSUE: Does a zoning ordinance that regulates the development of land for non-indigenous, non-natural uses constitute an unconstitutional constructive taking of the land where the ordinance is designed to prevent harm to public rights and resources, notwithstanding that the ordinance's restrictions may cause loss of economic value to the landowner by preventing the owner from changing the character of the land?

HOLDING AND DECISION: [Judge not stated in casebook excerpt.] No. A zoning ordinance that regulates the development of land for non-indigenous, non-natural uses does not constitute an unconstitutional constructive taking of the land where the ordinance is designed to prevent harm to public rights and resources, notwithstanding that the ordinance's restrictions may cause loss of economic value to the landowner by preventing the owner from changing the character of the land. Swamps and wetlands serve a vital role in nature, are part of the balance of nature and are essential to the purity of water in lakes and streams, and the exercise of the police power here is reasonable, as it prevents harm to public rights by limiting the use of private property to its natural uses so that the state's navigable waters are not harmed. This is not a case where an owner is prevented from using his land for natural and indigenous uses, as such uses are allowed without permit. The changing and filling of wetlands and swamps to the damage of the general public by upsetting the natural environment and the natural relationship is not a reasonable use of that land that is protected from police power regulation. Where such changing or filling does not cause harm, the ordinance allows it by special permit. In sum, destroying the natural character of a swamp or a wetland so as to make that location available for human habitation is not a reasonable use of that land when the new use, although of a more economical value to the owner, causes harm to the general public. Consequently, the exercise of the police power to prevent such destruction is reasonable, non-confiscatory, and constitutional. While it is true that the Justs' (P) land would be economically more valuable if filled and developed, and loss of value is to be considered in determining whether a restriction is a constructive taking, value based upon changing the character of the land at the expense of harm to public rights is not an essential factor or controlling. [The procedural result of the court's holding is not identified in the casebook extract.]

ANALYSIS

When the Wisconsin Supreme Court handed down this decision—in 1972—debates over sustainable development and

Continued on next page.

ecosystem health had largely not occurred. In this case of first impression, the court nevertheless intuited the importance of balancing development against harm to larger ecosystems. Other courts have drawn on this case to distinguish between natural and unnatural uses of land, holding that regulation of unnatural uses passes constitutional muster. Critics of this reasoning point out that it can be very difficult to distinguish between natural and unnatural uses for ecological purposes, as human habitation, at least on a small scale, can be considered consonant with most ecosystems.

Quicknotes

TAKING A governmental action that substantially deprives an owner of the use and enjoyment of his property, requiring compensation.

USE RESTRICTION A restriction on the right to utilize one's personal or real property.

Palazzolo v. State of Rhode Island

Landowner (P) v. State (D)

R.I. Super. Ct., C.A. NO. WM 88-0297 (2005).

NATURE OF CASE: Inverse condemnation action on remand from the state's highest court, as ordered by the U.S. Supreme Court, for a *Penn Central* determination.

FACT SUMMARY: Palazzolo (P) contended that the State of Rhode Island's (D) denial of his application to fill and develop salt marsh property constituted a taking for which he was entitled to compensation under the federal and state constitutions. The U.S. Supreme Court ordered the case remanded to the trial court for analysis consistent with *Penn Central Transportation Co. v. New York City*, 438 U.S. 104, 98 S. Ct. 2646 (1978).

RULE OF LAW

A denial of development pursuant to a land use regulation does not constitute an unconstitutional taking or inverse condemnation where: the development, if approved, would constitute a public nuisance; the state holds title to part of the land under the public trust doctrine, thus diminishing the owner's reasonable investment-backed expectations; and the owner may develop part of the land for a modest return on investment.

FACTS: Palazzolo (P) owned an 18-acre salt marsh parcel of land fronting a pond, almost all of which land was designated as coastal wetlands prior to his acquisition of the land. The land served as valuable habitat for wildlife, including birds and fish, and there had been almost no development of the salt marsh, which provided, inter alia, a valuable filtering system regarding water runoff containing pollutants and nitrogen from adjacent land. Palazzo (P) proposed to fill the land and build a substantial residential subdivision on it. It was determined that a sewerage system from his proposed development would add significant nitrogen to the pond, not to mention that the development would significantly reduce wildlife habitat. Additionally, the development would reduce the amenity value of the pond to other land owners in the area as well as the entire vacation/recreation community in the vicinity. After his development proposals for a residential subdivision were rejected by the Coastal Resources Management Council (CRMC), he filed suit in state court claiming the State of Rhode Island's (D) application of its wetlands regulations constituted a taking in violation of the Fifth Amendment's Takings Clause. The state's highest court rejected the claim that Palazzolo (P) was denied all economically beneficial use of the property since the uplands portion of the property could still be developed. The state court also ruled that because the regulation predated Palazzolo's (P) ownership of the property, he was precluded from bringing a takings claim challenging the regulation. Finally, the court also held that the case was not ripe for adjudication. Palazzolo (P) appealed to the U.S. Supreme Court, which ordered the case remanded for analysis by the state trial court under *Penn Central Transportation Co. v. New York City*, 438 U.S. 104, 98 S. Ct. 2646 (1978).

ISSUE: Does a denial of development pursuant to a land use regulation constitute an unconstitutional taking or inverse condemnation where: the development, if approved, would constitute a public nuisance; the state holds title to part of the land under the public trust doctrine, thus diminishing the owner's reasonable investment-backed expectations; and the owner may develop part of the land for a modest return on investment?

HOLDING AND DECISION: (Gale, J.) No. A denial of development pursuant to a land use regulation does not constitute an unconstitutional taking or inverse condemnation where: the development, if approved, would constitute a public nuisance; the state holds title to part of the land under the public trust doctrine, thus diminishing the owner's reasonable investment-backed expectations; and the owner may develop part of the land for a modest return on investment. Under *Lucas v. South Carolina*, 505 U.S. 1003 (1992), there can be no taking where a proposed use is prohibited ab initio by nuisance law. A public nuisance is an unreasonable interference with a right common to the general public: it is behavior that unreasonably interferes with the health, safety, peace, comfort or convenience of the general community. Here, clear and convincing evidence demonstrates that Palazzolo's (P) proposed development would constitute a public nuisance insofar as it would increase nitrogen levels in the pond and wreak ecological havoc on the pond and the salt marsh, harming wildlife and water quality. For this reason alone, the State's (D) denial of the proposed development cannot constitute a taking. The proposed development would not, however, create a private nuisance, i.e., a material interference with the ordinary physical comfort or the reasonable use of one's property. Although the proposed development, if built, would block all water views now enjoyed by land owners to the south of Palazzolo's (P) parcel, blocking a neighbor's view is not ordinarily considered a nuisance which is actionable at law. Another factor is that the public trust doctrine limits the title Palazzolo (P) took to his land in the first instance. In the state, land that is below mean high water and adjacent to a tidal body is held in trust by the State (D), and here there is overwhelming evidence that just about one half of the parcel at issue is below mean high water and next to the pond, which is a tidal body of water. Thus, the land is held in trust by the State (D) for the public good. The State (D) has never transferred its public trust rights, either in general or in relation to Palazzolo's (P) parcel, nor has there been either express or implied state approval or acquiescence to the filling of tidal waters upon which Palazzolo (P)

Continued on next page.

relied to his detriment. Moreover, Palazzolo (P) has not filled and improved his property with the permission or acquiescence of the State (D). Thus, as against the State (D), Palazzolo (P) gained title and the corresponding property rights to only one-half of the parcel in question. Although the public trust doctrine cannot be a total bar to recovery as to this takings claim, it substantially impacts Palazzolo's (P) title to the parcel in question and has a direct relationship to his reasonable investment-backed expectations. Furthermore, Palazzolo's (P) cost estimates were too low, and his net profit estimates too high—in part because if other landowners were able to build in the manner proposed by Palazzolo (P), there would be a glut of coastal homes on the market, which would diminish Palazzolo's (P) returns. Most significantly, since Palazzolo (P) did not have reasonable property expectations to fill tidal lands that were protected by the public trust doctrine or to cause a public nuisance, as already discussed, his reasonable investment-backed expectations were greatly reduced. Since he could still build a private residence on part of the land, he could net a modest return on his investment. In other words, constitutional law does not require the state to guarantee a bad investment, and, for all these reasons, Palazzolo (P) has not suffered a taking.

ANALYSIS

As remarked on by some commentators, this case demonstrates the relative ease that public nuisance law can be incorporated into a takings analysis and that ecosystem services can be integrated into public nuisance doctrine: "Palazzolo owned the marsh; the marsh filtered and cleaned runoff into the pond; those services were positive externalities flowing off of Palazzalo's property; the public in general enjoyed the economic benefits of that service; Palazzolo therefore had no property right to fill the marsh." J.B. Ruhl, "Making Nuisance Ecological," 58 *Case W. Res. L. Rev.* 753 (2008). By the same token, the case demonstrates the difficulty of integrating ecosystem services analysis into private nuisance law, in part because the government does not have the incentive under takings analysis to quantify economic harms to specific property owners. Once the government establishes a qualitative harm to the ecology, and, therefore, a public nuisance, it need go no further in defending the owner's takings claim since it has met the requirements of the *Lucas* takings defense.

Quicknotes

AB INITIO From its inception or beginning.

INTER ALIA Among other things.

INVERSE CONDEMNATION The taking of private property for public use so as to impair or decrease the value of property near or adjacent to, but not a part of, the property taken.

PUBLIC NUISANCE An activity that unreasonably interferes with a right common to the overall public.

PUBLIC TRUST DOCTRINE The government holds lands that are submerged beneath the water, or that are capable of being submerged, in trust for the public's benefit.

TAKINGS CLAUSE Provision of the Fifth Amendment to the United States Constitution prohibiting the government from taking private property for public use without providing just compensation therefor.

CHAPTER 38–39

Adverse Possession

Quick Reference Rules of Law

Tioga Coal Co. v. Supermarkets General Corp.

Adverse possessor (P) v. Property owner (D)

Pa. Sup. Ct, 519 Pa. 66, 546 A.2d 1 (1988).

NATURE OF CASE: Complaint seeking to quiet title by adverse possession.

FACT SUMMARY: Tioga Coal Co. (P) filed a complaint against Supermarkets General Corp. (Supermarkets) (D) seeking title by adverse possession to a paper street located within Supermarkets' (D) property.

RULE OF LAW

If the true owner has not ejected a trespasser in the time allotted for an action in ejectment, and all the other elements of adverse possession have been satisfied, hostility will be implied, regardless of the subjective state of mind of the trespasser.

FACTS: Tioga Coal Co. (Tioga) (P) filed a complaint against Supermarkets General Corp. (Supermarkets) (D) seeking title by adverse possession to a strip of land known as Agate Street, located within Supermarkets' (D) property and bordering Tioga's (P) property. Agate Street is a paper street forty feet wide, which was entered on the plan for the City of Philadelphia, but never opened to the public. On remand, the Chancellor concluded that the term for adverse possession was twenty-one years. He also found that around 1948 Tioga (P) took control of a gate controlling access to the street, put a lock on its gate, and maintained the lock until 1978, during which period it controlled ingress and egress. While Tioga's (P) possession was "actual, open, notorious, exclusive and continuous" for a period in excess of the required period, the Chancellor determined that Tioga (P) failed to show that its use was adverse or hostile. This court granted allocatur to determine whether the lower courts were in error as to the issue of the hostility required to perfect a claim of adverse possession.

ISSUE: If the true owner has not ejected a trespasser in the time allotted for an action in ejectment, and all the other elements of adverse possession have been satisfied, will hostility be implied, regardless of the subjective state of mind of the trespasser?

HOLDING AND DECISION: (Flaherty, J.) Yes. If the true owner has not ejected a trespasser in the time allotted for an action in ejectment, and all the other elements of adverse possession have been satisfied, hostility will be implied, regardless of the subjective state of mind of the trespasser. While intent is a requirement of adverse possession, how the state of mind requirement may be proved is a matter of debate. In *Schlagel v. Lombardi*, 337 Pa. Super. 83, 486 A.2d 491 (1984), the court stated that possession may be hostile even if the claimant knows of no other claim and falsely believes that he owned the land in issue. This implies that subjective intent is not required and hostility may be implied from compliance with the other requirements for adverse possession. The superior court required Tioga (P) prove its subjective hostility by showing such hostility was directed towards the true owner of the land, not the mistaken owner. The court stated that the doctrine of implied hostility was only applicable in cases involving boundary disputes or mistaken belief as to ownership. The court concluded that such circumstances were not present here. Tioga (P) argues the contrary. It is almost impossible to discern the mental state of an adverse possessor. The appropriate view is that set forth by Justice Holmes that, if an owner abandons his land and the land is possessed and used by another for the statutory period, beyond which the true owner no longer has a cause of action in ejectment, the trespasser has acquired the property through adverse possession, regardless of the trespasser's subjective state of mind. Reversed and remanded.

DISSENT: (McDermott, J.) In order to acquire title by adverse possession one must intend to take against the record titleholder. The majority's conclusion that one cannot glean a party's intent from his conduct is untenable.

ANALYSIS

The law of adverse possession is the result of the historical development of an action for ejectment. The two claims are intertwined, with the former often resulting from the unavailability of the latter.

Quicknotes

ADVERSE POSSESSION A means of acquiring title to real property by remaining in actual, open, continuous, exclusive possession of the property for the statutory period.

EJECTMENT An action to oust someone in unlawful possession of real property and to restore possession to the party lawfully entitled to it.

TITLE The right of possession over property.

TRESPASSER Person present on the land of another without the knowledge or express permission of the owner, and to whom only a minimum duty of care is owed for injuries incurred while on the premises.

Halpern v. The Lacy Investment Corp.

Adverse possessor (P) v. Property owner (D)

Ga. Sup. Ct., 259 Ga. 264, 379 S.E.2d 519 (1989).

NATURE OF CASE: Appeal of award of damages for slander of title and trespass.

FACT SUMMARY: Halpern (P) claimed certain property under adverse possession despite never having had a good faith belief in a claim of title.

RULE OF LAW

One cannot obtain title by adverse possession if he lacked a good faith belief that his claim was rightful.

FACTS: In 1960, Halpern (P) predecessor approached Lacy Investment Corporation's (Lacy) (D) predecessor about purchasing a lot adjacent to land owned by him. Lacy's (D) predecessor refused. Nonetheless, Halpern's (P) predecessor cleared the property and treated it as part of his backyard. Years later, Halpern (P) sued for title under adverse possession. Lacy (D) counterclaimed for damages for slander of title and trespass. The trial court, finding Halpern's (P) predecessor to have lacked a good faith belief in his claim of title, held that Halpern (P) could not have acquired title by adverse possession. Lacy's (D) causes of action were sustained, and Halpern (P) appealed.

ISSUE: Can one obtain title by adverse possession if he lacked a good faith belief that his claim was rightful?

HOLDING AND DECISION: (Gregory, J.) No. One cannot obtain title by adverse possession if he lacked a good faith belief that his claim was rightful. One of the elements of adverse possession is that such possession must be under a claim of right. Some jurisdictions hold hostile possession to be the equivalent of a claim of right, and Halpern (P) urges that this court concur. However, the court is not so inclined. To hold that mere hostility constitutes a claim of right would be to reward trespass and elevate a squatter to the level of titleholder, something this court will not do. Here, Halpern's (P) predecessor never had a good faith belief in a claim of right, so Halpern's (P) claim must fail. Affirmed.

ANALYSIS

The ruling here is fairly consistent with the purposes of adverse possession. Its primary purposes are to promote utilization of land and to remove doubts as to title. One not having a good faith claim of right is not as likely to exploit real estate as one who does.

Quicknotes

ADVERSE POSSESSION A means of acquiring title to real property by remaining in actual, open, continuous, exclusive possession of the property for the statutory period.

CLAIM OF RIGHT Made by a person claiming a right in property, who is in possession and intends to claim ownership of that property without regard to the record title owner.

SLANDER OF TITLE A defamatory statement made with the intent to disparage a party's title to real or personal property.

ITT Rayonier, Inc. v. Bell

Absentee owner (P) v. Hostile possessor (D)

Wash. Sup. Ct., *en banc*, 112 Wash. 2d 754, 724 P.2d 6 (1989).

NATURE OF CASE: Appeal of order quieting title to property.

FACT SUMMARY: An appeals court denied the claim of Bell (D) as an adverse possessor partially because Bell (D) had lacked a good faith belief in a claim of right.

RULE OF LAW

Hostile possession needed for title by adverse possession does not require a good faith claim to the property in question.

FACTS: In 1972, Bell (D) purchased a houseboat, which was moored adjacent to property belonging to ITT Rayonier, Inc. (P), an absentee owner. Bell (D) kept the houseboat situated continuously until the mid-1980s, when ITT Rayonier (P) filed a quiet title action. The trial court quieted title in favor of ITT Rayonier (P) because (1) Bell (D) was away for three consecutive school years, and (2) Bell (D) had not had a good faith belief in a claim of title. The state court of appeals affirmed on the same grounds. Bell (D) appealed.

ISSUE: Does hostile possession needed for title by adverse possession require a good faith claim to the property in question?

HOLDING AND DECISION: (Pearson, J.) No. Hostile possession needed for title by adverse possession does not require a good faith claim to the property in question. Adverse possession revolves around the character of possession, and it is difficult to see why a person's secret thoughts should have anything to do with it. A good faith belief that one owns property will not make it so if the elements of adverse possession are not satisfied. A corollary to this is that a lack of a good faith belief in ownership will not defeat an otherwise valid claim for adverse possession. The courts below were therefore in error in imposing this requirement. [The court went on to hold that Bell (D), by his periods of absence, had failed to show exclusive possession.] Affirmed in part; reversed in part.

ANALYSIS

Hostility can be approached either objectively or subjectively. The objective test looks only to the character of the adverse possession; the subjective test requires a good faith belief in a claim of right. The objective test is much easier to apply and is followed in most jurisdictions.

Quicknotes

ADVERSE POSSESSION A means of acquiring title to real property by remaining in actual, open, continuous, exclusive possession of the property for the statutory period.

CLAIM OF RIGHT Made by a person claiming a right in property, who is in possession and intends to claim ownership of that property without regard to the record title owner.

QUIET TITLE Equitable action to resolve conflicting claims to an interest in real property.

ITT Rayonier, Inc. v. Bell

Property owner (P) v. Adverse possessor (D)

Wash. Sup. Ct., 112 Wash. 2d 754 (1989).

NATURE OF CASE: Adverse possession case.

FACT SUMMARY: Bell (D) failed to establish that his possession of the subject property was exclusive, thereby entitling him to title by adverse possession.

RULE OF LAW

The test of possession is whether the party exercises dominion over the land in a manner consistent with actions a true owner would take.

FACTS: In 1972, Bell (D) purchased a houseboat, which was moored adjacent to property belonging to ITT Rayonier (P), an absentee owner. Bell (D) kept the houseboat situated continuously until the mid-1980s, when ITT Rayonier (P) filed a quiet title action. The trial court quieted title in favor of ITT Rayonier (P) because (1) Bell (D) was away for three consecutive school years, and (2) Bell (D) had not had a good faith belief in a claim of title. The state court of appeals affirmed on the same grounds. Bell (D) appealed.

ISSUE: Is the test of possession whether the party exercises dominion over the land in a manner consistent with actions a true owner would take?

HOLDING AND DECISION: (Pearson, J.) Yes. The test of possession is whether the party exercises dominion over the land in a manner consistent with actions a true owner would take. Possession is established only if it is of such a character as a true owner would make considering the nature and location of the subject property. Where the facts in an adverse possession case are not in dispute, whether adverse possession is established is a matter of law for the court to determine. Here the trial court concluded Bell (D) failed to establish that his possession of the property was exclusive. The court of appeals affirmed, finding that Bell's (D) shared use of the property with the Klocks and Olesens was not of the type expected of an owner. Their use constituted a shared occupation of land and not the exclusive use necessary for adverse possession. Affirmed.

ANALYSIS

While specific instances of property usage are evidence of possession, the hallmark of possession is exclusive dominion. This can only be shown by demonstrating that others were excluded from the property, such as by installing a fence or other barrier to intruders.

Quicknotes

ADVERSE POSSESSION A means of acquiring title to real property by remaining in actual, open, continuous, exclusive possession of the property for the statutory period.

Marengo Cave Co. v. Ross

Tour company (D) v. Landowner (P)

Ind. Sup. Ct., 212 Ind. 624, 10 N.E.2d 917 (1937).

NATURE OF CASE: Action to quiet title to that portion of a subterranean cave extending under plaintiff's land.

FACT SUMMARY: Marengo Cave Co. (D) conducted tours of a subterranean cave which extended under a portion of Ross's (P) land.

RULE OF LAW

Before the adverse possession period begins to run against subsurface land, the true owner must have knowledge of the trespass.

FACTS: Marengo Cave Co. (Marengo) (D) and its predecessors in interest owned and operated a cave tour. The cave was approximately 700 feet below the surface of the land. Both Marengo (D) and Ross (P) thought that the entire cave was on Marengo's (D) land. In actuality, a portion of the cave extended under Ross's (P) property. After some 40 years of use, Ross (P) became aware that a portion of the cave was under his land. Ross (P) brought suit to quiet title to that portion of the cave and a survey was ordered by the court. Marengo (D) defended on the basis that it had acquired title to the entire cave through adverse possession. The trial court found that the possession was not open and notorious as to Ross (P) and quieted title in him. Marengo (D) appealed on the basis that Ross (P) knew of the cave and had even visited it himself. It was Ross's (P) responsibility to determine whether any portion of the cave was on his land and, having failed to do so, Marengo (D) should acquire title through adverse possession.

ISSUE: Must the true owner have knowledge of the trespass before the adverse possession begins to run against subsurface land?

HOLDING AND DECISION: (Roll, J.) Yes. The requirement that possession be "open and notorious" is only satisfied where the owner has actual or constructive notice of the possession. On the land's surface, this is satisfied by ownership claims and open and continuous use. With respect to subsurface uses, an owner cannot determine, on his own, whether a trespass is taking place. He must hire an expert to survey the subsurface land in order to establish boundaries. Prior to the period for adverse possession to run, the true owner must actually be aware of the trespass. It is stipulated here that both Ross (P) and Marengo (D) thought the cave was solely on Marengo's (D) land. The cave was not separately taxed, nor was it assessed against either's property. Actual knowledge of the cave's existence does not equal knowledge that part of it is on his property. Finally, secret trespasses will not start the statute running. The adverse possessor must, through his actions, apprise the owner of his own claim to the land. The decision of the trial court is sustained.

DISSENT: Will adverse possession begin to run, as to subsurface land use, prior to the owner's learning of the trespass?

ANALYSIS

Where the mineral rights have been previously severed from the surface estate, the surface owner may not complain of the adverse possession of the subsurface. Also, the knowledge of the surface owner of a trespass to the subterranean land will not be imputed to the owner of the severed mineral estate unless there is an agency or fiduciary relationship between the two.

Quicknotes

ADVERSE POSSESSION A means of acquiring title to real property by remaining in actual, open, continuous, exclusive possession of the property for the statutory period.

CONSTRUCTIVE NOTICE Knowledge of a fact that is imputed to an individual who was under a duty to inquire and who could have learned of the fact through the exercise of reasonable prudence.

QUIET TITLE Equitable action to resolve conflicting claims to an interest in real property.

Howard v. Kunto

Owner of land (P) v. Grantee (D)

Wash. Ct. App., 3 Wash. App. 393, 477 P.2d 210 (1970).

NATURE OF CASE: Appeal from action granting a decree quieting title to real property.

FACT SUMMARY: Due to a mistake in survey, a summer cottage was constructed on the land of another.

RULE OF LAW

Part-time residency alone does not destroy the continuity of possession required to establish title by adverse possession if such residency is similar in nature to owners of like property.

FACTS: Due to a surveying error, Kunto's (D) grantor built a summer cottage on property located outside the boundaries of his land. The error was discovered some 30 years later. Howard (P), the owner of the land on which the cottage was built, sued. Kunto (D) attempted to establish adverse possession through "tacking" since he hadn't been in possession for the statutory period.

ISSUE: "Tacking" is the use of your predecessor's possession to meet the continuous possession requirement for adverse possession. The trial court permitted the tacking and held that there was sufficient privity between Kunto (D) and his predecessor in title, even though the deed did not contain the disputed property. It quieted title in favor of Kunto (D) and Howard (P) appealed.

ISSUE: Is tacking permitted where land is only used during a portion of the year and the deed of title does not contain the disputed property?

HOLDING AND DECISION: (Pearson, J.) Yes. Tacking, per statute, requires a "claim of right." Mere "squatting" is not sufficient to establish title by adverse possession. There must be privity between the "grantor" and "grantee" to establish privity. While the deed transferring the property does not contain any of the land in question, two factors require this court to find that privity existed to a sufficient extent as to allow tacking. First, Kunto (P) and his grantors acted in good faith, and, merely because of a surveying error, they cannot be considered squatters. Secondly, public policy favors early certainty as to the location of land ownership. The next question involves the fact that the land was only occupied during a portion of each year. To constitute adverse possession, the occupation must be actual, uninterrupted, open, notorious, hostile and exclusive, and under a claim of right made in good faith. It has become firmly established that the requisite possession is only to the extent that arbitrarily marks the conduct of owners in general who hold similar property. Since this property and other similarly situated property are used as summer residences, partial occupation during the summer months satisfies this requirement. For these reasons, the trial court was correct in its judgment quieting title. Reversed, with directions to dismiss plaintiff's action and to enter a decree quieting defendant's title to the disputed tract of land in accordance with the prayer of their cross-complaint.

ANALYSIS

If possession is interrupted for any reason, the statute of limitations starts to run all over again. Since all presumptions are made in favor of the real owner, even a short break in possession is held to destroy the adverse possessor's claim to the property.

Quicknotes

ADVERSE POSSESSION A means of acquiring title to real property by remaining in actual, open, continuous, exclusive possession of the property for the statutory period.

QUIET TITLE Equitable action to resolve conflicting claims to an interest in real property.

TACKING The attachment of periods of adverse possession by different adverse possessors in order to fulfill the requirement of continuous possession for the period prescribed by statute.

Ray v. Beacon Hudson Mountain Corp.

Adverse possessor (P) v. Landowner (D)

N.Y. Ct. App., 88 N.Y.2d 154, 666 N.E.2d 532 (1996).

NATURE OF CASE: Adverse possession suit.

FACT SUMMARY: The Rays (P) sought title by adverse possession to the land under a cottage owned by their mother on the basis that they used the cottage for one month each summer from 1963 until 1988.

RULE OF LAW

In determining whether the common-law requirement of "continuity of possession" has been met in an adverse possession claim to an estate in land, the court must consider not only the adverse possessor's physical presence on the land but also his other acts of dominion and control over the premises that would be appropriately undertaken by owners of properties of similar character, condition and location.

FACTS: The property subject to adverse possession claim is an improved parcel located in an area that was once a thriving summer resort community. Most of the property's neighboring structures have been destroyed by vandalism, fire or neglect. Prior to 1960, all the cottage owners occupied their property as lessees. Rose Ray came into possession of the subject premises under a lease that was assigned to her as lessee in 1931. Under that lease, she purchased the cottage located on the property and paid rent for use of the underlying property. The lease agreement stated that upon termination, any structures erected on the property would pass to the lessor who would pay the lessee the reasonable value of the improvements. The lessor terminated the leases of all occupants in the community in 1960 pursuant to an option clause in the lease. Ray died in 1962, never having been paid the reasonable value of the cottage. The site was purchased by Mt. Beacon, the contract of sale providing that all land and structures thereon pass to the purchaser. The Rays (P), son and daughter-in-law of Rose Ray, then reentered the premises and occupied the property for one month during the summer for each summer from 1963 to 1988. Beacon Hudson (D) acquired the property in 1978 after it was taken from Mt. Beacon for nonpayment of taxes. The Rays (P) commenced an adverse possession action against Beacon Hudson (D). Beacon Hudson (D) counterclaimed for ejectment. The Supreme Court held the Rays (P) were the rightful owners of the property. The appellate division reversed, noting that adverse possession could not be established by seasonal use of the property. The Rays (P) appealed.

ISSUE: In determining whether the common-law requirement of "continuity of possession" has been met in an adverse possession claim to an estate in land, must the court consider not only the adverse possessor's physical presence on the land but also his other acts of dominion and control over the premises that would be appropriately undertaken by owners of properties of similar character, condition and location?

HOLDING AND DECISION: (Titone, J.) Yes. In determining whether the common-law requirement of "continuity of possession" has been met in an adverse possession claim to an estate in land, the court must consider not only the adverse possessor's physical presence on the land but also his other acts of dominion and control over the premises that would be appropriately undertaken by owners of properties of similar character, condition and location. To acquire title to real property by adverse possession, the possessor must show that the character of the possession is hostile and under a claim of right, actual, open and notorious, exclusive and continuous for the statutory period. This means that there must be possession that would give the owner a cause of action in ejectment against the occupier throughout the prescriptive period. The acquisition to title by adverse possession is not favored under the law; thus the elements must be shown by clear and convincing evidence. The element of continuity will fail where the adverse possessor interrupts the period of possession by abandoning the premises, if an intruder's presence makes the possession nonexclusive, or where the record owner acts to eject the adverse possessor. The hostile claimant's actual possession of the property need not be constant to satisfy this element. The requirement of continuous possession is satisfied when the adverse claimant's acts of possessing the property are consistent with acts of possession that ordinary owners of like property would undertake. This depends on the character of the disputed property. The frequency and duration of acts of improvement are to be considered in conjunction with the claimant's other acts of dominion and control over the premises in determining whether possession is continuous. Here Beacon Hudson's (D) claim that the Rays' (P) possession was not continuous ignores the Rays' (P) other acts of dominion and control of the premises. The Rays' (P) installation of utilities and preservation of the cottage demonstrates continuous, actual occupation of land by improvement. Since Beacon Hudson (D) was clearly on notice of the Rays' (P) hostile claim of ownership, its failure to seek ouster within the statutory period results in the Rays' (P) acquiring title by adverse possession. Reversed.

ANALYSIS

This case indirectly involves the issue of "tacking." Tacking involves the joining of successive periods of adverse possession so as to satisfy the prescribed statutory period. Tacking is

Continued on next page.

permissible provided that privity of estate exists between the adverse possessors.

Quicknotes

ADVERSE POSSESSION A means of acquiring title to real property by remaining in actual, open, continuous, exclusive possession of the property for the statutory period.

EJECTMENT An action to oust someone in unlawful possession of real property and to restore possession to the party lawfully entitled to it.

TACKING The attachment of periods of adverse possession by different adverse possessors in order to fulfill the requirement of continuous possession for the period prescribed by statute.

CHAPTER 40

The Requirement of a Written Instrument

Quick Reference Rules of Law

PAGE

1. **A Written Invitation Is Not a Will.** A brief written invitation to live in a house as long as one wishes, does not create a life estate in the property. (In re O'Neil's Will) *186*
2. **Description of the Land.** A deed that does not identify the land sought to be conveyed does not act as notice to a bona fide purchaser for value. (Bowlin v. Keifer) *187*
3. **Conveyance of Land.** No technical words of grant are necessary to convey land. (Harris v. Strawbridge) *188*
4. **Statute of Frauds.** The Statute of Frauds will operate as a defense to an action for specific performance of an oral land sale contract unless the applicant can show that injustice can only be avoided by enforcement because of unavailability of other remedies, substantial and reasonable action or forbearance in reliance on the agreement, and clear and convincing evidence of the agreement. (Walker v. Ireton) *189*
5. **Oral Contract to Convey Real Estate.** An oral, arm's-length contract to convey real estate will not normally be enforceable. (Nessralla v. Peck) *190*
6. **Partial Performance of an Oral Land Sale Contract.** An oral land sale contract that has been partly performed may be enforced. (Gulden v. Sloan) *191*

In re O'Neil's Will

[Parties not identified.]

N.Y. Surr. Ct., 13 Misc.2d 796, 176 N.Y.S.2d 1022 (1958) *aff'd*, 8 A.D.2d 631, 185 N.Y.S.2d 393 (1959).

NATURE OF CASE: Probate of a will.

FACT SUMMARY: A testator's grandson claimed a life estate in a house based on the testator's one-sentence written invitation for the grandson and his family to live in the house as long as they wish.

RULE OF LAW

A brief written invitation to live in a house as long as one wishes, does not create a life estate in the property.

FACTS: Orva O'Neil wrote to her daughter, Tess, to invite Tess's son and his family to live in a house owned by O'Neil for "as long as they wish." After O'Neil died, her grandson used her brief letter to claim a life estate against proceeds from the sale of the property.

ISSUE: Does a brief written invitation to live in a house as long as one wishes, create a life estate in the property?

HOLDING AND DECISION: (Bennett, Surrogate) No. A brief written invitation to live in a house as long as one wishes, does not create a life estate in the property. O'Neil's grandson has no rights in the property because O'Neil's letter was only an innocent invitation. Claim denied.

ANALYSIS

Although O'Neil's brief letter was a writing, her will, which would have been witnessed, presumably contained either no provisions indicating an intent to devise a life estate to her grandson or provisions expressing an intent that precluded such a testamentary transfer.

Quicknotes

LIFE ESTATE An interest in land measured by the life of the tenant or a third party.

PROBATE The administration of a decedent's estate.

TESTAMENTARY INTENT A determination that the document was intended to be a will and, as such, reflects the writer's true wishes.

Bowlin v. Keifer

Grantee (D) v. Heir (P)

Ark. Sup. Ct., 246 Ark. 693, 440 S.W.2d 232 (1969).

NATURE OF CASE: Appeal testing the validity of a written instrument as a conveyance of real property.

FACT SUMMARY: Bowlin (D) contended that a contract conveying a son's interest in his father's estate, which did not describe the estate, cannot act as a deed conveying property.

RULE OF LAW

A deed that does not identify the land sought to be conveyed does not act as notice to a bona fide purchaser for value.

FACTS: George Wade was the father of Keifer (P) and Guy Wade. Guy Wade sold his interest in his father's estate to Keifer (P). This sale was evidenced by a contract of sale, which recited $300 as consideration, but did not describe the property involved. Guy Wade then died. Guy Wade's son, Victor Wade, conveyed his father's interest in his grandfather's land to Bowlin (D). Victor Wade gave Bowlin (D) a deed to the land which described a consideration of "one dollar and other valuable considerations." Keifer (P) brought a partition suit against Bowlin (D), claiming that Victor Wade had no interest in the land which he could sell to Bowlin (D).

ISSUE: Does a deed that does not identify the land involved act as notice to a bona fide purchaser for value?

HOLDING AND DECISION: (Fogleman, J.) No. A deed that does not identify the land sought to be conveyed does not act as notice to a bona fide purchaser for value. A contract for the sale of land will not be enforced unless the description of the land in it is as definite and certain as that required in a deed of conveyance. Keifer (P) acquired her interest in the land in a contract which did not describe the land. Therefore, the contract cannot be enforced against a bona fide purchaser (Bowlin [D]) who was not on notice that there was another claim to ownership of the property. The contract between Keifer (P) and Guy Wade is void as a conveyance of real property.

DISSENT: (Byrd, J.) Although the rule of law is correct, the majority has applied it incorrectly. Bowlin (D) is not a bona fide purchaser for value because he failed to sustain his burden of proof by showing that he paid a valuable consideration for the deed from Victor Wade. A grantor, or an heir claiming through him, is estopped to claim or assert anything in derogation of his deed or assignment. Therefore, Guy Wade could not challenge his own assignment to Keifer (P), and Victor Wade, his heir, has no better title than his father.

ANALYSIS

The basic law is that no conveyance is valid unless the description of the land sought to be conveyed is sufficient to identify the land. A deed which fails to describe a specific divided part of a larger tract but describes a distinct fractional part thereof may be upheld as a conveyance of an undivided part. Deeds describing land as "all my land" are considered valid if they are identified as within a particular city, town, county, or state.

Quicknotes

BONA FIDE PURCHASER A party who purchases property in good faith and for valuable consideration without notice of a defect in title.

BURDEN OF PROOF The duty of a party to introduce evidence to support a fact that is in dispute in an action.

CONVEYANCE The transfer of property, or title to property, from one party to another party.

DEED A signed writing transferring title to real property from one person to another.

Harris v. Strawbridge

Heir (D) v. Widow (P)

Tex. Ct. Civ. App., 330 S.W.2d 911 (1959).

NATURE OF CASE: Trespass-to-try title to land with a claim for damages.

FACT SUMMARY: Ethel Strawbridge (P) received some land from her husband in a deed in which the granting clause had been omitted, and she sought to recover title to that property.

RULE OF LAW

No technical words of grant are necessary to convey land.

FACTS: In 1928 Edward Strawbridge, now deceased, made a will leaving his land to various nieces and nephews, including Harris (D). In 1935, Edward married Ethel Strawbridge (P). In 1941, Edward sold part of the land to Ethel (P), but the conveying instrument, by mutual mistake, did not have a granting clause. Edward died in 1943, and the title to the land was at issue. Ethel Strawbridge (P) filed suit against Harris (D) to recover title to the property.

ISSUE: Are technical words of grant necessary to convey land?

HOLDING AND DECISION: (Bell, C.J.) No. No technical words are necessary to convey land. By the modern rule, the intention of the parties is determined by considering the whole instrument and arrangement, with observance of formal clauses, as required at common law, no longer the essence of a deed. Today, when the instrument itself makes it clear that it was the purpose of the grantor to convey the property to another, who is designated with reasonable certainty in the deed itself, the instrument will take effect as a conveyance. If operative words or words of grant appear anywhere in the instrument it suffices as a conveying deed. The evidence shows that a grantor and a grantee were named in the instrument, and the words "to have and to hold the above described land . . . unto the said Ethel Strawbridge, her heirs or assigns forever" show an intention to convey title in fee simple to Ethel Strawbridge (P). The instrument is a valid deed, the land belongs to Ethel Strawbridge (P) in fee simple, and the land does not pass under Edward Strawbridge's (P) will.

ANALYSIS

The purpose of construction in conveyances is to find the intention of the parties and all rules of construction are subservient to this purpose. A deed, such as the one in this case, is always construed against the grantor who has used the language therein. In construing an instrument of conveyance every part of it should be used to determine the meaning of the instrument as a whole.

Quicknotes

CONVEYANCE The transfer of property, or title to property, from one party to another party.

DEED A signed writing transferring title to real property from one person to another.

FEE SIMPLE An estate in land characterized by ownership of the entire property for an unlimited duration and by absolute power over distribution.

Walker v. Ireton

Potential purchaser (P) v. Farm owner (D)

Kan. Sup. Ct., 221 Kan. 314, 559 P.2d 340 (1977).

NATURE OF CASE: Appeal from denial of specific performance.

FACT SUMMARY: Walker (P) and Ireton (D) entered into a specific oral agreement for the sale of Ireton's (D) farm, but Ireton (D) refused any writing and would not accept tender of payment under the agreement and declined to go through with the deal, relying on the Statute of Frauds.

RULE OF LAW

The Statute of Frauds will operate as a defense to an action for specific performance of an oral land sale contract unless the applicant can show that injustice can only be avoided by enforcement because of unavailability of other remedies, substantial and reasonable action or forbearance in reliance on the agreement, and clear and convincing evidence of the agreement.

FACTS: Walker (P) and Ireton (D) engaged in negotiations for Ireton's (D) sale of his farm to Walker (P). Negotiations ended in agreement, and specific details for payment and delivery of possession were worked out. Ireton (D) put off signing any written contract on several occasions despite Walker's (P) requests. Ultimately, Ireton (D) refused to go through with the deal, though he had accepted a check (which he did not cash) for $50 deposit on the $30,000 sale price. Ireton (D) refused the tender of the next payment and refused to deliver possession. Walker (P) placed a hay rake on the property, but did not take further action to gain possession until maintaining this action for specific performance of the oral agreement. Ireton (D) asserted the Statute of Frauds as a defense, and obtained a summary judgment against any specific performance. Walker (P) appealed.

ISSUE: Will the Statute of Frauds operate as a defense to an action for specific performance of an oral land sale contract unless the applicant can show that injustice can only be avoided by enforcement because of the unavailability of other remedies, substantial and reasonable action or forbearance in reliance on the agreement, and clear and convincing evidence of the agreement?

HOLDING AND DECISION: (Prager, J.) Yes. Throughout American and English legal history, courts of equity have refused to apply the Statute of Frauds in cases where the purchaser under the oral contract performed acts required by it to such an extent that as to make it grossly unjust and inequitable to refuse enforcement. Modern law continues this practice. However, the Statute of Frauds will operate as a defense to an action for specific performance of an oral land sale contract unless the applicant shows that injustice can only be avoided by enforcement because of the unavailability of other remedies, substantial and reasonable action or forbearance in reliance on the agreement, and clear and convincing evidence of the agreement. Equity does not require this court to remove the Statute of Frauds defense from this action. Ireton (D) refused on five occasions to sign a written agreement and refused tender of the payment. Walker (P) moved a hay rake onto the property, but this can hardly be regarded as taking possession. Walker (P) does have a right to restitution of reliance expense on the basis of quantum meruit, however. Affirmed.

ANALYSIS

Part performance usually serves to take the contract out of the Statute of Frauds and permits enforcement. However, the part performance required in land sale contracts is normally the making of improvements on the land after taking possession. The court here finds Walker's (P) "performance" insufficient for this purpose, and implies that Ireton's (D) repeated refusal to sign a contract in writing was some indication of the unreasonableness of relying on the promise.

Quicknotes

CLEAR AND CONVINCING EVIDENCE An evidentiary standard requiring a demonstration that the fact sought to be proven is reasonably certain.

QUANTUM MERUIT Equitable doctrine allowing recovery for labor and materials provided by one party, even though no contract was entered into, in order to avoid unjust enrichment by the benefited party.

SPECIFIC PERFORMANCE An equitable remedy whereby the court requires the parties to perform their obligations pursuant to a contract.

STATUTE OF FRAUDS A statute that requires specified types of contracts to be in writing in order to be binding.

Nessralla v. Peck

Farm owner (P) v. Potential purchaser (D)

Mass. Sup. Jud. Ct., 403 Mass. 757, 532 N.E.2d 685 (1989).

NATURE OF CASE: Appeal of denial of specific performance of an oral land sale contract.

FACT SUMMARY: Nessralla (P) contended that Peck (D) had breached an oral arm's-length contract for the latter to sell certain real estate to him.

RULE OF LAW

An oral, arm's-length contract to convey real estate will not normally be enforceable.

FACTS: Nessralla (P) and Peck (D) entered an oral agreement that each would act as front men in purchases made on behalf of each other's corporation and would then convey the properties to these corporations. Nessralla (P) upheld his end of the deal. Peck (D), however, purchased with his own money the property Nessralla (P) wanted and then conveyed it to his own corporation. Nessralla (P) sued for specific performance. The trial court entered judgment in favor of Peck (D), and Nessralla (P) appealed.

ISSUE: Will an oral, arm's-length contract normally be enforceable?

HOLDING AND DECISION: (Hennessey, C.J.) No. An oral, arm's-length contract to convey real estate will not normally be enforceable. The Statute of Frauds requires a real estate contract to be in writing, and a contract not in writing will not be enforceable. It is possible, as Nessralla (P) argues, for a defendant to be estopped from raising the Statute as a defense. However, an estoppel requires some form of detriment by the aggrieved party. Here, Nessralla (P) did not incur expenses or obligations as a result of Peck's (D) breach, so an estoppel was not created. Further, neither a constructive nor resulting trust can be imposed upon the property. These remedies require a fiduciary or agency relationship between the litigants, which did not exist here. Consequently, no exception to the general rule against nonenforceability of land sale contracts existed here. Affirmed.

ANALYSIS

Constructive and resulting trusts are equitable remedies forcing one wrongfully possessing an asset to convey it to the rightful owner. A constructive trust is imposed when fraud or breach of fiduciary duty has occurred. The resulting trust is a device used when one purchases a thing with funds supplied by another. Neither device was applicable here.

Quicknotes

CONSTRUCTIVE TRUST A trust that arises by operation of law whereby the court imposes a trust upon property lawfully held by one party for the benefit of another, as a result of some wrongdoing by the party in possession so as to avoid unjust enrichment.

ESTOPPEL An equitable doctrine precluding a party from asserting a right to the detriment of another who justifiably relied on the conduct.

RESULTING TRUST An equitable trust that is established from the inferred intent of the parties to create a trust.

SPECIFIC PERFORMANCE An equitable remedy whereby the court requires the parties to perform their obligations pursuant to a contract.

Gulden v. Sloan

Lessee-sellers (P) v. Potential purchasers (D)

N.D. Sup. Ct., 311 N.W.2d 568 (1981).

NATURE OF CASE: Appeal of order specifically enforcing a land sale contract.

FACT SUMMARY: The Guldens (P) entered into an oral land sale contract with the Sloans (D), which the Sloans (D) partially performed.

RULE OF LAW
An oral land sale contract that has been partly performed may be enforced.

FACTS: The Guldens (P) leased a dwelling from Krueger. Krueger informed them that if they could find a buyer for the property, any amount over $62,400 would be theirs. James Gulden (P) approached the Sloans (D), with whom they were acquainted, about buying the property. The Sloans (D) lived in a mobile home. According to the Guldens (P), the Sloans (D) agreed to buy the house for $68,400, and to convey their mobile home to the Guldens (P). No written memorandum was drafted. The Sloans (D) subsequently vacated the mobile home and let the Guldens (P) move in, although title never passed, and the Sloans (D) eventually sold the mobile home. The Guldens (P) brought an action seeking (1) specific performance of the promise to convey the mobile home; and (2) damages because the Sloans (D) eventually purchased the home from Krueger for $61,556.62. The trial court denied specific performance as the Sloans (D) no longer had title, but awarded $6,000 damages. The Sloans (D) appealed.

ISSUE: May an oral land sale contract which has been partly performed be enforced?

HOLDING AND DECISION: (Erickstad, C.J.) Yes. An oral land sale contract which has been partly performed may be enforced. The Statute of Frauds requires that a contract involving the sale of land be in writing to be enforceable. The purpose of this law is to compel parties to furnish proof of such agreements. When a party sought to be charged with performance has, by his actions, provided proof of the contract, the proof usually provided by a memorandum has been supplied. Partial performance of the alleged terms of the agreement is a type of action constituting such proof. Here, the Sloans (D) moved out of their home and allowed the Guldens (P) to take occupancy, rent-free. This is consistent with the terms of the agreement as alleged by the Guldens (P) and denied by the Sloans (D). In light of this, the Statute of Frauds is not a defense to the Guldens' (P) action. Affirmed.

ANALYSIS

The Statute of Frauds was first enacted in England in 1677. At that time, it was as much a reaction to the political scene as an evidentiary rule. In its current form, it rears its head primarily in two contexts. This first is the situation here, a land sale contract. The second is in other contracts not capable of performance within one year.

Quicknotes

ORAL CONTRACT A contract that is not reduced to written form.

SPECIFIC PERFORMANCE An equitable remedy whereby the court requires the parties to perform their obligations pursuant to a contract.

STATUTE OF FRAUDS A statute that requires specified types of contracts to be in writing in order to be binding.

CHAPTER 41

Deed Descriptions

Quick Reference Rules of Law

Producers Lumber & Supply Co. v. Olney Bldg. Co.

Landowners (P) v. Builders (D)

Tex. Ct. Civ. App., 333 S.W.2d 619 (1960).

NATURE OF CASE: Action for damages resulting from the destruction of property.

FACT SUMMARY: Olney Building Company (D) built a house on Producers Lumber & Supply Company's (Producers) (P) land, and then tore it down. Producers (P) brought suit for damages.

RULE OF LAW

If a person improves the land of another in good faith he may ask for equitable relief, but he may not demolish the improvements without the consent of the landowner.

FACTS: Olney Building Company (Olney) (D) sold a lot to Producers Lumber & Supply Company (Producers) (P). Some months later, Olney (D) built a house on the lot in the good-faith belief that they still owned the lot. Olney (D) then tore down the house. Producers (P) sued Olney (D) for the resulting damages to the lot.

ISSUE: If a person improves the land of another in good faith may he either ask for equitable relief or in the alternative simply demolish the improvements?

HOLDING AND DECISION: (Murray, C.J.) No. If a person improves the land of another in good faith he may ask for equitable relief, but he may not demolish the improvements without the consent of the landowner. If the improver demolishes the improvements, he commits waste and can be required to pay the landowner for such waste. Olney (D) cannot seek equitable relief because it has "unclean hands" because it demolished the improvements on the lot. Producers (P) can recover the stipulated value of the dwelling that was demolished, plus damages and exemplary damages (to punish the defendant). The cost of the appeal is charged to Olney (D). Affirmed and amended.

DISSENT: (Barrow, J.) Courts of equity should make restitution and no reprisals. Producers (P) should recover damages only for the damages the lot suffered. It should not be entitled to compensatory damages for the removal of the house.

ANALYSIS

If a party builds on the land of another by mistake and the real owner allows the construction to be completed and says nothing, he will be estopped from denying that he commissioned the construction and will be liable in quantum meruit for the value of the construction. If the true owner is unaware of the construction, he may require it be removed and that damages to the land plus for trespass be assessed against the builder.

Quicknotes

COMPENSATORY DAMAGES Measure of damages necessary to compensate victim for actual injuries suffered.

EXEMPLARY DAMAGES Damages exceeding the actual injury suffered for the purposes of punishment, deterrence and comfort to plaintiff.

GOOD FAITH An honest intention to abstain from taking advantage of another.

Asotin County Port District v. Clarkston Community Corp.

Landowner (P) v. Property claimant (D)

Wash. Ct. App., 2 Wash. App. 1007 (1970).

NATURE OF CASE: Action to quiet title to land and reform a land deed.

FACT SUMMARY: Asotin County Port District (P) claimed title to land through a deed that merely designated the land as part of a larger tract.

RULE OF LAW

A description that designates the land conveyed as a portion of a larger tract without identifying the particular part conveyed is fatally defective.

FACTS: Asotin County Port District (Asotin County) (P) acquired land from its predecessor. The deed to the land merely described it as a part of a larger tract. Clarkston Community Corp. (Clarkston) (D), whose predecessor lost the land in a foreclosure action, contended that the description of the land in the deed was inadequate to convey the land. Asotin County (P) brought this action to: (1) quiet title to the land claimed to be owned by Clarkston (D), and (2) to reform the deed given by Clarkston's (D) predecessor.

ISSUE: Is a deed defective if the description of land conveyed is merely stated to be a portion of a larger tract without identifying the particular part involved in the conveyance?

HOLDING AND DECISION: (Munson, J.) Yes. A deed description that designates the land conveyed as a portion of a larger tract without identifying the particular part conveyed is defective and will fail to convey the land. Inadequate descriptions cannot be made specific. The evidence here showed that the description of the land in the deed was inadequate, and the tax rolls that were supposed to contain a more specific description of the land at the time it was conveyed had failed to do this. Asotin County (P) is denied judgment to title to the land and is denied reformation of the land deed. Title to the land in question is in Clarkston (D). Affirmed.

ANALYSIS

This case rule is contrary to the common-law rule that: "A deed which fails to describe a specific divided part of a larger tract but describes a distinct fractional part thereof may be upheld as a conveyance of an undivided part." *Bowlin v. Keifer*, 246 Ark. 693, 440 S.W.2d 232 (1969), uses the common-law rule as the basis upon which both parties rely. A basic proposition (that the court refused to apply in the *Asotin* case) is: if a person of ordinary intelligence and understanding can successfully use the description given in an attempt to locate and identify the particular property sought to be quieted title upon, then the description answers its purpose and must be held sufficient.

Quicknotes

QUIET TITLE Equitable action to resolve conflicting claims to an interest in real property.

Powell v. Schultz

Original owner of half (P) v. Deeded lot (D)

Wash. Ct. App., 4 Wash. App. 213 (1971).

NATURE OF CASE: Property line dispute.

FACT SUMMARY: "The Creek" is recited as the boundary line in deeds dividing two lots, but two creeks later existed on the land in question.

RULE OF LAW

Where a stream is a boundary, the centerline of the stream becomes the division between the properties.

FACTS: In 1910, the original owner deeded the southern one-half of lot 3 to Schultz's (D) predecessor. "The Creek" was designated as the dividing line between the two new lots. Unfortunately, two creeks now run through the original lot 3. The original owner's half belonged to Powell (P). Powell (P) brought this action to determine the actual boundary line. Both parties presented evidence bearing on the length of time the second stream had existed.

ISSUE: If a stream is used as the boundary line between two pieces of property, is the center of the stream the actual boundary line?

HOLDING AND DECISION: (Pearson, J.) Yes. If a stream is used as the boundary line between two pieces of property, the center of the stream becomes the division between the properties. Evidence was produced showing that the South or Rocky Creek was the proper boundary between the two pieces of land. The center of South Creek is the dividing line between the two pieces of land. Affirmed.

ANALYSIS

If the description of land in a deed carries it to or from a point on the side of a street, stream, road, or similar monument, and along such street, stream, road, or similar monument, the grantee should take title to the center of such monument under the common-law rule. When the boundary of a tract of land is the thread or center line of a stream or of water, such boundary is variable and changes with the thread of the stream. However, when a river by sudden and violent change (called avulsion) alters its course and overflows privately owned land the title to such lands is not changed.

Grand Lodge of Georgia v. City of Thomasville

Landowners (D) v. City government (P)

Ga. Sup. Ct., 226 Ga. 4 (1970).

NATURE OF CASE: Declaratory relief action to determine title to land.

FACT SUMMARY: Grand Lodge of Georgia, Independent Order of Odd Fellows (D), contended that the deed under which the City of Thomasville (P) claimed title to land was void for indefiniteness of description.

RULE OF LAW

To be effective as a conveyance of land, the deed must so describe the land as to identify it.

FACTS: The City of Thomasville (P) held a deed to land that described the length of the lot in terms of acres and did not identify the lot numbers of bordering lots that were used as reference points. The Grand Lodge of Georgia, Independent Order of Odd Fellows (D) contended that the deed was void for indefiniteness of description. This suit was brought to determine ownership of the land in question.

ISSUE: To be effective as a conveyance of land, must a deed describe the land so as to identify it?

HOLDING AND DECISION: (Mobley, J.) Yes. To be effective as a conveyance of land, the deed must so describe the land as to identify it. The deed in question here gives no beginning and ending points, and "about six acres" does not furnish a guide for measuring the distance of the land conveyed. The evidence shows that it would be impossible to locate the land in question from the description in the deed. The deed is so indefinite that it gives no means of identifying the land; it is void and is inoperative as a conveyance of title, or as color of title. The City of Thomasville (P) has no grounds to claim title to the land.

ANALYSIS

Parol evidence is not admissible to determine the identity of land described in a deed unless it is first found that the description is ambiguous. Even then it is not admissible to alter, but only to explain the ambiguity, unless the suit is in equity for reformation. The "course" of a line in a description means the direction it takes across the country and is usually determined by its angle with some other known line. The "distance" means the length of a line from one point to another point, and the "contents" means the area of a tract of land.

Quicknotes

CONVEYANCE The transfer of property, or title to property, from one party to another party.

DEED A signed writing transferring title to real property from one person to another.

PAROL EVIDENCE Evidence given verbally; extraneous evidence.

Ramsey v. Arizona Title Ins. & Trust Co.

Landowner (P) v. Title company (D)

Ariz. Ct. App., 10 Ariz. App. 538 (1969).

NATURE OF CASE: Appeal from summary judgment against plaintiff in an action to resolve a deed description dispute.

FACT SUMMARY: Ramsey (P) wished to sell his land. The deed described the property in a different manner than did the escrow instructions.

RULE OF LAW

Natural monuments, roads, etc., not a part of the property conveyed, may be used to describe the boundaries of the land.

FACTS: Ramsey (P) entered into a contract to sell his land. An escrow was opened and Arizona Title Insurance & Trust (Arizona Title) (D) conducted a title search in order to insure title. Their description of the property to be conveyed differed from the deed's description of the property. Arizona Title (D) used a street in its description. The street was a one-quarter-acre section line, but was not part of the property to be conveyed. All portions of the street were excepted from the grant, clearly indicating that it was merely intended to be a descriptive boundary reference. Ramsey (P) became worried over the discrepancy between the deed and the escrow title policy and brought suit against Arizona Title (D) to have its description reformed to comport with that given in the deed. The trial court granted summary judgment to Arizona Title (D) after finding that the property to be conveyed was the same.

ISSUE: May, natural or artificial monuments, not a part of the property to be conveyed be used to describe the property's boundaries?

HOLDING AND DECISION: (Cameron, J.) Yes. Although the grantor must be careful to convey only the property that he actually owns, descriptions of property may, at the outset, encompass other property for the purpose of accuracy in fixing the location of the property to be conveyed. The description in a deed is considered ambiguous and subject to construction only if it is not possible to relate the description to the land without inconsistencies. The evidence showed that the property described in the escrow instructions and the deed was the same. The two documents simply used different words to measure the land starting from the adjacent street, and then excepting the street from the land being conveyed. Summary judgment for Arizona Title (D) is affirmed.

ANALYSIS

Where monuments, e.g., streets, creeks, streams, etc., are used to describe the boundary of property, the grant is assumed to run to the center of the monument unless it is specifically excepted. If such a monument belongs to a governmental entity, the property owner has no right to it until it has been abandoned. He then may claim to the center of the monument (e.g., an alley is abandoned by the city).

Quicknotes

CONVEYANCE The transfer of property, or title to property, from one party to another party.

DEED A signed writing transferring title to real property from one person to another.

ESCROW A written contract held by a third party until the conditions therein are satisfied, at which time it is delivered to the obligee.

SUMMARY JUDGMENT Judgment rendered by a court in response to a motion made by one of the parties, claiming that the lack of a question of material fact in respect to an issue warrants disposition of the issue without consideration by the jury.

TITLE The right of possession over property.

CHAPTER **42**

Deed Must Be Delivered

Quick Reference Rules of Law

Williams v. Cole

Grantor (P) v. Grantee (D)

Mo. Ct. App., 760 S.W.2d 944 (1988).

NATURE OF CASE: Appeal of order denying petition to set aside a deed.

FACT SUMMARY: Williams's (P) decedent drafted a deed conveying certain property to Cole (D), but retained exclusive custody thereof.

RULE OF LAW

When a grantor retains exclusive custody of a deed, a conveyance is not effected.

FACTS: Johnny Williams executed a deed of certain property in favor of Cole (D); Williams retained custody of the will. Several times he suggested to Cole (D) that the latter take it and have it recorded, but Cole (D) never did. Eventually Williams passed away, and only then did Cole (D) take the deed. Lula Williams (P), Johnny's sister and heir, along with two other heirs, brought an action to set aside the deed. The trial court declined to do so, and Williams (P) and the other heirs appealed.

ISSUE: Is a conveyance effected when a grantor retains exclusive custody of a deed?

HOLDING AND DECISION: (Per curiam) No. When a grantor retains exclusive custody of a deed, a conveyance is not effected. For a conveyance to occur, the deed must be delivered. This can be as simple as the grantor handing the deed to the grantee. When this does not occur and the grantor retains custody of the deed, a presumption of nondelivery arises. The grantee can rebut this presumption, but there must be some evidence of acts reasonably constituting delivery. Here, the most that occurred was that Johnny told Cole (D) on several occasions that he should take the deed. Words do not constitute delivery, and so delivery never occurred. Consequently, the conveyance was never consummated. Reversed and remanded.

ANALYSIS

Delivery is an essential element of a conveyance in every jurisdiction. In its simplest form, all that is involved is the grantor handing the deed to the grantee. In matters involving escrow, the deed is handed to the escrow that eventually delivers it to the grantee. This sort of third-person delivery was permitted at common law from early times.

Quicknotes

CONVEYANCE The transfer of property, or title to property, from one party to another party.

DEED A signed writing transferring title to real property from one person to another.

ESCROW A written contract held by a third party until the conditions therein are satisfied, at which time it is delivered to the obligee.

Kresser v. Peterson

Purported heirs (P) v. Daughters (D)

Utah Sup. Ct., 675 P.2d 1193 (1984).

NATURE OF CASE: Appeal of order refusing to set aside a deed.

FACT SUMMARY: Pyper, decedent, deeded certain property to herself and two others without physically handing it to her cotenants.

RULE OF LAW

Physical handing of a deed to one's cotenants is unnecessary when the grantor reserves an estate.

FACTS: Edward Kresser and Della Pyper owned certain property as joint tenants. After Edward died, Della executed a will naming her daughters and Edward's sons as heirs. Seven years later, she executed a deed naming herself and her daughters as joint tenants. She recorded the deed and put it in a safe deposit box; the daughters were never handed the deed. After Pyper's death, the two sons, Delbert and Edward Kresser (P), sued to have the deed set aside on grounds of failure of delivery. The trail court denied such relief, and the Kressers (P) appealed.

ISSUE: Is physical handing of a deed to one's cotenants necessary when the grantor reserves an estate?

HOLDING AND DECISION: (Per curiam) No. Physical handing of a deed to one's cotenants is not necessary when the grantor reserves an estate. Delivery of a deed to one cotenant under a deed is deemed to constitute delivery to all. When a grantor reserves an estate in the deed, delivery is automatic, as the grantor retains custody of the deed at the moment of execution. Here, Pyper retained an estate, so the cotenants were deemed to have also accepted delivery. Affirmed.

ANALYSIS

In this particular case, Pyper had had the deed recorded. Recordation of a deed is generally deemed to constitute delivery. Consequently, several indicia of a valid delivery existed here. This case illustrates that the common belief that a deed must be handed over to constitute delivery is incorrect.

Quicknotes

CO-TENANT A tenant possessing property with one or more persons jointly or whose interest is derived from a common grantor.

DEED A signed writing transferring title to real property from one person to another.

GRANTOR Conveyor of property or settlor of a trust.

WILL An instrument setting forth the distribution to be made of an individual's estate upon his death; since a will is not effective until the death of its maker, it is revocable during his life.

Lenhart v. Desmond

Grantee (D) v. Grantor (P)

Wyo. Sup. Ct., 705 P.2d 338 (1985).

NATURE OF CASE: Appeal of order invalidating and returning title to the grantor.

FACT SUMMARY: A trial court ruled that Desmond (P) had proven nondelivery of a deed by a preponderance of evidence.

RULE OF LAW

One challenging the delivery of a deed may do so by a preponderance of evidence.

FACTS: Desmond (P) executed a deed granting certain real estate to his daughter, Lenhart (D). He intended that she receive the deed upon his death. At one point, when Desmond (P) was hospitalized, he gave Lenhart (D) the key to his safety deposit box so she could retrieve certain insurance policies for him. Apparently discovering the deed, she took it and recorded it. After Desmond (P) asked for the return of the property and Lenhart (D) refused, Desmond (P) sued to invalidate the deed, claiming nondelivery. The trial court, using a preponderance of evidence standard, declared the deed invalid. Lenhart (D) appealed.

ISSUE: May one challenging the delivery of a deed, do so by a preponderance of evidence?

HOLDING AND DECISION: (Cardine, J.) Yes. One challenging the delivery of a deed may do so by a preponderance of evidence. The rule in this area is that when the controversy is between the grantor and grantee only, a preponderance of evidence will suffice to prove nondelivery. When the rights of third parties are at stake, the proof must be clear and positive. Here, however, no third party interests are implicated, so the standard employed by the trial court was appropriate in this instance. Under this standard, the court's decision is certainly supported by a sufficiency of evidence. [The court went on to reject Lenhart's (D) contention of constructive delivery. Such delivery required a manifestation of an intent to deliver, which was absent here.] Affirmed.

ANALYSIS

Recordation provides a starting point for arguments regarding delivery. A deed recorded is presumed to be delivered. However, as the present case shows, this presumption can be rebutted. The standard of proof necessary to do so varies among the jurisdictions.

Quicknotes

DEED A signed writing transferring title to real property from one person to another.

PREPONDERANCE OF THE EVIDENCE A standard of proof requiring the trier of fact to determine whether the fact sought to be established is more probable than not.

Vasquez v. Vasquez

Beneficiaries (P) v. Grantee (D)

Tx. Ct. App., 973 S.W.2d 330 (1998).

NATURE OF CASE: Suit to determine owner of property.

FACT SUMMARY: Juanita Vasquez Carr executed a will leaving all her property to Ignacio and Jose Vasquez (P) as sole beneficiaries, then later, executed a quitclaim deed conveying the same property to Brigido Vasquez (D), to be held in custody by her attorney and filed upon her death.

RULE OF LAW

The delivery of a signed deed to one's attorney, with instructions to deliver the deed to the grantee upon the grantor's death, constitutes adequate delivery, rendering the grantee the rightful owner of the property.

FACTS: Juanita Vasquez Carr, the owner of the property at issue, executed a will naming Ignacio Vasquez as her independent executor and Ignacio and Jose Vasquez (P) as sole beneficiaries. Later she executed a quitclaim deed granting the same property to Brigido Vasquez (D). Carr left the quitclaim deed in the custody of her attorney with instruction not to file it until after her death. Upon Carr's death, the deed was filed and notice given to Brigido (D). The will was then executed and Ignacio executed a special warranty deed conveying the property to himself (P) and Jose (P). The trial court held that the deed was delivered when it was tendered to Carr's attorney, transferring the property to Brigido (D) as of that date. Ignacio (P) and Jose (P) appealed.

ISSUE: Does the delivery of a signed deed to one's attorney, with instructions to deliver the deed to the grantee upon the grantor's death, constitute adequate delivery, rendering the grantee the rightful owner of the property?

HOLDING AND DECISION: (Seerden, C.J.) Yes. The delivery of a signed deed to one's attorney, with instructions to deliver the deed to the grantee upon the grantor's death, constitutes adequate delivery, rendering the grantee the rightful owner of the property. While issue of whether there has been a delivery is one of fact, the issue of what constitutes a delivery is a question of law. The trial court concluded there was valid delivery of the deed to Carr's attorney. This conclusion must be upheld if it can be sustained on any legal theory supported by the evidence. In determining whether a deed has been delivered, the question is whether the grantor parted with all dominion and control over the instrument at the time of delivery to the third person with the intent that it takes effect as a conveyance at the very time of delivery. Thus the issue is whether Carr intended to relinquish all dominion and control over the quitclaim deed at the time she delivered it to her attorney. This finding is supported by the attorney's testimony that she delivered the signed deed to him with specific instructions. There was no mention of her power to recall the deed. While Carr did in fact remain in possession of the property until her death, possession is not determinative. Where the grantor delivers a deed to a third person with the intent to part with all control and without a reservation of a right to recall it, the legal effect of the transaction is equivalent to a delivery of the deed to the grantee, conveying a fee while reserving to the grantor the use and enjoyment of the land during his natural life. Affirmed.

ANALYSIS

Courts have reached different conclusions with respect to the same issue. In the case of a "gift causa mortis," or a gift made in contemplation of the grantor's death, the courts invoke more stringent standards than inter vivos gifts, gifts made during the grantor's lifetime, based on the potential for fraud.

Quicknotes

BENEFICIARY A third party who is the recipient of the benefit of a transaction undertaken by another.

DELIVERY The transfer of title or possession of property.

GIFT CAUSA MORTIS A gift made contingent on the donor's anticipated death.

INTER VIVOS GIFT A gift that is made, and is to take effect, while the parties are living.

QUITCLAIM DEED A deed whereby the grantor conveys whatever interest he or she may have in the property without any warranties or covenants as to title.

WARRANTY DEED A deed that guarantees that the conveyor possesses the title that he purports to convey.

WILL An instrument setting forth the distribution to be made of an individual's estate upon his death; since a will is not effective until the death of its maker, it is revocable during his life.

Rosengrant v. Rosengrant

Heir-at-law (P) v. Nephew of decedents (D)

Okla. Ct. App., 629 P.2d. 800 (1981).

NATURE OF CASE: Appeal from order invalidating a deed.

FACT SUMMARY: Harold Rosengrant purported to convey title to his nephew Jay Rosengrant (D) by executing a deed, handing it to Jay (D) to hold for a minute, and then giving it to a banker for safekeeping.

RULE OF LAW

A deed is not considered to be delivered if the grantor continues to exercise control over the property and the delivery is conditional on the grantor's death.

FACTS: Harold Rosengrant, an elderly individual, owned certain property. At one point he purported to convey the property to Jay Rosengrant (D). He arranged a meeting at a bank where he took a deed, handed it to Jay (D), took it back, and then put it in a safe deposit box. The understanding apparently was that the deed would pass to Jay (D) upon Harold's death. During the remainder of his life, Harold continued to live on the property and pay its expenses. Upon Harold's death, Jay (D) recorded the deed. A suit was then filed by other heirs (P) of Harold to void the deed. The trial court so ordered, and Jay (D) appealed.

ISSUE: Is a deed considered to be delivered if the grantor continues to exercise control over the property and the delivery is conditioned on the grantor's death?

HOLDING AND DECISION: (Boydston, J.) No. A deed is not considered to be delivered if the grantor continues to exercise control over the property and the delivery is conditional on the grantor's death. For a deed to convey title there must be an intent on the part of the grantor to convey title at time of delivery. If the grantor does not intend to presently convey title, no delivery occurs, and without delivery, no conveyance occurs. Here, Harold Rosengrant handed the deed to Jay (D), but he did not deliver it in a legal sense because he did not intend to part with title at that time. What he appeared to be trying to do was create a testamentary instrument passing title upon his death. Under Oklahoma law this cannot be done. A testamentary instrument must meet various statutory requirements that were not met here, so the purported deed was a legal nullity, and the property at issue remains in Harold's estate. Affirmed.

ANALYSIS

It seems that what the parties intended in the transaction at issue here was conveyance with retention of a life estate. Creation of such an estate in property is not particularly difficult, but it is quite likely that the parties here did not seek legal advice prior to their transaction. The lesson of this story is rather obvious.

Quicknotes

CONVEYANCE The transfer of property, or title to property, from one party to another party.

TESTAMENTARY INSTRUMENT An instrument that takes effect upon the death of the maker.

CHAPTER 43

Real Estate Brokers

Quick Reference Rules of Law

Ellsworth Dobbs, Inc. v. Johnson v. Iarussi

Real estate broker (P) v. Property owner (D) v. Potential buyers (D)

N.J. Sup. Ct., 50 N.J. 528, 236 A.2d 843 (1967).

NATURE OF CASE: Breach of contract suit.

FACT SUMMARY: Dobbs (P) brought suit against the Johnsons (D) and Iarussi (D) seeking payment of a commission allegedly owed him pursuant to a land sale contract.

RULE OF LAW

Absent default by the seller, the contract of sale must be performed by the buyer before liability for the real estate broker's commission is imposed upon the seller.

FACTS: Dobbs (P), a real estate broker, sued the Johnsons (D) and Iarussi (D) for commissions allegedly earned in a real estate transaction. The Johnsons and Iarussi (D) entered into an agreement to sell property owned by the Johnsons (D). Title did not close due to Iarussi's (D) inability to obtain financing and the Johnsons (D) released him from the contract. Dobbs (P) brought suit charging the Johnsons (D) with breach of an express agreement to pay a commission due for bringing about the contract of sale and charging Iarussi (D) with breach of an implied agreement to pay the commission if he failed to complete the purchase. The trial judge held that Dobbs's (P) commission claim against the Johnsons (D) vested upon the execution of the contract of sale. The jury concluded that the amount due Dobbs (P) was $15,000. The jury also found that Iarussi (D) was liable for payment of the commission since the implied agreement to perform the contract was breached by Iarussi (D). The appellate division reversed and Dobbs (P) appealed.

ISSUE: Absent default by the seller, must the contract of sale be performed by the buyer before liability for the real estate broker's commission is imposed upon the seller?

HOLDING AND DECISION: (Francis, J.) Yes. Absent default by the seller, the contract of sale must be performed by the buyer before liability for the real estate broker's commission is imposed upon the seller. This court rejects the proposition that whenever the owner-seller enters into a binding sale contract with the proffered customer, the broker's right of commission is complete unless the owner has expressly agreed that such right is contingent upon the closing of title. The basic law governing the owner-broker relationship is that absent default by the owner, the contract of sale must be performed by the buyer before liability for commission is imposed upon the owner. In entering into the contract of sale, the owner is entitled to assume that the customer is, or will be at the time fixed for closing, financially able to meet the terms of sale, and that he is now, and will be at performance time, willing to complete the transaction. Even if both broker and seller in good faith believe the buyer to be financially able to perform, and it turns out otherwise, the seller cannot be held liable for the commission. The issue then becomes, to what extent may the broker contract out of these general rules? Whenever the substantial inequality of bargaining power, position or advantage appears, a provision to the contrary in an agreement prepared or presented or negotiated or procured by the broker is to be deemed inconsistent with public policy and unenforceable. Here the claim against the Johnsons (D) must fail since title did not close solely as a result of the financial incapacity of Iarussi (D). No wrongful conduct on the part of the Johnsons (D) frustrated the closing of title. Where a broker's right to commission depends on the completion of the contract by the buyer, and the buyer fails or refuses to perform, the seller is under no duty to the broker to sue the buyer for damages or specific performance. He may accept forfeiture by the buyer, retain the down payment and not remain liable to the broker. If, however, he does sue for breach of contract and recovers damages therefore, he is deemed to have accepted the benefit of the broker's services and then is liable for the commission. Reversed and remanded.

ANALYSIS

The court also addresses the liability of the buyer to the real estate broker. When a prospective buyer solicits a broker to find or show him property to purchase, and the broker in fact finds such property (and the buyer knows that the broker will earn commission from the seller), there is an implied promise that the buyer will complete performance. If the buyer fails to complete performance without a valid excuse, he is liable to the broker for breach of that promise. Here Iarussi (D) made such an implied promise and became liable to Dobbs (P) for the commission.

Quicknotes

BREACH OF CONTRACT Unlawful failure by a party to perform its obligations pursuant to contract.

Easton v. Strassburger, Valley of California, Inc.

Buyer (P) v. Listing broker (D)

Cal. Ct. App., 152 Cal. App. 3d 90, 199 Cal. Rptr. 383 (1984).

NATURE OF CASE: Appeal from finding of liability in suit for fraud and negligence in the sale of residential property.

FACT SUMMARY: Agents of Valley of California, Inc. (Valley Realty) (D), the seller's real estate broker, refused to inquire further when warning signs of soil problems were uncovered, and subsequent landslides damaged the property severely.

RULE OF LAW

The duty of the real estate broker representing the seller to disclose facts includes the affirmative duty to conduct a reasonably competent and diligent inspection of the residential property and to disclose all facts materially affecting the value or desirability of the property that such an investigation would reveal.

FACTS: Easton (P) purchased an improved property, which included a large home, a pool, and a guest house, for $170,000. Shortly after the sale, there was a massive earth movement that damaged the house. Experts determined that the slide occurred because a portion of the property was fill that had not been properly engineered and compacted. Damage was so severe that the property was appraised as low as $20,000, and repair costs were estimated at $213,000. Valley of California, Inc. (Valley Realty) (D), a broker that sold the property to Easton (P), was represented in the sale by two agents. The agents made several inspections, and they were aware of certain "red flags" that should have indicated soil problems. Despite the indicators, the agents did not request a soil stability test, and they did not inform Easton (P) of the potential problem. Easton (P) filed suit against Valley Realty (D) for negligence and fraud. The judge at trial instructed the jury that the broker is under a duty to disclose facts materially affecting desirability or value that through reasonable diligence should have been known. Valley Realty (D) was found negligent and appealed.

ISSUE: Does a broker's duty of due care in a residential real estate transaction include a duty to conduct a reasonably competent and diligent inspection of property he has listed for sale in order to discover defects for the benefit of the buyer?

HOLDING AND DECISION: (Kline, J.) Yes. The duty of the real estate broker representing the seller to disclose facts includes the affirmative duty to conduct a reasonably competent and diligent inspection of the residential property and to disclose all facts materially affecting the value or desirability of the property that such an investigation would reveal. It is already law that a broker must disclose all facts known to him that affect the desirability or value of a property if those facts are accessible only to the broker or are not known or within reach of the buyer. But to this point, there has been no clear statement in the law that the broker is under a duty to disclose facts he should have known after reasonable efforts. If a broker were required to disclose only known defects, the incentive would be to rely on his own ignorance. Such a result is undesirable since the seller's broker is usually in the best position to discover and provide reliable information. In this case, Valley Realty's (D) agents were aware of warning signs in soil composition. They chose to turn a blind eye to the matter. Since they were clearly in the best position to investigate further, it is just to impose a duty of care upon them that requires a diligent search into the matter. Having imposed this duty, it is clear from the facts that it was not met. Affirmed.

ANALYSIS

This case was not greeted warmly by California brokers. The legislature, responding to brokers' lobbying efforts, enacted legislation that had the effect of limiting the scope of the duty of care to the discovery of visually identifiable defects only. See West's *Ann. Cal. Civil Code* § 2079. The same law also contains a two-year statute of limitation running from the time the buyer purchases the property.

Quicknotes

FRAUD A false representation of facts with the intent that another will rely on the misrepresentation to his detriment.

NEGLIGENCE Conduct falling below the standard of care that a reasonable person would demonstrate under similar conditions.

CHAPTER 44

Contracting for Marketable Title

Quick Reference Rules of Law

PAGE

1. **Marketability in a Land Sale Contract.** In a land sale contract defining "marketability" as acceptance of the title for insurance by a reputable title insurance company, the insurance company need not accept the title unconditionally to make the title marketable. (Laba v. Carey) *210*

2. **Reasonably Prudent Man Standard.** A title is considered unmarketable if a reasonably prudent man, under the circumstances, would refuse to accept title to the property in the ordinary course of business. (Madhavan v. Sucher) *211*

3. **Encumbrance on Marketability.** A zoning ordinance existing at the time a land sale contract is entered, and which regulates only the use of the property, is not an encumbrance making the title unmarketable. (Voorheesville Rod and Gun Club v. E.W. Tompkins Company) *212*

4. **Merchantable Title.** Merchantable title is such title that a reasonable person would accept as not subject to a doubt or cloud that would affect its market value. (Nelson v. Anderson) *213*

Laba v. Carey

Buyer (P) v. Seller (D

N.Y. Ct. App., 29 N.Y.2d 302, 277 N.E.2d 641 (1971).

NATURE OF CASE: Action to recover down payment and expenses incident to land sale contract.

FACT SUMMARY: Laba (P) refused a deed with minor defects, claiming unmarketability.

RULE OF LAW

In a land sale contract defining "marketability" as acceptance of the title for insurance by a reputable title insurance company, the insurance company need not accept the title unconditionally to make the title marketable.

FACTS: Laba (P), as buyer under a land sale contract, paid Carey (D) $5,700 down, plus the cost of a title search and land survey, the amounts to become a lien on the property and refundable in the event Carey (D) failed to perform. The sale contract contained a "subject to" clause, providing that Laba (P) would take the property subject to two tenancies, easements of record, and anything shown by an accurate survey that did not render the property unmarketable. The contract also contained an "insurance" clause providing that Laba (P) would take the property only if the title company agreed to insure the title. The title search uncovered a telephone easement and a "Waiver of Legal Grades," i.e., an agreement between Carey's (D) predecessor and the city to allow a sidewalk one foot below "legal grade" to match with neighboring sidewalks but binding the owner and his assigns to install a "legal" grade sidewalk whenever the Commissioner of Highways directed. The title company agreed to insure the title excepting only the telephone easement and the "Waiver of Legal Grades." The land survey found the building on the property to be above legal grade. At closing, Laba (P) rejected the deed, claiming failure to deliver marketable title, then, sued for return of his down payment and other expenses. The trial court dismissed, saying the items excluded from the title insurance were specifically accepted by Laba (P) under the "subject to" clause. Thus, reading the two clauses together, Laba (P) was tendered exactly what he agreed to accept under the contract. The appellate court reversed, holding the title unmarketable due to the insurance company's refusal to insure the title "unconditionally." Carey (D) appealed.

ISSUE: When a land sale contract defines "marketability" as acceptance of the title for insurance, must the insurance company accept the title unconditionally?

HOLDING AND DECISION: (Scileppi, J.) No. Contracts must be read to give the entire instrument effect. Thus, in order to ascertain the parties' intent as evidenced by the contract, the "insurance" and "subject to" clauses must be read together. Here, only those items—the easement and "Waiver of Legal Grade"—that Laba (P) agreed to accept under the "subject to" clause were excluded from the title policy obtained under the "insurance" clause, thus Carey's (D) tender was in complete conformity to the agreement in the sale contract. Furthermore, the "Waiver of Legal Grade" restriction in no way affects the use of the property. That Laba (P) might have to raise the sidewalk to conform to a future order of the Commissioner of Highways is only a normal incident of real property ownership and does not render the title unmarketable. The trial court's judgment, denying Laba (P) recovery of his down payment and expenses for failure to perform his contract, is reinstated. Reversed.

ANALYSIS

In *Laba*, the height of the sidewalk was not considered as making the title unmarketable. Marketability means property capable of being resold without undue difficulty. The standard is objective. There need not be actual or potential buyers waiting in the wings. If any reasonable doubt exists about the state of a seller's title, a buyer may refuse to accept tender. "A buyer may not be compelled to purchase a lawsuit."

Quicknotes

TITLE INSURANCE A policy insuring against loss incurred as the result of a defective title.

TITLE MARKETABILITY Title that, although not perfect, would be acceptable to a reasonably well-informed buyer exercising ordinary business prudence.

Madhavan v. Sucher

Potential purchasers (P) v. Potential sellers (D)

Mich. Ct. App., 105 Mich. App. 284, 306 N.W.2d 481 (1981).

NATURE OF CASE: Suit to recover deposit.

FACT SUMMARY: Plaintiffs brought suit to recover their $3,000 deposit for the purchase of defendants' home after refusing to close on the transaction on the basis that defendants' title was not marketable.

RULE OF LAW

A title is considered unmarketable if a reasonably prudent man, under the circumstances, would refuse to accept title to the property in the ordinary course of business.

FACTS: Plaintiffs executed an offer to purchase defendants' home and property. The purchase agreement provided that the sale was subject to the existing building and use restrictions, easements and zoning ordinances and required defendants to deliver a warranty deed conveying marketable title. Prior to closing the mortgagee disclosed to plaintiffs that a drainage easement encroached upon the property. Plaintiffs refused to close the transaction and defendants declared their $3,000 deposit forfeited. Plaintiffs brought suit to recover their deposit and the district court granted plaintiffs' motion for summary judgment on the basis that defendants were unable to convey marketable title due to the easement. Defendants appealed.

ISSUE: Is a title considered unmarketable if a reasonably prudent man, under the circumstances, would refuse to accept title to the property in the ordinary course of business?

HOLDING AND DECISION: (Cynar, J.) Yes. A title is considered unmarketable if a reasonably prudent man, under the circumstances, would refuse to accept title to the property in the ordinary course of business. Defendants were obliged to convey marketable title to plaintiffs. Marketable title is one that would assure the vendee the quiet and peaceful enjoyment of the property, which must be free from encumbrance. An encumbrance is anything that would constitute a burden on the title. It is not necessary that the title be bad in order to be unmarketable. The district court could reasonably determine that the drainage easement across the property constituted a significant encumbrance to render the title unmarketable. This is especially so since the title company refused to insure against the encumbrance. Affirmed.

ANALYSIS

The court did not hold here that title subject to any encumbrance would be unmarketable. A vendor is not required to convey title free from any easements; rather, the vendor is obligated to convey title that is marketable and fully insurable.

Quicknotes

TITLE MARKETABILITY Title that, although not perfect, would be acceptable to a reasonably well-informed buyer exercising ordinary business prudence.

Voorheesville Rod and Gun Club v. E.W. Tompkins Company

Potential purchaser (P) v. Landowner (D)

N.Y. Ct. App., 82 N.Y.2d 564, 626 N.E.2d 917 (1993).

NATURE OF CASE: Breach of contract suit.

FACT SUMMARY: Voorheesville Rod and Gun Club (P) sued for specific enforcement of a land sale contract or damages for breach of contract on the basis that E.W. Tompkins Company's (Tompkins) (D) title to the subject property was unmarketable due to Tompkins's (D) failure to obtain subdivision approval.

RULE OF LAW

A zoning ordinance existing at the time a land sale contract is entered, and which regulates only the use of the property, is not an encumbrance making the title unmarketable.

FACTS: Voorheesville Rod and Gun Club (Voorheesville) (P) signed a standard preprinted contract to purchase a portion of property owned by E.W. Tompkins Company (Tompkins) (D). The contract provided that the property would be conveyed by warranty deed subject to the covenants, conditions, restrictions and easements of record, so long as they did not render the title unmarketable. Prior to the closing date, Voorheesville's (P) attorney sent Tompkins's (D) attorney a copy of the Village of Voorheesville's subdivision regulations and requested that Tompkins (D) comply with them. Tompkins (D) did not seek such approval and sent Voorheesville (P) a time-of-the-essence notice, demanding the plaintiff close and, if it did not do so, it would be in anticipatory breach of contract. Voorheesville (P) failed to close and Tompkins (D) terminated the contract, returning the $5,000 deposit. Voorheesville (P) informed Tompkins (D) that termination of the contract was unacceptable since Tompkins's (D) failure to obtain subdivision approval rendered the title unmarketable and its bank was unwilling to close. Voorheesville (P) brought suit for specific performance of the contract or damages for breach and moved for partial summary judgment. The Supreme Court ordered the contract specifically performed and the appellate division affirmed. Then Voorheesville (P) moved for an order compelling Tompkins (D) to file the subdivision application and convey the property, which the supreme court granted.

ISSUE: Is a zoning ordinance existing at the time a land sale contract is entered, and which regulates only the use of the property, an encumbrance making the title unmarketable?

HOLDING AND DECISION: (Hancock, Jr., J.) No. A zoning ordinance existing at the time a land sale contract is entered, and which regulates only the use of the property, is not an encumbrance making the title unmarketable. The issue is whether the lack of subdivision approval renders the title to the subject property unmarketable. Nothing in the land sale contract itself imposes upon the defendant the affirmative obligation of obtaining subdivision approval. The contract, rather, provides that Voorheesville (P) was to purchase the property subject to the applicable zoning laws, which are closely related to the subdivision regulations. The rule is well established that where a person agrees to purchase real estate that is restricted by laws or ordinances, he is deemed to have entered into the contract subject to such restrictions and cannot later object. The only limitation placed on the plaintiff's duty to purchase the property subject to zoning laws is when the application of such laws would render the title unmarketable. The test of marketability of a title is whether there is an objection that would interfere with a sale or with the market value of the property. A marketable title is a title free from reasonable doubt, but not perfect title. The rationale is that the buyer should not be compelled to purchase property the title of which he may be later required to defend by litigation. He should have such title that is reasonably free from claim and any doubt that would have a negative effect on its market value. A zoning ordinance that exists at the time a contract was entered, which regulates only the use of the property, is generally not such an encumbrance making the title unmarketable. Reversed.

ANALYSIS

The court notes an exception where a contract expressly provides that the seller warrants and represents that the contract is not in violation of any zoning ordinance. In such cases the buyer may demand that the seller rectify the situation or return the money paid. Here the exception did not apply.

Quicknotes

BREACH OF CONTRACT Unlawful failure by a party to perform its obligations pursuant to contract.

TITLE MARKETABILITY Title that, although not perfect, would be acceptable to a reasonably well-informed buyer exercising ordinary business prudence.

ZONING ORDINANCE A statute that divides land into defined areas and which regulates the form and use of buildings and structures within those areas.

Nelson v. Anderson

Homeowner (P) v. Potential buyers (D)

Ill. App. Ct., 286 Ill. App.3d 706, 676 N.E.2d 735 (1997).

NATURE OF CASE: Merchantability of title.

FACT SUMMARY: The Andersons (D) sued to recover their deposit for the purchase of the Nelsons' (P) home, on the basis that the title to the property was unmerchantable.

RULE OF LAW

Merchantable title is such title that a reasonable person would accept as not subject to a doubt or cloud that would affect its market value.

FACTS: The Nelsons (P) contracted to sell their home to the Andersons (D). The contract required the Andersons (D) to pay a deposit of $1,500, with balance of the purchase price to be paid upon the delivery of a warranty deed conveying merchantable title. Closing was to be within thirty days of signing. The title report showed that the house was less than ten feet from the north lot line, in violation of an applicable setback covenant, prohibiting a building or any part of a building on any residential lot from being located less than ten feet from the property line of an adjacent owner. The Andersons (D) objected. The Nelsons (P) responded by obtaining written assurances from the title company that, for an additional fee, it would insure the building line exception at issue. The Andersons (D) were not satisfied with the condition of title, and filed suit to recover their deposit and the Nelsons (P) sued for damages. The cases were consolidated and each party moved for summary judgment. Judgment was granted in favor of the Andersons (D) on the ground that the sellers (P) did not provide merchantable title. The Nelsons (P) appealed.

ISSUE: Is merchantable title such title that a reasonable person would accept as not subject to a doubt or cloud that would affect its market value?

HOLDING AND DECISION: (Maag, J.) Yes. Merchantable title is such title that a reasonable person would accept as not subject to a doubt or cloud that would affect its market value. Merchantable title is not perfect title, but title reasonably secure against the hazard, annoyance and expense of future litigation. This is a question of law for the court. Here the title was encumbered by a violation of a restrictive covenant contained in the subdivision plat, which was recorded and thus ran with the land to bind the deeds of each lot in the subdivision. Violation of the covenant gives each owner in the subdivision the right to sue for its enforcement. Moreover, such cloud on the title would undoubtedly have a negative effect on the market value of the property. Thus, the title is unmerchantable. Affirmed.

ANALYSIS

The sellers' provision of assurances from the title insurance company did not affect a cure of the encumbrance on the title. Even if the sellers had provided cure that would indemnify the buyers from the costs of potential future litigation, courts recognize that buyers should not be bound to a transaction that is likely to result in future litigation.

Quicknotes

MERCHANTABLE TITLE Title that would be acceptable to a reasonably well-informed buyer exercising ordinary business prudence.

CHAPTER 45

Remedies for Breach of Marketing Contract

Quick Reference Rules of Law

PAGE

1. **Liquidated Damages.** In determining whether a contractual provision calls for liquidated damages, the court must view the transaction prospectively from the point of view of the parties on the particular facts of the case. (Covington v. Robinson) *216*

2. **Liquidated Damages.** Liquidated damages should not be awarded if the aggrieved party suffered no actual damages. (Colonial at Lynnfield, Inc. v. Sloan) *217*

3. **Actual Harm.** In order for a liquidated damages clause to be enforceable, the claimant must demonstrate that he has suffered actual harm. (Strouse v. Starbuck) *218*

4. **Specific Performance.** A contract to purchase a condominium unit may be specifically enforced even if the building containing the unit is used as rental housing instead. (Giannini v. First National Bank of Des Plaines) *219*

5. **Equitable Remedies.** Specific performance will not be granted if to do so would be inequitable or unfair. (Hilton v. Nelsen) *220*

Covington v. Robinson

Buyers (P) v. Property owner and seller (D)

Tenn. Ct. App., 723 S.W.2d 643 (1986).

NATURE OF CASE: Suit to recover earnest money deposited pursuant to a contract for sale of land.

FACT SUMMARY: Purchasers (P) of real property sought to recover $100,000 in earnest money deposited on the basis that it failed to obtain the necessary financing, which was a condition precedent to closing.

RULE OF LAW

In determining whether a contractual provision calls for liquidated damages, the court must view the transaction prospectively from the point of view of the parties on the particular facts of the case.

FACTS: Robinson (D) and Covington (P) contracted for the sale and purchase of property. The contract provided that it was contingent upon the buyers (P) obtaining a federal bank loan for 75 percent of the purchase price. The purchasers (P) posted $100,000 earnest money, which was to be divided equally between International Farm Management (D) and the sellers (D) upon default. Purchasers (P) declined to close the deal stating that the amount approved by the bank was slightly less than 75 percent. The earnest money was divided and plaintiffs brought this action. The trial court found that the loan money constituted 73.98 percent of the purchase price and that the purchasers (P) substantially complied with the contract. The court also found that the purchasers (P) failed to make a good faith effort to close the transaction and that retention of the $100,000 was reasonable. Purchasers (P) appealed.

ISSUE: In determining whether a contractual provision calls for liquidated damages, must the court view the transaction prospectively from the point of view of the parties on the particular facts of the case?

HOLDING AND DECISION: (McLemore, J.) Yes. In determining whether a contractual provision calls for liquidated damages, the court must view the transaction prospectively from the point of view of the parties on the particular facts of the case. Purchasers (P) contend that the $100,000 earnest money constituted a penalty that was unenforceable and that the trial court erred in finding the sum constituted liquidated damages. Furthermore, since defendants sold the property two months later, their damages should be limited to the difference in the contract sale price and the sale price to the third party, or $10,650. The law is well settled that a contractual provision will be construed as providing for liquidated damages where: (1) the parties contemplated that damages would flow from failure to perform; (2) such damages would be difficult to ascertain; and (3) the sum bears a reasonable proportion to the damages which the parties contemplated might flow from failure to perform. In determining whether a contractual provision calls for liquidated damages, the court must view the transaction prospectively from the point of view of the parties on the particular facts of the case. All the above factors are present in this case. There is nothing to indicate such amount is unconscionable or disproportionate to the damages likely to result from breach. Affirmed.

ANALYSIS

Where a purchaser defaults on a land sale contract, the seller is entitled to damages, so long as the applicable contract provision may be construed as a reasonable "liquidated damages" clause and not an unenforceable penalty.

Quicknotes

EARNEST MONEY A payment made by a buyer to a seller to evidence the intent to fulfill the obligations of a contract to purchase property.

LIQUIDATED DAMAGES An amount of money specified in a contract representing the damages owed in the event of breach.

Colonial at Lynnfield, Inc. v. Sloan

Hotel operators (P) v. General partner of prospective buyer corporation (D)

870 F.2d 761 (1st Cir. 1989).

NATURE OF CASE: Appeal of award of liquidated damages for breach of contract.

FACT SUMMARY: Liquidated damages for breach of a land sale contract were awarded to Colonial at Lynnfield, Inc. (P) even though it had suffered no actual damages.

RULE OF LAW

Liquidated damages should not be awarded if the aggrieved party suffered no actual damages.

FACTS: Colonial at Lynnfield, Inc. (Colonial) (P) operated a hotel in Lynnfield, Massachusetts. Facing a shortage of capital, it sought to sell an interest in the hotel. A contract was signed with Colonial Associates (Associates) (D), a limited partnership, for the latter to purchase a 49 percent interest in the hotel. The contract called for Associates' (D) obligation to arise only if sufficient limited partnerships were sold, and notification of this to be given by April 2, 1981. This date was extended, but Associates (D) never did notify Colonial (P) of its intention to proceed. The contract, calling for a $3,375,000 purchase price with a $200,000 liquidated damages clause, was declared in default by Colonial (P). Two months later Colonial (P) accepted a proposal from Lincoln National Development Corp. to purchase a 50 percent interest for $3.7 million. Colonial (P) sued to recover the $200,000 liquidated damages. The district court awarded the $200,000, and Associates (D) appealed.

ISSUE: Should liquidated damages be awarded if the aggrieved party suffered no actual damages?

HOLDING AND DECISION: (Coffin, J.) No. Liquidated damages should not be awarded if the aggrieved party suffered no actual damages. A liquidated damages clause is valid if it is a reflection of a legitimate estimate of an aggrieved party's damages; if it constitutes a penalty or forfeiture, it is invalid. Generally speaking, if it appears valid in light of what the parties knew at the time of contract formation, it will be held valid. Under Massachusetts law, however, which this court sitting in diversity must apply, actual damages can be easily ascertained and differ greatly from liquidated damages so as to make the liquidated damages into a penalty, the liquidated damages will be held invalid. Here, the contract price between Colonial (P) and Associates (D) called for a sale of 49 percent for $3,375,000. The subsequent sale to Lincoln of 50 percent for $3.7 million, even taking interest into account, resulted in a gain to Colonial (P) of $94,500 due to Associates' (D) breach. Since the breach did not cause a loss to Colonial (P), the liquidated damages clause should not be enforced. Reversed.

ANALYSIS

The rule employed here is not universal. Many jurisdictions do not permit the sort of retrospective analysis seen here. Moreover, some differentiate between residential and commercial property. With respect to goods, the Uniform Commercial Code would appear, per § 2-718, to permit either approach.

Quicknotes

BREACH OF CONTRACT Unlawful failure by a party to perform its obligations pursuant to contract.

LIQUIDATED DAMAGES An amount of money specified in a contract representing the damages owed in the event of breach.

Strouse v. Starbuck

Landowner (P) v. Potential purchaser (D)

Mo. Ct. App., 987 S.W.2d 827 (1999).

NATURE OF CASE: Petition seeking liquidated damages as the result of a breach of a real estate contract.

FACT SUMMARY: Strouse (P) brought suit against Starbuck (D) seeking liquidated damages, claiming that they failed to use reasonable diligence and good faith in obtaining financing.

RULE OF LAW

In order for a liquidated damages clause to be enforceable, the claimant must demonstrate that he has suffered actual harm.

FACTS: Strouse (P) brought suit against Starbuck (D) seeking liquidated damages as a result of a breach of a real estate contract. Starbuck (D) failed to obtain financing for the purchase of a 239-acre tract of land owned by Strouse (P) and informed Strouse one week prior to the closing date that that they would not be able to close on the contract. Clair Land held $10,000 in escrow, which it deposited with the court. The judgment ordered the $10,000 be released to Starbuck (D) and Strouse (P) appealed.

ISSUE: In order for a liquidated damages clause to be enforceable, must the claimant demonstrate that he has suffered actual harm?

HOLDING AND DECISION: (Prewitt, J.) Yes. In order for a liquidated damages clause to be enforceable, the claimant must demonstrate that he has suffered actual harm. Strouse (P) claimed that the trial court erred in failing to award him liquidated damages under the real estate contract. Missouri law requires a showing of actual harm to trigger a liquidated damages clause. This requires that Strouse (P) show not only that Starbuck (D) breached the contract, but that damages have accrued as a result. This is because while liquidated damages clauses are enforceable, penalty clauses are not, and in the absence of actual damages, a liquidated damages clause actually becomes a penalty clause and is unenforceable. Strouse (P) did not conclusively prove that he suffered any actual damage. We defer to the trial court's conclusion that Strouse's (P) testimony was insufficient to show he suffered actual harm. Affirmed.

ANALYSIS

Where a buyer breaches a contract for sale, the seller may be entitled to damages. Generally, the contract of sale provides that a deposit is to be retained by the seller upon breach by the buyer. Such clauses are enforceable so long as they are construed as liquidated damages and not an unreasonable penalty.

Quicknotes

BREACH OF CONTRACT Unlawful failure by a party to perform its obligations pursuant to contract.

GOOD FAITH An honest intention to abstain from taking advantage of another.

LIQUIDATED DAMAGES An amount of money specified in a contract representing the damages owed in the event of breach.

Giannini v. First National Bank of Des Plaines

Potential purchaser (P) v. Title holder (D)

Ill. Ct. App., 136 Ill. App. 3d 971, 483 N.E. 2d 924 (1985).

NATURE OF CASE: Appeal of dismissal of cause of action for specific performance in a breach of contract action.

FACT SUMMARY: Giannini (P) sought specific performance of a contract to purchase a condominium unit in a building that was originally planned as such but was made into rental property instead.

RULE OF LAW

A contract to purchase a condominium unit may be specifically enforced even if the building containing the unit is used as rental housing instead.

FACTS: Giannini (P) contracted with Stape Builders, Inc. (D) to purchase a condominium unit in a building it was erecting. Due to a poor market, an insufficient number of units was sold, and Stape Builders (D) eventually became insolvent and was later dissolved. Unity Savings (D), the mortgage holder, began operating the building as an apartment complex. Giannini (P), who had paid $62,330 down, sued for breach of contract, seeking specific performance or, in the alternative, damages and/or restitution. The trial court dismissed the specific performance cause of action as unavailable as a matter of law. Giannini (P) made an interlocutory appeal thereof.

ISSUE: May a contract to purchase a condominium unit be specifically enforced even if the building containing the unit is used as rental housing instead?

HOLDING AND DECISION: (Jiganti, J.) Yes. A contract to purchase a condominium unit may be specifically enforced even if the building containing the unit is used as rental housing instead. Generally speaking, a party is entitled to specific performance of a land sale contract as a matter of right, and a unit in a condominium is considered real estate. Unity Savings (D) contends that several reasons for not adhering to this rule exist in the context of a condominium building that is used as an apartment instead. The first is that specific performance is impossible because the condominium doesn't "exist." This is a specious argument, as the unit does exist; it is merely called something else. The next argument is that the requirement of mutuality of remedy is not fulfilled. However, this requirement is waived when the party invoking it is solely responsible for the breach, which is the case here. Finally, Unity Savings (D) argues against specific performance on the basis that it would be uneconomical. This is a factual issue properly decided at trial, not at the pleading stage. The trial court should consider the relative hardships involved; something it did not do. Consequently, the decision here was in error. Reversed and remanded.

ANALYSIS

Generally speaking, specific performance is available when damages for a breach would be inadequate. In the context of real estate, the legal notion is that each piece of property is unique, and damages cannot substitute therefor. Consequently, specific performance is generally available for breaches of land sale contracts.

Quicknotes

BREACH OF CONTRACT Unlawful failure by a party to perform its obligations pursuant to contract.

SPECIFIC PERFORMANCE An equitable remedy whereby the court requires the parties to perform their obligations pursuant to a contract.

Hilton v. Nelsen

Potential purchaser (P) v. Farm owners (D)

Minn. Sup. Ct., 283 N.W.2d 877 (1979).

NATURE OF CASE: Appeal from order of specific performance.

FACT SUMMARY: The Nelsens (D), after contracting to sell a farm to Hilton (P) on terms very favorable to Hilton (P), attempted to renege when they realized the nature of the terms.

RULE OF LAW

Specific performance will not be granted if to do so would be inequitable or unfair.

FACTS: The Nelsens (D), without counsel, contracted to sell a farm to Hilton (P) on terms very favorable to Hilton (P), who had counsel. The terms called for low down payment and long-term, low-interest financing, along with a unilateral right on Hilton's (P) part to back out under certain circumstances that were almost sure to occur, such as the Nelsens' (D) inability to completely clear the title. Closing was to be between May 1, 1975, and May 1, 1976, although the Nelsens (D) believed the prior date to be final. Hilton (P) did not close by May 1, 1975, and the Nelsens (D) later refused to consummate the sale. A pre-existing mortgage on the farm was foreclosed, and Hilton (P) bought it at the sale. Mandt (D) purchased the Nelsens' (D) redemption rights and redeemed the farm, later reconveying to the Nelsens (D). Hilton (P), who had intended to rent out the property, sued for specific performance, and the trial court granted it. The Nelsens (D) appealed.

ISSUE: Will a court grant specific performance in a land sale contract if to do so would be inequitable or unfair?

HOLDING AND DECISION: (Stone, J.) No. Specific performance will not be granted in a land sale contract when to do so would be inequitable or unfair. While the unique nature of land generally makes specific performance the preferred remedy in a land sale contract breach, it does not always. Due to the unequal sophistication of the parties as evidenced by the Nelsens' (D) lack of counsel, the rental purpose of the land, Hilton's (P) ability to unilaterally terminate, lack of mutuality of remedy, overreaching by Hilton (P) in the payment terms, and evidence that the Nelsens (D) never understood what they were signing, it would be unfair to specifically enforce the contract. While none of these would necessarily be determinative, their totality dictates that Hilton (P) seeks his remedy at law. Affirmed in part, reversed in part, and remanded.

ANALYSIS

This decision can be seen as an example of two very basic equitable doctrines. The first is that an equitable remedy will issue only if the legal remedy is inadequate. All Hilton (P) wanted out of the land was income, so therefore damages were adequate. Second, it illustrates the legal maxim, "He who seeks equity must do equity." Hilton (P) apparently took advantage of the Nelsens (D), and courts are loathe to help litigants in this position.

Quicknotes

FORECLOSURE An action to recover the amount due on a mortgage of real property where the owner has failed to meet the mortgage obligations, terminating the owner's interest in the property which must then be sold to satisfy the debt.

SPECIFIC PERFORMANCE An equitable remedy whereby the court requires the parties to perform their obligations pursuant to a contract.

CHAPTER 46

Introduction to Mortgages

Quick Reference Rules of Law

Peugh v. Davis

Grantor (P) v. Grantee (D)

96 U.S. (6 Otto) 332, 24 E.Ed. 775 (1877).

NATURE OF CASE: Appeal of defense verdict in action seeking redemption of mortgaged property.

FACT SUMMARY: Peugh (P) deeded certain real property to Davis (D) as security for a loan, and then sought to redeem it subsequent to his default.

RULE OF LAW

A party deeding property as security for a loan may redeem the property.

FACTS: Davis (D) loaned Peugh (P) $2,000. Peugh (P) deeded certain real estate to Davis (D) at the same time. When payment was made, the deed was returned. The same transaction was effected again, this time for $1,500. The loan was not repaid in a timely fashion. Several months later, Davis (D) advanced another $500. Subsequent to this, Peugh (P) offered the principal, plus interest, to redeem the property. Davis (D) refused. Peugh (P) brought an equitable redemption action. The trial court held the right of redemption not to exist, and entered judgment in Davis's (D) favor. Peugh (P) appealed.

ISSUE: May a party deeding property as security for a loan, redeem the property?

HOLDING AND DECISION: (Field, J.) Yes. A party deeding property as security for a loan may redeem the property. It is an established doctrine that a court will treat a deed, absolute in form, as a mortgage when it is executed as security for a loan. In being treated as a security transaction, the equitable right of redemption is available. This right cannot be forfeited, even upon the stipulation of both parties. In light of the fact that the deed had once been given contemporaneous to a prior loan, returned upon payment, and then given contemporaneous to the loan at issue, there can be no doubt that the deed was meant to secure the loan. Davis (D) argues that the subsequent advance of $500 was in consideration for a waiver of the right of redemption. While the right of redemption may be subsequently bargained away by the mortgagor, such waiver must be clear and unequivocal. No such evidence exists here. Reversed and remanded.

ANALYSIS

Redemption is an old common-law right. It arose in courts of equity, in much the same form it exists now. In many states, the common-law right has been superseded by statute. The terms tend to vary from state to state, but the right can be found in almost all jurisdictions, if not all.

Quicknotes

REDEMPTION The right to redeem or take back property or title that was issued pursuant to a document containing a reacquisition clause. Redemption rights may have a limited time period during which the right can be exercised.

SECURED TRANSACTION A transaction where security agreement provides for a security interest.

SECURITY INTEREST An interest in property that may be sold upon a default in payment of the debt.

Johnson v. Cherry

Farm owner (P) v. Bank director (D)

Tex. Sup. Ct., 726 S.W.2d 4 (1987).

NATURE OF CASE: Appeal of reversal of order canceling deed.

FACT SUMMARY: Johnson (P) contended that a deed given by him to Cherry (D) was in fact a mortgage.

RULE OF LAW

An instrument that appears to be a deed may in fact be a mortgage.

FACTS: Johnson (P) was in serious arrears on payments he owed on a 348-acre farm he owned, 200 acres of which were declared as a homestead. Johnson (P) agreed with Cherry (D) and Texas State Bank (Bank) (D) of which Cherry (D) was a director, that he would deed the property to the Bank (D) for $120,000, with an option to repurchase for $132,000 and reassumption of a note owed to his ex-wife, which was secured by the property. The transaction also called for a lease of one year by Johnson (P) with semi-annual payments of $12,510. Johnson (P) failed to pay the second installment, and the Bank (D) initiated eviction proceedings. Johnson (P) brought an action seeking to cancel the deed, claiming that the deed was in fact a mortgage, invalid because it covered homesteaded property. A jury found the instrument to be a mortgage rather than a deed. The trial court canceled the deed, awarded $9,612 to Johnson (P), and refused to enter a judgment in favor of the Bank (D) for the money loaned. The court of appeals reversed. Johnson (P) appealed.

ISSUE: May an instrument that appears to be a deed, in fact be a mortgage?

HOLDING AND DECISION: (Spears, J.) Yes. An instrument that appears to be a deed may in fact be a mortgage. An instrument that has the trappings of a deed may in fact be a mortgage, depending on the intention of the parties and the attending circumstances. Even when the instrument appears on its face to be a deed absolute, parol evidence is admissible to determine its status. The issue is one of fact. Here, the jury heard conflicting testimony and found the instrument to be a disguised mortgage. If supported by the evidence, such a finding will be sustained. Here, evidence was presented via Johnson's (P) testimony that the transaction was intended as a loan. While not conclusive, the transaction's structure is consistent with this contention. Since the jury's finding was supportable, it should have been sustained. [The court then reinstated the order canceling the deed but ruled that equity entitled the Bank (D) and Cherry (D) to the funds that they had loaned. The matter was remanded to the trial court with instructions to enter such an order, and giving Cherry (D) and the Bank (D) a lien on the homesteaded 148 acres.] Reversed and remanded.

ANALYSIS

The sale-leaseback option to repurchase type of transaction can be used for any number of reasons. Sometimes it has tax ramifications. Other times, and possibly here (it is unclear from the opinion), it is used to evade usury laws. In such circumstances, courts tend to look behind the form of the transaction to its substance.

Quicknotes

PAROL EVIDENCE Evidence given verbally; extraneous evidence.

CHAPTER 47

Covenants of Title

Quick Reference Rules of Law

Holmes Development, LLC v. Cook

Real estate buyer (P) v. Real estate seller (D)

Utah Sup. Ct., 48 P.3d 895 (2002).

NATURE OF CASE: Suit for breach of covenants of title in a warranty deed.

FACT SUMMARY: One developer granted a parcel of land to another developer by warranty deed. The purchaser later discovered defects in the quitclaim deed by which the seller had purported to acquire title to the parcel.

RULE OF LAW

A grantor breaches the covenants of seisin and right to convey in a warranty deed if the grantor does not own the land that the warranty deed purports to convey.

FACTS: Cook (D) purchased a 323-acre parcel and another parcel of 73 acres, and he conveyed both parcels to his company, Cook Development (D). Cook Development (D), in turn, formed two limited liability companies (LLCs) with Premier Homes: Lake Creek Farms (LC Farms) and Lake Creek Associates (LC Associates). Cook Development (D) then conveyed the 323-acre parcel to LC Farms and conveyed the 73-acre parcel to LC Associates. Eventually, Cook Development (D) and Premier decided to dissolve their two LLCs, which required that the two parcels be conveyed back to Cook Development (D). The quitclaim deed that purported to convey the 323-acre tract back to Cook Development (D) mistakenly showed that LC Associates, not LC Farms, was the grantor. Cook Development (D) then conveyed both properties to Holmes Development (P), who discovered, several months after the closing, that the quitclaim deed conveying the larger parcel back to Cook Development (D) was erroneous. The title insurance company tried to cure the defect with a revised quitclaim deed, but Premier refused to sign the new deed. Premier eventually purported to sell the 323-acre parcel to yet another developer, which brought a quiet title action on the property, immediately filing a lis pendens as notice of the quiet title suit; the lis pendens was filed after Cook Development (D) conveyed the parcel to Holmes (P). The trial court in the quiet title action found that title in the 323-acre property had vested in Holmes (P). During that suit, though, the lis pendens prevented Holmes (P) from selling any lots in the 323-acre parcel. Holmes (P) then sued Cook Development (D), alleging in part that the defendants had breached the covenants of title in conveying the larger property to Holmes (P). The trial court granted summary judgment for Cook Development (D) on that claim. Holmes (P) appealed.

ISSUE: Does a grantor breach any of the covenants of title in a warranty deed if the grantor does not own the land that the warranty deed purports to convey?

HOLDING AND DECISION: (Russon, J.) Yes. A grantor breaches the covenants of seisin and right to convey in a warranty deed if the grantor does not own the land that the warranty deed purports to convey. By Utah statute, a properly executed warranty deed inherently contains five covenants of title: covenants (1) of seisin, (2) of the right to convey, (3) against encumbrances, (4) of warranty, and (5) of quiet enjoyment. The parties raise no issue about the deed's validity or the validity of its execution, and accordingly the five covenants shall be deemed contained in the warranty deed in this case. The covenants of seisin and of the right to convey, which are essentially synonymous, ensure that the grantor can legally convey the property to the grantee. Cook Development (D) breached these two covenants here because it did not own the larger parcel when it delivered the warranty deed to Holmes (P). On this record, however, Cook Development (D) did not breach any of the other three covenants of title. There was no breach of the covenant against encumbrances because the lis pendens was filed after Cook Development (D) delivered the warranty deed to Holmes (P), and because Holmes (P) failed to show that any other encumbrance existed at the time of delivery. Similarly, summary judgment for Cook Development (D) was appropriate on claims for breaches of the covenants of quiet enjoyment and of warranty. On those covenants, Holmes (P) cannot meet the threshold requirement of showing a title paramount to its own for the 323-acre parcel; the quiet title action conclusively determined that Holmes (P) holds the paramount title to the property. Affirmed.

ANALYSIS

The appellate court affirmed summary judgment for Cook Development (D), even while finding a breach of the covenants of seisin and of the right to convey, because Holmes (P) was entitled only to nominal damages for the breach.

Quicknotes

COVENANT AGAINST ENCUMBRANCES A guarantee in a contract that the interest in property being conveyed is unencumbered.

COVENANT OF SEISIN A promise that the conveyor of property has the lawful right to convey the interest he is attempting to transfer.

LIS PENDENS A pending action.

WARRANTY DEED A deed that guarantees that the conveyor possesses the title that he purports to convey.

St. Paul Title Insurance Corp., as Subrogee of GECC Financial Services v. Owen

Title insurer (P) v. Grantee (D)

Ala. Sup. Ct., 452 So. 2d 482 (1984).

NATURE OF CASE: Appeal of defense judgment in action for damages based on breach of covenants of title.

FACT SUMMARY: St. Paul Title Insurance Corp. (P) sought to maintain a breach of covenant of title action against remote grantor Albert Owen (D).

RULE OF LAW

Under a warranty deed, a grantor may be liable to remote grantees for breach of title.

FACTS: Albert Owen (D) granted title to certain real estate under a warranty deed to James and Cheryl Owen (the Owens) (D). The property was then conveyed by statutory warranty deed to Carlisle, who mortgaged the property to GECC Financial Services (GECC). Title insurance was issued by St. Paul Title Insurance Corp. (St. Paul) (P). Carlisle defaulted on his loan. GECC sought to foreclose, but was unable to do so due to a defect in title that preceded Albert Owen's (D) title. St. Paul (P) indemnified GECC, and brought a subrogation action against the Owens (D) for breach of warranty of title. The trial court held that no action could be maintained against a remote grantor. St. Paul (P) appealed.

ISSUE: May a grantor under a warranty deed be liable to remote grantees for breach of title?

HOLDING AND DECISION: (Maddox, J.) Yes. A grantor under a warranty deed may be liable to remote grantees for breach of title. If a covenant runs with the land, a grantor executing a warranty deed may be liable to any remote grantee for any defect that existed at the time of the deed's execution. Here, the defect alleged is that of title. The covenants of quiet enjoyment and warranty of title, which are virtually synonymous, do run with the land. Since the claimed defect is one of title, an action can be maintained by St. Paul (P) against Albert Owen (D). As to James and Cheryl Owen (D), their deed was a statutory warranty deed, which differs from a general warranty deed in that it only warrants against defects created by the warranting grantor. Since the defect preceded their title, the Owens (D) cannot be liable. Reversed and remanded.

ANALYSIS

A difference of opinion exists as to the damages awardable against a remote grantor for breach of a covenant running with the land. Some courts permit recovery up to the aggrieved party's losses. Others limit damages to consideration received by the remote grantor.

Quicknotes

WARRANTY DEED A deed that guarantees that the conveyor possesses the title that he purports to convey.

Babb v. Weemer

Grantee (P) v. Grantor (D)

Cal. Ct. of App., 225 Cal. App. 2d 546 (1964).

NATURE OF CASE: Appeal from denial of damages.

FACT SUMMARY: Weemer (D) conveyed property to the Rosettes by a grant deed which failed to mention a trust deed on the property, and the Rosettes conveyed the property to the Babbs (P) by a grant deed which was subject to encumbrances of record.

RULE OF LAW

Covenants that land is free from encumbrances "are personal covenants not running with the land" (i.e., personal between the parties contracting for them), and, as such, they do not entitle a succeeding grantee or assignee to maintain an action in his own name for their breach.

FACTS: After Weemer (D) executed a first deed of trust on certain real property which he owned, he conveyed this property by grant deed to the Rosettes. In furtherance of this conveyance, the express written contract of sale, contained in the escrow instructions, fully set forth the existence of a deed of trust. The grant deed, though, contained no reference to the deed of trust. Later, the Rosettes conveyed the property to the Babbs (P) by a grant deed "subject to encumbrances and easements of record." Before the execution of this deed, the Babbs (P) searched the records and found the first deed of trust. After the execution of the deed, the Babbs (P) brought an action against Weemer (D) on the grant deed to the Rosettes. The Babbs (P) claimed that, since the original grant deed to the Rosettes contained no reference to the first trust deed, it carried an implied covenant that the property was free of such encumbrance. They further claimed that this implied covenant runs with the land, and, therefore, entitled them to sue personally for its breach. After the trial court held in favor of Weemer (D), the Babbs (P) appealed.

ISSUE: Does a covenant that land is free from encumbrances "run with the land" so that any succeeding grantee may bring an action for its breach?

HOLDING AND DECISION: (Burke, J.) No. Covenants that land is free from encumbrances "are personal covenants not running with the land" (i.e., personal between the parties contracting for them), and, as such, they do not entitle a succeeding grantee or assignee to maintain an action in his own name for their breach. Here, therefore, the Babbs (P) are not entitled to maintain such an action under the grant deed of the Rosettes. Furthermore, the Rosettes would not have been permitted to have maintained such an action in their own right. Although a grant deed is generally held to contain an implied covenant against encumbrances, whenever the parties expressly agree to the contrary there is no implied covenant. Here, the Rosettes expressly agreed, in the escrow instructions, to take the land subject to the first trust deed. Affirmed.

ANALYSIS

Statutes in many states provide that use of the word "grant" in a deed creates by implication two covenants of title, one of which is a limited form of the covenant against encumbrances (i.e., only against encumbrance suffered the grantor). Of the six possible covenants of title (all of which appear only in a general warranty deed), three do not run with the land: the covenant of seisin, the covenant of right to convey, and the covenant against encumbrances. In all three, however, disturbance of possession is not necessary for the covenant to be breached and damages to be recovered. The other three covenants of title, however, do run with the land (i.e., are enforceable by successive grantees). They are: covenant of quiet enjoyment, warranty, and further assurances. Furthermore, in all three, possession of the grantee must be disturbed (i.e., eviction) before damages for breach may be recovered.

Quicknotes

COVENANT AGAINST ENCUMBRANCES A guarantee in a contract that the interest in property being conveyed is unencumbered.

COVENANT OF SEISIN A promise that the conveyor of property has the lawful right to convey the interest he is attempting to transfer.

GRANT DEED A deed conveying an interest in real or personal property.

CHAPTER 48–49

Recording Statutes

Quick Reference Rules of Law

PAGE

1. **"Bona Fide Purchaser for Value."** A "bona fide purchaser for value" of real property takes free and clear of any encumbrances of which he does not have notice; but when such purchaser has sufficient information to put a reasonable "inquiry" as to the possibilities of an encumbrance, he (and any subsequent takers from him) are held to have notice of everything to which a reasonable inquiry would have led. (Jefferson County v. M.C. Mosley) *230*

2. **Master Lease and Sublease Contracts.** When a party succeeds to the master lease and sublease contracts of a seller-landlord, such party takes subject to the rights which the tenants of the premises hold against the seller-landlord. (Martinique Realty Corp. v. Hull) *231*

3. **Recordation and Option to Purchase.** An option to purchase leased premises that is not contained in the lease and not recorded is not enforceable against grantees of the lessor without actual notice of the option. (Gates Rubber Co. v. Ulman) *232*

4. **Grantor-Grantee Index System.** A transferee of real property pursuant to a quitclaim deed is not chargeable with notice by record of prior conveyances recorded before the grantor obtained title to the property, under a grantor-grantee index system of recordation. (Sabo v. Horvath) *233*

Jefferson County v. M.C. Mosley

Grantee (P) v. Landowner (D)

Ala. Sup. Ct., 284 Ala. 593, 226 So. 2d 652 (1969).

NATURE OF CASE: Appeal from a judgment denying the validity of a right-of-way.

FACT SUMMARY: Dillard conveyed a right-of-way to Jefferson County (P), and then conveyed his land to Mosley (D) "subject to all public roads, or easements or right-of-ways thereover," without mentioning the unrecorded right-of-way.

RULE OF LAW

A "bona fide purchaser for value" of real property takes free and clear of any encumbrances of which he does not have notice; but when such purchaser has sufficient information to put a reasonable "inquiry" as to the possibilities of an encumbrance, he (and any subsequent takers from him) are held to have notice of everything to which a reasonable inquiry would have led.

FACTS: On October 18, 1945, Lester Dillard conveyed by warranty deed to Jefferson County (P) a "right-of-way for public purposes" across his land. This right-of-way was subsequently used by Jefferson County (P) for a public road, but it was not recorded until April 2, 1953. Before the recordation of the right-of-way, Dillard conveyed his land by warranty deed to Mosley (D) "subject to all public roads, or easements and right-of-ways thereover." Dillard, though, did not tell Mosley (D) that Jefferson County (P) had a right-of-way over the property. After Mosley (D) recorded his deed on January 14, 1952, he conveyed a portion of the land to the Peoples (D) on May 26, 1952, and a portion to the Selfs (D) on June 26, 1953. After both the Peoples (D) and Selfs (D) recorded their deeds, Jefferson County (P) brought an action for a declaratory judgment that Mosley (D), the Peoples (D) and the Selfs (D) all had "actual, constructive or implied notice of sufficient facts to apprise them of, or place them upon inquiry as to, the existence and extent of the County (P) right-of-way." The portion of the land received by the Peoples (D) and the portion received by the Selfs (D) contained some of the land originally deeded to Jefferson as a right-of-way. The trial court, though, held against the County (P), and this appeal followed.

ISSUE: May the purchaser of real property be deemed to have "notice" of an encumbrance when he has knowledge of facts sufficient to put him on "inquiry" as to its existence?

HOLDING AND DECISION: (Lawson, J.) Yes. A "bona fide purchaser for value" of real property takes free and clear of any encumbrances of which he does not have notice; but when such purchaser has sufficient information to put a reasonable man on "inquiry" as to the possibilities of an encumbrance, he and any subsequent takers from him are held to have notice of everything to which a reasonable inquiry would have led. Of course, it is elementary that a person cannot convey better title than he has. Therefore, if a purchaser has notice of encumbrances, he and any subsequent purchasers from him take the property subject to those encumbrances. Here, although Mosley (D) had no actual or constructive notice of the right-of-way (i.e., Dillard did not mention it and it was not recorded when he received the land), his deed did state that it was "subject to all public roads, or easements and right-of-ways thereafter." Such a clause would have at least put a reasonable man on inquiry as to its purpose. Furthermore, the existence of the road on the right-of-way was sufficient to put Mosley (D) on inquiry as to all of the land described in his deed. Therefore, Mosley (D) and the subsequent purchasers from him took the land subject to the right-of-way. Reversed and remanded.

ANALYSIS

There are three types of notice which can prevent a subsequent purchaser from taking title to real property: actual, constructive (i.e., a recorded prior interest in the purchaser's chain of title), and inquiry notice. Generally, there are three ways in which a party can be put on inquiry notice. First, if he learns that a party other than the grantor is somehow "in possession" (e.g., user of an easement, etc.) of the property, he is on inquiry notice. Second, if he learns of another claim to the property through reference in a recorded instrument, not in his chain of title but of which he, in fact, learns, he is on inquiry notice. Third, in some jurisdictions, the purchaser of land by quitclaim deed is put on inquiry notice to make a reasonable inspection of the land. Note, however, that if a party on inquiry notice makes a reasonable inspection, he will not be held liable merely because he fails to discover anything.

Quicknotes

BONA FIDE PURCHASER A party who purchases property in good faith and for valuable consideration without notice of a defect in title.

ENCUMBRANCE An interest in property that operates as a claim or lien against its title potentially making it unmarketable.

WARRANTY DEED A deed that guarantees that the conveyor possesses the title that he purports to convey.

Martinique Realty Corp. v. Hull

Lessor (P) v. Tenant (D)

N.J. Super. Ct., 64 N.J. Super. 599, 166 A.2d 803 (1960).

NATURE OF CASE: Appeal from dismissal of action for rent.

FACT SUMMARY: Hull (D) paid an entire year's rent to Martinique's (P) predecessor in interest, who did not disclose this to Martinique (P), which then brought this action for rent allegedly due against Hull (D).

RULE OF LAW

When a party succeeds to the master lease and sublease contracts of a seller-landlord, such party takes subject to the rights that the tenants of the premises hold against the seller-landlord.

FACTS: The Martinique Realty Corp. owned an apartment building which it sold to Cambrian taking back long-term lease of that building. The leasehold was then sold to Martinique Realty Corp. (P), a separate entity. The Hulls (D) were a tenant of the building throughout these transactions. By agreement, the Hulls (D) paid Martinique the entire rental balance for a year for a 1½-room apartment. The Hulls (D) then exchanged their apartment for a larger one and paid the amount of increased rent and deposit by check and received acknowledgment of the prepayment. The Hulls (D) did not record their lease until after Martinique Realty (P), the ultimate purchaser of the master lease, searched the record finding no evidence of special arrangements for any tenants. (In any event, the Hulls' (D) lease recited monthly installments and ignored the prepayment arrangement.) Martinique Realty (P) brought this action for rent, and the Hulls (D) defended on the ground of payment. The Hulls' (D) motion for summary judgment of dismissal was granted and Martinique Realty (P) appealed.

ISSUE: When a party succeeds to the master lease and sublease contract of a seller-landlord, does such party take subject to the rights that the tenants of the premises held against such seller-landlord?

HOLDING AND DECISION: (Freund, J.) Yes. Martinique Realty (P) alleged that since prepayment of rent contravenes the lease as written and since it had the right to rely upon the covenants as written between Hull (D) and the predecessor in interest, then prepayment is no bar to an action for rent. There is a general rule, however, that the assignee of a contract right takes subject to all defenses valid against his assignor. This is codified by our statutes as to the lessor-lessee relationship. Martinique Realty (P) further argued that it had no notice of the arrangement and is thus not bound to it; but the mere examination of the record is insufficient to discharge the duty of inquiry with which it is charged based upon the degree of notice inferred from the tenants' possession. This duty obtains even in the large apartment or office building context. Thus, when a party succeeds to the master lease and the sublease contracts of a landlord-seller, such party takes subject to the rights which the tenants of the premises held against such landlord-seller. The prepayment by the Hulls (D) of their rent operates to bar Martinique Realty's (P) action for rent. Affirmed.

ANALYSIS

As the opinion notes, the result in this case is in line with the contract law notion that the assignee of a contract right takes subject to the defenses which can be validly asserted. Especially in the commercial context, the law of contracts has slowly been invading the real property field, generally producing more reasonable and predictable results. Here, for example, recordation of the lease, which did not reflect the agreement, would have been of little aid to either of the parties.

Gates Rubber Co. v. Ulman

Lessee (P) v. Lessor administrator (D)

Cal. Ct. App., 214 Cal. App. 3d 356 (1989), *review denied* (1990).

NATURE OF CASE: Appeal of denial of specific performance of a purchaser option.

FACT SUMMARY: Gates Rubber Co. (P), whose option to purchase leased property was not contained in the property lease and was unrecorded, sought to enforce it against Ulman (D), a grantee of the lessor, without actual notice of the option.

RULE OF LAW

An option to purchase leased premises that is not contained in the lease and not recorded is not enforceable against grantees of the lessor without actual notice of the option.

FACTS: Gates Rubber Co. (Gates) (P) signed a "triple net" lease of certain property owned by Lessor. The parties agreed that Gates (P) would have the option to purchase the property after twenty years at a set price. The option was not contained in the lease, but rather in a separate document. Neither the lease nor the option agreement was recorded. The property was sold and resold several times. It was eventually purchased by Charles Ulman in 1969. Ulman received a copy of the lease, but not the option agreement. In 1983, Gates (P) informed Harry Ulman (D), administrator of the late Charles Ulman's estate, that it was exercising the purchase option. Ulman (D) sent back the check, contending the option agreement to be a nullity. Gates (P) brought a specific performance action. The trial court held Charles Ulman to have been a bona fide purchaser, and that the option was not enforceable against his estate. Gates (P) appealed.

ISSUE: Is an option to purchase leased premises that is not contained in the lease and not recorded enforceable against grantees of the lessor without actual notice of the option?

HOLDING AND DECISION: (George, J.) No. An option to purchase leased premises that is not contained in the lease and not recorded is not enforceable against grantees of the lessor without actual notice of the option. A grantee who takes title to property without actual or constructive notice of another interest therein is a bona fide purchaser, and is not subject to that interest. The usual manner of constructive notice is recording. Here, neither the lease nor the option agreement was recorded. Gates (P) argues that its possession of the property put Charles Ulman on constructive notice that an opinion might exist. It is true that possession of property can impose constructive knowledge of any lease term not inconsistent with such possession. In this case, however, the option was not in the lease, but in a separate document. Possession alone cannot put a grantee on notice of an interest not in the lease. Since Charles Ulman was not on constructive or actual notice, the option is not enforceable against him. Affirmed.

ANALYSIS

Recordation constitutes constructive notice. The fact that a tenant is in possession does not create such notice, but rather a duty of inquiry. How far that duty goes is an issue both of fact and law. Here, the court was of the opinion that, as a matter of law, it could not go beyond the terms of the lease.

Quicknotes

BONA FIDE PURCHASER A party who purchases property in good faith and for valuable consideration without notice of a defect in title.

RECORDATION The recording of a document in the public record.

SPECIFIC PERFORMANCE An equitable remedy whereby the court requires the parties to perform their obligations pursuant to a contract.

Sabo v. Horvath

Recorder of quitclaim deed (D) v. Prior purchaser (P)

Alaska Sup. Ct., 559 P.2d 1038 (1976).

NATURE OF CASE: Appeal from order quieting title to real property.

FACT SUMMARY: One Lowery conveyed a parcel of land by quitclaim deed to Horvath (P) before Lowery was issued his government patent on the property, and later conveyed the same property by similar deed to Sabo (D); and both transferees recorded.

RULE OF LAW

A transferee of real property pursuant to a quitclaim deed is not chargeable with notice by record of prior conveyances recorded before the grantor obtained title to the property, under a grantor-grantee index system of recordation.

FACTS: One Lowery obtained title to a parcel of land by virtue of a government patent. Prior to issuance of the patent, Lowery, on January 3, 1970, transferred the property to Horvath (P), who recorded his quitclaim deed on January 5, 1970. The report of the authorities recommended issuance of the patent in 1968, but issuance did not take place until August 10, 1973. On October 15, 1973, Lowery conveyed the same premises by quitclaim deed to Sabo (D), who recorded on December 13, 1973. Horvath (P) brought suit to quiet title, and Sabo (D) counterclaimed to quiet his title on the grounds that (1) Horvath (P) did not obtain any interest inasmuch as Lowery did not have title at the time of his quitclaim conveyance to Horvath (P); and (2) the Horvath (P) deed was not discoverable by a search of the grantee-grantor index under Lowery's name and following, and was thus a "wild deed" outside the chain of title and capable of giving no notice. The trial court ruled that Lowery had transferred an equitable interest to Horvath (P) which was recorded first and gave Sabo (D) constructive notice thereof. Sabo (D) appealed the order quieting Horvath's (P) title.

ISSUE: Is a transferee of real property pursuant to a quitclaim deed chargeable with notice by record of prior conveyances recorded before the grantor obtained title to the property, under a grantor-grantee index system of recordation?

HOLDING AND DECISION: (Boochever, C.J.) No. Since Congress could have, but significantly did not, prohibit alienation prior to issuance of a patent, Lowery had an interest in land which could have been, and was, transferred to Horvath (P) in 1970. However, the quitclaim nature of the Sabo (D) deed did not preclude Sabo (D) from obtaining the protections of the recording statutes by giving some automatic constructive notice of other prior conveyances. Sabo (D), under the majority rule which is here adopted, could be an "innocent purchaser" for value. Alaska has a grantor-grantee index system of recordation. Thereunder, a title search begins at the time the grantor secured his title and covers all conveyances thereafter. Deeds granted by that grantor prior to his securing title, such as the Horvath (P) deed, is a "wild deed" which gives no constructive notice to a subsequent purchaser who duly records. Therefore, a transferee of real property pursuant to a quitclaim deed is not chargeable with notice by record of prior conveyances recorded before the grantor obtained title to the property, under a grantor-grantee index system of recordation. While it may not have been an undue burden to require Sabo (D) to go beyond the 1973 issuance of Lowery's patent to find a deed from some months previous to it, a general rule with such a requirement would lead to a significant burden on other purchasers and would lead to uncertainty as to real estate purchases. Sabo's (D) interest is entitled to prevail in this case. Reversed.

ANALYSIS

A tract index system of recordation would have produced a different result. In such an index, all documents regarding a particular tract are recorded in one place and searchable by looking up the tract, lot, or block in question. A tract index was in operation in the *Andy Associates* case, 399 N.E.2d 1160 (N.Y. 1979).

Quicknotes

CONVEYANCE The transfer of property, or title to property, from one party to another party.

QUIET TITLE Equitable action to resolve conflicting claims to an interest in real property.

QUITCLAIM DEED A deed whereby the grantor conveys whatever interest he or she may have in the property without any warranties or covenants as to title.

CHAPTER 50

Title Insurance

Quick Reference Rules of Law

Lick Mill Creek Apartments v. Chicago Title Ins. Co.

Developer (P) v. Title insurance company (D)

Cal. Ct. App., 231 Cal. App. 3d 1654, 283 Cal Rptr. 231 (1991).

NATURE OF CASE: Appeal from dismissal of action for indemnification for hazardous waste cleanup costs.

FACT SUMMARY: After paying for removal and cleanup of hazardous substances existing but unknown at the time a title insurance policy was issued on its property, Lick Mill Creek Apartments (P) sued Chicago Title Insurance Co. (D) for reimbursement, contending that the presence of hazardous waste rendered the title unmarketable and constituted an encumbrance on title.

RULE OF LAW

A title insurance company is obligated to protect the insured against defects in title but not against loss arising from physical damage to property.

FACTS: While acquiring lots for development, Lick Mill Creek Apartments (Lick Mill) (P) purchased title insurance from Chicago Title Insurance Co. (Chicago Title) (D). Before issuing the policy, Chicago Title (D) commissioned a survey and inspection of the entire site. Unbeknownst to Chicago Title (D) or Lick Mill (P), the government had been keeping records documenting the presence of hazardous substances in the soil, subsoil, and groundwater of the property. After Lick Mill (P) purchased the property, it incurred costs for removal and cleanup of the hazardous materials. It then sought indemnity from Chicago Title (D) for the cost of the cleanup, arguing that the presence of hazardous substances rendered the title defective or unmarketable within the terms of the title insurance policy. Lick Mill (P) also contended that liability for the costs of the cleanup constituted an encumbrance on title. The trial court concluded that Chicago Title's (D) insurance policy did not cover the costs of removing hazardous substances. Lick Mill (P) appealed.

ISSUE: Is a title insurance company obligated to protect the insured against defects in title but not against loss arising from physical damage to property?

HOLDING AND DECISION: (Agliano, J.) Yes. A title insurance company is obligated to protect the insured against defects in title but not against loss arising from physical damage to property. Title insurance covers title marketability, which relates to defects affecting legally recognized rights and incidents of ownership. Title insurance does not cover market value. It is possible to hold perfectly marketable title to valueless, unmarketable land. Here, the presence of hazardous material may affect the market value of Lick Mill's (P) land, but it does not affect the title to the land. Chicago Title (D) was obligated, under its policy, to insure Lick Mill (P) against unmarketability of title. But since marketability of title and the market value of the land itself are separate and distinct, Lick Mill (P) could not claim coverage, under the policy, for the property's physical condition. Furthermore, it could not claim coverage for an encumbrance where no lien has been filed against the property. "Encumbrances" include only liens, easements, restrictive covenants, and other such interests in or rights to the land that are held by third persons. The mere possibility that the state may attach a lien in the future to secure payment of cleanup costs is not sufficient to create an encumbrance on title. Affirmed.

ANALYSIS

Title insurance reflects the faith of the insurer in the validity of title, not the physical condition of the property. Title insurance policies are contractual devices. Most courts will construe policies to insure only what they say they insure. This will be true even if the court subscribes to the presumption that policies are to be strictly construed in favor of the insured and against the title insurance company.

Quicknotes

DEFECT Lacking in some manner; imperfection.

INDEMNITY The duty of a party to compensate another for damages sustained.

TITLE INSURANCE A policy insuring against loss incurred as the result of a defective title.

TITLE MARKETABILITY Title, which although not perfect, would be acceptable to a reasonably well-informed buyer exercising ordinary business prudence.

Holmes v. Alabama Title Company

Landowners (P) v. Mineral rights holders (D)

Ala. Sup. Ct., 507 So. 2d 922 (1987).

NATURE OF CASE: Appeal of summary judgment dismissing a series of consolidated property damage actions.

FACT SUMMARY: Landowners (P) whose title arose from a grant exculpating the mineral rights owner from liability to surface title owners sought to hold the title insurance companies liable for not notifying them of the exclusionary provisions.

RULE OF LAW

A title insurance company may not be liable for failing to notify subsequent purchasers of language in a deed in the chain of title that limits the purchaser's right to seek property damage compensation.

FACTS: Certain land was held by Woodward Iron Company (Woodward). In 1943, Woodward conveyed the surface rights to one Patton, reserving mineral rights. The deed contained a covenant that Patton and subsequent grantees would have no cause of action for property damage occasioned by exploitation of the mineral rights. The land was eventually subdivided. In 1983 land subsidence attributable to mining operations occurred, causing considerable property damage. One hundred twenty-eight landowners (P) filed suit against USX Corp. (D), successor to the mineral estate, Alabama Title Company (D) and Commonwealth Land Title Insurance Co. (D), contending that the companies were under a duty to advise them of the mining. After USX (D) obtained summary judgment, the landowners (P) contended that the title companies (D) should have advised them of the exculpatory language. The trial court granted summary judgment, and the landowners (P) appealed.

ISSUE: May a title insurance company be held liable for failing to notify subsequent purchasers of language in a deed in the chain of title that limits the purchasers' right to seek property damage compensation?

HOLDING AND DECISION: (Shores, J.) No. A title insurance company may not be held liable for failing to notify subsequent purchasers of language in a deed in the chain of title that limits the purchasers' right to seek property damage compensation. The purpose of title insurance is not to protect the insured against loss arising from property damage; rather, it is to protect the insured against defects in title. Title companies are not required to explain the significance of language found in deeds during the title search on how property damage causes of action may be affected. Here, the claims of the landowners (P) had nothing to do with title, and consequently the title companies had no duties with respect to the language at issue. Affirmed.

ANALYSIS

Policies of title insurance exist to fit a specific type of loss, that arise from the defects in title. Even as to those defects, the defects must be found in instruments in the chain of title. Nonetheless, the presence of a title company makes a tempting target for one not having the foresight to obtain property damage or liability insurance, and suits such as the present one are not uncommon.

Quicknotes

SUMMARY JUDGMENT Judgment rendered by a court in response to a motion made by one of the parties, claiming that the lack of a question of material fact in respect to an issue warrants disposition of the issue without consideration by the jury.

TITLE INSURANCE A policy insuring against loss incurred as the result of a defective title.

Note: There are no principal cases in chapter 51 of the casebook.

CHAPTER 52

The Time Between the Contract and Deed: The Doctrine of Equitable Conversion

Quick Reference Rules of Law

DiDonato v. Reliance Standard Life Ins. Co.

Potential purchasers (P) v. Landowners (D)

Pa. Sup. Ct., 433 Pa. 221, 249 A.2d 327, 39 A.L.R. 3d 357 (1969).

NATURE OF CASE: Appeal from refusal to rescind a contract of sale.

FACT SUMMARY: After the DiDonatos (P) agreed to purchase industrial zoned property from the Reliance Standard Life Insurance Co. (D), the property was rezoned residential, but such rezoning was not recorded until after the sale was completed.

RULE OF LAW

After a contract for the sale of real property has been made, the purchaser becomes the equitable or beneficial owner through the doctrine of equitable conversion and, in the absence of some expression in the contract to the contrary, bears the risk of loss for injury to the property between the time of the execution of the contract and the actual conveyance (i.e., settlement).

FACTS: On August 4, 1965, the Reliance Standard Life Insurance Co. (D) entered into an Agreement of Sale with the DiDonatos (P) for industrial zoned land. On September 22, 1965, though, before the sale was settled an ordinance was enacted which changed the zoning of the land to residential. Furthermore, at the time the transaction was settled, a certification from the Department of Licenses and Inspections of the city of Philadelphia erroneously indicated that the property was still zoned industrial. Subsequently, in 1967, the DiDonatos (P), for the first time, discovered the zoning change when they contracted to sell the property. Thereafter, when they were unable to sell the property, the DiDonatos (P) brought an action against the Reliance Standard Life Insurance Co. (D) to rescind the contract of sale. The lower court, though, refused to rescind the contract, and this appeal followed.

ISSUE: Does a purchaser of real property bear the risk of any loss resulting from zoning changes occurring between the execution of the sale contract and settlement?

HOLDING AND DECISION: (Eagen, J.) Yes. After a contract for the sale of real property has been made, the purchaser becomes the equitable or beneficial owner through the doctrine of equitable conversion and, in the absence of some expression in the contract to the contrary, bears the risk of loss for injury to the property between the time of the execution of the contract and the actual conveyance (i.e., settlement). There is no reason for treating losses resulting from zoning changes any differently from casualty or other kinds of loss. Here, therefore, since the DiDonatos (P) did not state otherwise in the contract for sale, they are liable for any loss resulting from the zoning change which occurred after the execution of the contract. Affirmed.

ANALYSIS

This case illustrates the general rule (i.e., equitable conversion). Under this rule, the seller, after the execution of the contract, is only the owner of a chose in action, and the purchaser is the real owner of the property. Note, though, that a minority of jurisdictions place the risk of loss on the seller until the buyer actually takes possession of the property. The Uniform Vendor and Purchaser Risk Act (followed in some jurisdictions) is a form of this minority rule. Under this Act "if, when neither the legal title nor the possession of the subject matter of the contract has been transferred, all or a material part thereof is destroyed without fault of the purchaser or is taken by eminent domain, the vendor cannot enforce the contract, and the purchaser is entitled to recover any portion of the price he has paid."

Quicknotes

EQUITABLE CONVERSION Once property is sold pursuant to a land sale contract, equitable title passes to the buyer and legal title remains in the seller as security until the remainder of the purchase price is tendered.

ZONING Municipal statutory scheme dividing an area into districts in order to regulate the use or building of structures within those districts.

Skelly Oil Co. v. Ashmore

Prospective buyer (P) v. Seller (D)

Mo. Sup. Ct., 365 S.W.2d 582 (1963).

NATURE OF CASE: Appeal from an award of specific performance and damages.

FACT SUMMARY: Skelly Oil Co. (P) contracted to purchase certain land and a building from Ashmore (D), but before the sale was closed the building was destroyed by fire.

RULE OF LAW

A sales contract for buildings and land is no longer binding upon the vendee or vendor if the buildings are destroyed by fire before the conveyance and if the value of the buildings constitutes a material part of the total value of the estate and an important part of the subject matter of the contract; but if the buildings do not constitute a material part of the value of the estate or an important part of the sales contract, the vendee may have the contract specifically enforced, with abatement for any loss.

FACTS: Skelly Oil Co. (P) contracted to purchase certain land "together with the buildings, driveways, and all construction thereon" from Ashmore (D), with the intent of constructing a service station on such land. This contract, however, made no provision for allocating the risk of loss to the property before the completion of the sale, and, before the sale was completed, the central building upon the land was destroyed in a fire. Thereafter, since Ashmore (D) had insurance on the building, he collected $10,000 in insurance proceeds. Subsequently, Skelly Oil (P) brought an action to recover the insurance proceeds from Ashmore (D) and to have the land contract specifically enforced. In response, Ashmore (D) claimed that the contract became void when the building was destroyed by fire. After the trial court decided in favor of Skelly Oil (P), Ashmore (D) brought this appeal.

ISSUE: Is any sales contract for land and buildings automatically void if the buildings are destroyed by fire prior to the conveyance of the land?

HOLDING AND DECISION: (Hyde, J.) No. A sales contract for buildings and land is no longer binding upon the vendee or vendor if the buildings are destroyed by fire before the conveyance and if the value of the buildings constitutes a material part of the total value of the estate and an important part of the subject matter of the contract; but, if the buildings do not constitute a material part of the value of the estate or an important part of the sales contract, the vendee may have the contract specifically enforced, with compensation in the form of abatement for any loss. Of course, under this rule, the loss by fire falls on the vendor, but this is only equitable since it is not fair to make the vendee pay the vendor for something which the vendor cannot give him. Here, since Skelly Oil (P) intended to use the land for a "Service Station Site," the value of the building (which would have to be torn down) did not constitute a material part of the value of the estate or an important part of the sales contract. As such, Skelly Oil (P) is entitled to specific performance of the contract with compensation for the loss of the building. Furthermore, it is only equitable that the insurance proceeds received by Ashmore (D) be given to Skelly Oil (P) as compensation for the building, since Ashmore (D) will still receive the full amount for which he contracted to sell the property. Affirmed.

DISSENT: (Storckman, J.) Although the majority of the court here states the Massachusetts rule, they do not follow it. Here, there was no showing that Skelly Oil (P) was actually damaged by the fire in the amount of the insurance proceeds received by Ashmore (D), especially since Skelly Oil (P) planned to tear down the building which was destroyed by the fire. Any vendee, though, who is allowed to enforce a contract for land and buildings after the buildings are destroyed by fire, should only be allowed compensation if he also establishes the manner and amount of damage he suffered.

ANALYSIS

This case illustrates only one manner of allocating the burden of fortuitous loss between vendor and vendee of real estate, when such loss occurs before the property contracted for is actually conveyed. The other views are as follows: (1) that from the time of the contract of sale of real estate the burden of loss is on the vendee even though the vendor retains possession until closing (i.e., the doctrine of "equitable conversion"); (2) the burden of loss should be on the vendor "until legal title is conveyed, and thereafter on the vendee unless the vendor be in such default as to preclude specific performance" (such view has been advocated, but is not followed by the courts); (3) the burden of loss is on the party in possession, whether the vendor or vendee; and (4) the burden of loss should be on the vendor "unless there is something in the contract or in the relation of the parties from which the court can infer a different intention" (this view, also, has not been followed by many courts). Note that the doctrine of "equitable conversion" is the majority view and the Massachusetts rule (in this case) is the minority rule.

Continued on next page.

Quicknotes

CONVEYANCE The transfer of property, or title to property, from one party to another party.

DAMAGES Monetary compensation that may be awarded by the court to a party who has sustained injury or loss to his person, property or rights due to another party's unlawful act, omission or negligence.

EQUITABLE CONVERSION Once property is sold pursuant to a land sale contract, equitable title passes to the buyer and legal title remains in the seller as security until the remainder of the purchase price is tendered.

SPECIFIC PERFORMANCE An equitable remedy whereby the court requires the parties to perform their obligations pursuant to a contract.

Lucenti v. Cayuga Apartments, Inc.

Potential purchaser (P) v. Seller (D)

N.Y. Ct. App., 48 N.Y.2d 530, 423 N.Y.S.2d 886, 399 N.E.2d 918 (1979).

NATURE OF CASE: Appeal from modified order of specific performance with abatement of land sale contract.

FACT SUMMARY: After Lucenti (P) contracted to purchase Cayuga's (D) two buildings, Lucenti (P) brought this suit for specific performance with an abatement of the purchase price.

RULE OF LAW

The purchaser of realty which is materially destroyed before title passes may specifically enforce the land sale contract with an abatement of the purchase price.

FACTS: Lucenti (P) agreed to purchase two contiguous parcels of land with a building on each parcel. A land sale contract was executed between Lucenti (P) as purchaser and Cayuga Apartments, Inc. (Cayuga) (D) as vendor of the properties. Before title closed, however, the older of the two buildings was destroyed by fire. Cayuga (D) proposed rebuilding with the insurance proceeds, retention of the proceeds by Cayuga (D) as against the purchase price, and rescission of the contract. No agreement was reached, and the parties decided to wait until the insurance settlement was paid. Upon collection of $45,000 by Cayuga (D), it mailed Lucenti (P) a check for his $1,000 deposit and purported to rescind. Lucenti (P) returned the check and demanded conveyance of the property with an abatement of the purchase price. Upon refusal, Lucenti (P) brought this suit to obtain this result. The trial court dismissed the suit, the appellate division reversed, and on remand, the trial court fixed the abatement of $19,500. Lucenti (P) appealed, and the appellate division increased the abatement to $27,500. Cayuga (D) sought review.

ISSUE: May the purchaser of realty which is materially destroyed before title passes specifically enforce the land sale contract with an abatement of the purchase price?

HOLDING AND DECISION: (Meyer, J.) Yes. The purchaser of realty which is materially destroyed before title passes may specifically enforce the land sale contract with an abatement of the purchase price. This rule of the General Obligations Law § 5-1311 does not, however, abrogate the common-law rule that the purchaser may specifically enforce the contract with an abatement of the purchase price. Here, one of the buildings under contract was destroyed, this being a material destruction of the property involved. Lucenti (P) had not taken possession nor acquired title at that time. The purchaser of realty which is materially destroyed before title passes may specifically enforce the land sale contract with an abatement of the purchase price. Affirmed.

ANALYSIS

The doctrine of equitable conversion placed the risk of loss on the purchaser during the existence of the land sale contract on the theory that the purchaser is the beneficial owner. The Uniform Vendor and Purchaser Act, applied in this case, bars the vendor from enforcing the contract against the purchaser in the event of destruction prior to the passing of title. This can be viewed as a protection for the purchaser, who can waive the protection and specifically enforce the contract with abatement.

Quicknotes

ABATEMENT A decrease or lessening of something; in equity, a suspension or dismissal of a cause of action.

CONVEYANCE The transfer of property, or title to property, from one party to another party.

EQUITABLE CONVERSION Once property is sold pursuant to a land sale contract, equitable title passes to the buyer and legal title remains in the seller as security until the remainder of the purchase price is tendered.

SPECIFIC PERFORMANCE An equitable remedy whereby the court requires the parties to perform their obligations pursuant to a contract.

CHAPTER **53**

After the Closing: Implied Warranty of Fitness and the Duty to Disclose

Quick Reference Rules of Law

Lempke v. Dagenais

Purchaser (P) v. Builder (D)

N.H. Sup. Ct., 130 N.H. 782, 547 A.2d 290 (1988).

NATURE OF CASE: Appeal of dismissal of action against a contractor for unworkmanlike performance.

FACT SUMMARY: Lempke (P) sought to recover from Dagenais (D) the cost of rebuilding a garage Dagenais (D) had built for the prior owner, which Lempke (P) claimed had been built in a substandard manner.

RULE OF LAW

A subsequent purchaser of property may recover from one performing defective contractor services for the prior owner if the work contained latent defects not apparent at the time of purchase.

FACTS: Lempke's (P) predecessor contracted with Dagenais (D) for the latter to build a garage, which he did. After Lempke (P) purchased the property, structural problems appeared which Lempke (P) claimed were due to substandard work by Dagenais (D). Lempke (P) sued Dagenais (D) for the cost of repair and/or replacement. The trial court dismissed the complaint, ruling that privity was a condition precedent to a cause of action against a builder for unworkmanlike performance. Lempke (P) appealed.

ISSUE: May a subsequent purchaser of property recover from one performing defective contractor services for the prior owner if the work contained latent defects not apparent at the time of purchase?

HOLDING AND DECISION: (Thayer, J.) Yes. A subsequent purchaser of property may recover from one performing defective contractor services for the prior owner if the work contained latent defects not apparent at the time of purchase. New Hampshire, like most states, recognizes in building construction work an implied warranty of workmanlike quality. Much debate has been generated as to whether this warranty is a creature of tort or contract, on the notion that the latter would require privity. However, in a final analysis, the implied warranty, be it tort or contract, arises by operation of law as a matter of public policy. Consequently, whether privity is required is determined by a reference to policy. In this respect, numerous policy reasons for not imposing a privity requirement exist. First, our society is increasingly mobile, and a builder/vendor should not be surprised by a change in ownership. Second, experience teaches us that latent defects often will not show up for years, so a sale to an unsuspecting purchaser is not unlikely. Third, a builder is in a better position to control the quality of the work than a subsequent buyer. Fourth, a contractor is already under an obligation to perform in a workmanlike manner, so the nature of his obligation is not changed by dispensing with privity. Finally, to impose a privity requirement would encourage sham first sales. These policy concerns lead this court to conclude that privity should not be required for a homeowner to sue a vendor/builder for latent defects resulting from substandard work. [The court went on to hold that the measure of damages would be the cost of repair or replacement, and also noted that a vendor/builder's duty did not go on indefinitely, but only for a reasonable time.] Reversed and remanded.

ANALYSIS

All jurisdictions recognize some form of implied warranty such as that discussed here. Whether privity is required to assert it varies among the jurisdictions. The trend is generally toward disposing of the requirement. Some jurisdictions take the warranty out of contract and put it into tort. Others simply dispense with the requirement, as this court did.

Quicknotes

CONTRACT An agreement pursuant to which a party agrees to act, or to forbear from acting, in exchange for performance on the part of the other party.

PRIVITY Commonality of rights or interests between parties.

TORT A legal wrong resulting in a breach of duty by the wrongdoer, causing damages as a result of the breach.

Reed v. King

Grantee (P) v. Grantor (D)

Cal. Ct. App., 145 Cal. App. 3d 261, 193 Cal. Rptr. 130 (1983).

NATURE OF CASE: Appeal of dismissal of action seeking damages against a seller of real property for nondisclosure of detrimental facts.

FACT SUMMARY: Reed (P) sued King (D), former owner of her residence, for failing to disclose to her that a quintuple murder had occurred there.

RULE OF LAW

A purchaser of real estate may maintain an action against the seller for failing to disclose that a murder had occurred there.

FACTS: Reed (P) purchased a residence from King (D). Subsequently, she was informed by neighbors that the house was infamous locally because of a murder of a woman and her four children that had occurred there. Reed (P) brought an action against King (D) and his real estate agents, contending that the house's history affected its value and that they had been under a duty to disclose the house's history. The trial court sustained King's (D) demurrer and dismissed the action. Reed (P) appealed.

ISSUE: May a purchaser of real estate maintain an action against the seller for failing to disclose that a murder had occurred there?

HOLDING AND DECISION: (Blease, J.) Yes. A purchaser of real estate may maintain an action against the seller for failing to disclose that a murder had occurred there. A seller is under a duty to disclose to buyer material information affecting the value or desirability of the property that is not reasonably within the reach of the purchaser. Whether an item of information is material depends upon the facts of each case. Factors include the gravity of harm inflicted by nondisclosure, fairness of imposing a duty of discovery on the buyer, and the impact on the stability of the contracts. In this instance, Reed (P) alleges that the house's history has a detrimental effect on its value, an allegation that for demurrer purposes must be accepted as true. Diminution of a property's market value is a fairly serious consequence of nondisclosure. Further, murders are sufficiently uncommon that imposing a duty of disclosure will not greatly affect stability of contracts. In short, if Reed (P) can prove that the house's value has been diminished, she should be allowed to do so. Reversed.

ANALYSIS

With respect to real estate, the old concept of caveat emptor has largely been jettisoned. Recognizing that purchasers simply are not in a position to ascertain many facts about a property, a duty of disclosure has been imposed in all jurisdictions, either by statute or decision. How far this duty goes varies from state to state. As the present case illustrates, California has taken this duty to a fairly extreme limit.

Quicknotes

DEMURRER The assertion that the opposing party's pleadings are insufficient and that the demurring party should not be made to answer.

DIMINUTION IN VALUE A measure of computing damages pursuant to a breach of contract representing the decrease in the value of the subject matter of the contract as a result of the breach.

DUTY TO DISCLOSE The duty owed by a fiduciary to reveal those facts that have a material effect on the interests of the party that must be informed.

Frickel v. Sunnyside Enterprises, Inc.

Buyers (P) v. Sellers (D)

Wash. Sup. Ct., 106 Wash. 2d 714, 725 P.2d 422 (1986).

NATURE OF CASE: Appeal of damages awarded for breach of warranty of habitability.

FACT SUMMARY: The Frickels (P), purchasers of apartment buildings from Sunnyside Enterprises, Inc. (Sunnyside) (D), sought to hold Sunnyside (D) liable for structural defects despite a contractual disclaimer of responsibility therefor.

RULE OF LAW

A contractual disclaimer may absolve an owner/builder of responsibility for defects in a premises.

FACTS: Sunnyside Enterprises, Inc. (Sunnyside) (D) was engaged in the business of developing and operating apartment buildings. At one point the Frickels (P), in search of a real estate investment, approached Sunnyside (D) about purchasing a complex. A transition was effected. The contract of sale contained a clause to the effect that the buyer (the Frickels) (P) had made a full inspection, and the sale was on an "as is" basis. After the sale, structural problems began to manifest themselves. The Frickels (P) brought suit, seeking damages for breach of warranty of habitability. The trial court, after a trial, awarded damages. Sunnyside (D) appealed.

ISSUE: May a contractual disclaimer absolve an owner/builder of responsibility for defects in a premises?

HOLDING AND DECISION: (Brachtenbach, J.) Yes. A contractual disclaimer may absolve an owner/builder of responsibility for defects in a premise. The imposition of an implied warranty of habitability is predicated on public policy grounds, based on the recognition that a builder/vendor is in a much better position to determine the quality of the work on a home, and therefore should bear responsibility for substandard work. The vendees in such situations generally will have neither the expertise nor resources to ensure adequate workmanship. When the parties are of relatively equal bargaining power, however, and a sale is effected via an arm's-length transaction, the policy reasons for imposing a nonwaivable warranty of habitability disappear. In such a situation, parties are free to allocate the risk of loss as they see fit. The Frickels (P), who were represented by counsel, contracted to accept the rise of loss associated with defects in the premises. They should be held to the terms of the bargain into which they entered. Reversed.

DISSENT: (Pearson, C.J.) A contractual disclaimer cannot absolutely void potential warranty of habitability claims of a purchaser.

ANALYSIS

It should be noted that the court here departed from usual nomenclature in this area. "Warranty of habitability," as it is usually understood, refers to a warranty running in favor of a residential tenant from landlord that a premises will be kept in a minimally liveable condition. The warranty designated "warranty of habitability" here is better known as the implied warranty of fitness or implied warranty of workmanlike quality.

Quicknotes

IMPLIED WARRANTY OF FITNESS An implied promise made by a merchant in a contract for the sale of goods that such goods are suitable for the purpose for which they are purchased.

WARRANTY OF HABITABILITY An implied warranty owed by a landlord to a tenant to provide premises in a properly maintained habitable condition at time of leasing and during the term of the lease.

CHAPTER 54

Liability For Toxic Wastes

Quick Reference Rules of Law

United States of America v. Monsanto Co.

Federal government (P) v. Lessees (D)

858 F.2d 160 (4th Cir. 1988).

NATURE OF CASE: Appeal from summary judgment holding landowners liable under CERCLA.

FACT SUMMARY: Seidenberg (D) and Hutchinson (D) leased land and a small warehouse they owned to a chemical company which later deposited chemical waste on the land, waste from which hazardous substances were released into the environment.

RULE OF LAW

Any person who owned a facility at a time when hazardous substances were deposited there may be held liable for all costs of removal or remedial action if a release or threatened release of a hazardous substance occurs.

FACTS: The Columbia Organic Chemical Company (COCC) executed a lease with Oscar Seidenberg (D) and Harvey Hutchinson (D) (landowners) for the purpose of storing raw materials and finished products in the warehouse on their land. COCC expanded its business to include the disposal of toxic waste, and haphazardly deposited more than 7,000 fifty-five gallon drums of chemical waste on the landowners' land. Hazardous substances leaked from decaying drums and oozed into the ground. They also mixed with incompatible chemicals that escaped from other containers, creating a toxic cloud, fires, and explosions. In 1980, the Government (P) filed suit under § 7003 of the Resource Conservation and Recovery Act (RCRA), and South Carolina (P) intervened in the pending action. After the Comprehensive Environmental Response, Compensation, and Liability Act (CERCLA) was enacted in the December of 1980, the federal and state governments filed an amended complaint under § 107(a) of CERCLA, alleging that the landowners and waste-generators were jointly and severally liable for the costs expended in completing the surface clean-up of the site. The landowners contended they were innocent absentee landlords unaware of and unconnected to the waste disposal activities that took place on their land. But they admitted that they had become aware of waste storage in 1977, and that they had accepted lease payments until 1980. The district court granted the Government's (P) summary judgment motion on CERCLA liability, finding that no sufficient evidence to support an affirmative defense under § 107(b)(3) had been presented, and finding it sufficient that Seidenberg (D) and Hutchinson (D) owned the land at the time the hazardous substances were deposited there.

ISSUE: May any person who owned a facility at a time when hazardous substances were deposited there be held liable for all costs of removal or remedial action if a release or threatened release of a hazardous substance occurs?

HOLDING AND DECISION: (Sprouse, J.) Yes. Any person who owned a facility at a time when hazardous substances were deposited there may be held liable for all costs of removal or remedial action if a release or threatened release of a hazardous substance occurs. (CERCLA § 107(a)). The plain language of § 107(a) clearly defines the scope of intended liability under the statute. The overwhelming body of precedent has interpreted § 107(a) as establishing a strict liability scheme. Under such a scheme, the landowners are within the class of owners Congress intended to hold liable, regardless of their degree of participation in the subsequent disposal of hazardous waste. Further, under no view of the evidence could they satisfy the proof requirements of § 107(b)(3) which sets forth a limited affirmative defense based on the complete absence of causation. Thus, the district court committed no error in entering summary judgment against the landowners. Affirmed.

ANALYSIS

Partly to give innocent landowners protection from the harsh outcome of § 107(a)(2), Congress amended CERCLA in 1986 through enactment of the Superfund Amendments and Reauthorization Act of 1986 (SARA). To CERCLA § 101(35), SARA added a new defense for purchasers of property who acquire such property without "reason to know" that hazardous substances were disposed of on the property. However, in order to demonstrate the purchaser had no "reason to know," SARA also requires the purchaser to undertake, at the time of purchase, all appropriate inquiry into the previous ownership and uses of the property consistent with good commercial or customary practice in an effort to minimize liability. This second requirement makes it virtually impossible for a purchaser to qualify as an innocent landowner under SARA.

Quicknotes

STRICT LIABILITY Liability for all injuries proximately caused by a party's conducting of certain inherently dangerous activities without regard to negligence or fault.

SUMMARY JUDGMENT Judgment rendered by a court in response to a motion made by one of the parties, claiming that the lack of a question of material fact in respect to an issue warrants disposition of the issue without consideration by the jury.

CHAPTER 55

Trademark Law

Quick Reference Rules of Law

Jordache Enterprises, Inc. v. Levi Strauss & Co.

Jeans manufacturer (P) v. Jeans manufacturer (D)

841 F. Supp. 506 (S.D.N.Y. 1993).

NATURE OF CASE: Motion for summary judgment in trademark infringement suit.

FACT SUMMARY: Jordache Enterprises, Inc. (P) filed an intent to use application to register the mark "Jordache Basics 101 with star and wing design," which was opposed by Levi Strauss & Co. (D) which claimed that it infringed Levi's (D) "501" mark in violation of the Lanham Act.

RULE OF LAW

In order to state a claim for trademark infringement, a party must show likelihood that ordinary prudent consumers are likely to be misled or confused as to the source of the goods in question.

FACTS: Jordache Enterprises, Inc. (Jordache) (P), a nationally known jeans manufacturer, commenced use of the trademark "Jordache Basics 101," and ran a television commercial that Levi Strauss & Co. (Levi) (D) claimed to be a simulation of the style of its Levi's "501 Blues" advertising campaign. Jordache (P) applied to register with the Patent and Trademark Office (PTO) the trademarks "Jordache Basics 101," "Jordache 101," and "Basics 101." Levi (D) filed notices of opposition to each of the marks, claiming Jordache's (P) use of the number "101" was similar to Levi's (D) family of three digit trademarks, and therefore likely to confuse or mislead the public into believing the jeans either originated from, or were sponsored by Levi (D). Jordache (P) then abandoned its trademark application, but reserved the right to use the mark. Jordache (P) filed intent to use application with the PTO to register the mark "Jordache Basics 101 with star and wing design" for use with jeans and jeans apparel. Jordache (P) moved for summary judgment and Levi (D) opposed the motion and cross-moved for summary judgment.

ISSUE: In order to state a claim for trademark infringement, must a party show likelihood that ordinary prudent consumers are likely to be misled or confused as to the source of the goods in question?

HOLDING AND DECISION: (Kram, J.) Yes. In order to state a claim for trademark infringement, a party must show likelihood that ordinary prudent consumers are likely to be misled or confused as to the source of the goods in question. The Lanham Act prohibits the use of any reproduction of a registered mark if it is "likely to cause confusion, or to cause mistake or to deceive." Types of confusion that constitute trademark infringement include when (1) prospective purchasers believe the senior user sponsored or otherwise approved the junior user's trademark; (2) potential consumers are initially attracted to the junior user's mark by virtue of its similarity to the senior user's mark, and (3) customers are confused as to the source of the junior user's product when this product is observed in the post-sale context. The court must consider several factors in deciding the issue of likelihood of confusion: (1) strength of the mark, (2) degree of similarity between the two marks, (3) proximity of the products, (4) likelihood the prior owner will bridge the gap, (5) actual confusion, (6) defendant's good faith, (7) quality of defendant's product, and (8) sophistication of buyers. The first factor weighs heavily in Levi's (D) favor. The strength of a mark is defined as its tendency to identify the goods sold as originating from a particular source. The strength of a mark is a function of its distinctiveness and is generally classified as follows: (1) generic, (2) descriptive, (3) suggestive, (4) arbitrary, and (5) fanciful. Arbitrary and fanciful marks are stronger and, when registered, afforded the highest degree of protection. These marks consist of words that neither suggest nor describe any characteristic of the particular good or service. The "501" is in fact arbitrary and fanciful as it does not describe any particular quality or characteristic of the jeans or apparel. With respect to the second factor, the court must look to the effect of the mark upon consumers and determine whether a consumer will know the difference. Since there is a factual dispute as to the degree of similarity between these two marks, summary judgment is not proper. Third is whether the proximity of the products in the marketplace will lead consumers to be confused as to their source. Factors to be considered include appearance, style, function, fashion appeal, advertising orientation and price. There is an even greater likelihood of confusion where the junior user's product competes for a slightly different market segment than the senior user. This factor favors Levi (D). Under the fourth factor, if the trademark owner can show that it intends to enter the market of the infringer, such showing is indicative of future likelihood of confusion as to source. As stated earlier, while both parties are competing in the jeans market, it is unclear whether the two address different market segments and, thus, this constitutes a question of fact. Fifth, there is no evidence of actual confusion; however, this factor does not weight in Jordache's (P) favor since the "101" mark has not infiltrated the jeans market. Sixth, the existence of good faith on the part of Jordache (P) is disputed and must be resolved at trial. The seventh factor, the quality of the junior user's product, favors Levi (D) since the fact that the goods are of corresponding quality supports the inference that they emanate from the same

Continued on next page.

source. Last, the sophistication of consumers factor, weighs in Levi's (D) favor. While jeans purchasers are found to be highly sophisticated consumers, it is more likely that they will be confused by jeans containing nearly identical back pocket stitching pattern. While three factors weigh heavily in Levi's (D) favor, summary judgment here is inappropriate. Summary judgment in favor of either party is denied.

ANALYSIS

Trademark law is the body of law that protects symbols used in conjunction with the marketing of a product or service. A trademark is defined as "any word, name, symbol, or device, or any combination thereof" which is used to "identify and distinguish" and "indicate the source" of the particular goods or services. The hallmark for trademark infringement is the likelihood of consumer confusion.

Quicknotes

SUMMARY JUDGMENT Judgment rendered by a court in response to a motion made by one of the parties, claiming that the lack of a question of material fact in respect to an issue warrants disposition of the issue without consideration by the jury.

TRADEMARK Any word, name, symbol, device or combination thereof that is either currently utilized, or which a person has a bona fide intent to utilize, in commerce in order to distinguish his goods from those of another.

TRADEMARK INFRINGEMENT The unauthorized use of another's trademark in such a manner as to cause a likelihood of confusion as to the source of the product or service in connection with which it is utilized.

Packman v. Chicago Tribune Co. and Front Page News, Inc.

Trademark holder (P) v. Newspaper publisher (D)

267 F.3d 628 (7th Cir. 2001).

NATURE OF CASE: Suit for trademark infringement.

FACT SUMMARY: A newspaper celebrated a professional basketball team's sixth championship with a banner headline that proclaimed, "The joy of six." The newspaper reprinted its headline on promotional memorabilia, and the owner of the trademark for the phrase "the joy of six" sued the newspaper for infringement.

RULE OF LAW

The use of a trademarked phrase does not constitute infringement if the use was a fair use and created no likelihood of confusion among consumers.

FACTS: Packman (P) registered a federal trademark for the phrase "the joy of six" for uses in connection with "entertainment services" related to football and basketball games. She used the mark with groups of friends and family to, for example, announce gatherings for watching football games or attending basketball games; she also sold hats and t-shirts as part of these promotional efforts. Packman's (P) husband also eventually sold t-shirts containing the phrase to a homeless street vendor. The record contained no evidence of either how many people attended the gatherings or of how much revenue the sales involving the phrase had generated for Packman (P). The record did show, however, that Packman (P) had written to the Chicago Tribune Co. (Tribune) (D) specifically to encourage the newspaper to use the phrase in describing the Chicago Bulls' expected sixth league championship. After the Bulls did win their sixth championship, the Tribune (D) printed a front-page headline that announced "The joy of six." Following its customary practice in the wake of a local professional sports championship, the Tribune (D) reprinted, on various promotional memorabilia, the front page that announced the Bulls' sixth championship. Eighteen months after the Tribune (D) used "The joy of six" on its front page, Packman (P) sued the Tribune (D) and one of its vendors, alleging federal trademark infringement and unfair competition under state law. Packman (P) challenged only the use of the trademarked phrase on the promotional memorabilia, not the use on the Tribune's (D) front page. The trial court entered summary judgment for the defendants, reasoning that the uses of the phrase either constituted fair use or failed to create a likelihood of confusion for consumers. Packman (P) appealed.

ISSUE: Does the use of a trademarked phrase constitute infringement if the use was a fair use and created no likelihood of confusion among consumers?

HOLDING AND DECISION: (Ripple, J.) No. The use of a trademarked phrase does not constitute infringement if the use was a fair use and created no likelihood of confusion among consumers. A trademark claim under the Lanham Act requires a plaintiff to establish that the mark is protectable and that the defendant's challenged use is likely to confuse consumers. Registration of a mark creates a presumption of validity; a defendant can excuse its use of a presumptively valid mark, though, by showing that the use was a fair use. Applying these standards to this record, the trial judge correctly granted summary judgment for the Tribune (D). The Tribune's (D) fair use defense requires that the use was not a trademark use, that the phrase described the Tribune's (D) goods or services, and that the Tribune (D) used its own masthead, not the trademarked phrase, to identify itself as the source of the memorabilia. Packman (P) also admitted, in her deposition, that the phrase generally can denote happiness about six of anything. Furthermore, the Tribune (D) used the phrase only descriptively, not to take advantage of a secondary meaning for the phrase—a merely asserted secondary meaning for which Packman (P) produced no evidence. Finally, the use on the promotional memorabilia occurred in good faith: the only way to show bad faith is to probe a defendant's subjective purpose for the use, and here the Tribune's (D) use of its own distinctive masthead defeats any claim of bad faith. The Tribune (D) employee who authorized producing the memorabilia knew nothing of Packman's (P) trademark, and the sportswriters' awareness of the mark does not suffice to show bad faith. Moreover, there was no likelihood of confusion among consumers regarding Packman's (P) and the Tribune's (D) uses of "the joy of six." Courts review seven factors when assessing the likelihood of confusion: similarity of appearance and suggestion, similarity of products, the area and manner of the uses, how careful consumers likely would be, how strong the plaintiff's mark is, actual confusion, and the defendant's intent. Of the seven factors, the marks' similarity, the defendant's intent, and actual confusion receive special consideration. Here, the uses were not similar. Packman's (P) use presented the phrase vertically and employed a larger typeface for "joy" and "six"; the Tribune (D) printed the phrase horizontally and in a black typeface typically associated with newspapers. The Tribune's (D) intent in using the phrase appeared in its use of its own masthead and in using the phrase only descriptively. Packman (P) also failed to show any actual confusion; even if her four friends and relatives who asked

Continued on next page.

about her "deal" with the Tribune (D) did qualify as Lanham Act "consumers," the evidence of actual confusion was de minimis. Packman (P) likewise failed to show any likelihood of confusion on the other four factors: the products' manners of appearance were distinctively different, no evidence showed that the parties' distribution or advertising of their products overlapped, no evidence established a genuine issue of fact on consumer sophistication, and Packman's (P) mark was weak. For all these reasons, summary judgment for the Tribune (D) and its vendor was appropriate. Affirmed.

ANALYSIS

An otherwise prohibited use of a presumptively valid trademark will be considered fair if the second user does not deprive the trademark holder of the benefits of the mark. As *Packman* shows, courts determine whether such a benign use occurs by asking whether the second use was a trademark use, whether the second use merely describes the second user's goods or services, and whether the second use was made in good faith.

Quicknotes

DE MINIMIS Insignificant; trivial; not of sufficient significance to require legal action.

FAIR USE An affirmative defense to a claim of copyright infringement providing an exception from the copyright owner's exclusive rights in a work for the purposes of criticism, comment, news reporting, teaching, scholarship or research.

GOOD FAITH An honest intention to abstain from taking advantage of another.

LANHAM ACT Name of the Trademark Act of 1946 that governs federal law regarding trademarks.

TRADEMARK Any word, name, symbol, device or combination thereof that is either currently utilized, or which a person has a bona fide intent to utilize, in commerce in order to distinguish his goods from those of another.

TRADEMARK INFRINGEMENT The unauthorized use of another's trademark in such a manner as to cause a likelihood of confusion as to the source of the product or service in connection with which it is utilized.

Silverman v. CBS, Inc.

Scriptwriter (P) v. Television studio (D)

870 F.2d 40 (2d Cir. 1989).

NATURE OF CASE: Suit seeking declaratory judgment.

FACT SUMMARY: Silverman (P) brought suit seeking a declaration that the "Amos 'n' Andy" radio programs aired from 1928 to 1948 were in the public domain.

RULE OF LAW

Abandonment of a trademark is established by showing that the mark has been abandoned once use has been discontinued with intent not to resume use in the reasonable future.

FACTS: Gosden and Correll created the "Amos 'n' Andy" characters in 1928 and assigned all their rights in the "Amos 'n' Andy" scripts and radio programs to CBS, Inc. (D) in 1948. In 1981, Silverman (P) began writing a script for a Broadway musical based on the "Amos 'n' Andy" characters. He filed suit for a declaration that the "Amos 'n' Andy" radio programs broadcast from 1928 and 1948 are in the public domain and that CBS (D) has no rights in these programs. The court rules that, with respect to the trademark aspects of the case, the name "Amos 'n' Andy" as well as the names and appearances of the characters and other distinctive features from the shows are protectable marks. The judge also concluded that CBS (D) had not abandoned its trademarks. Silverman (P) appealed.

ISSUE: Is abandonment of a trademark established by showing that the mark has been abandoned once use has been discontinued with intent not to resume use in the reasonable future?

HOLDING AND DECISION: (Newman, J.) Yes. Abandonment of a trademark is established by showing that the mark has been abandoned once use has been discontinued with intent not to resume use in the reasonable future. Silverman (P) challenged the district court's ruling that CBS (D) had protectable marks and that it has not abandoned such marks. This court agrees that CBS (D) abandoned the marks. Lanham Act § 45 provides that a mark is abandoned "when its use has been discontinued with intent not to resume. Intent not to resume may be inferred from the circumstances. Nonuse for two years shall be prima facie abandonment." CBS (D) made a conscious decision to take the "Amos 'n' Andy" television programs off the air in response to complaints of several civil rights organizations that the programs were demeaning to Blacks. CBS (D) argued that even though it has not used the mark for 21 years, it always intended to continue using them at some point in the future. We conclude that the applicable standard is whether the mark has been abandoned once use has been discontinued with intent not to resume use in the reasonable future. A proprietor who temporarily suspends use of a mark can rebut the presumption of abandonment by showing reasonable grounds for the suspension and plans to resume use in the reasonably foreseeable future when the conditions requiring suspension abate. The proprietor may not protect a mark, however, if he discontinues use for more than 20 years and has no plans to use or permit its use in the reasonably foreseeable future. An assertion of possible use is not sufficient. Thus, CBS (D) abandoned the marks.

ANALYSIS

The court recognizes that if the applicable standard were "intent never to resume use" this would be virtually impossible to establish circumstantially. Even after a period of prolonged nonuse, and no plans to reinstate use, a company could always truthfully assert that it had intent to resume use at some point in the future.

Quicknotes

DECLARATORY JUDGMENT A judgment of the court establishing the rights of the parties.

PRIMA FACIE On its face, at first sight.

TRADEMARK Any word, name, symbol, device or combination thereof that is either currently utilized, or which a person has a bona fide intent to utilize, in commerce in order to distinguish his goods from those of another.

CHAPTER 56

Copyright Law

Quick Reference Rules of Law

PAGE

1. **What is Copyrightable?** To be copyrightable, a work must be original and possess at least some minimal degree of creativity. (Feist Publications, Inc. v. Rural Telephone Service Co.) *258*

2. **Artwork.** Under common-law agency principles, one who creates an artwork at the behest of another retains copyright thereon unless he was an employee of that other. (Community for Creative Non-Violence v. Reid) *260*

3. **Copyright Infringement.** A literary work can be copyrighted even if it prescribes a primarily factual process; and, if the work is copyrighted, unauthorized wholesale copying of the work need not be permitted as a fair use even if the copying was done for non-commercial purposes. (Religious Technology Center v. Lerma) *261*

Feist Publications, Inc. v. Rural Telephone Service Co.

Publishing company (D) v. Phone book publisher (P)

499 U.S. 340 (1991).

NATURE OF CASE: Appeal from grant of summary judgment to plaintiff in suit for copyright infringement.

FACT SUMMARY: After Feist Publications, Inc. (Feist) (D) took 1,309 listings from Rural Telephone Service Co.'s (Rural) (P) white pages when compiling Feist's (D) own white pages, Rural (P) filed suit for copyright infringement.

RULE OF LAW

To be copyrightable, a work must be original and possess at least some minimal degree of creativity.

FACTS: As a certified telephone service provided in northwest Kansas, Rural Telephone Service Co. (Rural) (P) published a typical telephone directory as a condition of its monopoly franchise. The white pages alphabetically listed the names, towns, and telephone numbers of Rural's (P) subscribers. Feist Publications, Inc. (Feist) (D) was a publishing company specializing in area-wide telephone directories. The Feist (D) directory that was the subject of this litigation contained 46,878 white pages' listings, compared to Rural's (P) approximately 7,700 listings. Feist (D) approached the 11 northwest Kansas telephone companies and offered to pay for the right to use their respective white pages listings. When only Rural (P) refused to license its listings, Feist (D) used them without Rural's (P) consent. A typical Feist (D) listing included each individual's street address, while most of Rural's (P) did not. Of the 46,878 listings in Feist's (D) 1983 directory, 1,309 of those listings were identical to listings in Rural's (P) white pages. Rural (P) sued for copyright infringement. The district court granted summary judgment to Rural (P), and the court of appeals affirmed. Feist (D) appealed.

ISSUE: To be copyrightable, must a work be original and possess at least some minimal degree of creativity?

HOLDING AND DECISION: (O'Connor, J.) Yes. To be copyrightable, a work must be original and possess at least some minimal degree of creativity. This case concerns the interaction of two well-established propositions. The first is that facts are not copyrightable; the other, that compilations of facts generally are. There is an undeniable tension between these two propositions. The key to resolving the tension lies in understanding why facts are not copyrightable. No one may claim originality as to facts because facts do not owe their origin to an act of authorship. Factual compilations, on the other hand, may possess the requisite originality. Compilations were expressly mentioned in the Copyright Acts of 1909 and 1976. Even a directory that contains absolutely no protectable written expression, only facts, meets the constitutional minimum for copyright protection if it features an original selection or arrangement. If the selection and arrangement are original, these elements of the work are eligible for copyright protection. No matter how original the format, though, the facts themselves do not become original through association. There is no doubt that Feist (D) took from the white pages of Rural's (P) directory a substantial amount of factual information. The question that remains is whether Rural (P) selected, coordinated, or arranged these uncopyrightable facts in an original way. It did not. Rural (P) simply took the data provided by its subscribers and listed it alphabetically by surname. There is nothing remotely creative about arranging names alphabetically in a white pages directory. Rural (P) expended sufficient effort to make the white pages directory useful, but insufficient creativity to make it original. Thus, because Rural's (P) white pages lack the requisite originality, Feist's (D) use of the listings cannot constitute infringement. Copyright rewards originality, not effort. Reversed.

ANALYSIS

In the words of the Court, copyright ensures authors the right to their original expression, but encourages others to build freely upon the ideas and information conveyed by a work. This principle, known as the idea/expression or fact/expression dichotomy, applies to all works of authorship. As applied to a factual compilation, assuming the absence of original written expression, only the compiler's selection and arrangement may be protected; the raw facts may be copied at will. This is the means by which copyright advances the progress of science and art by encouraging creativity with the reward of exclusive rights for the original creation.

Quicknotes

COPYRIGHT Refers to the exclusive rights granted to an artist pursuant to Article I, Section 8, clause 8 of the United States Constitution over the reproduction, display, performance, distribution, and adaptation of his work for a period prescribed by statute.

COPYRIGHT INFRINGEMENT A violation of one of the exclusive rights granted to an artist pursuant to Article I, Section 8, clause 8 of the United States Constitution over the reproduction, display, performance, distribution, and adaptation of his work for a period prescribed by statute.

Continued on next page.

SUMMARY JUDGMENT Judgment rendered by a court in response to a motion made by one of the parties, claiming that the lack of a question of material fact in respect to an issue warrants disposition of the issue without consideration by the jury.

Community for Creative Non-Violence v. Reid

Nonprofit organization (P) v. Sculptor (D)

490 U.S. 730 (1989).

NATURE OF CASE: Review of order adjudicating copyrights with respect to a sculpture.

FACT SUMMARY: Reid (D), who had created a sculpture on commission from Community for Creative Non-Violence (P), contended that since he had not been an employee of it under common-law agency principles, he owned the copyright thereon.

RULE OF LAW

Under common-law agency principles, one who creates an artwork at the behest of another retains copyright thereon unless he was an employee of that other.

FACTS: The Community for Creative Non-Violence (CCNV) (P) was a nonprofit organization dedicated to advocacy for the cause of the homeless in the United States. It negotiated with Reid (D), a sculptor, for the latter to fashion a variation on the classic nativity scene, depicting homeless individuals. Agreement was finally made, and Reid (D) fashioned the sculpture out of a bronze-like material. The work was done by Reid (D) in his studio, with minimal direction from CCNV (P). After the unveiling, Reid (D) registered a copyright on the work. Subsequent to this, a disagreement arose between CCNV (P) and Reid (D) who had taken custody of the sculpture, over future exhibition thereof. CCNV (P) filed an action seeking to obtain possession of the work. The district court held CCNV (P) to have the right to exhibit the statute. The Federal Circuit of the Court of Appeals reversed, and the U.S. Supreme Court granted review.

ISSUE: Under common-law agency principles, does one who creates an artwork at the behest of another retain copyright thereon unless he had been an employee of that other?

HOLDING AND DECISION: (Marshall, J.) Yes. Under common-law agency principles, one creating an artwork at the behest of another retains copyright thereon unless he had been an employee of that other. 17 U.S.C. § 201(a) provides that copyright ownership vests initially in the work's author, something Reid (D) in this instance indisputably was. Section 101 of the 1976 Copyright Act creates an exception to this in the case of works created "for hire." Section 101(2) mandates copyright vestiture in the case where the author is an independent contractor of another, in specific instances not applicable here. Section 101(1) provides that the work is one created "for hire" if the work is created by an employee within the scope of his employment, and this subsection is the only one which can divest Reid (D) of copyright therein. "Employee" is not defined in the section. This being so, the rule comes into play that words used in a statute will be presumed to possess their normal meanings. Contrary to CCNV's (P) assertions, "employee" is a narrower term than one over whom another exercises a measure of control. Rather, "employee" has a particular meaning, derived from common-law agency principles, wherein one party performs labor for another under circumstances in which that other exerts substantial control over the work environment on the laborer, as well as the manner of performance. Numerous factors figure in this equation, such as the level of skill required, tax treatment of the putative employee, the singleness of the assignment, and the source of the instrumentalities of the labor. Here, the work was highly skilled, Reid (D) was retained only for this single assignment, was not treated as an employee for tax purposes, and supplied his own tools and work area. The conclusion is mandated that, under agency principles, Reid (D) was not an employee of CCNV (P). Therefore, the § 101 (1) exception to § 201(a) does not apply, and the copyright belongs to Reid (D). Affirmed.

ANALYSIS

Sections 101(1) and 101(2) were the result of lengthy debate and compromise in Congress. Prior to 1955, any commissioned work belonged to the hiring party. For the next several years, changes in this rule were proposed numerous times. Not until 1965 was the substantive embodiment of current law enacted.

Quicknotes

AGENCY A fiduciary relationship whereby authority is granted to an agent to act on behalf of the principal in order to effectuate the principal's objective.

COPYRIGHT Refers to the exclusive rights granted to an artist pursuant to Article I, Section 8, clause 8 of the United States Constitution over the reproduction, display, performance, distribution, and adaptation of his work for a period prescribed by statute.

INDEPENDENT CONTRACTOR A party undertaking a particular assignment for another who retains control over the manner in which it is executed.

Religious Technology Center v. Lerma

Copyright protector (P) v. Online poster (D)

40 U.S.P.Q.2d 1569 (E.D. Va. 1996).

NATURE OF CASE: Copyright infringement suit.

FACT SUMMARY: Religious Technology Center (P) brought suit against Lerma (D) for his posting of the Church of Scientology's sacred texts and materials on the Internet.

RULE OF LAW

literary work can be copyrighted even if it prescribes a primarily factual process; and, if the work is copyrighted, unauthorized wholesale copying of the work need not be permitted as a fair use even if the copying was done for non-commercial purposes.

FACTS: Lerma (D) acquired and posted on the Internet texts that the Church of Scientology considers sacred and protects from unauthorized disclosure. The church charged Religious Technology Center (RTC) (P) with securing the texts and aggressively policing any breaches in security or unauthorized disclosures. RTC (P) brought suit against Lerma (D) and both parties moved for summary judgment.

ISSUE: Is a literary work automatically uncopyrightable because it prescribes a primarily factual process; and, if the work can be copyrighted, must unauthorized wholesale copying of the work be permitted as a fair use even if the copying was done for non-commercial purposes?

HOLDING AND DECISION: (Brinkema, J.) No. A literary work can be copyrighted even if it prescribes a primarily factual process; and, if the work is copyrighted, unauthorized wholesale copying of the work need not be permitted as a fair use even if the copying was done for non-commercial purposes. In order to establish copyright infringement, a plaintiff must show: (1) ownership of a valid copyright; and (2) unauthorized copying. Lerma (D) challenged the copyrightability of the work on the basis that it was not copyrightable under the merger doctrine of the idea/expression dichotomy. The idea/expression dichotomy precludes copyright protection for any "idea, procedure, process, system, method of operation, concept, principle or discovery, regardless of the form in which it is . . . embodied in the work." 17 U.S.C. § 102(b). Where the author's expression is so closely entertwined with the idea, the two are said to have merged and the expression becomes uncopyrightable. Lerma (P) argues that the merger doctrine applies and thus RTC's (P) copyright infringement claim is invalid. The court concludes that the merger doctrine does not apply here. The ideas and concepts of the Scientology religion may be discussed independently of their documents. Lerma (D) next argues that even if the works are copyrightable, his copying was lawful under the "fair use" defense. To determine whether a use of a copyrighted work is fair, the court must consider four factors: (1) the purpose and character of the use, (2) the nature of the copyrighted work, (3) the amount and substantiality of the portion used in relation to the work as a whole, and (4) the effect of the use on the potential market for or value of the work. With respect to the first factor, Lerma (D) argued that his use of the work constituted criticism, comment, news reporting and scholarship, the classic fair use categories listed in section 107. While Lerma's (D) use was not commercial and there is no evidence of his profiting directly from the use, this one factor is not dispositive. The second factor, the nature of the copyrighted work, recognizes that some works are closer to the "core of intended protection" than others. The fair use defense is broader with respect to factual than creative or literary works. The works here are intended to be informational rather than creative and a broader fair use approach is appropriate in this respect, however, the works here have not been "published." RTC (P) has not, and does not plan to, release these works to the public. Lerma (D) argued that since the works were available in a court file and on the Internet, that this constituted publication. This argument is not convincing. The third factor is the amount and substantiality of the portion copied. This factor has both a qualitative and quantitative element so that a use is considered unfair is it goes to the "heart" of the copyrighted work. In addition, wholesale copying generally precludes use of the fair use defense. Although Lerma (D) did not post each batch in its entirety, he did post the entirety of certain discreet subparts of the series. Both the Code of Federal Regulations and pertinent case law find that each of the series is to be considered as a separate work. Thus Lerma's (D) infringement is clear. Last, the court must consider the effect that the infringing material has on the market for, or value of, the copyrighted work. Lerma (D) correctly argues that any economic harm resulting from legitimate commentary is permissible. While it is difficult to measure the market impact of the use in this case, the potential for economic harm to RTC (P) must also be considered. This requires the plaintiff to show that should the conduct become widespread, it would adversely affect the potential market for the work. RTC (P) is unable to show concrete evidence of the economic effect of Lerma's (D) postings. Based on the four factors together, Lerma's (D) use was not fair. Summary judgment for RTC (P).

ANALYSIS

A copyright owner may seek actual damages and any additional profits received by the infringer or statutory damages under 17 U.S.C. § 504(a). Since actual damages

Continued on next page.

and profits are not readily measurable, RTC (P) must seek statutory damages. Statutory damages are based on three issues: (1) to what extent the works infringe the copyrights; (2) number of infringing acts; and (3) the willfulness of the infringement.

■═■

Quicknotes

COPYRIGHT Refers to the exclusive rights granted to an artist pursuant to Article I, Section 8, clause 8 of the United States Constitution over the reproduction, display, performance, distribution, and adaptation of his work for a period prescribed by statute.

COPYRIGHT INFRINGEMENT A violation of one of the exclusive rights granted to an artist pursuant to Article I, Section 8, clause 8 of the United States Constitution over the reproduction, display, performance, distribution, and adaptation of his work for a period prescribed by statute.

FAIR USE An affirmative defense to a claim of copyright infringement providing an exception from the copyright owner's exclusive rights in a work for the purposes of criticism, comment, news reporting, teaching, scholarship or research.

■═■

CHAPTER 57

The Right of Publicity

Quick Reference Rules of Law

National Basketball Assn. and NBA Properties, Inc. v. Motorola, Inc.

Sporting associations (P) v. Pager company (D)

105 F.3d 841 (2d Cir. 1997).

NATURE OF CASE: Copyright infringement suit.

FACT SUMMARY: The National Basketball Assn. and NBA Properties, Inc. (P) brought suit against Motorola, Inc. (D) claiming misappropriation of their broadcasts for the purpose of transmitting game information via handheld pagers.

RULE OF LAW

A state law "hot news" misappropriation claim survives preemption by the federal Copyright Act of 1976.

FACTS: Motorola. Inc. (D) sold and marketed a handheld pager under the name "SportsTrax," displaying updated information of professional basketball games in progress. Sports Team Analysis and Tracking Systems (STATS) supplies the game information transmitted to the pagers. SportsTrax's operation relies on a "data feed" supplied to them by STATS reporters, who relay the information via modem to STATS' host computer. The computer compiles, analyzes and formats the data for retransmission to a common carrier which sends it via satellite to various FM networks that emit the signal to the pagers. The court found Motorola (D) and STATS (D) liable for misappropriation and permanently enjoined them from transmitting scores or other data regarding NBA games without authorization by the National Basketball Assn. and NBA Properties, Inc. (NBA) (P). Motorola and STATS (D) appealed.

ISSUE: Does a state law "hot news" misappropriation claim survive preemption by the federal Copyright Act of 1976?

HOLDING AND DECISION: (Winter, J.) Yes. A state law "hot news" misappropriation claim survives preemption by the federal Copyright Act of 1976. The 1976 Act contained provisions preempting state law claims that enforced rights equivalent to exclusive copyright protections of the work to which the state claim was being applied fell within the area of copyright protection. The Act expressly affords copyright protection to simultaneously recorded broadcasts of live performances such as sports events. Recorded broadcasts of NBA (P) games are also entitled to copyright protection. The district court, however, correctly held that Motorola and STATS (D) did not infringe the NBA's (P) copyright since they only reproduced facts from such broadcasts, not the expression of the game that constitutes the broadcast. This principle is known in copyright law as the "idea/expression" dichotomy. Since the SportsTrax device reproduces only factual information from the broadcasts and none of the copyrightable expression of the games, the defendants did not infringe the NBA's (P) copyright. The district court's injunction, however, was based on its conclusion that defendants unlawfully appropriated the NBA's property rights in the games under state law. The district court held that the NBA's (P) misappropriation claim was not preempted by the 1976 Act and that defendants engaged in unlawful misappropriation under state law. This court disagrees. Under the 1976 Act, a state law claim is preempted when (1) the state law claim seeks to vindicate legal rights equal to those protected by copyright law (general scope requirement), and (2) the particular work falls within the type of works protected (subject matter requirement). Here the subject matter requirement is met as to both the broadcasts and games. Certain forms of commercial misappropriation, however, will survive preemption if an extra element test is met. The elements of a "hot news" misappropriation are as follows: (1) the plaintiff generates or collects information at some cost or expense; (2) the information's value is time-sensitive; (3) the defendant's use of the information constitutes free-riding on the plaintiff's costly efforts to collect it; (4) the defendant's use of the information is in direct competition with a product or service offered by plaintiff; and (5) the ability of others to free-ride on the plaintiff's efforts would so reduce the incentive to produce the product or service that its existence is threatened. Those additional elements that allow a "hot news" claim to survive include: (1) the time-sensitive value of factual information, (2) free-riding by the defendant, and (3) the threat to the existence of the service or product. Defendants have not engaged in unlawful misappropriation under this test. Defendants cannot be said to be free-riding, enabling the defendants to produce a directly competitive product at lower cost. Injunction vacated.

ANALYSIS

In *Feist Publications, Inc. v. Rural Telephone Service Co.*, 499 U.S. 340 (1991), the Supreme Court held that facts are in the public domain and not copyrightable. Preemption of state law is expressly provided for in the 1976 Act § 301 to the extent the state rights seek to protect rights equivalent to copyright. These include the right to reproduce, distribute, create derivative works, display, and perform the copyrighted work.

Continued on next page.

Quicknotes

COPYRIGHT Refers to the exclusive rights granted to an artist pursuant to Article I, Section 8, clause 8 of the United States Constitution over the reproduction, display, performance, distribution, and adaptation of his work for a period prescribed by statute.

COPYRIGHT INFRINGEMENT A violation of one of the exclusive rights granted to an artist pursuant to Article I, Section 8, clause 8 of the United States Constitution over the reproduction, display, performance, distribution, and adaptation of his work for a period prescribed by statute.

The Elvis Presley International Memorial Foundation v. Elvis Presley Memorial Foundation, Inc.

Nonprofit organization (P) v. Memorial corporation (D)

Tenn. Ct. App., 733 S.W.2d 89 (1987).

NATURE OF CASE: Appeal from grant of summary judgment motion in right of publicity action.

FACT SUMMARY: The Elvis Presley International Memorial Foundation (International) (P) appealed from a decision granting summary judgment to the Elvis Presley Memorial Foundation, Inc. (Foundation) (D), in its unfair competition action, contending that there was no descendible right of publicity recognized in this jurisdiction.

RULE OF LAW

The right of publicity is decidable upon death, and can be devised accordingly.

FACTS: Elvis Presley International Memorial Foundation (International) (P) formed in 1979 as a non-profit group to support a new trauma center in the community. Their application for charter as a non-profit corporation was denied in 1980 when they were informed that the name "Elvis Presley" could not be used in the charter. The Presley estate offered to give International (P) a limited, royalty free license to use the singer's name and likeness but the offer was turned down. Shortly thereafter, Elvis Presley Enterprises, Inc. (D) was incorporated. Two days later, in a reversal, a corporate charter was issued to International (P). Elvis Presley Memorial Foundation, Inc. (Foundation) (D) was then formed and incorporated as a not-for-profit corporation in 1985, to solicit funds to construct a fountain across from Elvis Presley's home. International (P) then filed the present action for unfair competition, seeking to dissolve Foundation (D) and to enjoin it from using a deceptively similar name. Enterprises (D) intervened, indicating that it had granted permission to Foundation (D) to use the Presley name, but not to International (P). Foundation (D) successfully moved for summary judgment and succeeded in dismissing the complaint, and International (P) appealed, contending that there was no descendible right of publicity and that Elvis Presley's name and image entered into the public domain upon his death.

ISSUE: Is a person's right to publicity descendible upon his/her death?

HOLDING AND DECISION: (Koch, J.) Yes. The right of publicity is descendible upon death, and can be devised accordingly. The right of publicity involves an individual's right to capitalize upon the commercial exploitation of his name and likeness and to prevent others from doing so without his consent. The value in the right of publicity is unquestioned. Although the right of publicity originally evolved from the right of privacy, and was not independently recognized for some time, courts from other jurisdictions have uniformly held that the right of publicity is a separate and independent right. The state's common law embodies an expansive view of property, and since a person's right of publicity has all the attributes of property, we recognize it as a species of intangible personal property. Recognizing its descendibility is consistent and promotes several important state policies, tied together with individual rights and expectations associated with other forms of property. Therefore, since the right of publicity is descendible, Elvis Presley's right of publicity survived his death and is enforceable by his estate. [The court then made clear that its decision was based on the recognition of the right under common law, but vacated the lower court judgment and remanded the case to resolve issues of material fact concerning International's (P) laches defense.] Vacated and remanded.

ANALYSIS

The court in the present case expressly declined to base its decision upon state statute, even though the issue was raised by Foundation's (D) countercomplaint. Counsel for Foundation (D) has suggested that this was done so that the court did not wish to make a decision regarding the retroactivity of the statute. The rule in the present case is rapidly becoming the majority view throughout the country.

Quicknotes

RIGHT OF PUBLICITY The right of a person to control the commercial exploitation of his name or likeness.

SUMMARY JUDGMENT Judgment rendered by a court in response to a motion made by one of the parties, claiming that the lack of a question of material fact in respect to an issue warrants disposition of the issue without consideration by the jury.

UNFAIR COMPETITION Any dishonest or fraudulent rivalry in trade and commerce, particularly imitation and counterfeiting.

White v. Samsung Electronics America, Inc.

Game-show celebrity (P) v. Consumer electronics company (D)

989 F.2d 1512 (9th Cir.) *cert. denied*, 508 U.S. 951, 113 S. Ct. 2443 (1993).

NATURE OF CASE: Suit for infringement of the right of publicity.

FACT SUMMARY: [Facts not stated in casebook excerpt.]

RULE OF LAW

An advertisement that parodies a celebrity by evoking her personality infringes upon her right of publicity.

FACTS: [Facts not stated in casebook excerpt.]

ISSUE: Does an advertisement that parodies a celebrity by evoking her personality infringe upon her right of publicity?

HOLDING AND DECISION: (Kozinski, J.) Yes. An advertisement that parodies a celebrity by evoking her personality infringes upon her right of publicity.

DISSENT: (from the denial of a petition for rehearing en banc): (Kozinski, J.) The original panel majority's opinion in favor of Vanna White (P) is deeply flawed, and it deserves a more thorough en banc review. Protecting White (P) from Samsung Electronics America, Inc.'s (Samsung) (D) parody satisfies neither the Copyright Act nor the Copyright Clause of the U.S. Constitution, and it implicates disturbing First Amendment concerns. The trial judge correctly entered summary judgment against White (P) because Samsung (D) did not use her name, likeness, voice, or signature—considerations that used to establish the boundaries of the right to publicity under California law. The panel of this Court that heard the appeal, however, reversed the trial judge's perfectly reasonable judgment because the panel majority was concerned that Samsung's (D) ad had "evoked" White's (P) personality. Intellectual property must include balances, such as fair use and parody. But such a ruling goes even further and ignores the constitutional underpinnings of intellectual property by restricting the very creativity that the Copyright Clause strives to foster. Furthermore, First Amendment issues raised by the panel majority's opinion are staggering: *White* cannot, consistent with any known First Amendment jurisprudence, control our mere thoughts. Parody is an essential component of robust free speech, even if the speech is only marginally protected commercial speech as Samsung's (D) was in this case. At a minimum, then, this case should receive a much more considered review than it has received thus far.

ANALYSIS

White does at least implicate all the issues so vigorously raised by Judge Kozinski. Considering the breadth with which other courts have interpreted the right of publicity though, *White*'s right of publicity ruling seems to fit comfortably within the mainstream of such cases.

Quicknotes

APPROPRIATION In governmental accounting, an expenditure authorized for a specific amount, purpose and time.

COMMERCIAL SPEECH Any speech that proposes a commercial transaction, or promotes products or services.

RIGHT OF PUBLICITY The right of a person to control the commercial exploitation of his name or likeness.

Glossary

Common Latin Words and Phrases Encountered in the Law

A FORTIORI: Because one fact exists or has been proven, therefore a second fact that is related to the first fact must also exist.

A PRIORI: From the cause to the effect. A term of logic used to denote that when one generally accepted truth is shown to be a cause, another particular effect must necessarily follow.

AB INITIO: From the beginning; a condition which has existed throughout, as in a marriage which was void ab initio.

ACTUS REUS: The wrongful act; in criminal law, such action sufficient to trigger criminal liability.

AD VALOREM: According to value; an ad valorem tax is imposed upon an item located within the taxing jurisdiction calculated by the value of such item.

AMICUS CURIAE: Friend of the court. Its most common usage takes the form of an amicus curiae brief, filed by a person who is not a party to an action but is nonetheless allowed to offer an argument supporting his legal interests.

ARGUENDO: In arguing. A statement, possibly hypothetical, made for the purpose of argument, is one made arguendo.

BILL QUIA TIMET: A bill to quiet title (establish ownership) to real property.

BONA FIDE: True, honest, or genuine. May refer to a person's legal position based on good faith or lacking notice of fraud (such as a bona fide purchaser for value) or to the authenticity of a particular document (such as a bona fide last will and testament).

CAUSA MORTIS: With approaching death in mind. A gift causa mortis is a gift given by a party who feels certain that death is imminent.

CAVEAT EMPTOR: Let the buyer beware. This maxim is reflected in the rule of law that a buyer purchases at his own risk because it is his responsibility to examine, judge, test, and otherwise inspect what he is buying.

CERTIORARI: A writ of review. Petitions for review of a case by the United States Supreme Court are most often done by means of a writ of certiorari.

CONTRA: On the other hand. Opposite. Contrary to.

CORAM NOBIS: Before us; writs of error directed to the court that originally rendered the judgment.

CORAM VOBIS: Before you; writs of error directed by an appellate court to a lower court to correct a factual error.

CORPUS DELICTI: The body of the crime; the requisite elements of a crime amounting to objective proof that a crime has been committed.

CUM TESTAMENTO ANNEXO, ADMINISTRATOR (ADMINISTRATOR C.T.A.): With will annexed; an administrator c.t.a. settles an estate pursuant to a will in which he is not appointed.

DE BONIS NON, ADMINISTRATOR (ADMINISTRATOR D.B.N.): Of goods not administered; an administrator d.b.n. settles a partially settled estate.

DE FACTO: In fact; in reality; actually. Existing in fact but not officially approved or engendered.

DE JURE: By right; lawful. Describes a condition that is legitimate "as a matter of law," in contrast to the term "de facto," which connotes something existing in fact but not legally sanctioned or authorized. For example, de facto segregation refers to segregation brought about by housing patterns, etc., whereas de jure segregation refers to segregation created by law.

DE MINIMIS: Of minimal importance; insignificant; a trifle; not worth bothering about.

DE NOVO: Anew; a second time; afresh. A trial de novo is a new trial held at the appellate level as if the case originated there and the trial at a lower level had not taken place.

DICTA: Generally used as an abbreviated form of obiter dicta, a term describing those portions of a judicial opinion incidental or not necessary to resolution of the specific question before the court. Such nonessential statements and remarks are not considered to be binding precedent.

DUCES TECUM: Refers to a particular type of writ or subpoena requesting a party or organization to produce certain documents in their possession.

EN BANC: Full bench. Where a court sits with all justices present rather than the usual quorum.

EX PARTE: For one side or one party only. An ex parte proceeding is one undertaken for the benefit of only one party, without notice to, or an appearance by, an adverse party.

EX POST FACTO: After the fact. An ex post facto law is a law that retroactively changes the consequences of a prior act.

EX REL.: Abbreviated form of the term "ex relatione," meaning upon relation or information. When the state brings an action in which it has no interest against an individual at the instigation of one who has a private interest in the matter.

FORUM NON CONVENIENS: Inconvenient forum. Although a court may have jurisdiction over the case, the action should be tried in a more conveniently located court, one to which parties and witnesses may more easily travel, for example.

GUARDIAN AD LITEM: A guardian of an infant as to litigation, appointed to represent the infant and pursue his/her rights.

HABEAS CORPUS: You have the body. The modern writ of habeas corpus is a writ directing that a person (body) being detained (such as a prisoner) be brought before the court so that the legality of his detention can be judicially ascertained.

IN CAMERA: In private, in chambers. When a hearing is held before a judge in his chambers or when all spectators are excluded from the courtroom.

IN FORMA PAUPERIS: In the manner of a pauper. A party who proceeds in forma pauperis because of his poverty is one who is allowed to bring suit without liability for costs.

INFRA: Below, under. A word referring the reader to a later part of a book. (The opposite of supra.)

IN LOCO PARENTIS: In the place of a parent.

IN PARI DELICTO: Equally wrong; a court of equity will not grant requested relief to an applicant who is in pari delicto, or as much at fault in the transactions giving rise to the controversy as is the opponent of the applicant.

IN PARI MATERIA: On like subject matter or upon the same matter. Statutes relating to the same person or things are said to be in pari materia. It is a general rule of statutory construction that such statutes should be construed together, i.e., looked at as if they together constituted one law.

IN PERSONAM: Against the person. Jurisdiction over the person of an individual.

IN RE: In the matter of. Used to designate a proceeding involving an estate or other property.

IN REM: A term that signifies an action against the res, or thing. An action in rem is basically one that is taken directly against property, as distinguished from an action in personam, i.e., against the person.

INTER ALIA: Among other things. Used to show that the whole of a statement, pleading, list, statute, etc., has not been set forth in its entirety.

INTER PARTES: Between the parties. May refer to contracts, conveyances or other transactions having legal significance.

INTER VIVOS: Between the living. An inter vivos gift is a gift made by a living grantor, as distinguished from bequests contained in a will, which pass upon the death of the testator.

IPSO FACTO: By the mere fact itself.

JUS: Law or the entire body of law.

LEX LOCI: The law of the place; the notion that the rights of parties to a legal proceeding are governed by the law of the place where those rights arose.

MALUM IN SE: Evil or wrong in and of itself; inherently wrong. This term describes an act that is wrong by its very nature, as opposed to one which would not be wrong but for the fact that there is a specific legal prohibition against it (malum prohibitum).

MALUM PROHIBITUM: Wrong because prohibited, but not inherently evil. Used to describe something that is wrong because it is expressly forbidden by law but that is not in and of itself evil, e.g., speeding.

MANDAMUS: We command. A writ directing an official to take a certain action.

MENS REA: A guilty mind; a criminal intent. A term used to signify the mental state that accompanies a crime or other prohibited act. Some crimes require only a general mens rea (general intent to do the prohibited act), but others, like assault with intent to murder, require the existence of a specific mens rea.

MODUS OPERANDI: Method of operating; generally refers to the manner or style of a criminal in committing crimes, admissible in appropriate cases as evidence of the identity of a defendant.

NEXUS: A connection to.

NISI PRIUS: A court of first impression. A nisi prius court is one where issues of fact are tried before a judge or jury.

N.O.V. (NON OBSTANTE VEREDICTO): Notwithstanding the verdict. A judgment n.o.v. is a judgment given in favor of one party despite the fact that a verdict was returned in favor of the other party, the justification being that the verdict either had no reasonable support in fact or was contrary to law.

NUNC PRO TUNC: Now for then. This phrase refers to actions that may be taken and will then have full retroactive effect.

PENDENTE LITE: Pending the suit; pending litigation under way.

PER CAPITA: By head; beneficiaries of an estate, if they take in equal shares, take per capita.

PER CURIAM: By the court; signifies an opinion ostensibly written "by the whole court" and with no identified author.

PER SE: By itself, in itself; inherently.

PER STIRPES: By representation. Used primarily in the law of wills to describe the method of distribution where a person, generally because of death, is unable to take that which is left to him by the will of another, and therefore his heirs divide such property between them rather than take under the will individually.

PRIMA FACIE: On its face, at first sight. A prima facie case is one that is sufficient on its face, meaning that the evidence supporting it is adequate to establish the case until contradicted or overcome by other evidence.

PRO TANTO: For so much; as far as it goes. Often used in eminent domain cases when a property owner receives partial payment for his land without prejudice to his right to bring suit for the full amount he claims his land to be worth.

QUANTUM MERUIT: As much as he deserves. Refers to recovery based on the doctrine of unjust enrichment in those cases in which a party has rendered valuable services or furnished materials that were accepted and enjoyed by another under circumstances that would reasonably notify the recipient that the rendering party expected to be paid. In essence, the law implies a contract to pay the reasonable value of the services or materials furnished.

QUASI: Almost like; as if; nearly. This term is essentially used to signify that one subject or thing is almost analogous to another but that material differences between them do exist. For example, a quasi-criminal proceeding is one that is not strictly criminal but shares enough of the same characteristics to require some of the same safeguards (e.g., procedural due process must be followed in a parole hearing).

QUID PRO QUO: Something for something. In contract law, the consideration, something of value, passed between the parties to render the contract binding.

RES GESTAE: Things done; in evidence law, this principle justifies the admission of a statement that would otherwise be hearsay when it is made so closely to the event in question as to be said to be a part of it, or with such spontaneity as not to have the possibility of falsehood.

RES IPSA LOQUITUR: The thing speaks for itself. This doctrine gives rise to a rebuttable presumption of negligence when the instrumentality causing the injury was within the exclusive control of the defendant, and the injury was one that does not normally occur unless a person has been negligent.

RES JUDICATA: A matter adjudged. Doctrine which provides that once a court of competent jurisdiction has rendered a final judgment or decree on the merits, that judgment or decree is conclusive upon the parties to the case and prevents them from engaging in any other litigation on the points and issues determined therein.

RESPONDEAT SUPERIOR: Let the master reply. This doctrine holds the master liable for the wrongful acts of his servant (or the principal for his agent) in those cases in which the servant (or agent) was acting within the scope of his authority at the time of the injury.

STARE DECISIS: To stand by or adhere to that which has been decided. The common law doctrine of stare decisis attempts to give security and certainty to the law by following the policy that once a principle of law as applicable to a certain set of facts has been set forth in a decision, it forms a precedent which will subsequently be followed, even though a different decision might be made were it the first time the question had arisen. Of course, stare decisis is not an inviolable principle and is departed from in instances where there is good cause (e.g., considerations of public policy led the Supreme Court to disregard prior decisions sanctioning segregation).

SUPRA: Above. A word referring a reader to an earlier part of a book.

ULTRA VIRES: Beyond the power. This phrase is most commonly used to refer to actions taken by a corporation that are beyond the power or legal authority of the corporation.

Addendum of French Derivatives

IN PAIS: Not pursuant to legal proceedings.

CHATTEL: Tangible personal property.

CY PRES: Doctrine permitting courts to apply trust funds to purposes not expressed in the trust but necessary to carry out the settlor's intent.

PER AUTRE VIE: For another's life; during another's life. In property law, an estate may be granted that will terminate upon the death of someone other than the grantee.

PROFIT A PRENDRE: A license to remove minerals or other produce from land.

VOIR DIRE: Process of questioning jurors as to their predispositions about the case or parties to a proceeding in order to identify those jurors displaying bias or prejudice.

Casenote Legal Briefs

Administrative Law	Breyer, Stewart, Sunstein & Vermeule
Administrative Law	Cass, Diver, Beermann & Freeman
Administrative Law	Funk, Shapiro & Weaver
Administrative Law	Mashaw, Merrill & Shane
Administrative Law	Strauss, Rakoff & Farina (Gellhorn & Byse)
Agency & Partnership	Hynes & Loewenstein
Antitrust	Pitofsky, Goldschmid & Wood
Antitrust	Sullivan, Hovenkamp & Schelanski
Bankruptcy	Warren & Bussel
Business Organizations	Allen, Kraakman & Subramanian
Business Organizations	Bauman, Weiss & Palmiter
Business Organizations	Hamilton & Macey
Business Organizations	Klein, Ramseyer & Bainbridge
Business Organizations	O'Kelley & Thompson
Business Organizations	Smiddy & Cunningham
Civil Procedure	Field, Kaplan & Clermont
Civil Procedure	Freer & Perdue
Civil Procedure	Friedenthal, Miller, Sexton & Hershkoff
Civil Procedure	Hazard, Tait, Fletcher & Bundy
Civil Procedure	Marcus, Redish, Sherman & Pfander
Civil Procedure	Subrin, Minow, Brodin & Main
Civil Procedure	Yeazell
Commercial Law	LoPucki, Warren, Keating & Mann
Commercial Law	Warren & Walt
Commercial Law	Whaley
Community Property	Bird
Community Property	Blumberg
Conflicts	Brilmayer & Goldsmith
Conflicts	Currie, Kay, Kramer & Roosevelt
Constitutional Law	Brest, Levinson, Balkin & Amar
Constitutional Law	Chemerinsky
Constitutional Law	Choper, Fallon, Kamisar & Shiffrin (Lockhart)
Constitutional Law	Cohen, Varat & Amar
Constitutional Law	Farber, Eskridge & Frickey
Constitutional Law	Rotunda
Constitutional Law	Sullivan & Gunther
Constitutional Law	Stone, Seidman, Sunstein, Tushnet & Karlan
Contracts	Ayres & Speidel
Contracts	Barnett
Contracts	Burton
Contracts	Calamari, Perillo & Bender
Contracts	Crandall & Whaley
Contracts	Dawson, Harvey, Henderson & Baird
Contracts	Farnsworth, Young, Sanger, Cohen & Brooks
Contracts	Fuller & Eisenberg
Contracts	Knapp, Crystal & Prince
Copyright	Cohen, Loren, Okediji & O'Rourke
Copyright, Patent, and Trademark	Goldstein & Reese
Criminal Law	Bonnie, Coughlin, Jeffries & Low
Criminal Law	Boyce, Dripps & Perkins
Criminal Law	Dressler
Criminal Law	Johnson & Cloud
Criminal Law	Kadish, Schulhofer & Steiker
Criminal Law	Kaplan, Weisberg & Binder
Criminal Procedure	Allen, Stuntz, Hoffmann, Livingston & Leipold
Criminal Procedure	Dressler & Thomas
Criminal Procedure	Haddad, Marsh, Zagel, Meyer, Starkman & Bauer
Criminal Procedure	Kamisar, LaFave, Israel, King & Kerr
Criminal Procedure	Saltzburg & Capra
Debtors and Creditors	Warren & Westbrook
Employment Discrimination	Friedman
Employment Discrimination	Zimmer, Sullivan & White
Employment Law	Rothstein & Liebman
Environmental Law	Menell & Stewart
Environmental Law	Percival, Schroeder, Miller & Leape
Environmental Law	Plater, Abrams, Goldfarb, Graham, Heinzerling & Wirth
Evidence	Broun, Mosteller & Giannelli
Evidence	Fisher
Evidence	Mueller & Kirkpatrick
Evidence	Sklansky
Evidence	Waltz, Park & Friedman
Family Law	Areen & Regan
Family Law	Ellman, Kurtz, Weithorn, Bix, Czapanskiy & Eichner
Family Law	Harris, Carbone & Teitelbaum
Family Law	Wadlington & O'Brien
Family Law	Weisberg & Appleton
Federal Courts	Fallon, Meltzer & Shapiro (Hart & Wechsler)
Federal Courts	Low & Jeffries
Health Law	Furrow, Greaney, Johnson, Jost & Schwartz
Immigration Law	Aleinikoff, Martin & Motomura
Immigration Law	Legomsky
Insurance Law	Abraham
Intellectual Property	Merges, Menell & Lemley
International Business Transactions	Folsom, Gordon, Spanogle & Fitzgerald
International Law	Blakesley, Firmage, Scott & Williams
International Law	Carter, Trimble & Weiner
International Law	Damrosch, Henkin, Murphy & Smit
International Law	Dunoff, Ratner & Wippman
Labor Law	Cox, Bok, Gorman & Finkin
Land Use	Callies, Freilich & Roberts
Legislation	Eskridge, Frickey & Garrett
Oil & Gas	Lowe, Anderson, Smith & Pierce
Patent Law	Adelman, Radner, Thomas & Wegner
Products Liability	Owen, Montgomery & Davis
Professional Responsibility	Gillers
Professional Responsibility	Hazard, Koniak, Cramton, Cohen & Wendel
Property	Casner, Leach, French, Korngold & VanderVelde
Property	Cribbet, Johnson, Findley & Smith
Property	Donahue, Kauper & Martin
Property	Dukeminier, Krier, Alexander & Schill
Property	Haar & Liebman
Property	Kurtz & Hovenkamp
Property	Nelson, Stoebuck & Whitman
Property	Rabin, Kwall, Kwall & Arnold
Property	Singer
Real Estate	Korngold & Goldstein
Real Estate Transactions	Nelson & Whitman
Remedies	Laycock
Remedies	Shoben, Tabb & Janutis
Securities Regulation	Coffee, Seligman & Sale
Securities Regulation	Cox, Hillman & Langevoort
Sports Law	Weiler, Roberts, Abrams & Ross
Taxation (Corporate)	Lind, Schwartz, Lathrope & Rosenberg
Taxation (Individual)	Burke & Friel
Taxation (Individual)	Freeland, Lathrope, Lind & Stephens
Taxation (Individual)	Klein, Bankman, Shaviro & Stak
Torts	Dobbs, Hayden & Bublick
Torts	Epstein
Torts	Franklin & Rabin
Torts	Henderson, Pearson, Kysar & Siliciano
Torts	Schwartz, Kelly & Partlett (Prosser)
Trademark	Ginsburg, Litman & Kevlin
Wills, Trusts & Estates	Dukeminier, Sitkoff & Lindgren
Wills, Trusts & Estates	Dobris, Sterk & Leslie
Wills, Trusts & Estates	Scoles, Halbach, Roberts & Begleiter